Jeroen Warner is Assistant Professor of Disaster Studies at Wageningen University in the Netherlands. He has written extensively on the politics of water and is editor of *Multi-Stakeholder Platforms for Integrated Catchment Management* and co-editor of *The Politics of Water.*

INTERNATIONAL LIBRARY OF POLITICAL STUDIES

Series ISBN: 978 1 84885 226 6

See www.ibtauris.com/ILPS for a full list of titles

37. *Choosing Slovakia: Slavic Hungary, the Czechoslovak Language and Accidental Nationalism*
Alexander Maxwell
978 1 84885 074 3

38. *Khatami and Gorbachev: Politics of Change in the Islamic Republic of Iran and the USSR*
Zhand Shakibi
978 1 84885 139 9

39. *Critical Turns in Critical Theory: New Directions in Social and Political Thought*
Séamus Ó Tuama (Ed)
978 1 84511 559 3

40. *Nationalism and Identity in Romania: A History of Extreme Politics from the Birth of the State to EU Accession*
Radu Cinpoeş
978 1 84885 166 5

41. *Democracy, Sovereignty and Terror: Lakshman Kadirgamar on the Foundations of the International Order*
Adam Roberts (Ed)
978 1 84885 307 2

42. *Democracy or Autocracy in Algeria: Political Change, Civil War and the Islamist Movement*
Noura Hamladji
978 1 84885 334 8

43. *The Emergence of Nationalist Politics in Morocco: The Rise of the Independence Party and the Struggle Against Colonialism after World War II*
Daniel Zisenwine
978 1 84885 323 2

44. *Fundamentalism in the Modern World Vol 1: Fundamentalism, Politics and History: The State, Globalisation and Political Ideologies*
Ulrika Mårtensson, Jennifer Bailey, Priscilla Ringrose and Asbjørn Dyrendal (Eds)
978 1 84885 330 0

45. *Fundamentalism in the Modern World Vol 2: Fundamentalism and Communication: Culture, Media and the Public Sphere*
Ulrika Mårtensson, Jennifer Bailey, Priscilla Ringrose and Asbjørn Dyrendal (Eds)
978 1 84885 331 7

46. *Welfare Policy under New Labour: The Politics of Social Security Reform*
Andrew Connell
978 1 84885 389 8

47. *Constructing Political Islam as the New Other: America and its Post-War on Terror Politics*
Corinna Mullin
978 1 84885 268 6

48. *Choosing the Labour Leader: Labour Party Leadership Elections from Wilson to Brown*
Timothy Heppell
978 1 84885 381 2

49. *From Pitt to Peel: Conservative Politics in the Age of Reform*
Richard A. Gaunt
978 1 84885 437 6

50. *The Labour Party in Britain and Norway: Elections and the Pursuit of Power between the World Wars*
David Redvaldsen
978 1 84885 540 3

51. *Revolution and Reform in Russia and Iran: Modernisation and Politics in Revolutionary States*
Ghoncheh Tazmini
978 1 84885 554 0

52. *Media and Politics in Latin America: Globalization, Democracy and Identity*
Carolina Matos
978 1 84885 612 7

53. *Ethnicity, Nationalism and Conflict in the South Caucaus: Nagorno-Karabakh and the Legacy of Soviet Nationalities Policy*
Ohannes Geukjian
978 1 84885 643 1

54. *Power Hierarchies and Hegemony in Afghanistan: State Building, Ethnic Minorities and Identity in Central Asia*
Shah Mahmoud Hanifi (Ed)
978 1 84885 693 6

Flood Planning

The Politics of Water Security

Jeroen Warner

Published in 2011 by I.B.Tauris & Co Ltd
6 Salem Road, London W2 4BU
175 Fifth Avenue, New York NY 10010
www.ibtauris.com

Distributed in the United States and Canada Exclusively by Palgrave Macmillan
175 Fifth Avenue, New York NY 10010

International Library of Political Studies: 30

ISBN: 978 1 84511 817 4

A full CIP record for this book is available from the British Library
A full CIP record is available from the Library of Congress

Library of Congress Catalog Card Number: available

Printed and bound in Great Britain by CPI Antony Rowe, Chippenham

CONTENTS

LIST OF TABLES AND BOXES

LIST OF FIGURES

PREFACE

After a destructive flood or drought, the drive to mount a project that will end all insecurity is enormous. Politicians promise quick and dirty solutions in the national interest, engineers rise to the occasion, ask their lawyers to make their plan lawsuit-proof and organise road shows to promote the project to the local stakeholders. Post-crisis planning and decision-making is not the best time for scholarly reflection, public consultation, and hard-nosed economic weighing of costs against benefits. The cases in this book however show that in the aftermath of the storm, a clear-headed perspective is in order, as details skipped now will come back to haunt the project planner later. The proverbial retired engineer, geography teacher, environmental NGO or disgruntled gravel king will find ammunition against a project. The present book sketches how the political will rears its head even in the most 'closed' administrative systems.

I looked into six major projects in five very different countries. Apples and pears inevitably got to be compared, along with bananas and watermelons. Nevertheless, some arresting commonalities jump out, which makes me believe that planners who read Habermas and Healey on collaborative planning should also be reading Mouffe and Flyvbjerg on conflict. Like floods, conflict can destroy and traumatise decision-makers, but also fertilise discussion, breathing new life into a static landscape. As the Japanese say: *ame futte chi katamaru* (雨降って地固まる) – after a storm, things will stand on more solid ground.

All errors of fact and judgment are, as ever, my sole responsibility.

1

INTRODUCTION

POLITICS OF FLOODS AND FEAR

> . . . the analysis of the political strategies surrounding the construction of insecurity is necessary to understanding some of the most influential social and political processes of our time. This is why more research on the politics of insecurity is needed. (Béland, 2005: 20)

1.1 Introduction: Floods and Fear

'One person in 10 worldwide, including one in eight city-dwellers, lives less than 10 metres above sea-level and near the coast'.[1] Flooding is the most common type of natural disaster worldwide – 40 per cent of all natural disasters (www.floodsafety.com). Floods account for 15 per cent of all deaths related to natural disasters, famines for 42 per cent. From 1992 to 2001, developing countries accounted for 20 per cent of the total number of disasters, but over 50 per cent of all disaster fatalities – approximately 13 times more people die per reported disaster in developing countries than in developed countries.

The five deadliest floods listed by Wikipedia (Table 1.1) are all in China, especially on the Yangtze and Yellow rivers. Number 7 on the list is the St Felix's storm surge in the Netherlands in 1530 taking over 100,000 people with it. The 2007 land flood in the UK, with 11 victims, pales by comparison, but the terror and loss felt by these families are enormous. Floods may be expected and accepted with fatalism, while smaller floods can lead to clamour and outrage.

The blame for the increased number of floods in the UK is routinely laid at the doorstep of climate change, which, in turn, is attributed to industry and carbon fuels. But the trend in flood figures is the object of political contest. While green scientists routinely quote alarming figures to support

Death Toll	Event	Location	Date
2,500,000–3,700,000	1931 China floods	China	1931
900,000–2,000,000	1887 Yellow River flood	China	1887
500,000–700,000	1938 Yellow River flood	China	1938
231,000	Banqiao Dam failure, result of Typhoon Nina. Approximately 86,000 people died from flooding and another 145,000 died during subsequent disease.	China	1975
145,000	1935 Yangtze River flood	China	1935

Table 1.1: ***The deadliest floods of all time according to Wikipedia***

their agenda to take action to prevent climate change, free-market organisations, including oil companies, are interested. Earthquakes and tropical cyclones may claim more lives than floods, but floods appear to affect more lives than the other geophysical hazards (Parker, 2000). But some counter-intuitive information is trickling through. The number of people killed each year by weather-related disasters is actually falling.[2] Deaths in such disasters peaked in the 1920s and have been declining ever since, claims the report by the Civil Society Coalition on Climate Change, a grouping of 41 mainly free-market bodies:

> Average annual deaths from weather-related events in the period 1990–2006 – considered by scientists to be when global warming has been most intense – were down by 87 per cent on the 1900–89 average. The mortality rate from catastrophes, measured in deaths per million people, dropped by 93 per cent.

Compared with the peak of mortality rate, from weather-related events in the 1920s, which reached nearly 500,000 a year, the death toll during the period 2000–06 averaged 19,900. The number of deaths had fallen sharply due to better warning systems, improved flood defences and other measures. Poor countries remained most vulnerable.

Meanwhile Britain experienced the wettest May to July period ever recorded (records began in 1776). Some areas received as much precipitation in a single day as they normally would in a month, and parts of Yorkshire, Lincolnshire and the Midlands more than ever, while on the whole England got more than twice as much rain as the average.[3] These extremes translated into crisis situations: civil and military authorities were called out for the biggest rescue operation since the war (Wikipedia on English floods of 2007, last consulted on 1 October 2010).

> A 28-year-old man died in Hull after becoming stuck in a drain despite the attempts of rescuers to free him. Also in Sheffield, a body has been found after a 13-year-old boy was swept away in a river, and a 68-year-old man died getting out of his car in floods. ('Three dead following flood chaos', BBC News, 26 June 2007)

One of the affected sites was the town of Maidenhead, where homes were flooded in the Wootton Way area. We will see later in this volume that recurrent floods revived flood protection plans dismissed earlier – and fears about those plans.

The UK was not alone in suffering torrential rains. At the same time as the UK, southern Asia has been suffering, with flash floods ravaging central Afghanistan (70 fatalities), cyclone Yemyin hitting coastal areas of Pakistan's Sindh and Baluchistan provinces, before moving into eastern Iran (12 deaths), while 32 fisherman caught up in the storm are thought to have drowned. A few days previously, floods in Karachi killed 230 people in the city's shanty towns. Another storm killed 45 people in India's southern states of Andhra Pradesh, Kerala and Karnataka, displaced tens of thousands and killing an estimated 400 people, and affected 4 million people. Floodwaters breached drinking water supplies, and rescue efforts were made even more perilous by snakes and scorpions in the water. Floods and landslides affected China, where one-tenth of the population was affected. New Zealand, Panama and Ecuador experienced floods, while in the USA heavier rain has been exacerbating the floods across the southern Great Plains, particularly Texas.[4] With the current state of technology, there is little we can do against water extremes, but we can do a lot about how they affect us.

For decades, the UK considered itself flood-free. But since Easter 1998, the country has been hit every two or three years by water masses affecting properties and taking lives of those unfortunate enough to be trapped. Climate change promises hotter climates, but also more rain in already flood-prone countries like Britain, Holland but also Bangladesh.

The severity of the flood impact is closely related to social and infrastructural resilience. The 2007 UK flood was particularly damaging when it exposed the fragility of critical infrastructure. In the Midlands, water supply and sewerage systems broke down, affecting hundreds of thousands who were otherwise outside the flood zone. A police station, a vital coordination point in disaster response, was flooded in Hull.[5]

This is not accidental. In Rotterdam, Netherlands, the flood coordination centre's central computer is in the basement, several metres below sea level. The city of Venlo gave permission to build a new hospital in a flood-prone area. Perrow (1984) calls our attention to Normal Accidents – hazards that are built into our society – a point picked up later by Beck (1992) in his 'world risk society'.

In Perrow's model, characteristic features of a normal accident are:

- Unexpected and complex interactions between faults that are tolerable individually.
- *Tight coupling* allowing little opportunity for mitigation or defence once a fault occurs.

Accidents do not occur because people gamble and lose, they occur because people do not believe that the accident that is about to occur is possible.

In the USA, the war on terrorism, a human-made disaster, has perversely weakened planning for natural disasters. Perrow (2007) notes: 'Grants that once went to train and equip first responders to disasters are now funding antiterrorism efforts of dubious efficacy, leaving a government that is at all levels less competent to plan for and respond to disasters.' Perrow cites as a sorry example the US Federal Emergency Management Agency (FEMA). A competent agency for disaster management under the Clinton Administration, FEMA was subsumed under the Department of Homeland Security (DHS) in a massive reorganisation after the 2001 terrorist attacks. As its focus shifted to terrorism, FEMA was caught unawares by Katrina (Birkland, 2006).

In August 2005 Hurricane Katrina, one of the most famous disaster events in recent times, was rated a 'Category 4' hurricane. As only people affected by Category 1 through 3 events qualify for public protection, the citizens of New Orleans were on their own (Lukes, 2005a). As it was a 'normal' mishap under formal rules, authorities decided to treat the event as a normal event rather than bypassing procedure, as they would have, had the hurricane been labelled a catastrophe.

The US Federal Government elected not to send the Army in to evacuate the city, while it was otherwise engaged in Iraq and Afghanistan, a (non)-decision satirised in a fundraising pop video.[6] Yet, at the same time, there was criticism of the security measures that *were* taken. Not only floods, but also flood response, deprived people of their basic rights and dignity – they found themselves jam-packed in sports complexes without basic services, stopped by military men at state borders, dispersed across the country without a plan for return. Rumours that dikes were deliberately dynamited to save rich areas from flooding highlighted the socio-economic distribution effects of floods as well as flood response.

Nevertheless, it is too simplistic to blame only the authorities as Spike Lee film, *When the Levees Broke*, argues. People want maximum security and maximum freedom (Boutellier, 2002) – it is a fine balance between control and abandonment. There was advance flood warning, evacuation service and road capacity, but no coercion to leave. As a consequence, 200,000 people stayed on (HKV Lijn in Water 2007).[7] Seeking to make up for past mistakes, the state of Louisiana decided to evacuate forcibly when another hurricane closed in on New Orleans in the Summer of 2008. But this time, the hurricane and the floods passed the Jazz City by.

The Americans had been seen as progressive by changing from investment in structures to flood zoning and incentives in the 1960s. But post-Katrina, the paradigm changed back to dike building. The Dutch were called in, personified by Arcadis environmental consultants, on a US$150 million project to design a security system . . . the actual building of flood defences would come later. In the Netherlands itself, the philosophy also shifted back. Since 1995, a risk-accepting policy to 'Make Room for the River', a greener, more local and participatory approach to river management, seemed to become hegemonic, but was challenged by a powerful lobby to strengthen sea defences, build new developments on 5-m mounds and generally invest in security infrastructure, legitimised by climate-change-induced sea level rise. To the as-yet-undecided battle between those two attractors I will return time and again in the present book. A key lever in this respect is 'national security' – those who see it threatened see the water as an enemy to fend off; those who do not, seek peace and accommodation.

1.1.1 Why Flood Politics?

Flood politics are not like normal politics – they are about survival, they are security issues. Security is being 'without a care' (*s(in)e cura*) – in German *Sicherheit* is safety, security and certainty in one (Bauman, 1999). Floods deeply challenge *Sicherheit* in each of its three meanings. Similar to other complex emergencies like earthquakes or wars, extreme floods reduce people to vulnerable existence, surviving in a situation where normal rules and laws no longer obtain. The way hydrological risks are dealt with is of decisive influence on how secure people feel.

The present book will look at the political aspect of flood protection, which shapes the decisions on dealing with risk. Floods not only frighten people in society, they incite fear of social chaos and societal ungovernability in authorities, who are expected to provide security within their territory. The public outcry after flood events can seriously challenge a governmental body's legitimacy, which may be blamed for unsatisfactory warning or ineffective flood protection.

But the role of protector, taking responsibility, can also bring extra legitimacy. If a flood happens, someone gets blamed, but if it is contained, someone takes the credit. In drought- or flood-prone states, river projects can play a key role in legitimising the hegemonic rule of water agencies. Water is a political good that can enhance (or reduce) a political actor's legitimacy base (Donahue and Johnston, 1998).

Despite advanced techniques of risk assessment and management that give the appearance of controlling the future, bids for security (its supply and demand) cannot be based on 'objective facts'. Risk is about what *might* happen and therefore about fear and anxiety. The analysis treats risk and security as constructs, as *frames* that give meaning to a bewildering reality. I propose this sense-making may have a political instrumentality to it: it legitimises certain agendas over others. Even if the frames ultimately prove unsuccessful, they may reap the desired effect of landing the issue high on the political agenda. The present study seeks to bring a coherent theorisation and conceptualisation of the political construction of security and risk in water management, responding to Béland's observation that '[t]he construction of threats and insecurity through framing processes is a major aspect of the politics of insecurity' (Béland, 2005).

The study focuses on infrastructural projects designed to prevent traumatic flood events happening. In response to criticism of a technocratic outlook, engineers now increasingly devise participatory processes promoting stakeholder involvement. The five schemes I researched for this study (and one that never made it), several were prize-winning designs involving a degree of public participation. Still, each provoked a level of controversy (politicisation) unforeseen by its initiators.

The study sketches the genesis, conflicts and outcome of six river plans: the Toshka project in Egypt, the Ilısu hydropower dam in Turkey, the FAP-20 compartmentalisation pilot project in Bangladesh, river widening and deepening on the Maas and controlled flood storage in the Ooij polder in the Netherlands, and the Maidenhead, Eton and Windsor Flood Alleviation Scheme in Britain.

When I started studying these cases at the turn of the Millennium, I could not have predicted that all the cases studied were going to end up heavily dented:

- Most of the consortium walks out and the project is shelved for five years (Turkey).
- Phase One is completed, but many wonder if the next phases will ever be carried through (Egypt).
- The project is completed but never sees its follow-up (Bangladesh).
- The project is reduced and much of its 'green' content cut (Netherlands, Maas).
- The infrastructure for controlled flooding never even gets built (Netherlands, Ooij).
- The infrastructure is completed, but crumbles at its first test (Britain).

Flood projects bring contest over the risk, over who should be protected by whom at what sacrifice. These issues are so fundamental they warrant intense political debate and action. It is therefore prudent to anticipate that such projects will always be politicised, although this rarely really means the end of the project.

The analysis shows that such politicisation is always to the apparent surprise of project initiators. They may be dismayed to learn that not even a well-organised trust-building participation process, 'joint' or 'open planning', will exempt river planners from such a political process.

I propose that a crucial factor explaining this is that flood projects not only promote some people's security, they often significantly reduce the security of others. A river regulation plan that regulates floods and promises economic development for the area is not necessarily appreciated, given recurring social and environmental protests against dams, embankments, spillways and detention basins as unrequited interference in local affairs. The projects appear to have disregarded essential values of project-affected stakeholders, inciting anxiety, anger and conflict.

In the present study, we shall encounter spaces where some stakeholders blame government for failing to stop the flood or even starting it, some dread the invasion of their space and freedoms, making them feel fenced in, 'enclosed', and still others who feel deprived of protection, bereft of basic political rights, either in the name of security or efficiency. All of these however can 'speak security' to try and turn the tables.

In *Security: A New Framework for Analysis*, Barry Buzan, Ole Wæver and Jaap de Wilde claim that saying 'security' legitimises extraordinary measures that are otherwise impossible to achieve (Buzan, et al., 1998). The speech act of 'securitisation' is a powerful move for closure, foreclosing political debate and choice for the sake of swift emergency action. While states are mandated to declare threats, so can others (Litfin, 1999). Still, not everyone advocates 'securitising' environmental issues (Krause and Williams, 1997). If river schemes can make one more rather than less vulnerable, it is tempting to distrust the political process and argue against state involvement in flood security. I will argue, though, that one should not throw the baby called Security out with the bathwater. We need a well-coordinated and accountable collective security apparatus to counter collective insecurity (see also Béland, 2005). While Béland rightly reminds us that state protection also has an oppressive side, it is not so clear that flood victims are better off if condemned to the alternative – self-help.

1.1.2 Theoretical Relevance

Risk studies and security studies traditionally study phenomena of danger at different geographical levels: the local and international level, respectively. Recently, the two disciplines seem to be drawing towards each other as local risks take on international or global dimensions (global warming; environmental refugees), whereas security studies increasingly recognise the sub-state and non-military dimensions of conflict – and indeed, are developing an understanding of security which goes beyond (violent) conflict. In both disciplines, the legitimacy of social arrangements for dealing with security and risk, and in some cases even of the political system as a whole, are now debated, resulting in the identification of risk as the new danger for states (Giddens, 1999) and a plethora of new understandings of 'security'. The so-called Copenhagen School of peace research has given a fresh impetus to security studies that also places environmental politics in a different light. Regrettably, the focus of the research and debate on the Copenhagen approach is very much concentrated on Europe, specifically on issues of identity, integration and migration issues (Wilkinson, 2007). The approach however merits wider application, both in terms of geography and subject matter. Not only has 'securitisation' become a household word in International Relations and peace studies, it echoes in other disciplines such as cultural and media studies and human geography. The approach has become more current in international hydro-political analyses (Turton, 2001; Jägerskog, 2003; Phillips, et al., 2006), but these studies applied security concepts to situations of scarcity rather than excess, i.e. floods. The present approach sheds light on the framing and legitimisation and delegitimisation of proposed 'solutions' to disaster challenges. A comparative approach highlights similarities and differences in context.

Given the proximity of wars and emergencies in their potential for social disruption, it is surprising that the securitisation approach has not made similar inroads in disaster studies literature. The constructivist approach underlying securitisation theory permits a dispassionate account and analysis of the politics of emergency.

The present study applies the approach to natural hazards and river development as potential sources of securitisation, given the existential threat, urgency and exceptional measures taken to contain rivers. Drawing on three current international narratives of 'water wars' and peace (in Section 1.3), I will identify three similar narratives of (de)securitising floods. The study tests this idea on the basis of an analysis of six recent infrastructural river interventions in five countries – two in Western Europe, one in South Asia and two in the Middle East. The latter two regions have often been singled out as flashpoints for international water conflict.

On the basis of security literature, the present research starts from the proposition that 'saying security' would successfully legitimise river management projects, close the debate, and boost the role of the securitising agent in the river management regime. This leads me to a central research question: *What role do 'security' frames play in (de)legitimising flood management projects, and how does this affect the political and river management regime context?*

To help answer this question, I develop a conceptual framework around concepts of regime, crisis, framing, closure and hegemony, applied to six case studies in five different countries.

1.1.3 Organisation of the Book

The remainder of this chapter is devoted to conceptual development and case selection. The next section will first look at the importance of security to the state and the challenges of the changing 'security governance regime' (Section 1.2), in its administrative and technological sense. It introduces the idea of *closure* and notes the role of crisis events like floods, or even a flood project, in 'opening up' the regime overnight.

As a crisis can be 'constructed', the focus turns to the role of discourse and (strategic) framing of risk and security issues (Section 1.3). The section goes into contest over frames, the formation of discourse coalitions and hegemonic strategies, and closes with a definition of politics of flood insecurity. Section 1.4 makes methodological observations on a constructivist 'positioning' approach and pointers of identifying successful and unsuccessful securitising moves. The final section explains the case study selection process and goes into more detail about the research methods employed.

The remaining chapters will analyse the six case studies, starting with the two Middle East ('dry basin') studies discussed in Chapters 2 and 3 (Egypt, and Turkey). The politics of the Toshka river diversion scheme and the Ilısu hydroelectric dam are discussed at the domestic and international levels.

Chapter 4 to 7 discuss four 'wet basin' studies: Bangladesh, the Netherlands (Ooij polder and Maaswerken) and England. Flood Action Plan 20, the disputed project discussed in Chapter 4, compartmentalised an existing polder in Central Bangladesh, seeking to a safer environment for food production and to democratise decision-making on when to drain monsoon water. The Maaswerken (Chapter 5), deepened and widened the river Maas in the south of the Netherlands to provide a safer but also more natural river environment. While the Maas is a natural border with Belgium, the Ooij polder, on the Rhine, connects the Netherlands with Germany. The polder was slated for controlled emergency flood storage in case of extreme events but as Chapter 6 discusses, the polder dwellers refused to be sacrificed. The final case study zooms in on the river Thames where a flood relief channel to protect Maidenhead, Eton and Windsor caused a commotion.

Chapter 8 brings all cases together and develops three flood narratives. Chapter 9 concludes by linking back the findings from the river management studies to debates in the security field.

1.2 The Flood Regulation Regime: Controlling Rivers and People

Flood managers may be the only people who pray for a really good periodic disaster. The Dutch paraphrase 'Give us our daily bread and a flood every ten years' will sound familiar to civil engineers in Britain, Bangladesh and in many other settings, even Egypt, where one might prefer the flood to appear every single year.

Flood experts however do not normally make the rules, and they do not always have their way. The way environmental hazards like floods are managed is a reflection of how society is organised, the governance arrangement or *regime* – the division of labour and responsibility between public and non-public actors to provide stability of expectations, and thus durably legitimising certain solution alternatives over others.

Security politics has important consequences for the decision arena: who can take decisions, who has responsibility, and what options for redress are there? As a regime provides stability of expectations, it durably legitimises certain solution alternatives over others (Bijker, 1995). The ensuing resource distribution can become 'closed' and 'fossilised', until a new frame or crisis event opens the regime up again.

Disasters are moments when nature escapes human control; it is hard to imagine effective disaster management policies without the aim of control (Hilhorst, 2003: 6). Engineers are trained to look at the world as a control system, in which they manipulate parameters and solve problems (e.g., see Geldof, 1994) so that the system will not be overwhelmed. Yet the only really effective way to impress on people that action is urgently needed is the arrival of a high water event. While the flood stays away, it is hard to convince decision-makers to agree to interventions to manage the river. Other concerns always seem more important than containing the river, which costs large amounts of money and interferes with people's everyday lives. When the flood calls, it is a rare and limited window to 'do something', to intervene and avert the threat or seize a development opportunity. The window is brief, so best to make good use of it.

Given the state's identity as security provider, the 'marketing' of security by playing on insecurities to generate or foreground 'demand for security' is part and parcel of politics. The present section will therefore first discuss the role of the *state*, then changes in the governance arrangement thereafter and then the role of a crisis.

1.2.1 Security Governance

Historically, states have not always enjoyed supremacy, and have often needed to legitimise themselves through warfare (Tilly, 1985). Currently, citizens have no choice but to be protected by the state, unless they stage a coup d'état. The Westphalian state system, instated in 1648 to put an end to several long European wars, vests the legitimate use of the means of violence and the power to declare a state of exception solely in the sovereign state. This power to instate or shore up the rule of law states can make, but also break the law for the sake of order in the face of perceived chaos, constitutes the very essence of sovereignty. According to the German political philosopher Carl Schmitt (Schmitt, 1922), this *decision* is even the very essence of the political: it determines the distinction between friends and enemies, reconstituting actors as political actors (those with rights) and outcasts (those without rights) who find themselves reduced to what the Italian philosopher Giorgio Agamben (1998) has called 'bare life'. The normal order is dependent on this power. While European states have rarely experienced states of emergency of late, it is far more frequent on other continents. Bangladesh, for example, declared a state of emergency in 2006 to deal with political chaos.

The urgency of a threat or crisis justifies bypassing normal political debate, budget considerations and public accountability and transparency, as well as civil rights like privacy and a voice in decisions affecting them. Under an authoritarian regime, political contest, consultation and cooperation with stakeholders would be an anomaly. This may suit some states well, as states cannot always be sure of their monopoly on sovereignty.

'Weak states' may feel threatened and in competition at the domestic level with regional strongmen, separatist forces or religious movements that do not recognise their authority. As Agamben (1998) has warned, a state which has security as its sole source of legitimacy is a fragile organism: it can always be provoked by terrorism to become terrorist itself. The state can act destructively to save the population from destruction. An insecure state, beleaguered from all sides, may seek certainties by pursuing dangerous routines and fall into a pattern of regression (Mitzen, 2005) and repression. Chapters 2 and 3 will investigate to what extent Egypt and Turkey are such 'security states', while the other cases assess if, and how, flood defence plays a role in the legitimacy of the other states, especially their water departments.

A state of emergency or state of war is not cast in stone; a state can change its 'mind', its self-image as a consequence. A currently influential school of Constructivism in international relations (Wendt, 1999; Checkel, 2001) claims that states have identities and security needs, especially a need for stability of expectations. If these needs can be met otherwise, there is no need to work in security mode. Threats may become less threatening over time, conflictive relations may become friendly. Reframing an issue as 'non-security' opens the political arena up: it can promote the role of non-state actors and bring in governance alternatives and other non-military foci for protection. When there is no clear enemy or crisis to deal with, the united societal front against the challenge dissipates into factions (Roe, 2004). The liberal (Lockeian) project found in European democracies is a contest between a plurality of contenders.

Discussions of contemporary security studies have involved both 'wideners' and 'deepeners' (Hough, 2004):

- 'Deepeners': 'deepening' security referents to include sub-state categories, that is, communities or individuals rather than states become the focus for protection.

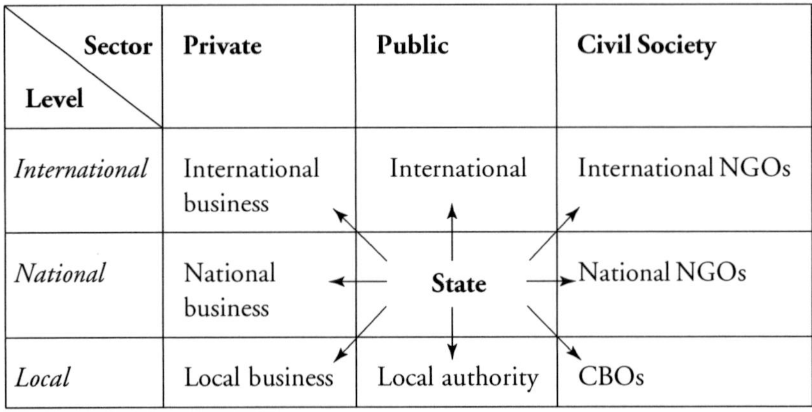

Level \ Sector	Private	Public	Civil Society
International	International business	International	International NGOs
National	National business	State	National NGOs
Local	Local business	Local authority	CBOs

NGO = Non-governmental organisation, CBO = Community-based organisation

Table 1.2: ***Horizontalisation and verticalisation of governance***

- 'Wideners': 'widening' security categories (beyond the military domain) economic, environmental, societal, political security may be deemed survival issues. The 'new security agenda' is focussed on *societal* emergencies and vulnerabilities.

A governance focus finds that there is not only a 'widening and deepening' of security 'referents', but also of 'security suppliers'. 'Security governance' is a newly emerging, and therefore still underdeveloped, concept to analyse new social arrangements for security provision (Krahmann, 2003). Modern states are faced with demanding citizens and lobbies, and with knotty policy issues that reflect the increasing complexity, diversity and dynamics in today's societies (Kooiman, et al., 2000). They find it hard to meet the presumed or expressed demand for security alone. To fill the gap between demand and supply, non-state actors present themselves and may be enlisted or co-opted to help out in providing security. The police, prisons, protection and intelligence services are currently being (part-)privatised in several countries while the war in Iraq is fought enlisting private companies (Table 1.2). Private and NGO actors are likewise of growing importance in humanitarian relief after disasters. This may improve the governability of danger and risk, but also present problems of transparency and accountability, control, coordination and efficiency (Krahmann, 2003).

A currently popular narrative claims that the world is becoming increasingly 'flat' (Friedman, 2005): power distances get smaller, unilateral control is relaxed. The (contestable)[8] 'government to governance' narrative paints a picture of a past where public services were rendered in a vertical manner, and now are increasingly horizontalised: less hierarchy, more lateral coordination.

However, the vertical aspect may be as important to the analysis. A twin trend towards decentralisation and internationalisation of policy suggests a concomitant vertical differentiation of governing powers at work. Thus, the European Union's subsidiary principle stipulates that policy should be made and implemented at the lowest relevant level, placing more decision power in the hands of local authorities and participating citizen organisations. Meanwhile, the overlay of international actors, notably the European Union (the European Framework Directive of 2000 and the High Water Directive of 2006), set standards that impinge on member states' national policies while donors and consultants may overrule the (de)securitising moves of statesmen. The European Union is also seeking to make transnational civil defence arrangements (Ekengren, 2004).

While relations between 'partners in governance' are unlikely to be egalitarian, their roles may be fluid. The governance domain begins to look like an open 'network' that is in flux but has a degree of close coupling between actors. Karen Bakker, et al. (2006) perceive this movement more like a shift in emphasis, from the vertical levels of governance to the functional mechanisms of government. There is no 'either/or' but 'and-and': both state and non-state actors take roles: they coordinate with each other in top-down hierarchy, but also horizontal 'heterarchy' and 'free interaction' in society (Kooiman, et al., 2000). While such authors appear to project their hopes for a better world onto governance, others are sceptical. Bustamante and Palacios (2005), for example, are concerned that the concept depoliticises essentially political issues of distributive justice and rights. In the present study, an analytical rather than normative approach to governance will be attempted (Hood, Rothstein and Baldwin, 2001).

The new, dynamic arrangements for security at different geographical levels have given rise to a blending of the literature on governance in Public Administration and regimes in International Relations. As a result, there are various ways of conceptualising the mechanisms of risk and responsibility to provide order and stability of expectations in an issue-area, such as environmental policy arrangements (Arts and Tatenhove, 2000) and risk regulation regimes (see Hood, Rothstein and Baldwin, 2001). For the purposes of this study, the 'regime' for dealing with an issue-area such as river management will combine and integrate three foci of 'patterned behaviour' (Puchala and Hopkins, 1983) noted in regime theory: a regime will be said to consist of the *actor* coalition involved, the *rules and roles* they take on with respect to each other, and their *knowledge* and action capacities (after Hasenclever, et al., 1997). While regimes describe cooperation in interstate relations, the literature on governance looks at multiple levels of organisation. They tend to focus on the horizontal and vertical moves away from the state, as pictured in Table 1.1.

While painting a more intricate picture of how security issues are dealt with, such a picture underexposes two important groups: the expert community and local, disaster-affected stakeholders. Buzan, et al. (1998: 72) note that the way academic agenda structures the political agenda is 'exceptional'. Given the long and prominent history of *experts* in (infra)structural river management, the role of science and technology in the way flood hazards are dealt with merits special attention. Our focus on *projects*, moreover, means a focus on the project's interface with the stakeholders in the *local* domain.

Following Hilhorst (2003), I shall therefore focus on the interactions within three specific social domains that share practices with respect to hazard management:

- *governance sector* (decision-makers, funders and bureaucrats),
- *security experts* (scientists and managers),
- *local actors* at risk from floods, or as the case may be, from flood projects.

Actors within these domains are supposed to be coordinated and cooperative, but as Hilhorst notes, this is an exception rather than a rule.

Having discussed the governance sector at some length, I will now turn to the domain of experts and technology. The local domain will be discussed in Section 1.2.3.

1.2.2 Science and Technology

A central concept in the study is '(en)closure', taken here in both its technical, political and discursive sense. If you close off a river and enclose its stream by *technological* means, you capture a resource that others see as a common pool resource. *Political closure* disenfranchises actors from having a 'voice' in decision-making. Weber (1947) highlighted the concept of *social closure* which creates in- and out-groups, selective or all-inclusive participation. Closure has a distribution effect on who gets 'voice', responsibilities, resources and constraints, and which actors, factors and alternatives are excluded. *Discursive* (rhetorical) closure, finally, excludes debate and alternatives and puts the audience in a position from which everything is 'obvious' (Chandler, 2007: 127). It was noted that a core frame, technology or axiom, once selected, tends to reinforce itself and becomes almost unassailable. Narratives undergirding these frames may become 'canonised' in institutions and 'normalised' in everyday institutional practices (Miller, 2000). We will return to discursive closure in Section 1.3.

The water projects under review can all be seen as technological innovations, intervening in a social reality but also shaped by that reality (Pinch and Bijker, 1984). Science and Technology studies show that technology is never politically neutral – dikes and dams are 'thick with politics' (Bijker, 2007). Thus new 'paradigms', new ways of dealing with a technological challenge, are not merely the result of progressive insight, but of contest. Pinch and Bijker (1984) show that a great number of actors are involved in the development of a knowledge claim or technology, which shows up conflicting interests and power relations. Bruno Latour, a protagonist of Science and Technology Studies, conceives of innovation as the continuation of politics by other means (Latour, 1987). As it arrives on the scene, a new knowledge claim or technology has different meanings for different groups (interpretative flexibility). The *type of solution* needs to be facilitated and legitimised, which means it will not only be judged on its technical merits. Therefore, there is likely to be debate, or even conflict, over this claim. The debate can be cut short either through rhetorical closure (explicitly or implicitly declared closed) or the problem being redefined (defined away). Once selected, a core technology or axiom, tends to reinforce itself and becomes almost unassailable. A 'paradigm', an exemplar of how things should be done, emerges. This creates a stable environment. *Socio-technical regimes* are networks of rules and assumptions in which an established technique gets its stability (Geels, 2004). Rival technologies will remain underfunded and underexplored. Developments within this dominant paradigm tend to be incremental in nature rather than radical (shock-wise) until further optimisation is no longer possible and a 'shock' or challenge opens the 'frame' up. This phenomenon is known as *closure* (Pinch and Bijker, 1984).

The type of technological regime has environmental as well as institutional and social consequences. Mumford (in Miller, 1986) argues that large, closely coupled technologies are more compatible with top-down bureaucratic (centralised) management, while dispersed technologies are more democratic, as they can be controlled locally. In the water sector, we can juxtapose high dams with groundwater pumps and flood walls and flood-proofing of individual neighbourhoods and arrive at the same conclusion.

Particular technologies thus serve some groups better than others. Physical infrastructure creates what Callon (1986) has termed 'obligatory passage points' or nodes. The illuminating concept of 'pipelines of power' (after Turton, 1999) captures the fact that infrastructural layout has distributive consequences: who controls, who gets resources first, who gets them later and who never gets them. Egypt, but also India, Israel and indeed the Netherlands built their interlinked water grid so that they can move water around from any location to another, to bring it where it is needed or to drain it where it is in excess, or – in the Dutch case – as a water defence line to stop enemy invasions. In times of crisis, governments decide who gets priority treatment – who continues to receive water in times of drought, or which areas will be saved in times of flood.

We can visualise a continuum denoting whether the chosen technology constraints and controls the river (e.g., a flood wall) or frees up the river (a dike relocation to widen the channel), which relate with the regime's treatment of the river as a danger or an opportunity, as enemy or friend (Figure 1.1A).

A state that takes the lead in controlling and developing all water resources on the territory to guarantee the security of supply, is said, after Mark Reisner's (1993: 112–114) phrase, to be on a 'hydraulic mission'. This is a highly 'closed', Etatist form of river governance – open-ended in its ambitions and interventionism, but one-dimensional in its state–society relations, as it mobilises people

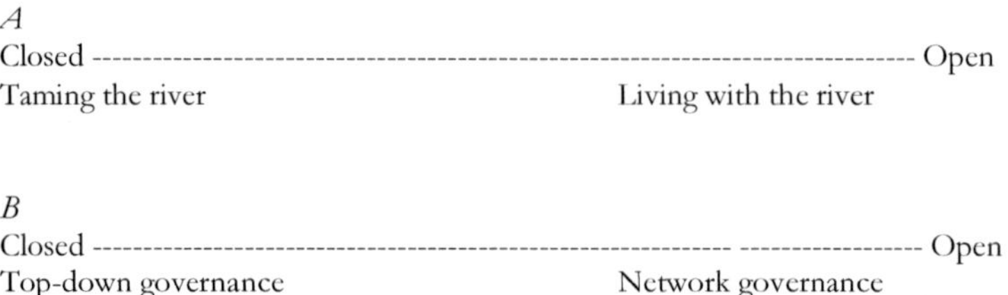

Figure 1.1: ***A: Stream intervention continuum; B: Social intervention (governance) continuum***

and resources in a top-down, command-and-control fashion to realise its development schemes for irrigation and hydropower production (Wittfogel, 1957). A state can bring water to people through infrastructure, or people to water through resettlement. Either way, the control of water is thus closely related with the control of people.

But while under the hydraulic mission the sky appears to be the limit, many twentieth-century developments ran up against 'closing basins'. This is said to have triggered a different, 'reflexive' form of management, more aware of the limits of environmental carrying capacity for water development and the need to diversify. It opened up the regime to more economically rational water management, environmental conservation and stakeholder participation with stakeholders (Meissner and Turton, 2003). In terms of my focus on closure, this brought an 'open' form of water governance; limited in its ambitions for control, intervention and expansion, open-ended in the range of alternatives. Water is no longer a resource, but is recognised for other values too, and alternative uses. A continuum is pictured in Figure 1.1.

So far, we have discussed the role of scarcity management in river control. In flood management, dealing with temporary excess, the state likewise has more 'open' and 'closed' control strategies that keep the river away from people or people away from the water. By influencing people's risky behaviour, security policy is hoped to reduce risk to life and assets. While drought is a creeping catastrophe, floods are sudden and immediate, with a capacity to overwhelm the social system in one fell swoop. The potential for such crisis events to change and open up the scene has been subject to much speculation.

1.2.3 Local Domain

Faced with a disaster, it is the local domain that bears the brunt of immediate coping and relief efforts (Kirschenbaum, 2004). A 'from government to governance' approach backgrounds that before governments became involved in security management, people developed and institutionalised local responses to hazard on the basis of their local knowledge of the area, to survive in the most adverse environments (van Dijk and de Bruijn, 1995). When central states initiate disaster management approaches, these are set in a particular technological frame that may be at odds with local responses, peculiarities and perceptions of insecurity. However, of late, project initiators have sought to make their projects more participatory and interactive, so that local people may have a voice in decision-making that affects their lives. The present study does not so much concentrate on charting these coping mechanisms but rather on the interaction between the central and local levels when a project is planned and implemented.

1.2.4 Calling a Crisis

The decision-making regime, it was noted above, may fossilise and in so doing prevent innovation. But political actors may seize on a *crisis* to enter, leave or improve their position, while others use the same event to reinforce theirs or stifle alternatives.

A disaster is a crisis of control. A crisis, in turn, is

> an event, concentrated in time and space, which threatens a society or relatively self-sufficient subdivision of society with major unwanted consequences as a result of the collapse of precautions which had hitherto been culturally accepted or adequate. (Turner, 1976)

Crises expose and question the taken-for-granted arrangements in society (the regime and the governance set-up), and provide windows for changing them. They reveal and call into question social arrangements that in normal situations remain unnoticed or undisputed. 'Abnormal times' can bring to consciousness alternative conceptions of the world (Gramsci quoted in Lukes, 2005). If system legitimacy itself remains intact, the legitimacy of specific actors may be at stake.

The public outcry after flood events challenges the legitimacy of a governmental body or the technological frame, which may be blamed for unsatisfactory warning or malperformance of the flood protection system. Others within and outside the ruling regime may present themselves as alternative security suppliers. This (de)legitimisation drive is often fanned by non-participant intermediaries such as the press, who amplify risks (Pidgeon, et al., 2003) and as a rule paint conflicts in shrill colours (Vultee, 2007).

The present research looks at floods as focusing events that may break the status quo. According to Punctuated-Equilibrium Theory (PET), a crisis disturbs the equilibrium and opens windows of opportunity for another coalition pushing for radical, self-reinforcing change (positive feedback), 'punctuating the equilibrium' (Baumgartner and Jones, 1991). A new problem definition can destabilise the status quo in the decision-making regime such that actor coalitions are realigned and new actors find their way into the process (Baumgartner and Jones, 1991). Both in flood policy and in regimes this has certain inevitability: if you repress risk and tension, the crisis will only be bigger when it happens – you have only displaced the risk from 'high-incidence, low-consequence' to 'low-incidence, high-consequence' (Bak, 1996 calls this 'organised criticality').

Radical change after a crisis clearly cannot be taken for granted. Pelling and Dill (2006) note that disaster enables political leaders to regain or even enhance their legitimacy and repress spontaneous social action. A flood, or the fear of one, can then be expected to open a considerable window of opportunity in which governments can get away with draconic emergency measures and schemes, without political fallout.

Declaring and responding to an environmental crisis, such as a drought or flood, can thus unfold either to maintain or change the status quo. But while declaring a crisis brings advantages and resources, it also carries special responsibilities, so that *not* declaring a crisis where others would declare one can be preferable to a political actor. Some high-water events and hurricanes are called crises, some are not, as illustrated by Hurricane Katrina. The hurricane was not awarded national disaster status, which led to a much-criticised delay in crisis response.

After all, short of an acute threat – a loaded gun pointed at one's head, a tsunami wiping out a town – many 'dangers' and 'crises' are ambiguous. A crisis is only a crisis when a situation is declared and accepted to be one. Given this unpredictability, I decided to see what happened in actual high-water events.

Meijerink (2005) and Johnson, et al. (2005) analyse floods as windows of opportunity for a new river management philosophy. (Liberal) regime theory also teaches that a 'catalytic shock' can turn the decision-making regime upside down (Young, 1994).[9] But they did not look at the potential of flood projects for overturning the regime. Lowry (2006) sees *both* disasters *and* river regulation schemes as 'focusing events' that can herald major change. This widens our scope to the regime change potential of conflict. A flood scheme can also call into question the local social arrangement of rules, roles and knowledge in managing the resource, i.e. the regime, and *changes people's (perceived) security positions*. As a result the project itself is a 'risk' (both in the sense of a threat and an opportunity) to stakeholders in flood management.

Political ecologists have noted that a crisis can be *constructed* and declared for a particular goal. The flexibility of the 'crisis' label allows declaring some issues security issues and ignoring others. Political ecologists show that calling an environmental crisis and/or securitising biodiversity (wildlife conservation) decisively changes power relationships between socio-economic groups (Lees, 2001)[10]. A 'crisis', a successful representation of urgency, works like a tin opener or window smasher to break the closure, with important political and institutional consequences.

The next section will explore the concept of construction and framing in more detail, along with the associated body of knowledge on how people create stories and narratives to make sense of the world. It will especially zoom in on one particular frame possessing particular 'political magic': the security frame. This brings us to a short exposition of the constructivist approach of the Copenhagen School exemplified by Barry Buzan, Ole Wæver and Jaap de Wilde's framework.

1.3 Moves for Closure: Strategic Frames, Narratives and Security Speech Acts

'What man desires is not knowledge but certainty.'

– Bertrand Russell

> There are not only struggles over security among nations, but also struggles over security among notions. Winning the right to define security provides not just access to resources but also the authority to articulate new definitions and discourses of security, as well. (Lipschutz, 1995)

1.3.1 Why Frames?

Cultural anthropologists teach us that we do not perceive the world 'as it is' – rather, we devise stories about the world that make sense of the messy reality we are presented with. People tend to dread uncertainty and ambiguity: the fundamental *uncertainty* over the future procures an existential feeling of not being in *control* (Lupton, 1999). (For the difference between uncertainty and risk, see Box 1.1.)

Risk is about fear of loss, but without meaning, we ourselves are lost. We construct a coherent world view that lends logic, a meaning to our existence. Given the amount of uncertainty, people create cause-and-effect stories to 'fill in the blanks'. Frames mobilise the values against which 'risks' and policy 'problems' are judged to exist, and point at a way out. These stories have important social effects, since the way the problem is *framed* delineates the range

Box 1.1 Risk and Uncertainty

Risk and uncertainty are commonly defined as follows (after Knight, 1921):

1. If you know for sure what is going to happen, that is *certainty*.
2. If you do not know for sure what will happen, but you know the odds, that is *risk*.
3. If you do not even know the odds, that is *uncertainty*.

of alternatives considered and the division of responsibilities in the governance regime.

In their interaction with the world, people create representations that become legitimate (Berger & Luckmann, 1991 [1966]: 110ff) and try to convince others that it is the proper view. A *frame* is a persuasive device used to 'fix meanings, organise experience, alert others that their interests and possibly their identities are at stake, and propose solutions to ongoing problems' (Barnett, 1999: 25). Frames are incorporated categories of perception. 'Norm entrepreneurs' promote new ideas such that they resonate with the intended audience (Nadelmann, 1990: 482). This skill is known in organisational management studies as the 'management of meaning' (Smircich and Morgan, 1982; Czarniawska-Joerges, 1988).

1.3.2 Security Frames

The work of Buzan, Wæver and de Wilde (1998) suggests that security and risk frames are a special frame category. By putting the issue into the domain of the absolute and non-negotiable, such frames can move a decision-making process to a degree of closure that other types of frames cannot achieve because they are about life and death issues. It sacrifices choice for the sake of necessity.

Security, for Buzan, et al., is a speech act (Austin, 1962), that is, a way of using language that changes the world by uttering it. While everything we say has the potential of influencing the world around us, some categories have a far more powerful 'social magic' than others. Like making a promise, naming a ship and declaring a couple married, calling something a security issue in the right context, given the right stage, to the right audience makes it so. The 'social magic' of speech acts is that they create and legitimise facts on the ground, can make it so. Saying 'security' forecloses choice and contradiction: it becomes an absolute that overrides everything else where others might like to dispute aspects of the proposed projects.

Security successfully presents a values as absolute and inviolable, reducing the *range of alternatives and of actors* (and their say) involved in decisions to a minimum. It splits the world into *black and white*: if you are not for it, you are against it; if you are not part of the solution, you are part of the problem. A security speech act does not tolerate half measures – it calls for the 'neutralisation, elimination or constraint of that person, group, object or condition which engenders fear' (Dillon, 1995).

This type of closure depoliticises the issue; it does not, however, kill politics. Rhetorical closure does not necessarily mean that the issue has been 'solved' or even accepted. It is also possible that someone succeeded in 'putting a lid on it' through skilful use of discourse. The united front of discursive closure therefore may obscure power inequalities and the exclusion of alternatives proposed by less powerful actors. Security absolutes may get things done and clear up ambiguity, they can also create antagonism. Where there are winners, there are also losers, where there is inclusion, there is exclusion. 'Risk-talk implicitly empowers some people as experts and excludes others as inarticulate, irrelevant or incompetent' (Jasanoff, 1999: 96).

Dangers to security issues are usually far from 'clear and present', they need to be framed as such. One issue will become elevated to security status ('securitised'), while another remains unaddressed. Douglas and Wildavsky (1983) have argued that out of the many threats we are faced with, we select only those that protect the (political) community. An instrumentalist (strategic) perspective however does not rule out the possibility that actors project threats for their own political gain. The power to 'close' the frame not only ends quarrelling but also gives access to the resources of security (for oneself or one's constituency) – legal, financial, informational and institutional. This makes it attractive to seek to shape the closure. But the speech does not have to be successful: people do not always spring to attention when a little boy cries 'wolf'. Buzan, et al. (1998) call the successful performance of this speech act *securitisation*.

A securitising move does not become a successful securitisation[11] without the consent, however grudging, from others. This points at the rather underappreciated roles of *audience* and *social context* in successful securitisation (Balzacq, 2005). It takes a receptive audience to turn word into action, to become *hegemonic* in an arena of competing discourse coalitions.

1.3.3 Finding an Audience: Hegemonic Coalition Building

Security framing takes place within a 'field of power struggles in which securitising actors align on a security issue to swing the audience's support toward a policy or course of action' (Balzacq, 2005: 173). The fragmented *political infrastructure* in liberal democracies can contribute to the need to spread a 'sense of crisis' to get anything done (Béland, 2005). This can 'distort' the message significantly. Moreover, different messages may be intended for different audiences.

Public speech acts are always uttered with an *audience* in mind. Burton and Carlen (1979) show how official discourse is an 'exercise in legitimation', incorporating 'discrepant' discourse and achieving 'discursive coherence'. An emergency, a crisis, a threat to survival, is most likely to generate general consensus (Buzan, et al., 1998). Providing and taking *responsibility* for security can procure the provider *legitimacy*, which increases an actor's power (Donahue and Johnson, 1998). Legitimacy is 'the extent to which social or political norms are accepted, especially those applying to the exercise of power or domination of some individuals or groups of individuals by others' (Rush, 1992: 53). All hierarchical power relations must be legitimated at every level of social life from the smallest scale to the level of multinational regimes (Beetham, 1991). Even

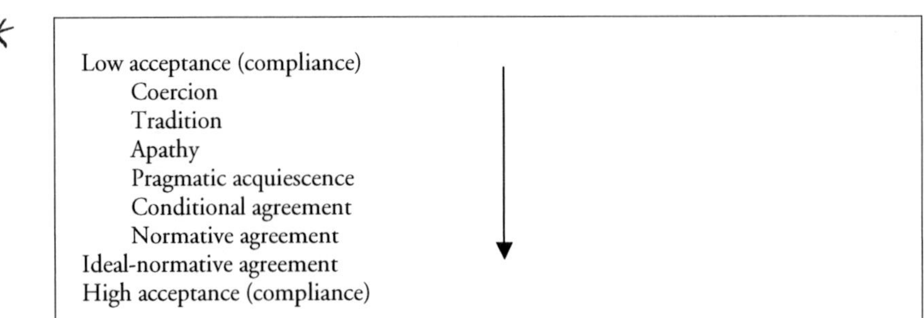

Figure 1.2: ***A ladder of compliance***

Machiavelli recommended that the Prince who seizes power by force cultivate belief that his actions are just and legitimate. It is easier to govern society when authority is accepted than when it is *imposed:* the costs of imposing one's dominance to obtain compliance are higher than those of cementing a platform on which everyone can agree. As Rush (1992: 21) suggests, fear, an unwillingness to accept the consequences of non-acceptance, apathy or cynicism (the opportunity costs of acceptance) can lead to *de facto* acceptance. He contrasts this with *de jure* authority: acceptance of the exercise of power as right or justified by those to whom it is administered (Rush, 1992: 52). Compliance with a securitisation may thus be impelled by a hegemonic securitisation – not complying means endangering the hegemonic relationship (Stahl, 2007).

A widely accepted taxonomy of authority acceptance is David Held's (1984) continuum of social-political compliance (Figure 1.2).

How does a discourse gain acceptance as authoritative? Different speakers/authors can take an infinite number of positions with regard to the concept. But unless they already dominate the scene, they will need to strike a discursive alliance to promote one's agenda. Discourse coalitions form around what Barthes has called 'empty signifiers' (quoted in Chandler, 2007), that is, words that do not refer to something very specific, so that they can be filled in different ways by different people. This reduces the number of positions in the arena (shades of grey) to a manageable number.

Forging a discourse coalition or discourse alliance is likely to involve pandering to other actors' agendas that are not too much at odds with your agenda. To enable this, you need to construct a *political formula* to combine threats into a totality that captures these agenda elements, but in which your agenda, and your leadership is seen as the common good. A hegemon – from the Greek *hegemoon*, guide – is the (durably) predominant actor or actor coalition, not in terms of material and coercive power – although that certainly helps – but in terms of authority that can command compliance with his or her rule.

The neo-Gramscian school of International Political Economy, which analyses hegemony, took the stage around the same time the aforementioned linguistic turn in management literature became influential. The discipline (re)discovered the work by the Italian revolutionary thinker Antonio Gramsci on hegemony. Gramsci was inspired by the conservative Mosca, who, not unlike today's managerial literature, analysed the strategic construction of political formulas to build and cement hegemonic leadership coalitions enabling a minority to stay in control. By contrast, Gramsci, imprisoned by the regime of Benito Mussolini, theorised hegemony with a view to subverting it (Cox, 1981). A concept of control is a *settlement* (a deal) that stabilises or balances socio-economic forces. Gramsci noted that hegemonic ideas underlying this deal are reproduced not only by states but by societal institutions such as the church, schools and trade unions, who had accepted the agenda of the ruling coalition as the general interest. The resulting sense of solidarity (normative agreement) facilitates compliance and forestalls the threat of political resistance. Gramsci pointed at Fordism, named after the car maker who offered his workers five dollars a day so that they could save up for a Ford car, as an increasingly internationally successful socio-economic 'deal' in his day, a hegemonic concept of control.

This influential approach reminds us that the ideational level is never very remote from practices and material capabilities: the call for arms uttered by an army general is likely to have more influence than that of a schoolboy. The context of (material) power relations may influence the results of a frame contest (Marullo, Pagnucco and Smith, 1996: 3). Yet neither can a supremo durably command the compliance of others in the political arena by relying on the use of force only (hard power), they have to employ a discursive strategy ('soft power') to attract and persuade. Hegemonic rule is thus a judicious combination of coercion and consent. Nevertheless, neither the legitimacy of a security frame nor that of a security provider has to be accepted. The below will go into the different forms of rejecting a security frame – these will be especially interesting for the present study where those rejections themselves use the language of security.

1.3.4 Contested Security

Margaret Thatcher became famous for her favourite categorical claim: 'There is no alternative', whose acronym is 'TINA'. But as her visionary compatriot and contemporary, the cyberneticist Stafford Beer (in van Gigch, 1987)[12] has argued, there is *always* an alternative, even if it is politically more opportune to disallow it. Frames always compete with counter-frames to provide singular interpretations of problems and appropriate solutions. New social groups (discursive alliances) will inevitably form and bring other (environmental, economic and cultural) security values to bear. In any engagement and negotiation process, actors bring new frames into play all the time, foregrounding certain aspects and backgrounding others. It does not mean that security issues have disappeared, but rather that the interpretation of the threat and its solution become more flexible and negotiable. This 'interpretative flexibility' enables the reframing of conflictive situations as non-conflictive and vice versa. In a securitised situation this flexibility means they are subject to desecuritisation processes; if the context was never securitised to begin with, it means unsuccessful securitisation (that is: successful non-securitisation). The move is disarmed, life goes on like before.

While the securitiser may find it strategically opportune to frame an issue as a security issue, this audience may thus find it strategically opportune to accept or reject the speech act. Unintended (possibly uninvited) 'audiences' may join the fray to contest and reframe the security claim. In analysing the contest over flood management projects, I have looked into the 'counter-frames' offered in the public arena, and have left the possibility open that stakeholders could 'counter-securitise' and, as a consequence, politicise an issue just as well as project initiators.

Constructivists tend to present reframing as a process of 'social learning' – the process of arriving at complementary mindsets (or 'reasons for action') in a network of interdependent stakeholders (Leeuwis, 2004). While the term conjures the image of a studious group seeking to understand the world, a reframing process is equally likely to involve conflict and struggle where power differences make themselves felt (Proost and Leeuwis, 2006). The research indeed zooms in on multiple instances of conflict over river management projects, where securitising moves were strongly contested.

Conflict is 'a social situation in which a minimum of two actors (parties) strive to acquire at the same moment in time an available set of scarce resources' (Wallensteen, 2002). It reflects and reproduces 'incompatible subject positions', that is, of a diametrical opposition between Us and Them, Self and Other(s), with clearly defined boundaries between them. Such 'pre-productions' tend to escalate, so that conflict over one issue becomes antagonism over everything else. While the conflict may be over only one aspect, the parties involved find themselves at daggers drawn over all possible issues: everything else collapses into two categories: black and white, friend and foe. One actor who feels impeded by the presence of an 'other' will start to project all fears and undesirables on this Other. This 'logic of equivalence' (Laclau and Mouffe, 1993) stands in clear contrast with a 'logic of difference', which accepts more shades of grey. Communication breaks down, antagonists speak about each other but rarely with each other. In such a conflict situation, it is not one but two coalitions that need to convince their audience that their non-negotiables should be honoured.

1.3.5 Competing Water (Meta-)narratives

Security moves and stories are set in larger (global) narratives, which lend a 'deep structure' and, hence, coherence to ambiguous, uncertain situations. Narratives allow storytellers to be certain about what is essentially uncertain. Like the speech act, the story frames particular solutions in terms of influencing or neutralising action – curbing opportunities for resistance and alternative conceptions (closing the frame) or pushing for particular measures to check, debate and correct security measures (opening the frame).

War or Peace?

National or basin borders are far from impermeable to ideas. In this context I take issue with the view that there is a basically uncontested set of prevailing (hegemonic) ideas in the 'water discourse' (Du Plessis, 2000; Furlong, 2006). While concepts such as integrated water resources management are currently almost unassailable (Wester and Warner, 2002), what constitutes hegemonic water discourse in the 'International Water Relations' community appears to be more in flux than the water discourse authors claim (Warner and Zeitoun, under review). There appears to be a change of 'grand narratives' giving meaning to experienced reality.[13]

The end of the 1980s saw a sense of crisis and confusion in both the security and water sector. The can-do mentality – the feeling that every problem can be fixed – that long prevailed in the water world eroded after a succession of setbacks. The Water Decade had brought water to many, but many more were still without water. The years 1989–2001 marked a period of relative 'anarchy', with no clearly hegemonic arrangement.

Global 'anarchy' brought, in broad strokes, three types of response and two contenders for discursive hegemony. The first narrative is that of '*water wars*', a Malthusian tale that considers water as a high-politics (security) issue. Robert Kaplan (1994) predicted a 'coming' anarchy and ungovernability while many popular books appeared predicting 'resource wars' (Starr and Stoll, 1988; Bulloch and Darwish, 1993; de Villiers, 1999). I will argue that (physical, political and discursive) 'closure' and its close cousin, 'enclosure' are at the heart of this narrative at the level of the project and at the level of the national and basin governance context. In the twenty-first century, climate change put the fear of 'water wars' back on the political map.

On the other hand, an increasingly influential 'water peace' camp made itself heard, which saw the post-Cold War period as an opportunity for reform towards environmentally sound, participatory, integrated, cooperative basin water management. Water pricing, virtual water and shared benefits are catchwords of this world view. The state was no longer seen as the natural water manager, and security and development not necessarily its domain. 'The Turning of the Screw' narrative, proposed by Leif Ohlsson and Tony Turton (1999), will be presented as an exponent of this view.

At the same time, a 'counterculture' against liberalisation and privatisation as well as large dams (Narmada, Arun) became increasingly vocal and at times successful. Taken to its extreme, it can be summarised as '*plus ça change, plus c'est la même chose*'. This is the *hydro-hegemony* thesis: hegemony is expressed in ever more subtle forms of control over water – and over society. But hegemony, as we saw, is always contestable, and a global movement against the hegemony of what its opponents see as water capture has made itself felt in the past two decades. This presents a completely different take on 'water wars' (Shiva, 2002), not between countries, but between the global and the local.

It turns out that these discourses give different meanings to what the 'politics of flood security' constitute, what 'cooperation regimes' mean and how flood management may be labelled as

- a security imperative (the water wars narrative),
- an engine for cooperation and sustainable development (the water peace narrative),
- an instrument of control and locus for contest (the water hegemony narrative).

Natural or Social?

The phrase 'complex emergency' captures war and disaster, which both invite the state of exception. Given that the two are close cousins, I looked for narratives in the discipline of disaster studies as foci for flood security that would be compatible to the above three narratives. Candidates are the 'structural', 'behavioural' and 'vulnerability' approach (Hilhorst, 2003; Johnson, et al., 2005).

The *structural* paradigm is the result of modern science, which saw the flood as a force of nature to be tamed with physical infrastructure. Rulers and their bureaucracies sought to eliminate uncertainty by calling on science and expertise to avoid relying on the fickleness of nature and of human passions. River regulation in flood-prone or drought-prone areas easily becomes a matter of central government concern. The first centralised states developed from the perceived need to regulate rivers for collective development. Water bureaucracies ('hydrocracies'; Wester, 2008), often related with the military sector (US Corps of Engineers in the USA and DSI in Turkey), would take care of civil defence against flood threats as part of homeland security. The downside of machine bureaucracies, however, is that they are rarely well-equipped to deal with crises; they tend to handle crises the same way as normal situations (Crozier, 1964).

Dissatisfied with the performance of flood defences, an American liberal school of human geographers (G. White, 1954; Burton, Kates and White, 1993) focussed on human *behaviour* and choice. Institutional regulation (zoning) and incentives (subsidies) influence the preferences within the range of alternatives individuals have at their disposal, to make up for people's 'bounded rationality' (see also Johnson, et al., 2005). Collective insurance and national reinsurance complements the set of instruments.

A vulnerability approach, finally, critiqued this approach in the 1980s, arguing that disadvantaged groups in society do not have a choice, but end up in the most hazard-prone locations because of their position in the political economy (Hewitt, 1983; Blaikie, et al., 1994). As they identify with local actors and initiatives rather than the state, I see strong parallels with the (anti-)hegemony perspective on 'water wars'.

1.3.6 Beyond Talk: Practices of Security and Conflict

So far, the discussion in this section has focussed on words, as used in speech acts, frames, stories, narratives. It has been noted with some frequency, however, that focusing on speech acts only privileges the verbal over the non-verbal. This not only ignores the power of images (M. Williams, 2003), but also backgrounds the practical institutionalisation of security and external conditions (Léonard, 2004; Floyd, 2007). Bigo (2002) has noted that to understand securitisation, we should not just look at the success of speech acts but at the *practices* of security professionals, their everyday practices in the security field at the micro level, not only at the macro-level studies of political discourses.[14] While politicians and other public speakers speak (or picture) security, security experts more quietly handle the technologies of security. Securitisation discourses are embedded in technology, which not only comprises instruments to implement policy decisions, but also 'shape the options available to decision-makers' (Léonard, 2004).

The present study focuses on such practices by way of *projects:* proposed technological interventions. A channel, an embankment, is planned in a cycle of situation analysis, project identification, selection of options, implementation and evaluation. At each of these stages, decisions are made and alternatives and actors included or excluded. Unlike Bigo (2002), however, I maintain it is not only the recognised security professionals, but also their opponents who shape the discourse and practice of security with securitisations and counter-securitisation. Project-affected stakeholders can voice approval or stage vocal protest, but also more quietly display 'compliance' or 'deviance'. Depending on the protection frame's felicity with the intended audience, a major infrastructural flood management project helps or hinders the legitimacy of its initiators and objectors and the constellation (decision-making regime) in which they operate.

I reasoned that the best way of eliciting security practices is by focusing on actual river management schemes. To promote development and guarantee protection, a river scheme almost inevitably involves 'taking (someone's) space'. (River) *regulation* projects are 'sites of struggle over the definitions of uses and the boundaries of the zones which have material effects on the use and perception of space' (Bierschenk, 1988). This is notably where a flood project meets the domain of local stakeholders. Spatial planning is about 'making space' using concepts that reflect an actor's ambitions with that space (Hagens, 2007): a 'hub', a 'park' or even a 'new civilisation', but also 'ancestral commons' (Bierschenk, 1988). In so doing, the planner meets others who have other plans for the space at issue, or resist what they see as the invasion of their space and territorial control. Projects are thus essentially contested (Bierschenk, 1988)and it is this contest that can reveal the practice of security interventions.

The self-image of the planning discipline has seen major change in the past decade: From rationality-based social engineering. One such change is the way it now engages with power. Booher and Innes (2002) note that planners try to think comprehensively in the public interest, but are frustrated that they do not have the politicians' ear, and are forced to work by the agencies that are organised on a piecemeal approach to the world. Booher and Innes claim that planners do exercise power on an everyday basis, they shape the flow of it. But they are not in charge. Innes & Booher point at the 'power-to' procured by collaborate network planning, as the distributed capacities are productively coordinated. The Habermasian implication would be that collaborative planning would make things more rational, due to better communication and argumentation which come with more interaction and trust. Flyvbjerg (1998) however very much doubts the rationality of planning because of the power play at work – not only on the part of politicians, but of planners themselves.

Planners, then, are part of the political arena, and seek to work the terrain to their advantage, collaboratively or otherwise. Public, but also non-state actors can use crisis and danger vocabulary to make their claim to power or legitimacy of a certain solution and delegitimise others. Project-affected actors, or those speaking for them, may claim the intervention makes them more insecure rather than more secure. This can lead to negotiation and accommodation or negation, but also to an escalating crisis. The present analysis tests Lowry's interpretation of a Focusing Event as an *opportunity* for actors to promote or even impose previously impossible agendas.

1.3.7 In Search of Politics

What, then, is the politics of flood security? Having defined 'flood' and '(in)security', the present study treats the security arena as a special kind of 'politics'. There are a great many conceptualisations of politics, ranging from party politics to all human relations. For the purposes of the present study, I will bring together some of those strands.

Many might subscribe to Wishnick's (2005) cynical interpretation of politics: an actor's manipulation of a problem for political ends. This however is not a usual interpretation in political science. A preliminary view of politics, steeped in the Greek tradition, is what delineates the public from the private sphere. The political is what promotes the public common good (what constitutes 'the good life') in the *polis*. This normative content is reflected in the definition of politics as the 'authoritative allocation of values' (Easton, 1953). Politics is the contest over the distribution of scarce resources (Haywood, 1998) – or 'the shaping, distribution and exercise of power' (Lasswell and Kaplan, 1950: 75). It is the answer to Harold Lasswell's (1936) question: 'Who gets what, where, when, why and how', summarised as *cui bono* (in whose interest)?

Dye, Zeigler and Lichter (1992) rephrase Lasswell's question as: 'who says what; in which channel, to whom, and with what effect?' Politics is *communication* – politics takes shape through discourse, visuals and dramaturgy (staging) (Hajer, 1995, 2001). Hajer (1995: 59) defines politics as the struggle for discursive hegemony in which actors struggle to secure support for their definition of reality.

While for Buzan, et al. (1998: 23–24), 'politicised' means 'subject to public policy and debate'. I will follow Guzzini's (2005) wider understanding of politicisation as 'making political', the imagination of *alternatives* which open the frame, and Mouffe (2005) in being alive to the polarising effects that, she claims, are only proper to actual political interaction. The politics of flood insecurity, then, is the contest (foreclosure and opening) over alternatives (which I will take to mean frames, actors and options) for flood management, and their distributive effects between stakeholders.

The present study takes up Buzan, et al.'s (1998: 25) rejoinder to concentrate on *discourse* and the *political constellation* when studying the effect of a security argument, if without much guidance on how this might be done. Above, I have explained how I conceptualise the central analytical elements of the two – frames, narratives, governance and regimes. The final section of the chapter will explain in more detail how I conceived the methodology.

1.4 Constructivism and Positioning

Following Buzan, et al. (1998), I shall take a constructivist approach to risk and security. In constructivism there is no objective truth, only interpretation. Constructivists (Berger and Luckmann, 1991 [1966]) see the world not as something static, something that 'is', but something that 'becomes'. Change is normal, we should be on the alert if something remains the same for very long.

Because we cannot explain and validate constructions, we can only try to understand and interpret what may have been on an actor's mind (Smith and Hollis, 1990). Discourse analysis, such as securitisation analysis, helps us 'disclose' what was consciously or subconsciously closed. By naming a threat, it makes explicit what was hidden, and in so doing the speaker gives us a piece of his or her mind (Miniotaite, 2000). Buzan, et al. (1998) remind us not to look specifically for the word 'security', but rather for 'arguments that take the rhetorical and logical form defined [by them] as security' (Buzan, et al., 1998: 177). This is their recipe for *securitisation*:

> . . . follow the security form, the grammar of security, and construct a plot that includes existential threat, points of no return, and a possible way out – the general grammar of security as such plus the particular dialects of the different sectors, such as talk identity in the societal sector, recognition and sovereignty in the political sector, sustainability in the environmental sector, and so on (. . .) (I)t is implicitly assumed that if we talk of *this* (. . .), we are by definition in the area of urgency: by saying 'defence' (or in Holland, 'dikes'), one has implicitly said security and priority. (Buzan, et al., 1998: 27)

How does one operationalise this rather broad portrait (*signalement*) of social and linguistic felicity conditions for securitisation in the water sector and critically engage with it? As a first clue, Buzan, et al. (1998) explicitly relate security to survival issues. 'Survival' is the point of no return, everything else will be irrelevant. Gromes and Bonacker interpret this as follows:

> Phrases [. . .] close to 'to be or not to be' are death, end, annihilation, extinction [. . .] Loss of self-determination is inflicted by notions as loss of freedom [. . .], oppression [. . .] and proper names that refer to well-known examples. (Gromes and Bonacker, 2007)

In addition, I proposed above to relate securitisation to closure, the disallowance of contending alternatives, actors and issues, that is, the delegitimisation of choice. To me (Warner, 2004a), 'There Is No Alternative' (TINA) sums up the exemplar of a securitisation: it shuts out alternatives, breaks normally binding rules of engagement, such as exchange, debate and openness, that might bring in other colours.

Since no one in the security studies, to my knowledge, appears to have done this so far, I developed the below diagram (Table 1.3), which provides a provisional heuristic of the characteristics of the (ideal-typical) practice of securitised and desecuritised decision-making, compiled on the basis of the principles laid out in the literature, especially Buzan, et al. (1998) and Roe (2004).

Constructivist political science maintains that political actors (individuals, groups or states, as in International Relations) not only, and not always, play power games, they also puzzle, which may change actors' interest definition,

	Logic of Securitisation ('war' and 'emergency')	Logic of Non-securitised Policymaking ('peace' and 'routine')
Applicability	For extraordinary, urgent events	For ongoing concerns
Governance	Vertical (top-down management, patronage in protection)	Network (co-management, negotiation among autonomous actors)
Degree of power sharing	Bypassing democracy and stakeholder participation	Stakeholder participation and influence
Role of market	Bypassing market mechanism and cost-benefit analysis	Market for security goods and services
Mode of securing compliance	Compliance through force and rules	Compliance through persuasion and marketing of security
Transparency	Secrecy, information distribution on need to know basis and unaccountability	Openness, free exchange of information & public accountability

Table 1.3: ***Logics of securitised and non-securitised policymaking***

therefore their compliance with a particular policy issue (Checkel, 2001) and, as a result, their positioning. A constructivist approach means that actors can learn and change their perspective in interaction with others, such that it changes their role, their position with respect to those others. We can expect the definition and identity of 'who' in Lasswell's question (who gets what) as well as in van Eeten's (1997) 'stories' to be in flux rather than a static entity. Political actors develop identities in their interaction and interrelation with each other, so that they themselves can be 'changed by the distributional games in which they participate' (I. Neumann, 1999). The same actors can act as friends or enemies, as Englishmen or Europeans. Since, according to Buzan, et al. (1998) the security speech act is an 'act' with special force, the present study zooms in on the consequences of this particular positioning. The enemy can be the flood, but also the flood manager, whose actions (or non-action) may be seen to bring insecurity rather than security. Speech acts are embedded in what Jasanoff (1999) has called 'songlines' and others storylines. Uttering a specific element from that storyline (say, Buzan, et al.'s examples of Dutch dikes), a whole storyline is effectively reinvoked that lends credence to some (security) actors and delegitimises others (see Hajer, 1995: 62, 67).

But security language is not cast in stone. Slocum and van Langenhove's (2003) suggestions for a positional methodology may be helpful here. Whether social interactions are conflictive or peaceful depends upon how people attribute meanings to their interactions and situation. Discourse is a fishnet-like structure of knots (objects) connected by threads (relations) (Lindahl and Sundset, 2003). An actor in the fishnet has a 'subject position' from which (s)he sees and categorises the world, the rest of the net and positions others. Slocum and Langenhove's Positioning Triangle consists of Actors, Acts and Narratives. The Acts, such as speech acts, set in a particular setting (narrative) (re)constitute the actors in particular positions, roles, identities with respect to each other: 'leader', 'protector', 'expert', 'victims' with the help of specific lexical supports (frames and plots). In the context of the present research, it can also reconstitute the frames with respect to water: 'enemy', 'friend' or 'resource'.

By positioning oneself, one also positions others in the arena. Parties in conflict co-define each other's goals and identities (Kriesberg, 1986). In this respect, I am inspired by van Eeten's (1997) narratological analysis of conflict on water management in the Netherlands. Van Eeten shows how flood-risk stories ('fairy tales') take the same narrative form, the discourse coalitions mirror each other even though the discursive coalitions finds themselves diametrically opposed to each other: the hero of one story is the villain in the other: the former's problem is the latter's solution. Van Eeten's approach points at the embeddedness of individual speech acts in security stories, a point I will elaborate in the next section.

Not all securitising moves are successful, not all stories are believed. Attribution of a threat does not necessarily lead to counteraction. In that case, there is security discourse, but no 'performativity'. Securitisation is a 'call and response' between enunciator and intended audience. The authority relation between the securitising actor and the audience may play a part, or the audience does not respond as expected, that is, does not accept the securitising move, or there is no follow-up that reproduces the discourse and translates word into action. In that case, there is no legitimation for extraordinary measures (Roe, 2004). Gromes and Bonacker (2007) therefore also identity non-securitising moves:

- denying the existence of an existential threat,
- claiming the addressed audience does not possess the legitimacy to decide on the adoption of extraordinary means,
- recommending the addressed audience to reject the call to 'panic politics',
- resisting the implementation of extraordinary measures.

If *non*-securitisation failed, *de*securitisation is the undoing of an existing securitisation:

Country	Project	Project Core	Start of Project	(Projected) End of Project
Egypt	New Valley Project	Toshka Channel	1998	2017
Turkey	Greater Anatolia Project	Ilısu Dam (first major dam on Tigris)	2001	2014?
Bangladesh	Flood Action Plan	Compartment-alisation Pilot Project (CPP)	1991	(2000)
Netherlands – Maas	Maaswerken	Border Meuse	1995	2015
Netherlands – Ooij	Controlled Emergency Flood Storage	Ooij polder	2000	Aborted
UK	Integrated Catchment Management	Jubilee Channel	1999	2001

Table 1.4: ***List of case studies discussed in this book***

- not to talk (any more) about issues in terms of security to keep responses in forms that avoid vicious spirals to move security back into normal politics (Roe, 2004).

1.4.1 The Cases

The study involves six cases of flood-related politics in five countries. Allowing for considerable differences between projects and *modus operandi*, all the studies are concerned with national projects presented as new, innovative (non-standard) ways of dealing with flood water challenges. The first five studies concern the biggest river management project in that country in recent times – all started after 1990 – but were in fact the largest since the 1960s (Table 1.4). A sixth study looks into the proposed revival of a flood protection measure (emergency storage) that had fallen into disuse for fifty years. The five countries studied are plotted in the below matrix for their variation on the two variables 'stream intervention' and 'openness of governance system' that can be plotted on the two continua introduced in Section 1.2.2. All selected countries can be said to be on the continuum of governance ranging from states with a 'closed' (state-dominated) to a more 'open' governance regime introduced above.

The first two studies, Egypt and Turkey, based on desk research, appear 'closed systems' in terms of technical and political control, if with considerable nuances. They are states where, due to earlier interventions, flood risk is not a great challenge anymore. Egypt, commonly regarded as dependent on only one source of water, the Nile, is downstream to nine countries, and therefore can be expected to make continued access to water a security issue. This case is contrasted with Turkey, a state that has rain as well as the geopolitical advantage of being upstream. Due to this third dimension, 'river position', the two countries can be expected to take a different view of the role in national security.

The felicity of security speech depends very much on what is normal speech in a particular setting and rhetorical tradition. Security framing in the *press* is a crucial *mediator* of security speech acts (Vultee, 2007) exerting a heavy influence on whether an issue will be a security issue. Wilkinson (2007: 10) notes that in non-European cultures, freedom of speech may be constrained so it may not be possible for actors to engage in security speech. Indeed Turkey and Egypt may be researched as political cultures with repressive traits. In such cases, protest may express a community perceiving an existential threat. Power holders then will label protesters as appearing a threat to the regime. Protesters will have to 'desecuritise' their opposition by stressing their allegiance to shared values (protective frame) to avoid being securitised themselves (Paltemaa and Vuori, 2006).

The four remaining case study countries concern downstreamers with riverine flood risk in 'wet' basins – the Netherlands on the Rhine and Meuse, England downstream to Wales on the Thames, and Bangladesh to Brahmaputra, Indus and Meghna. In Bangladesh, despite thousands of miles of dikes and embankments, floods invade large swathes of territory every year. Flood protection depends very much on external funds so that conditionality as regards the flood management philosophy is high. In the Netherlands, half the territory is below sea level and potential flood risk from river is large, but flood control has been so extensive that floods had been thought to be under control. The UK, finally, is a country with low water intervention in which the private (insurance) rather than the public sector appears to be charged with risk management.

Mitchell reminds us that flood management happens in a physical as well as a political, socio-cultural, etc. context (B. Mitchell, 1990). Any analysis of flood politics should take full cognisance of this context. For example, even though England is in the same moderate flood risk-prone category as the Netherlands and floods have claimed lives and assets, the degree of public intervention displays great difference between the two countries. The Netherlands and

Bangladesh are both deltas with waterways wherever one looks, but the socio-economic and political setting is completely different.

Since no one in security studies, to my knowledge, appears to have done this so far, I developed the below diagram (Table 1.3) which provides a provisional heuristic of the characteristics of the (ideal-typical) practice of securitised and desecuritised decision-making, compiled on the basis of the principles laid out in the literature, especially Buzan, et al. (1998) and Roe (2004). The study is based on extensive documentary research and, in the latter four case studies (Chapters 5–8) field visits and interviews with decision-makers and stakeholders. Following Michael Williams (2003), I have taken discourse to mean both textual and visual discourse, taking due note of the staging (Hajer, 2005) of the security discourse, which enhance or defeat their felicity.

2

MIDNIGHT AT NOON? THE TUSSLE OVER TOSHKA, EGYPT

Moving to the desert is a must. There is no better way to inspire people than through a dramatic announcement. The President knows his people. Egyptians tend to join hands when they are inspired by an urgent national project. (Egyptian government official quoted in Bush, 2007)

When the emperor claims it's midnight at noon, the wise man says: behold the moon. (Omar Khayyam, *Rubaiyat*)

2.1 Introduction: Closing the River

Had the High Aswan Dam not blocked the river Nile, floods would have wreaked havoc in Egypt in 1975, 1988, 1998 and 1999. Now Lake Nasser, the giant reservoir behind the dam, stores surface floodwater for dry years. But in 1998, Egypt experienced such an exceptional peak discharge that even this mega-reservoir might have overflowed. Previously, such excess water would have been drained via a spillway straight into the desert, but the Egyptian government felt this was a waste of a precious resource. This time, therefore, Egypt embarked on a giant desert reclamation plan, presented with much fanfare as a 'new civilisation on the Nile'. The plan is far more than an irrigation plan: the government hopes to house millions of Egyptians in a new city in the Western desert, creating additional space to relieve the pressure on the small strip of inhabitable Nile flood plain. The Toshka project, however, will require far more water than the occasional flood can provide, and in so doing has the unique feature of planning for *more* than the maximum.

In the well-known phrase of the Greek philosopher Herodotos, 'Egypt is the gift of the Nile,' (quoted in Schiffler, 1997) but another image comes to mind – that of a diver depending on his oxygen supply. This extreme dependence has inspired dozens of journalistic accounts and scientific studies of violent water conflict potential with upstream countries – 'The Nile is a war waiting to start' (cited in MacNeill, et al., 1991: 56). Despite numerous verbal attacks between riparians, these wars never happened. Blanket statements, such as 'scarcity leads to war', are clearly too simplistic.

The 'project of the millennium'[1], however (once more), set Egypt on a collision course with Ethiopia, which claims more Nile water for its own agrarian development. If all nine upstream Nile states were substantially to develop the waters flowing through their territory for economic development, Egypt would find itself in dire straits. Nevertheless, Ethiopia is not the only country to complain. A half-century after Egyptian independence, Nile relations are still largely governed by colonial treaties concluded on behalf of Egypt by Great Britain, and the 'Full Utilisation of the Nile' treaty concluded to placate Sudan in 1959. These agreements oblige the upstream riparians not to 'arrest' the flow of the Nile. In 1961, Julius Nyerere, president of what was to become Tanzania, proclaimed in the 'Nyerere Doctrine on State Succession' that he would abrogate the treaties after two years:

> As regards bilateral treaties validly concluded by the United Kingdom on behalf of the territory of Tanganyika, or validly applied or extended by the former to the territory of the latter, the Government Tanganyika is willing to continue to apply within its territory on a basis of reciprocity, the terms of all such treaties for a period of two years from the date of independence – unless abrogated or modified earlier by mutual consent. At the expiry of that period, the Government of Tanganyika will regard such of these treaties which could not by the application of rules of customary international law be regarded as otherwise surviving, as having terminated. (Quoted in Phillips, et al., 2006)

Still, despite many protestations to the contrary, no upstream country has seriously cancelled the colonial moratorium on upstream development on the Nile that Egypt still invokes.

Why does Egypt embark on a project that, experts argue, will claim even more water when Egypt is already approaching water and cash shortage? Are the motives domestic or do external Nile relations play a part? Are there opposing voices or is the issue depoliticised in the spirit of the saying from the *Rubayyat*: 'if the ruler claims it's midnight at noon, the wise man says: behold the moon'?

This chapter will argue that the scheme serves *multiple goals*, of which 'greening the desert' is only one. A parallelism between domestic and foreign policy strategies seems to lend the project an unstoppable dynamics.

The chapter will first outline the scope of Toshka and its accompanying mega-projects in the Egyptian deserts. Thereafter, it will introduce and apply the concept of 'closure' in decision-making. As the Egyptian state is acutely aware of its vulnerability with regard to the water resource, one expects Egypt to exert tight technical control of the river, but also of its population and of its riparian neighbours. To what extent does this hold true in practice? The second half of the chapter inventories Egyptian relations with its upstream neighbours, assessing the Nile basin Initiative (NBI) as a cooperation regime. *How does Egypt ensure the compliance of its co-riparians and citizens, and what is the role of securitisation and closure in this?*

2.1.1 The Nile: Best Friend or Worst Enemy

For five thousand years, Nile floods carried much-needed water as well as a sediment-load of basalt, rich alluvial soil and silts to a dry and desert area, and flushed out the salt left behind by high evaporation in the intense heat and capillary rise in fine-grained, waterlogged soils (Murakami, 1999). In ancient times, there was a fragile balance between too much and too little. The ideal flooding height was 7–8 metres. 'When the flood was too low, cultivated acreage might be halved, causing widespread famine; when the flood was too high, small-scale riverine irrigation works were destroyed and fields were swamped, also causing widespread famine' (Shapland, 1997: 60).

Egypt only needs to point at its neighbours' predicament to feel justified in building the mega dam to control excess water. In Sudan, floods continue to cause damage and to claim lives. In its capital Khartoum, where the Blue and White Nile branches meet, 1.5–2 million, out of the 4.5 million inhabitants at the time, were displaced by the flood of 1988.[2] The 2005 floods left 1,000 families homeless in Khartoum and killed 8 persons and left 2,000 homeless in Darfur.[3] In Uganda, Nile floods had devastating effects in 1964 and 1998.

The other extreme, intense drought claimed 1 million Ethiopian lives from famine in the 1980s. While disaster experts have shown that the mechanisms underlying famine are far more complex than water shortage, food scarcity can also be due to bad infrastructure and hoarding by traders (see Sen, 1981, on entitlements); this 'detail' is easily lost in the political discourse.

Egypt feels particularly vulnerable because it has few alternatives to the Nile. Since average rainfall in Egypt is only 60 mm/year and it may not rain for years on end in the desert, the only significant addition to the 55.5 km^2 (=55 billion cubic metres) coming in at Aswan these days is the reuse of return flows from municipalities, industry and agriculture. These extremes make the river both Egypt's worst enemy and its life support. This, in turn, makes regulating the river Nile the central focus of Egypt's *water security* strategy, which hinges on three pillars: *river development, groundwater development* and *rationalisation* of use (Murakami, 1999). We will encounter each of those three in the course of the chapter.

	Domestic Developments	Basin Developments
1953	General Nasser comes to power	
1956	Nationalisation of the Suez Canal; European intervention	
1958		Coup in Sudan Start of American dam study for Ethiopia
1959	Creation of New valley Governorate	'Full Utilisation of the Nile Waters' agreement
1960–1972	Building Aswan dam and spillway	
1961		Nyerere Doctrine defies colonial treaties
1973	*Infitah:* economic liberalisation reforms after war on Israel	
1980–1988	Lake Nasser saves Egypt from drought	Famine in Ethiopia
1981	President Sadat killed; state of emergency pronounced	
1983		UNDUGU initiative for the Nile
1985		Discontinuation of Sudan's Jonglei project after SPLA attack
1987		Hydromet initiative for the Nile
1992		The first Nile 2002 conference
1995	Egyptian president escapes attack in Addis Ababa	Accusations between Nile states after attack on the president
1997	Construction of Zayyed Channel	Four years of abundant Nile flow

Table 2.1: ***Chronology of domestic and basin events on the Nile***

To contend with the precariousness of exposure to floods and droughts, Egypt has a millennial history of advanced water regulation. Egypt and Mesopotamia are commonly bracketed together as the first 'hydraulic civilisations'. However, the 'hydraulic imperative' only became an issue in the past century, when Egypt was under foreign rule. First, Muhammad Ali, the Ottoman viceroy, connected Alexandria (Iskanderiyya) with the Nile for irrigation purposes. Then, at the turn of the twentieth century, when there was a relative shortage of cotton on the world market, the Englishman William Willcocks built the first Aswan dam to ensure the Lancashire mills in Britain would be supplied with a constant supply. King Cotton also gave the impetus for the Gezira project in the Sudan and, more recently, the Ethiopian Awash irrigation project (Ward, 1997: 113). The original Aswan dam was built in 1902 to trap excess autumn floods to use in the dry season. Before the High Aswan Dam (Sadd el-Aali in Arabic), 'a third of the Nile water coming from Ethiopia flowed into the Mediterranean without being tapped.' To gain complete control of the river, Egypt replaced the 'low' Aswan Dam in the 1960s by a huge rockfill barrage, the High Aswan Dam, and impounded Lake Nasser. Completed in 1970, the colossal storage reservoir inundated a 'land described as the cockpit of the ancient world and both the connection and the buffer between the ancient Mediterranean civilisations and the vanished high cultures of Black Africa' (Schleifer and Bursch, 2005). A historical heritage like the Abu Simbel temples, which the lake would submerge, were rebuilt 210 metres to the west of the original location. All temples were relocated except the monuments of Qasr Ibrim, which was built on top of an 80-metre-tall rock formation above the Nile's level[4]. Moreover, 50,000 Nubians were resettled in government housing, and many have indicated wanting to return (Moll, 2004).

The project was paid for by the Soviet Union, to the tune of US$1 billion plus technical assistance, plus US$650 million coming from Nasser's nationalisation of the Suez Canal in 1956. Regulation for storage was never the only objective for Aswan Dam; faced with a rising population, vast tracts of desert land were developed in the 1960s for irrigation with Aswan water.

In principle, the 5-kilometre-long and 100-metre-high High Dam finally secured total flood protection by stopping the floodwater altogether. When Egyptians planned the 565-kilometre-long Lake Nasser reservoir on the Sudanese border, they had not counted on its 163,000 km^3 capacity to be too *small.* The upshot is unexpected excess water that needs to go somewhere – either passing through the dam into Egypt if it opens the floodgates, or allowed to backflow into Sudan, where it would cause major trouble. To make absolutely sure, between 1966 and 1978, as part of the Aswan project, the Egyptians excavated a 14-mile canal through Khor (Bay) Toshka on the western shore of Lake Nasser, to spill any excess water into the Toshka Depression (*wadi*). As the overflow channel was completed at the start of a decade of very dry years, it remained inoperative for many years.

The Dam tided Egypt over the long spell of drought which hit Africa in the 1980s. Due to heavy rains over the Blue Nile and the Atbara, which joins the Nile in Sudan, the Nile discharge in 1988 was 106 km^2. This heralded a return of a series of high inflows – 1994 (91.9 km^3), 1996 (92.2 km^3), 1998 (121 km^3) and 1999 (95.2 km^3) (Collins, 2003).

The 1996 flood tested the carrying capacity of the earth underneath Lake Nasser, which displayed geologic faults vulnerable to fracture from the increasing weight of the lake. Then Minister of Public Works, Radi, declared a state of emergency for Upper Egypt (Collins, 2003). The inflow was so high that the dam's overflow channel had to be opened to ease the pressure (back-flooding) on Sudan. In 1998, the waters rose even higher, and while the excess water was drained into the Toshka depression, the floodwater still affected 40 tribal houses.

But more was yet to come. The one-in-a-hundred-year flood of 1998, thought to be attributable to the El Niño southern oscillation, was followed by two La Niña flood years. The excess water – a total of 80 billion cubic metres (BCM) of water – was again duly discharged through the spill channel into the desert. But that raised an already rising water table due to the progressive 'sealing' of the bottom of Lake Nasser, while infiltration in aquifers is very limited due to impermeable limestone underlying the Toshka depression. Four new lakes appeared in the Kiseiba-Dungul Depression[5] – the first (at 172 m above sea level) in 1998, the others in 2000. A fifth lake briefly emerged to the northwest up in 2001. The lakes are subject to huge evaporation losses: 87 per cent between 1998 and 2001. 'Now we have salt marshes there, good for duck hunting but not much else' (Taher Muhammad Hassan cited by Werner and Bubriski, 2007).

Rather than let all this precious water go to waste, the Egyptian government decided for a four-year spillway construction project (1998–2002) to utilise the floodwater to 'green the desert'. A new Toshka channel was constructed from 1998 to turn an exceptional inflow into a rule: it counts on a structural inflow of 300 m^3 per second into a whole new irrigation scheme. In so doing, it reverses a very old historic flow: while Wadi Toshka used to feed the Nile in ancient times, the Toshka depression will now be used to pump water in the opposite direction,aiming to 'eventually create a second branch to the River Nile in the western desert of Egypt, parallel to its prehistoric main course'.[6]

It is not hard to see wider implications for Toshka than agricultural opportunity, however. The chapter will first look into the planning history and *domestic* background to the Toshka project. Thereafter, the *external* conflict potential with nine riparians is looked into.

2.1.2 What is the Toshka project? History and Alternatives

The exact scope of the Toshka project (Lonergan and Wolf, 2001: 590) seems to change and grow as it comes along.

> Part of the confusion surrounding the project relates to the lack of detailed plans for all aspects of development and implementation [. . .] and the lack of information provided to donor groups, potential investors, and other governments regarding specific details of the development project. (Lonergan and Wolf, 2001: 591)

To add to the confusion, the project is also known under different names: the National Project for the Development of Upper Egypt (NPDUE), the South Valley Development Project, or South Egypt Development Project. It is best known as the Toshka project, after Wadi Toshka – although Tosca, Tushka, Tashka, Toshki, Tushcan and Tashkan are also among the spellings used (Lonergan and Wolf, 2001).

Plans for a 'New Valley Project' date back to the 1950s when Egypt was pursuing a *groundwater development* strategy. A first version of the New Valley Project consisted of efforts to expand the abstraction from groundwater wells, for which the groundwork was laid in 1958. In 1959 the New Valley governorate was created. As I will discuss below, the timing, in the middle of grave water and territorial conflict with Sudan, does not seem coincidental.

The groundwater-based approach, however, quickly ran into problems of salinisation and loss of hydraulic head (pressure), and artesian wells stopped to flow (Murakami, 1999). Water taken from the massive Nubian Sandstone aquifer, which Egypt shares with Libya, Chad and Sudan, is non-renewable. Drawing it down could not just lead to an unwelcome drop in the groundwater table but in due course also spark conflict between Egypt and its neighbour to the west, Libya.

Faced with these early setbacks, the Egyptians redrafted the project. Geological and soil surveys carried out by the Public Authority for Desert Reconstruction (PADR) in the early 1960s were followed by more studies between 1971 and 1973 confirming that a third of the Toshka Depression would be arable if irrigated (Collins, 2003). The Planners Association proposed to extend the existing Toshka Channel beyond the depression into the western oases of the New Valley, over a 310-kilometre stretch, to provide half the water needed – the rest still has to come from the finite, aquifers, mostly running underneath the Nile.

In 1997, construction of the Sheikh Zayyed Canal was begun. The 70-kilometre trunk canal has four 28-kilometre branches and is designed to convey 5 billion cubic metres of water a year to the New Valley Project. The canal

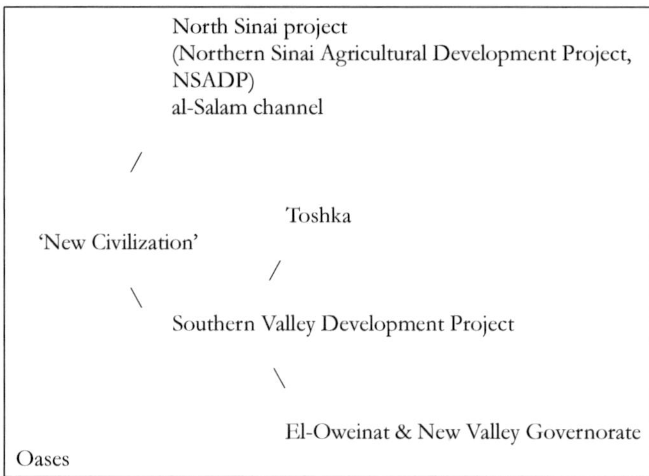

Figure 2.1: ***Schematic overview of Egypt's New Civilisation***

water will have to be pumped up an average of 21 to 53 m to get across the intervening section of the Nubian Plateau. The channel was shortened by half, from a planned length of 158 km to 72 km as the rest was 'not necessary' (El-Din, 1999).

The late 1990s saw several floods so that the spillway could be used in the last four years of the twentieth century. It captured 35 per cent of discharge to Egypt or 20 BCM. However, in the past years there have not been excess floods. A complicating factor is that a climate change-induced variation of 10 or 20 per cent in rainfall leads to 40–50 per cent variation in the inflow in Lake Nasser (WL: Delft Hydraulics, 2005).

In the meantime, the bigger picture got ever bigger. Figure 2.1 shows how Toshka fits into Egypt's grand plans for a 'New Civilisation'[7] in the desert.

The envisaged 'civilisation' consists of a northern and a southern valley project. The Northern Sinai Agricultural Development Project (NSADP) targets to resettle 750,000 Egyptians. Its core is the al-Salam Canal running from the Damietta Branch of the Nile, fifteen miles from Port Said, diving underneath the Suez Canal and emerging to irrigate 92,000 ha west of Suez and 168,000 ha of reclaimed land in the Sinai: the Suez Canal Region Development Project. In the context of the peace accords with Israel in 1979, President Sadat hinted that Nile water might be diverted to the South of Israel. The diversion of 'holy' Nile water to the 'Zionist state' elicited strong protests from Arab countries, but also from the Egyptian army, and after rumours of several plotted coups surfaced (Allouche, 2003), Sadat abandoned the diversion idea, but the al-Salam canal went ahead. An Environmental Assessment drafted for the Government of Egypt by the World Bank was suppressed in 1992 but leaked by activist Nabil El-Khodari, who, being especially concerned about the Sinai project's outcome for local indigenous Bedouin (El-Khodari, 2003a), posted the Environmental Impact Assessment on the Internet.

The *Southern* or *New Valley* project in turn is conceived in two phases, which, in turn, consist of three stages. Stage 1 is the *Toshka project* itself, the centrepiece of the project. It consists of the Toshka Channel and Mubarek (Mubarak) pumping station, launched on 9 January 1997 and consisting of the biggest pumping station in the world – a US$500 million, 24-pump structure near Abu Simbel – prepared by Lahmeyer of Germany and built by a consortium of the Norwegian-British company Kvaerner (inlet), Hitachi of Japan (pumps) and Egypt's Arabian International Construction, which would draw water from a point at 147.5 m above sea level into the canal. Asea Brown Boveri is responsible for the electrical engineering.

According to original plans (Lonergan and Wolf, 2001), 300 m^3/s of surface water was to be drawn from the Lake at a site upstream from the High Aswan Dam through six tunnels, each 1.5-kilometre long, and then lifted up 56 m via the pumping station (this in itself requires 200–375 MW), then through a channel into the desert. In so doing it extends the Aswan spillway westward into the Toshka depression, 'a sand-filled, dry-wash tributary of the Nile 34 km north of Abu Simbel' (Vance Haynes, 1980), which takes its name from the mythical Egyptian queen Tosca. The channel resuscitates what is believed to be an old *wadi* (a seasonal river valley) which, according to feasibility studies, had served to drain water from lakes *into* the Nile in ancient times. Annually, this diversion would amount to 5.5 million m^3, one-tenth of Egypt's ration under the 1959 Full Utilisation of the Nile agreement.

Stage 2 of the Southern Valley project, Toshka's 'sister', aims to reclaim the governorate of el-Oweinat (or Aweinat) and the oases of the New Valley governorate, if possible fed by groundwater only. The New Valley Canal is to be dug north to three oases, then northwest to three more beyond the end of the 50-kilometre-long, US$1.2 billion Zayyed Canal (Collins, 2003).

These projects together – Toshka, Oweinat and the New Valley oases (total cost: $2 billion) – form the first phase of a $90-billion package, scheduled to be finished in 2017, which would convert about half of Egypt's surface into agricultural and industrial areas. Agricultural expansion is only the basis of the comprehensive project: 'Industry, mining, alternative energy production, and possibly oil and gas production and tourism, are part of the vision, with plans for desert safaris, car rallies, conferences and medical tourism, such as sand burial for skin diseases' (Noeman, 2000; Pratt, 2001).

Stages 2 and 3[8], however, have been put on hold due to financial constraints. It cannot have helped that the Toshka Lakes are receding, leaving a 'bath tub ring' of wetlands.[9] A consultant observes that the pumps, which commenced action in March 2005, operate only half a day per month to guarantee a minimum flow into the irrigation channels. But 2007 promised to be a high-discharge year

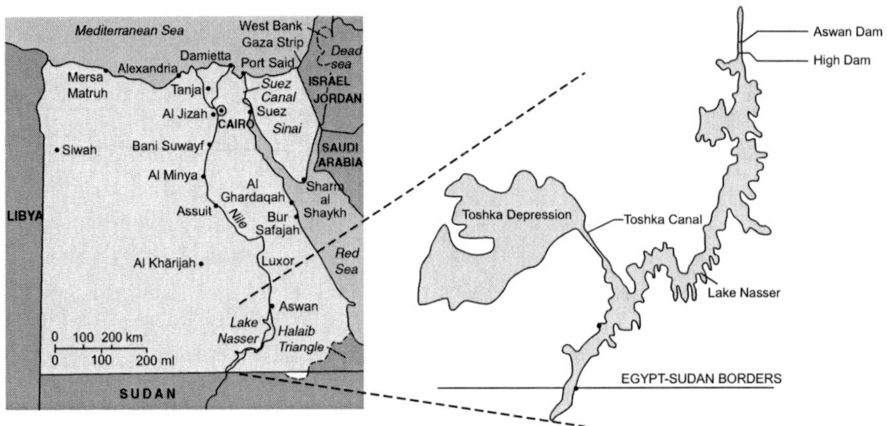

Figure 2.2: ***Location of the new lakes supplied by the Toshka project***

again; the stage of Lake Nasser was so high that the Qasr Ibrim monument overlooking it was flooded (el-Aref, 2007).

Certainly, a 'second Nile' is a dream many like to believe in – Sheikh al-Sayyid (Zayyed) bin-Sultan Al-Nahayan, president of the United Arab Emirates, made a US$100 million investment to enable the main cataract. The Saudi prince and maverick investor, Al-Walid bin Talal bin Abdul Aziz al-Saud, through his Kingdom Agricultural Development Company (KADCO) purchased 100,000 acres for a mega-farm in the New Valley to the tune of US$300 million, and contracted Sun World, a subsidiary of Cadiz of California, to help him grow cotton and watermelons, grapes, citrus, strawberries and tomatoes – many of these out of season – for export to Europe (Cowper, 2000). Due to the high temperatures, four to five harvests a year would be possible. Despite the savings from drip irrigation (Collins, 2003), the new firm is predicted to require 1 per cent of the entire Egyptian water quota.[10] The world food organisation, FAO, also showed great enthusiasm (Lonergan and Wolf, 2001) and the Turkish GAP administration signed a collaboration agreement in 2000, labelling both the Turkish and Egyptian projects 'sustainable and integrated'.

But the project has elicited considerable scepticism as well. When a US Congress delegation visited the project in early 1998, its unpublished report concluded that KADCO, responsible for project development and management, had failed to honour its promise to make an Environmental Impact Assessment once its development plan is ready. As the 'necessary feasibility studies' had not been done, the delegation advised American companies not to invest' (Young, 1999).

International Nile experts have voiced damning criticism. Dale Whittington and John Waterbury doubt the project's sustainability even for the short run, claiming 'the Tushka canal spillway will probably never be used again' (Waterbury, 1997: 279–298, fn. 2), while Tony Allan has called the project 'preposterous, a national fantasy... Egypt is going to have less water, not more.'[11]

The experts' criticism suggests that Egypt has embarked on a chimera. The project calls to mind the historian Donald Worster (1985)'s description of the delusions of the American West – the belief that if you settle a parched area, the water for irrigation will come in due course when you have God on your side. Similar 'magic thinking' seems to have the Egyptian government in thrall, planning to green the desert without the necessary water.

The next section will discuss how the state counters this criticism by securitising its water resources and its project. A securitising move seeks to realise discursive closure to legitimise extraordinary actions. With amazing political elasticity, closure on living space is given emphasis (foregrounded) while ignoring (backgrounding) physical closure with respect to water availability in legitimising the Toshka project.

2.1.3 Governance Context: Political Structures

Egypt became a republic when General Gamal Nasser staged an army coup overthrowing King Faisal. Nasser established a nationalist-patriarchal ideology, where 'the interests of the regime (as patriarch) are identified with the nation's interests', a statist economic system, and a corporatist institutional framework. After the Suez Crisis, Egypt became a socialist one-party state. Once they had the money and technology for the High Aswan Dam, the Egyptians switched back to the capitalist world. Since the 1970s, the Egyptian government has allowed a process of *infitah* (open door). Under IMF pressure, two waves of economic reforms have further liberalised the Egyptian economy, with severe repercussions on the agricultural sector.

The governance context thus seemed to open up. However, the liberalisation was offset by strict state control of food imports. State-controlled corporatist structures remained in place, giving rise to an arrangement where the Egyptian government pretends to liberalise while the business sector pretends to invest (Waterbury, 1993). State powers were extended in 1981, after the assassination of President Anwar Sadat, the *state of emergency* was declared and has not been lifted since. This allows indefinite imprisonment of opponents of state policies. According to Collins (2003), Egyptian state control has become stricter rather than looser of late:

> The monolithic regime of Egypt today and its structured bureaucracy is more reminiscent of Rameses II in the thirteenth century before Christ than the socialists and communists of the twentieth century after him. The central government of Egypt appoints its powerful provincial

> governors, the mayors of its 4,000 villages, those who preach in the 60,000 mosques, and the presidents of its fifteen universities. They are supported by an inflated bureaucracy encrusted through time like a Red Sea coral reef with volumes of regulations that stifle initiative, discourse, and dissent. Entangled in a legal and regulatory cobweb spun by the spiders of Arab, Turkish, French, and British rulers, a third of the Egyptian people are underpaid civil servants with security of employment that often perpetuates their officious and mediocre performance.

In 2002 Egypt tightened the reins on NGOs, banning them from foreign funding and political activities. 'This law seeks to impose the hegemony of executive power on civil society,' says Hafez Abu Saada, secretary general of the Egyptian Organization of Human Rights.[12] A rationale for this is that NGOs 'de-essentialise' Egypt as a society of multiple groups and classes with different needs and rights (Pratt, 2001),[13] a plurality that might question the unity of the nation-state and thus promote politicisation. The state prefers avoiding any issue becoming political.[14]

The Toshka project remains non-negotiable for the Egyptian government. Irrigation Minister Abu Zayd 'ruled out any attempt to reconsider the project'; President Mubarak said it was 'an irreversible venture'; Prime Minister Kamal el-Ganzouri said: 'Raising doubts about Toshka harms the interest of the nation'; and his successor Atef Obeid claimed in 2003: 'Our commitment to success in Toshka is incontrovertible, for moving out of the Nile Valley into the desert is not only an economic necessity but a social and security issue'.[15]

The depoliticisation of social issues is rooted in a long line of historic experiences. *Rebus sic stantibus*, it is unsurprising that the Toshka project has faced relatively little criticism within the political elite. The elevation of the river Nile to the national interest requires a loyalty to Egypt's water strategy that forecloses any questioning of the sense of its hydraulic projects. As an Egyptian state spokesman, explaining the need for the Toshka Project in Thatcherite style, pronounced, 'There is no alternative' (*World Water Shimbun*, 2003). Is pharaonic etatism so entrenched in Egypt that everyone involved is prepared to claim it is 'midnight at noon' because President Mubarak says so?

A Toshka Debate?

Above, we saw that projects like Toshka are depoliticised and 'securitised' as national security issues. But the state's tight grip on parliament, media and society does not preclude occasional grumbles about the cost and effectiveness of the project.

Rushdi Said, an Egyptian hydro-geologist, feels that the employment projections are overrated, and is quoted (in Cooperman, 1997) as warning that '(t)his project is going to employ thousands of people, not millions.' Egyptian hydrologists also worry about evaporation and degradation of soils, and health experts see stagnant water leading to increasing schistosomiasis (bilharzia). A full environmental impact analysis has not been made, while ecologists worry about flora and fauna of the western desert (Collins, 2003), which could bring an 'environmental crisis' (Bush, 2007: 1610). Since international funding agencies have declined to fund the project, Egypt will have to raise the money alone, making some commentators fear the project would be 'sucking the lifeblood out of the economy' (Noeman, 2000).

A window of opportunity to domestic opposition to Toshka opened when in the summer of 1998, Egypt indeed faced a *cash flow* crisis. As the cost of the Toshka project spiralled, opposition appeared to be growing to the principle and the cost of the scheme, as well as other projects such as the East of Port Said hub port project within the ministries, both in the nation's four oppositional newspapers and its scientific community. After President Ganzouri left office, the project's detractors in the Egyptian opposition wasted no time in denouncing the project(s), through the oppositional press, as megalomaniac and nepotistic.

Both the three governmental and four oppositional papers are owned and printed by the government, so that it has full control. Still, this is relative: Napoli and Amin (1997) call Egypt's press the most liberal in the Middle East, in the sense that many things can be said if certain lines are not crossed. The Toshka project is an interesting example of this.

In 1999 Abbas Al-Tarabili, the editor of the Wafd opposition party's eponymous newspaper published two front-page editorials claiming that insufficient feasibility studies had been carried out for the Toshka project, that the terrain is much harsher than expected (with granite and an unforeseen depression) causing the project to fall behind schedule, and that project implementation is 'rife with (financial) irregularities'. Irrigation Minister Abu Zayd, denied all problems while President el-Ganzouri's government decried the 'hostile campaign' as directed against the national interest (El-Din, 1999). Zakaria Azmi, chief of the presidential staff, requested a series of hearings (El-Din, 1999). On 6 April 2006, the Egyptian Parliament again discussed Toshka, as Members of Parliament tabled memoranda on corruption, arguing the plots had been sold way too cheaply. The Muslim Brotherhood's Health Commission Deputy El-Shaer called Toshka a 'nightmare' that failed to meet any of its objectives. *Al-Ahram Weekly* reports every year there are complaints that New Valley areas do not receive enough irrigation water.[16] Within the government, there appeared some fission too. By February 2006 the Minister of Irrigation announced

Water Sources	**Million m^3/year**	**Uses**	**Share in Total Use**
- Nile water	55.5	Agriculture	85.0 %
- Rain and floods water	1.0	Industry	9.5 %
- Subterranean water (valley and delta)	6.5	Potable water	5.5 %
- Deep subterranean water in New Valley, Oases and Sinai	1.0		
- Agricultural drainage water	5.0		
- Recycled agricultural drainage water	0.7		
Total	69.7		100.0 %

Table 2.2: ***Water resource use in Egypt, 2002/03***

that just 23,000 feddans had been brought into cultivation. Minister Abu Zayd disputed the figures, claiming the project had already met 85 per cent of its targets.[17]

The cost issue is particularly painful because the project banks on private capital to supplement a maximum of 25 per cent public investment. Egypt further liberalised its investment policies to find the money needed to supplement funding for the New Valley project, Egypt's Law No. 8 of 1997 deregulated investment and offered tax breaks. However, foreign direct investment was falling in the 1990s from $2.5 billion to 1 billion in 2000.

In the New Valley, the state has a hands-off policy. While a minor percentage is held back for smallholders and graduates, to attract investors for the scheme it has been decreed that private enterprises cannot be nationalised or expropriated. Thus, the public sector cannot interfere with management practices and firms can import whatever they like.

Nonetheless, Flemings, an international credit bank, downgraded Egypt as its economy is groaning under a host of punishing projects, of which Toshka is only one (Cowper, 2000). 'Opposition politicians, banks and development specialists have attacked them [the mega-projects] for being grandiose, impractical and a severe drain on limited government resources' (Cowper, 2000).

Where Will the Water for Toshka Come From?

In Section 2.1, we have seen that Toshka project depends on infrequent floodwater and non-renewable groundwater (Figure 2.2). It is notable that 55.5 billion m^3/year at current population figures is about 800 m^3/year per capita. If this were Egypt's only source of water, the country would be severely water stressed.

Where will Egypt find the 5–10 billion m^3 extra water needed to complete the project? Could Egypt diversify? Egypt does have desalination plants near Hurghada on the Red Sea coast and Marsa Matruh on the Mediterranean. Desalination is still costly and relatively small-scale in terms of yield. Egypt has so far not used much of its *groundwater* resources, but will draw on those a great deal more (Hvidt, 1995).

Of course, Egyptian water managers recall that the High Aswan Dam and Lake Nasser may have tided Egypt over the extreme droughts of 1979–88, but that in 1988 the water level in the reservoir reached a critical low (150 m), endangering electricity generation (2.1 million kW annually) by its 12 generators. The state therefore seeks to diminish its dependence on hydropower from Lake Nasser, which takes care of 50 per cent of the country's energy supply[18] and is using its oil and gas supplies. A dramatic *rationalisation* programme has been started aiming for a less water-intensive type of agriculture – notably cuts in rice and cane sugar, improved drainage, stepped-up recycling efforts to reuse reclaimed wastewater, and levelling of arable land to slow down the level of evaporation – though plans for night-time irrigation have met with resistance from farmers. After all, out of the 85 per cent taken by the agricultural sector, a high percentage is lost because of inefficient sheet irrigation practised by the *fellahin* (peasants and labourers, from Arabic *fellah*: ploughman or tiller). High-tech solutions such as drip irrigation and even better Nilometers are envisaged. There are plans to store water in the Lakes Manzal and Barlus on the Mediterranean coast, to repair leaky pipes and line ditches (Cooperman, 1997). Egypt will economise, recycle, and modernise its way out – and save, according to Abdelrahman Salabi, water policy advisor to Minister Abu Zayd, 20 BCM.[19] Users of Toshka water, however, are not expected to have to pay for it, though, so conservation is unlikely to happen there.

Clearly, these measures are efficiency boosters, not structural measures. Like many of its neighbours, Egypt has officially not really begun to contemplate the kind of 'demand management' all water-poor states will eventually have to accept. However often sections of the academic community (e.g., Gleick, 1993) may sound alarms about water shortages in the region, the Egyptian state has different ideas. 'The idea that there should be a water shortage is absurd', says a Ministry of Public Works and Water Resources expert.[20]

2.1.4 *Not Enough Water; Not Enough Space? Is Egypt Overpopulated?*

It is tempting to see the New Valley as 'Mubarak's pyramid', a prestigious French-style *grand travail* – a lasting memory of his presidency to follow in the footsteps of his predecessors General Nasser (the High Aswan Dam) and Anwar Sadat (Abu Simbel) and his neighbour, President Muammar Gaddafi of Libya (the Great Man-Made River).

But its advocates claim there is an urgent practical reason for the mega-project. A major legitimiser of the New Valley project is the supposed overpopulation on a narrow strip of land. According to Cowper, referring to Toshka, '(f)ear of a demographic and food security time-bomb lies at the heart of the argument in favour of two of the most controversial mega-projects' (Cowper, 2000). The project's advocates claim it seeks to create some *space* to prevent social tensions as a consequence of demographic pressure on a tiny strip of land. Each year, some 20,000 ha are lost due to urbanisation. Just 5 per cent of Egypt's territory (an area the size of Switzerland) is inhabited by some 63 million Egyptians. In 2017, this number will have grown to 140 million. The Egyptian 'decentralisation policy' has resettled several hundreds of thousands of Egyptians and seeks to resettle millions more (Lonergan and Wolf, 2001). Thus the new project would not only put 250,000 ha of land into production but also enable 5–7 million Egyptians to move into the New Valley within the next two decades[21] – though Lonergan and Wolf (2001) note that the size of the Egyptian population will have increased by five times that number by then. The project would quadruple Egypt's inhabited space[22] so that land occupation would rise to 25 per cent.

On the other hand, we should not be taken in by the word 'overpopulated' – while we should not necessarily reach for a revolver when we hear it, as Susan George of the Transnational Institute has it (in Mitchell, 1995: 131), it is wise to reach for the calculator. Egypt is still less densely populated than Belgium, and on its arable area produces three times as much crop per hectare as Bangladesh (Mitchell, 1995). Mitchell's (1995) analysis of World Bank documents shows that the portrayal of Egypt as a space-constrained country in need of development is an unfounded case of 'spin'.

Even if we accept the *Lebensraum* argument as valid, will 5 million Egyptians move into the desert – 3 million to the Southwestern Desert and 2 million to the Sinai? 'Historically, Egyptians resist moving from their homes to new settlements in the desert, and the Toshka project is no exception.' (Wahby, 2004: 90) So far only 15,000 had settled there by 2006.[23]

Is Egypt in a Food Crisis?

As for the other argument for the desert reclamation projects – the 'food security time-bomb' thinking also seems selective. Food self-sufficiency is an important Egyptian policy goal and Toshka is part of the 'horizontal agricultural extension' to achieve it.[24] Egypt has not been self-sufficient in food since the 1970s, this deficit is more than made up for by the global food market. But the new crops are mainly horticultural crops for export purposes.

Tony Allan (1997) has given an influential explanation of the workings of a political taboo. The autocratic technology-driven leadership Egypt has traditionally practised makes it hard to garner societal support and legitimacy for a change of mindset toward demand management. This adaptation would take money as well as goodwill and adaptability on the part of the population. The only regional state to have started such a process was Israel in the early 1990s (Allan, 1997). But in Egypt, the dream of 'water sufficiency' is alive and well while Egypt's *fellahin* 'adapt' by abandoning the land. Despite increasing 'water poverty' (Ramadan, n.d.), the notion of water scarcity remains undebatable. This is made possible by backgrounding an ever greater reliance on 'virtual water'.

If you stop exporting water-intensive agricultural products (*encapsulated water*) and take full advantage of low international wheat prices, a huge percentage of irrigational demand is avoided. By switching from food export to food import Egypt saved billions of m^3 of premium water. Food constitutes 10.8 per cent of Egypt's total imports bill (OECD, 2004/2005). Thanks to American food aid and the availability of cheap grain on the world market, Egypt became less and less dependent on its own water. This way, a silent revolution realised economic adaptation which spares the government an embarrassing political debate on the question whether the state is accountable for a looming water shortage.[25]

Up to the 1970s, it was possible for the Middle East to augment the water supply by finding or mobilising new resources to ensure food self-sufficiency. Since around 1972, Egypt switched to importing, which means importing encapsulated water. Nowadays, imports meet half of Egypt's food requirements, and '(m)ore water "flows" into the Middle East each year as "virtual water" than flows down the Nile into Egypt for agriculture' (Allan, 1997).

This dependence on food imports evidences a national economic vulnerability (dependence on the rest of the world) that Egyptian officials prefer to keep politically silent about. Egyptian water professionals, who are quite well represented in the international water and donor community,[26] have not wanted to discuss virtual water for many years and – until the fourth World Water Forum in 2006 – kept it off the agenda where they could.

Apart from its political silence, there is another advantage to a virtual water strategy. As Alan Richards and John Waterbury (1990) have noted in passing, food imports have proved an ideal control mechanism – it is easier to control the distribution of imported food than of food produced by millions of *fellahin* (peasants) in the countryside. In 1977 the Egyptian government cut subsidies, which doubled the prices of food in the cities and 'bread riots' broke out after draconian price rises following IMF-imposed structural adjustments. Egypt's geography allows all food imports to come in at a central location (sea port) and distributed for food coupons to the urban poor, thus preventing future riots. Like the High Dam at Aswan, this creates what Callon would call an obligatory passage point (Callon, 1987). In this respect, virtual water can also play a role in maintaining state control.

A (not-so-)Silent Revolution?

What Allan (2001 and elsewhere) has repeatedly described as the 'economically invisible and politically silent revolution' of virtual water has propelled an economic adaptation process that spares the government an embarrassing political debate on the question whether the state is accountable for a looming water shortage and dependency on the rest of the world, that Egyptian officials prefer to keep silent about. But how silent is this revolution in the countryside?

In that context, a prescription that Egypt should turn to the world market to import virtual water more is anathema. When Beyene and Wadley (2004) discuss this as an option, they voice concern that the market mechanism does 'not account for the different social meanings attributed to water across state boundaries. [. . .] It is hard to predict . . . how far the Egyptian farmers are ready to buy the idea of detaching themselves from producing agricultural products, should the Egyptian government agree to implement the "virtual water" scheme' (Beyene and Wadley, 2004).

But what seems to have escaped Beyene and Wadley is that, in fact, Egyptian food producers – whether they 'buy' the idea or not – have already been adjusting to a virtual strategy for the last 30–35 years.

The *fellahin* are a powerful symbol for Egypt, and when Gamal Abdel Nasser came to power, he sought a political support base in the countryside by pushing for land reform. This reform proceeded only haltingly, sustaining absentee landownership, but the overall effect of land redistribution and collectivisation of the agricultural sector was to create a clientele for the state, which had nurtured a class of small-time farmers (*fellahin*) and guaranteed a good price for their corn and cotton (Weinbaum, 1982. See also: Beblawi and Luciani, 1987). Egyptian irrigation is still heavily subsidised – Kagwanja (2007) quotes a $5 billion per year figure.

As a consequence, the first wave of economic liberalisation initially progressed only slowly. But after the 1977 food riots, the Egyptian state responded by a policy of subsidies and social welfare programs for the urban electorate – combining welfare and developmental roles (Abdelazim, 2002) in such a way that the infrastructural links with and investments in the countryside were neglected. Imported food brought wealth to harbours, not to farmers, so that farmers' bargaining power was eroded, leading to further marginalisation.

In a second IMF-impelled wave of reforms, Egypt liberalised its agrarian policies, abandoning fixed supply and price support in wheat and maize from 1987. After the Land Law (No. 96 of 1992) previous subsidies on farming inputs were cut. This subsidy cut was especially meaningful since disappearance of fertile sediment from the Nile due to the Aswan Dam, 99 per cent of which is now trapped in lake Nasser, had to be compensated for by chemical fertiliser. Even worse, land tenure was reformed: over a five-year period, tenants had to return their land to the landowners. They had rented this land for 40 years at fixed rates; now the rents were allowed to skyrocket. Evicted farming families have resisted the police, which has given rise to a 'silent civil war' in the Egyptian South: widespread violence in the countryside has been reported due to police-assisted evictions of tenants. The inevitable outcome was for tenants to swell the shanty towns of Cairo (Bush, 2004, 2005; see also OMCT, 2006) and, who knows, Toshka – had they only been notified at all of the possibility and the very short time window, not to mention very different farming methods and start costs (Hill, 2000: 23, 29).

The virtual water (import) strategy thus appears to have supported urban political control while widening the socio-economic gap between mega-city and countryside. Egypt is a semi-*rentier state* (Beblawi and Luciani, 1987), developing with easily obtained income from running the Suez Canal, oil production, Western aid, remittances and tourism. Relying on external rents and a 'bubble economy' (T. Mitchell, 2002), Egypt now seeks to attract foreign investment in projects like the New Valley to generate foreign currency from horticulture and cotton. But rather than attracting farmers to produce food, the state appears to gamble on 'rural development without farmers' (Bush, 2005). New Valley plots are rather larger than those made available in earlier development projects, such as 1- to 2.5-acre plots at Nourabayya in the 1980s. A 100,000-acre plot was sold to Saudi Prince Al-Walid bin Talal bin Abdul Aziz al-Saud. But despite the tax breaks, Toshka only attracted one significant investor:

> [Sun World] was to invest no money of its own in the Toshka project... In the excitement of the government's announcement that the project had found an American partner, the reason for this went unnoticed: Sun World had no money. (T. Mitchell quoted in Bush, 2007)

The Muslim Brotherhood MPs have taken the Egyptian state to task for not having sold land on the market but directly awarding it to Kingdom Agricultural Company (KAC) while preaching market liberalisation.

In the Egyptian welfare state, taxation remains low, urban subsidies are high, state control of the economy remains considerable while leaving farmers to their own devices. Beblawi and Luciani have argued, and Dorman confirmed for Egypt that *rentier* states like Egypt can exempt themselves from the need to develop strong state–society relations. The state exerts control, but it is not ingrained: it can rely on continuing patronage relations. It tolerates a huge informal economy – Dorman (2007) maintains the whole Cairian economy is informal. The state may be everywhere, but it can be co-opted and subverted by locals. While open discontent in the streets is stamped down, hidden deviance is tolerated: if you do not visibly avoid the law, you are not branded an 'outlaw'. People retain their rights in a political sense if they keep their heads down (Dorman, 2007).

An Alternative Explanation

We have thus seen that 'closure' is an elastic discourse strategy – Egypt's space and food insecurity, which are contestable, can be invoked to legitimise a project, while water closure (shortage) cannot, because it is a carefully maintained taboo. The project makes neither hydrological nor economic sense. At the time of writing, the Ministry of Agriculture appears to 'behold the moon', labelling Toshka a model of agricultural investment (State Information Service, 2007). But Toshka is not related with the Ministry of Water Resources or even the Ministry of Agriculture; it is a Presidential project (Egypt State Information Service, 2007). Modern Egyptian rulers continue to have a taste for building pyramids. It may serve a political goal, as a symbol for state prowess – not by the ancient mode of exploiting the population – but neither by creating a bustling investment market.

The role of the army may be a clue here. Since Sadat's assassination in 1981, Egypt has been under a state of emergency. The president is head of the army and relies on their support, knowing that the forces can be a danger: in 1985 the Central Security services plotted a failed coup. In the 1990s, the army's budget has been cut, but at the same time its mandate has been expanded.

The Egyptian army is heavily involved in the business of 'butter'; not just 'guns' (Frisch, 2001; Dorman, 2007: 209). Quite literally so: its mandate extends to 'basic needs like agriculture, irrigation and land reclamation'. Armies got monopolies in non-military sectors like agro-industry in the new development schemes. Given the scarcity of land, the Army profited from sale of military terrains and the development of new lands. The army is heavily involved in the agro-industry on land reclaimed by the al-Salam canal and Toshka, for which the military is responsible for planning, canal construction and earth removal; giving water to nomads and 'educating Upper Egypt' (Frisch, 2001). This raises the alternative hypothesis that Toshka provides self-sustaining income for an army that sees its budget cut.

Moreover, the location of the project so close to the Sudanese border does not seem accidental. The importance of a desert development project with questionable economic prospects to national *security* makes more sense from the perspective of controlling border areas: the Sudan for the Southern Valley project, and likewise areas close to Israel in the Northern Sinai project. This brings in a foreign policy (geopolitical) angle on the Toshka story. For a broader perspective, we thus have to look at Egypt's external affairs.

An international approach can also shed more light on the heated response of, especially Egypt, to the Toshka project. If Egypt is no longer an agriculturally based society, as Selby (2005) observes, it could afford to grant some water to upstream countries. However, the signs do not evidence this. To help us understand how Egypt manages to prevent sharing much, the remainder of the chapter will first look into the international overlay of Nile politics.

2.2 External Hydropolitics

> 'The Nile is Egypt's lifeline, so it can't accept any decline or decrease of water', says Ahmed El-Naggar of the Al-Ahram Centre for Political and Strategic Studies in Cairo. 'Each country has water rights, but if any country takes more than its rights, Egypt will not forgive it.' (*Sudan Tribune*, 16 February 2004)

> 'Any action that would endanger the waters of the Blue Nile will be faced with a firm reaction on the part of Egypt, even if that action should lead to war.' (Former President Anwar Sadat, cited in Kendie, 1999)

> 'The Egyptians treated the waters of the Nile as though they were a purely Egyptian affair rather than one concerning all states in the basin [. . .] And they created facts on the ground that make matters very difficult for the future. Hence, we felt we had entered into a game stupidly. We were talking about sharing resources, while the Egyptians were making that impossible in future. Therefore continuing with the technical talks became, quite simply, a waste of time.' (Ethiopian president, Meles Zenawi in 1999)[27]

2.2.1 International Overlay

The position of Egypt in the international system remains important, and as a consequence, so does the overlay of global geopolitics. The Aswan Dam, for example, would not have been possible without the Cold War. Although Nasser won the stand-off with Britain and France over Suez in 1956, it proved a pyrrhic victory as it nearly bankrupted Egypt when the West responded with a crippling economic boycott. General Nasser still wanted his dam and in 1959 the Soviet Union stepped in, willing and able to supply the money and technology. Six years on, USSR president, Khrushchev, was present at the High Dam's inauguration.[28] Once the High Aswan Dam had become operative – it came fully on stream in 1970 – Egypt returned to the capitalist camp and started very carefully to liberalise its economy: the 'open door' (*infitah*) policy. The return to the West seems to have been inspired by both economic as well as political motives.

When Egypt was defeated in the 1967 war against Israel, the country also lost some of its international prestige. The Gulf states' oil boycott in 1973, as bold a move as Egypt's nationalisation of the Suez Canal, stole Egypt's thunder. On the back of its newly found riches Saudi Arabia became the new regional leader. Peace with Israel in 1979 (the Camp David agreement) won President Sadat a Nobel Peace prize but lost his country even more Arab credibility. During the Camp David talks it was also proposed to divert 1 per cent of the Nile influx, some 500 million m^3 annually, to the densely populated, heavily saline Gaza strip – the al-Salam canal running into the Sinai as part of the above-mentioned *Northern Valley* project (see above) would not have to be extended by much to reach Rafah, on the Egyptian-Israeli border. The peace move made Egypt an outcast among its Arab friends but had other dividends: while Arab development aid dried up, Egypt soon became a top-three recipient of American aid.

There were limits, however, to the degree Egypt was prepared to alienate the Arab world. After President Sadat was killed, relations with Israel became tenser under Mubarak, and his Water Minister, Abu Zayd, let it be known that Egypt is not going to be made to supply Israel with water.[29] As expected, relations with the Arab states and Iran improved as a result.

Of course Egypt continues to keep a keen eye on the remunerative relation with the USA, of which it is still a major recipient while Egypt remains a cornerstone of US policy to moderate the Middle East. When Egypt joined the Allied forces and even sent soldiers to fight in the Gulf War of 1990–91, US$7.5 billion of its debt burden was scrapped while Sudan, which had sided with Saddam, was punished. But now that America no longer gives Egypt food aid, the spending strategy will only work with the help of oil exports (Egypt is a member of the Organization of Arab Petroleum Exporting Countries, OAPEC), and/or extensive foreign support (Beblawi and Luciani, 1987).

2.2.2 Conflict or Cooperation?

In water literature, a sometimes unhelpful distinction is frequently made between conflict and cooperation between states. When one state is significantly stronger than the others, the way states 'cooperate' with each other may be suspiciously like the way a detainee 'cooperates' with his captors. Conversely, 'conflict' sometimes looks like a staged theatrical act to get outside attention and funding. A cursory glance at the Nile basin reveals a coexistence of professed cooperation and professed conflict, which highlights that both 'conflict' and 'cooperation' are political discourses, constructed for specific audiences. Egypt has made threats to upstreamers, several riparians have made angry noises since independence; news that the Nile riparians were close to signing a Nile agreement in early 2007 therefore generated considerable international excitement – but at the time of writing of this chapter, the agreement still seemed outstanding. The following sketches a background to these 'signs' and seeks to explain them in the context of Egypt's role in the Nile community.

The upstream Nile riparians profess to be far from happy with the status quo on the Nile. As the last port of call before the Nile reaches the Mediterranean Sea, Egypt depends on what the upper riparians leave. It seems daring – if not foolhardy – for Egypt to claim even more water.

The next sections will analyse Egypt's relationships with upstream countries Ethiopia (2.2.3), Sudan (2.2.4) and Uganda, Kenya and Tanzania (2.2.5). Ethiopian opposition to the Toshka project will be discussed in the context of upstream resistance to Egypt's insistence on upholding colonial treaties. But also relations with Sudan, which Egypt needs on its side to get a greater share of the Nile, are highly volatile, while three East African upstreamers, Kenya, Uganda and Tanzania, have become more assertive. The next sections go into Nilotic conflict as well as cooperation.

2.2.3 Acrimony with Ethiopia

The Nile catchment extends way down to Burundi in Central Africa and to Eritrea in the Horn. It does so on the basis of colonial treaties, economic and, if need be, military dominance. Out of ten riparians – Kenya, Tanzania, Burundi, Rwanda, Zaire, Uganda, Ethiopia, Eritrea, Sudan and Egypt – Ethiopia would seem to warrant the biggest claim by far on the Nile. The Ethiopian Highlands are the primary source of the Blue Nile, contributing 76 per cent to the annual flow of the Blue Nile – during the flood period Ethiopian sources even provide 95 per cent of the flow of the Blue Nile, and 50 per cent of the White Nile through the Machar marsh and Sobat river (Haynes and Whittington, 1981).[30]

A bewildering historic heritage enables Egypt to keep its nine neighbours in check. Egypt's dependence on Europe and France started in 1879 with Egypt's bankruptcy in that year, after a failed campaign of Khedive Ismail to conquer Ethiopia and make the Nile an Egyptian river.[31] In 1902, still in the colonial age, England (on behalf of Egypt and Sudan) concluded a treaty with Italy (on behalf of Ethiopian King Menelik II) stipulating that any upstream 'arrest' of the waters would not be permissible. The English sought to secure the continued production of cotton for its Lancashire mills. Almost a century down the road, Egypt still stands by this document. Ethiopia, unsurprisingly, is piqued by the situation, as they thwart its development plans. Like Kenya and the Belgian Congo, Ethiopia was not a party to the Nile treaty of 1959 – and has refused to accept it. The treaty allocated what has become a 'non-negotiable' (Collins, 2003) 55.5 km^3 a year to Egypt, 18½ to Sudan, which theoretically left something over 10 million m^3 for all other riparians, given the average 84 km^3 measured (on average) at Aswan annually. Ethiopia has never lodged a formal complaint about the distribution agreement, but is well aware of its upstream position. Kendie (1999) cites an early instance of linkage politics in the fourteenth century when the Negus of Ethiopia threatened to retaliate by diverting the Nile if Egypt did not refrain from persecuting its Christian (Coptic) minority. Still, Ethiopia's interest in seriously developing the Nile materialised as recently as 1956 when Emperor Haileselassie established the Ministry of Public Works, recast in 1971 as the National Water Resources Commission.

According to Collins (2003) the aforesaid agency and its offspring, such as the Valley Agricultural Development Authority, lacked sufficient technological knowledge. Only in 1990 a *Preliminary Water Resources Development Master Plan* (PWRD) was drawn up. However, the overlay of the Cold War encouraged external drafts in support of Ethiopian water plans. By 1959, Egypt had joined the socialist bloc, cemented by financial and technical aid for the High Aswan Dam from the Soviet Union. In retaliation, the West, annoyed over the loss of a strategic ally, decided to support upstream Ethiopia. In the early 1960s, the US Bureau of Reclamation advised the Ethiopian emperor on the development of the Blue Nile.

Between 1958 and 1963 a comprehensive plan for 33 dams (the Blue Nile Development Plan, to irrigate 434,000 ha) was developed for the Emperor by the US Bureau of Reclamation, to be funded with a loan from the African Development Bank. 'During the next decade the French reported on the Blue Nile, the Italians on the Beles, and the Dutch on the Tekeze' (=Atbara) (Collins, 2003). These plans were never realised – while Egypt returned to the Western camp, Ethiopia joined the Soviet sphere losing the loan. During Mengistu's reign of terror, a shouting match erupted over the Nile between Egypt and Ethiopia. A minor diversion by Ethiopia of the waters of the Blue Nile and the Sobat River in the late 1970s triggered threats from President Anwar Sadat of Egypt and Minister of State Boutros-Ghali, with Egypt warning Addis Ababa that it was prepared to declare any Ethiopian water diversions a casus belli, a reason to go to war (Phillips, et al., 2006). Mengistu defiantly responded that the Nile was Ethiopian heritage.

After the Mengistu dictatorship was deposed in 1991, relations between Ethiopia and Egypt warmed significantly. Egypt concluded a non-binding general agreement on cooperation and use of the Nile with Ethiopia on 1 July 1993,

Country	Total Area of the Country (km^2)	Area of the Country within the Basin (km^2)	As Per Cent of Total Area of Basin (per cent)	As Per Cent of Total Area of Country (per cent)
Burundi	27,834	13,260	0.4	47.6
Rwanda	26,340	19,876	0.6	75.5
Tanzania	945,090	84,200	2.7	8.9
Kenya	580,370	46,229	1.5	8.0
Zaire	2,344,860	22,143	0.7	0.9
Uganda	235,880	231,366	7.4	98.1
Ethiopia	1,100,010	365,117	11.7	33.2
Eritrea	121,890	24,921	0.8	20.4
Sudan	2,505,810	1,978,506	63.6	79.0
Egypt	1,001,450	326,751	10.5	32.6
Nile basin		3,112,369	100.0	

Table 2.3: ***Area of the states of the Nile basin (FAO, 1997)***

but no quota. But Ethiopia was clearly 'not amused' by Egypt's announcement of the Toshka scheme in 1997. In 1998 Ethiopian Minister Seyoum Mesfin wrote a protest letter with copies to Salim Ahmed Salim, Secretary General of the Organization of African Unity, Kofi Annan, then his counterpart at the UN, and James Wolfensohn, the president of the World Bank at the time, saying Ethiopia will not accept its water share to be affected by the Toshka project. But the Bank is not funding Toshka, so it cannot veto it. Until recently, Ethiopia, on the contrary, was too destitute to build big dams unassisted. As the lending institute will not fund regionally controversial projects, this has effectively stopped international donations to Ethiopian projects of any significance.[32] So, in practice, it is the Egyptians who find the World Bank uncritically on their side. As Tony Allan has often claimed, the World Bank may need Egypt more than Egypt needs the World Bank – to the extent that the Bank, too, appears to think it wise to 'behold the moon'. All in all, the treaties and threats effectively boil down to a veto on upstream water resource development.

How can downstream use affect upstream rights? Under 'equitable use' principles, Egypt would need to share its surplus with upper riparians in periods of slack. Further Egyptian reliance on virtual water could create such slack (Waterbury, 2002: 87). Both countries accuse the other of seeking to strengthen its hand in the negotiations by diverting water, which could later count as 'prior use'.

In response, an increasingly self-confident Ethiopia called for the revision of the 1959 treaty. 'It is time to build dams', said Foreign Minister Mesfin (George, 1998), no doubt mindful that famines have precipitated the downfall of Haileselassie and Haile Mariam Mengistu in earlier decades (Collins, 2003). To this, Mubarak threatened to bomb Ethiopia, whereupon the Ethiopian leadership claimed that nothing and no-one could stop it.

Ethiopia has responded with contempt and assured that 'there is no earthly force that can stop Ethiopia from benefiting from the Nile' (ibid.: 664) and that 'We [Ethiopia] will use the Nile waters within our territory. We will not go to war unless they [Egypt] prevent us from using it'. (Prime Minister Meles Zenawi, May 1997, cited by Westermann (2003)).

However, if Ethiopia's response was 'tit-for-tat', as Waterbury claims (Waterbury, 2002: 83), it acted in a pussyfooting kind of way. Ethiopia pressed ahead with the Tekeze River dam in Tigray – but that is a hydroelectric project, not an irrigation project – which stalled due to the territorial war with Eritrea (Waterbury 2002: 120). The second response has been for the country to embark on a series of small-scale dams (Waterbury and Whittington, 1998).[33] The advantages of a micro-dam strategy for Ethiopia are obvious: they do not need international funding, they are relatively more efficient, they are hardly vulnerable to military attack, and the compounded downstream effects are hard to quantify – they are estimated at 2–3 BCM (Waterbury and Whittington, 1998). Ethiopia is loath to give information about the dams, although it is not clear whether this is because the information is 'securitised' or because there is no data (Mason, 2004: 171).

Under the more relaxed atmosphere facilitated by the Nile basin Initiative (see Section 2.3), Egypt will support non-subtractive water uses like hydropower projects at the Blue Nile Falls (Tis Abay II, US$63 million, 450 MW). Moreover, Ethiopia has meanwhile been enmeshed in repeated wars with Eritrea, so that it had other concerns than negotiating with Egypt.

2.2.4 *Strong-Headed Sudan*

Apart from Ethiopia there is another tough customer to appease: Sudan. The Blue and White Nile join forces at Khartoum, Sudan's capital city. As Sudan controls both branches of the river, a healthy relation with its next-door neighbour is of great importance to Egypt, the country however continues to benefit from a shared colonial past with Sudan. Hydraulic cooperation led to the construction of various dams for Egypt's benefit, which, however, have not always been very well coordinated (Waterbury, 1979).

Britain recognised the potential for political blackmail of the Nile to play the countries off against each other at an early stage. In 1924 the governor of Sudan was killed by an Egyptian. A furious British High Commissioner for Egypt then announced that Sudan could have as much water as it wished. At that time, however, Sudan laid very little actual claim on the river.

Egypt had gained independence from England in February 1922, but remained a *de facto* protectorate. In 1929 Egypt signed a highly favourable agreement with Great Britain, which then controlled Sudan, Uganda, Kenya and Tanganyika (future Tanzania). The treaty gave Egypt 48 BCM and Sudan only 4 BCM as measured at Aswan. But as Sudan developed its cotton potential (the Gezira Project), that situation changed. Tensions with Sudan mounted between 1954 and 1958. After independence in 1956, the new Sudanese government called for the revision of the 1929 Nile treaty.

Egypt withdrew its support for the Roseires dam, which Sudan had built without consultation, and moved army forces to the border. At the same time, Sudan worried over the impact of the envisaged High Aswan Dam, whose storage lake straddles the border with Sudan and could easily flood parts of its territory. In 1958 reclamation reconnaissance began and in 1959 the governorate of the New Valley was created, adjacent to Sudan. A coup in 1958 brought Sudan more Egypt-friendly rulers, who concluded a new agreement with Egypt in 1959, the Treaty for the Full Utilisation of the Nile, which had a 30-year validity. The bilateral agreement included the establishment of a Permanent Joint Technical Commission.

Full utilisation meant that previously unallocated Nile water was now carved up between Sudan (14.5 BCM) and Egypt (7.5 BCM) (Hornstein, 1999). Significantly, Ethiopia was not party to the treaty. While the allocation in principle left some 'slack' for Ethiopian use and future expansion, the Full Utilisation of the Nile treaty was not given its name thoughtlessly: 'the Egyptian Government has been extremely vigilant in ensuring that all waters are currently used' (Allan, 1999). The 1959 Agreement set out a 50–50 share of both the costs of the canalisation projects in the *Sudd* ('blockade') marshes in South Sudan, and the allotment of newly accrued water. The technical committee established by it, the Joint Permanent Joint Technical Commission (PJTC), functioned until 1984.

One reason why Egypt thinks it can claim so much more Nile water for Toshka is that much water gets 'lost' along the way. As the Nile passes through Sudan, it loses much of its momentum – and its discharge – in the Sudd marshes.

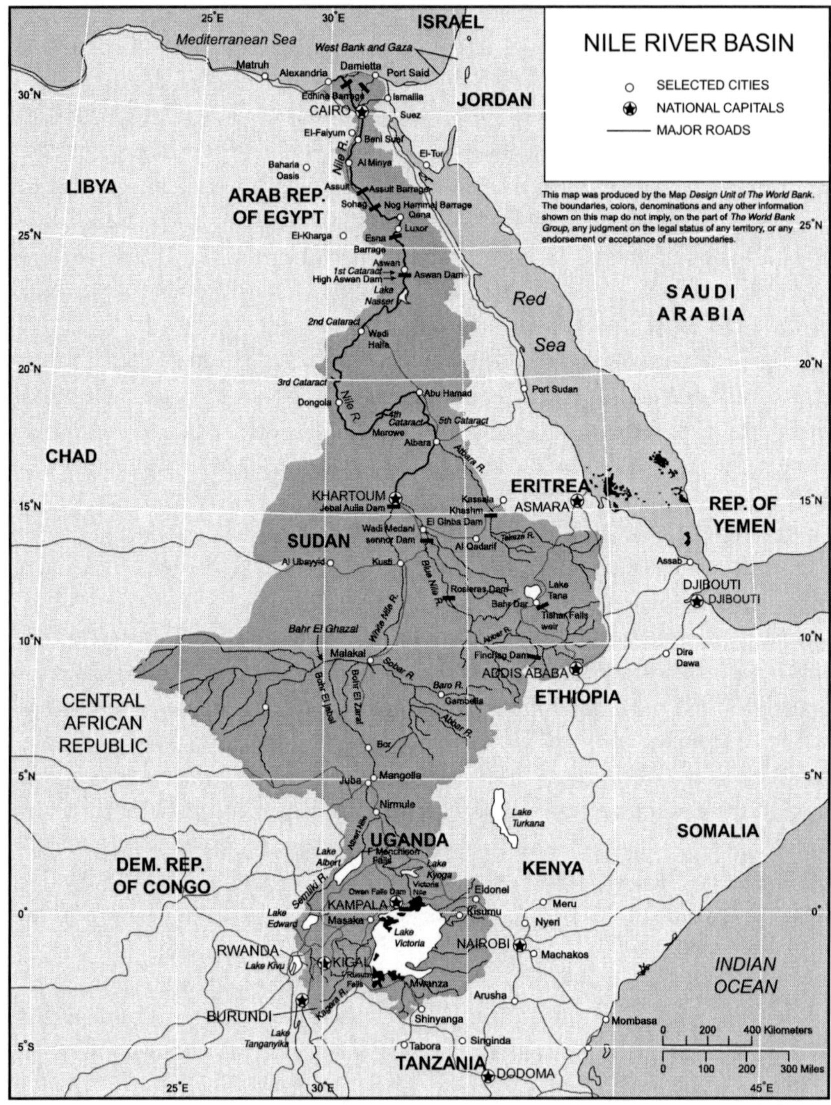

Figure 2.3: ***Nile River Basin***

The flow is so slow there that 50 per cent of the White Nile flow evaporates under the cloudless sunlight. Much evapotranspiration would be avoided if the Sudd marshes could be bypassed – the estimated 5 km^3 gain would just offset the extra demand resulting from the Toshka lakes project. A planned bypass running from Bor to Malakal would bring an additional 4 billion km^3 each year into Egypt, improve navigation between South and North Sudan and irrigate 200,000 acres in South Sudan.

But the 360-kilometre Jonglei Canal project, started in 1979, was destined for trouble. First, because it cuts right through the migration routes of transhumant Southern tribes (Nüer, Dinka and Shilloth), destroying their livelihoods, subject large areas to desiccation and jeopardise swamp fishing livelihoods. A smaller-scale version was tabled to remedy some of those defects in 1979, but that plan was rejected by the south because too much water would still drain to the north and Egypt, rather than fulfilling southern dreams of agricultural development (Hornstein, 1999). The leader of the southern separatist movement, SPLA, John Garang, even devoted his PhD thesis at an American university to a critique of the Jonglei Canal (Hornstein, 1999). However, the canal had become a flashpoint of conflict in the broader struggle between the Arabic, Islamic north and the black, Christian and animist south. SPLA armed attacks to stop construction works were successful in 1985, leaving a half-finished canal and a giant 'bucketwheel' cutter, used to cut through the dense growth, rusting in the marshes (Hvidt, 1995).

Perhaps this resistance was to be expected, and one may wonder why Sudan concurred with turning the ecosystem into a 'ditch' (Hornstein, 1999) to give Egypt extra BCMs. There may be a return of favours, as Egypt had intervened twice, militarily, to rescue al-Numayri's regime, in 1971 and July 1976, so it stands to reason that in exchange for Egypt's help, Sudan concurred with the Jonglei channel (Swain, 1998).

Sudan borders six Nile countries and is hydrologically well placed for exploiting the river's water resource. Two out of three Sudanese work in agriculture. Recurring famine and malnutrition provide ample legitimation for water development. Sudan's population of 40 million is growing at a rate of 2 to 2.4 per cent per year. South Sudan's estimated population of 7 million is set to increase with the return of up to 4 million southern refugees. This demographic pressure will further stress Sudan's Nilotic water resources.

Since the fundamentalist Islamic revolution overthrowing Numeiri in 1985, relations between Egypt and Sudan have almost gone back to square one. In 1989 Sudan decided not to renew the cooperation agreement and agreed to a Declaration of Friendship and Peace with Addis Ababa[34] to establish a Blue Nile Valley Organisation and study joint projects in 1991.

Egyptian relations with Sudan worsened steadily in 1994 and 1995. The oil-rich Halaib Triangle is disputed between Egypt and Sudan – both countries invoke mutually contradicting colonial treaties. The unresolved territorial conflict led Egypt to populate the area. In 1995, Mohammed Ibrahim Soliman, Minister of State for Reconstruction and New Communities, announced that Egypt would erect three settlements there housing a total of 70,000 people. In this context, the impression comes to mind that Egypt intends to create facts on the ground – Egypt actually plans airports and a road in Halaib. Egyptian and Sudanese troops clashed in Halaib the day after the

Egyptian president, Mubarak, barely survived an assault in the Ethiopian capital of Addis Ababa in June 1995. Egyptian fingers pointed at the Sudanese government, accusing it of sponsoring terrorism. Sudan responded by calling off the Nile treaty. The new Sudanese leader, Hassan al-Turabi, declared: 'Sudan has full control of the Nile', whereupon Egyptian Minister Muhammad Mussa rebutted:

> If Sudan wants to play with water, it is playing with fire. [. . .] Any step taken to this end will force us into confrontation to defend our rights and our life. Our response will be beyond anything they can imagine. (Schiffler, 1997)

In spite of its bold language (Belshaw and Belshaw, 1999), Sudan so far has built little infrastructure to back up its tough words, though. It lacks the obstructive upstream power that, for example, Turkey has developed in the Euphrates-Tigris basin. Even when the new, 83-metre Hamlab or Meroe (Merowe) dam will have been completed, Sudan will not be able to store a whole season's Nile discharge (Schiffler, 1997). The Meroe Multi-Purpose Hydro Project, near the confluence of the White and Blue Nile on the 4th cataract of the River Nile in North Sudan, was inaugurated in March 2009 with bilateral funding from both the Gulf region (a loan from the United Arab Emirates, (Collins, 2003) and China, the latter no doubt in exchange for a share of Sudan's oil wealth. Once completed, the Meroe Dam can impound 20 per cent of annual Nile flow and produce an annual electricity yield of 5.5 TWh). Preparations for the Kajbar Dam at the third cataract of the Nile are started as well.

When Sudan's warring factions signed the Comprehensive Peace Agreement on 9 January 2004, bringing Sudan's long civil war to an end, this opened up – in principle – South Sudan's vast water resources for development. The peace brokered between North and South may open the door to completion of the canal. A referendum will decide the possible secession of South Sudan in 2011. Since the south is also where much of the oil is, secession would be a sensitive economic loss. Moreover, Egypt still has its eyes on the Sudd and wants to revive the Jonglei (Jangali) Canal. Also projects in the White Nile basin, in Machar Marshes and Bahr el Ghazal are counted on to increase the efficiency of discharge towards Egypt (Waterbury, 1998) – which could create just enough slack to accommodate Ethiopia's claim for 9.5 km^2 without needing to change the 1959 treaty (El-Khodari, 2003b). Egypt is well aware that it will be very hard to achieve anything in the way of pan-Nilotic cooperation without Sudan. When in 1998 a shuttle diplomacy between Cairo and Khartoum resumed and Sudan extradited a dozen Islamic activists to Egypt (Egypt accuses Sudan of aiding and abetting Egyptian Islamism), this also boded well for long-cherished development initiatives for the Nile basin (Alterman, 1998). Sudan therefore had little incentive to grumble about Toshka.

2.2.5 The East African Community

In addition to uneasy relationships between Egypt, Sudan and Ethiopia, the past few decades have seen the fledgling formation of a second power block, the East African Community – Kenya, Uganda and Tanzania. Rainfall there is much more reliable than in the Eastern Nile, so that the aspiration for irrigation is lower. But crucially, the three countries are co-riparians to Lake Victoria, which is fed by 40 small rivers and is considered the *de facto* source of the Nile. To forestall a possible counteroffensive and secure permission to access this source, Egypt has long used carrots and some sticks to keep control. In 1950 Egypt secured access to Uganda's water posts at all times to capture meteorological and hydrological data from the East African Lakes basin, including Lake Victoria. This would help Egypt 'determine the amount of water it could receive from the upper reaches of the Nile, and thus would allow them effective long-term planning' (Okidi, 1994). In return, Egypt would contribute to the upkeep of the gauging of the posts. Meanwhile, Egypt seeks to influence any plans for upstream hydroelectricity generation. Since electricity generation, unlike irrigation, is not consumptive (it does not abstract from the quality or quantity of available flow), Egypt is not too worried about the dam, and might in fact benefit from upstream regulation, but feels the need to make sure it was in control. Thus, Egypt was negotiating with the British government between 1948 and 1953 on Uganda's Owen Falls Dam, intended for the generation of electricity (Howell and Allan, 1994).

After independence in 1963, however, the government of Uganda declared in a letter to the Secretary General of the UN that all colonial era treaties would be considered 'terminated' unless modified by agreement with the government. But like in so many other riparian countries, Uganda's war (with Sudan) and domestic strife have taken attention away from the Nile, and in practice Uganda stuck to the agreements with Egypt and reaffirmed them in 1991. Egyptian–Ugandan cooperation continued including plans to clean out weeds that clogged Lake Victoria and Kyoga and caused local floods in Uganda. However, the 1990s have seen a more assertive Uganda. Uganda's parliament in 2004 proposed to rescind the treaty and charge Egypt and Sudan for water use.

In December 2003 the Kenyan minister of foreign affairs stated that 'Kenya will not accept any restrictions on the use of Lake Victoria or the River Nile' and Chris Oboru, a Kenyan MP, said, 'This is a human rights issue. Egypt cannot continue wallowing in wealth, while Kenyans are languishing in poverty'. Egypt did not take kindly to these words and threatened economic and political sanctions.[35]

The boldest move was made further south: Tanzania is reported to have launched a $27.6 million project to divert water from Lake Victoria to Kahama in the Shinyanga region, in contravention of two colonial treaties Britain signed with Egypt and Sudan controlling the use of water from the lake.

> Tanzania . . . [has lost] patience with talks involving Kenya, Uganda and Egypt over the validity of the two [colonial] agreements signed . . . Despite engaging in lengthy negotiations over the use of waters from Lake Victoria and the Nile, Tanzania has maintained that the two [colonial] agreements were illegal. (Beyene and Wadley, 2004)

However, Tanzania was quick to point out that its $27.6 billion project would not affect the lake or the Nile flow: 'The water we get from Lake Victoria is such a small amount of water anyway and it does not affect water coming to Egypt.'[36]

In 1999 the three countries revived the East Africa Community which had broken down in 1977 (Kagwanja, 2007). After three years of drought, from 2005 to 2007, the upstreamers intensified their ties. Joining upstream forces could in principle strengthen their hand in making a stance in negotiations with downstream Egypt and Sudan, but in practice appears to have led to careful manoeuvering. The next section briefly sketches the history and results of Nilotic cooperation.

2.3 The Road to the Nile basin Initiative

The intermittent collision course outlined above has not been lost on the international world. Under the Clinton administration, environmental security has become a key issue in American foreign policy. Water scarcity, it is feared, could be an occasion for violence, and the United States appointed twelve problem areas as 'environmental hubs'.[37] Addis Ababa, the Ethiopian capital, is one of those hotspots.

But it is mostly World Bank dignitaries that are now busily shuttling between Cairo and Addis. After a series of public relations disasters (Narmada, Arun II), the World Bank seems desperate for something to succeed and is betting on the Nile basin Development Plan. Significantly in this respect, Egypt has succeeded in catapulting its leaders on strategic global positions in water and environment policy fora (see also Allan, 1990): Boutros Boutros-Ghali (former Secretary-General, United Nations), Ismail Serageldin (Vice-Director, World Bank) and, more recently, Egypt's Water Minister, Mohamed Abu Zayd (president of World Water Forum 2000 in The Hague). Egypt's *de facto* veto on World Bank support for upstream projects on the Nile has been a most effective tactic, as Ethiopia lacks Sudan's pulling power for drumming up counteracting international support.

Nile cooperation has a pedigree. Undugu ('brotherhood'), an Egyptian initiative, operated under the auspices of the Organisation of African Unity since 1983 – but without the participation of Ethiopia, Kenya and Tanzania. Within this forum Egypt floated daring plans such as an electricity grid from Lake Victoria down to Aswan. A *Century Storage Plan* for storing water near Lake Tana in Ethiopia and Lake Victoria even dates back from 1904. Ethiopia has always approached such fora with scepticism, seeing them as a vehicle for Egyptian hegemony (Stroh, 2003). Indeed they have not been very successful so far, and neither have other technical fora such as Hydromet and Tecconile,[38] especially when a long dry spell put all countries under stress. However, a window of opportunity opened in the early 1990s. After a long period of drought, Lake Nasser started to rise, easing the pressure on Egypt. In 1993 Egypt offered its upstream riparians financial support for projects, as long as they would not divert Nile waters. Within the six-country Tecconile group, and with the support of the Canadian International Development Agency, the US$100 million Nile basin Action Plan was launched in 1994. The United Nations Development Programme (UNDP) created the so-called 'D3' initiative to facilitate the first ever meeting of all Nile riparians (Westermann, 2003), and after international experts called for the NBAC's 22 disparate infrastructural projects into a Shared Vision, presented at the Second World Water Forum in 2000. The initiative's role in guiding the mission was authorised by the 3rd Council of Ministers meeting in February 1999. The World Bank, Cida and UNDP now put considerable effort into promoting the ensuing NBI, which was enthusiastically condoned by all states in 2001.

The enthusiasm may well be related to the funds made available in this project, as well as by its non-threatening nature. Egypt's *Al-Ahram Weekly* newspaper (2001) sees a considerable role of transnational contracting and water industries in the genesis of the NBI: 'They lobbied to promote these plans and succeeded in obtaining the agreement of the Nile basin states to enter a joint initiative to develop the river as a whole.'

The initiative is resolutely non-threatening, first because technical cooperation carries less risk and also less political weight – but also because upstream irrigation is resolutely on the non-agenda. Important options are still beyond the pale. To address the problem of evaporation and seepage from Lake Nasser (12–14 per cent of the annual input, according to Dasgupta and Chattopadhyay (2004)), the most effective option would be to move water storage to reservoirs under cloudier skies. This takes considerable international political will. Still, the initiatives seem to have helped *desecuritise* information: 'The establishment of a grid of sensors all over the Nile to accurately measure water level/flow and to predict flooding/drought is another achievement.' At one point these data were considered 'national secret' in the case of Egypt. *Al-Ahram Weekly* however still complained about a lack of transparency over the Nile initiatives.[39]

This gives us a perspective on the form Nile cooperation is taking. While a paper on the 8th Nile 2002 Conference contrasts 'hydro-cooperation' with 'hydro-politics' (Girma, 2000), I would argue that cooperation is hydropolitics too. A striking aspect of Nile cooperation is that it is focussed on improving water quality or exploiting non-consumptive water quantities (hydroelectricity), never on the distribution of water between the countries. Egypt is also very willing to initiate projects with joint benefits that will increase the amount of water flowing into Egypt. For example, it is interesting to see that the Jonglei Canal is one of the NBI's projects, and that a second Jonglei channel is being considered. Egypt's role in peace building in Sudan appears very closely linked to a (Egypt's) desire to have the canal completed and indeed Egyptian experts will be involved in new dam plans.

In terms of epistemic communities, all kinds of technical cooperation (Tecconile, NBI) make sure that experts keep exchanging information, even when political communication breaks down. It also ensures a 'sanctioned discourse' that prevents a frank debate on the terms of Nile cooperation. So while learning and shared benefits are certainly within reach, they do not take away from their role of propping up Egypt's primacy.

Hegemonic Stability or Change?

However, while belligerent discourse is repeatedly voiced both up- and downstream, the Nile has seen no armed conflict so far, and is unlikely to do so in future, despite increasing upstream assertiveness. All involved seem to cooperate, more or less happily, in the continuation of a conflict, which takes on aspects of a ritual, as well as bringing attention and, potentially, donor funds.

Waterbury, in this context, warns that '(a)symmetrical rewards always characterise the potential outcomes of cooperation in international river basins' (quoted in Lindemann, 2005). Whether hegemonic stability is evaluated positively or negatively depends on whether non-hegemons perceive benefit in the status quo. Perspective is decisive for this normative evaluation. Non-hegemons are obviously interested in blowing up the perspective of conflict, while hegemons are interested in projecting an image that all is plain sailing. Thus, an Ethiopian newspaper could write:[40]

> The arithmetic of the waters of the Blue Nile River is, therefore, a zero-sum game, which Egypt is determined to win. It must have a hegemonic relationship with the countries of the Nile Valley and the Horn of Africa. When, for instance, Ethiopia is weak and internally divided, Egypt can rest. But when Ethiopia is prosperous and self-confident, playing a leading role in the region, Egypt is worried.

In response, Marawan Badr, the Egyptian Ambassador to Ethiopia, wrote:

> Such political commentary, or more correctly, political trash, cannot come [except] from a sick and disturbed mind. Egyptian–Ethiopian relations are not in a crisis. We do not even have problems. There are serious issues, which need to be addressed. (quoted in Kendie 1999: 141–142)

Egypt's Water Minister and Third World Water Forum chairman, Mohammed Abu Zayd, expressed more politely that 'there is no conflict or struggle between Egypt and any other Nile basin country' (quoted in Brunnée and Toope, 2002).

The denial of alternatives to the harmonious discourse of course does not mean they are not there. According to Waterbury (2002), Ethiopia and Sudan are intent on changing the Nile regime, while Uganda and Kenya are not. Ethiopia however lacks the material basis that Sudan has, oil, and that allows it to escape, circumvent established systems of patronage. Sudan's position is still unclear after John Garang died under mysterious circumstances in 2005, while domestic war and suffering in Darfur continues. It is not unimportant that Sudan is a target on America's rogue state list. According to El-Khodari (2003b), Egypt was unhappy with the USA giving $2 billion in military aid to Ethiopia, Eritrea and Uganda, and intervening in Sudan's civil war in favour of southern Sudan's liberation army, SPLA-M. If South Sudan will be given independence in 2011, the new political entity is likely to pursue its own hydraulic mission on the basis of John Garang's vision, which could in turn change the dynamics, and might side with Ethiopia.

2.4 Conclusion – Midnight at Noon or Out of Time?

Having reviewed Egypt's domestic and external strategy, we are now in a better position to explain why Egypt might insist on the Toshka scheme in what is surely one of the most inhospitable places on earth.

The sense of the Toshka project is hard to defend. The lack of space is contestable, and living conditions in the new area are such that it is unlikely to attract millions of new dwellers. Instead, it seems to serve foreign hydropolitics, inspired by a 'prior use' strategy to safeguard acquired water rights to Nile water rather than meaningful domestic development, and a domestic strategy to create work for the army and construction sector.

The present contribution concurs with Whittington and Waterbury's (1998) claim that the Toshka channel project is best explained as one plank of a basin strategy to make a claim to prior use of Nile floodwaters and in so doing safeguard claims for the long term. Egypt's domestic, regional and international position is strong enough to risk short-term conflict over this move, keeping the pressure on by using the Nile's floodwater as fully as it can. Internationally, an ongoing position play of threatening language and cooperative agreements can obfuscate the ongoing hegemony Egypt enjoys in the Nile. While offering its cooperation to upstreamers and initiating Nilotic cooperative initiatives and organisations, Egypt can also be said to hegemonise this regime by suppressing alternative discourses. In the international arena, Egypt's hegemonic position at home and abroad is strong enough to be able to claim that there is no conflict on the Nile. Renouncing treaties and threatening military action have been a popular but pretty meaningless gesture for upstream Nile riparians. Now that political relations between Egypt and Ethiopia have been normalised to some degree, some sort of treaty cannot be too far away. The Blue Nile states are also talking about three-way cooperation on both the Blue Nile and three of its tributaries.[41]

It is telling that most mega-plans under the NBI concern the White Nile, where upstream states are less vocal. The US and World Bank interest in regional stability has provided a financial and/or diplomatic incentive to this process. The Bank seems determined not to let this basin plan fail because of neighbourly squabbles.

Under the bright rhetoric on cooperation lies the reality that the NBI has not led to talks on sustainable reallocation of the Nile flow. When the push comes to shove, both Egypt and Ethiopia have so far lent substance on the ground to prior-use claims in preference to coordinated management. The New Valley projects only really make sense in this context.

Various forms of (regime) closure are part of the country's water security strategy in the face of the unpredictability of the resource and of upstream state behaviour. In addition to its co-riparians, Egypt also keeps a tight rein on its own population, and firm control on the waters coming in at Aswan. To pull off its international strategy, Egypt keeps tight control of the scheme and forestalls or co-opts opposition or alternatives to the project. The securitisation of space and development supports a normative consensus, so that domestic and riparian control is maintained without resorting much to outright coercion and repression. This has included foreclosing a public discussion of the alternative of virtual water, and of what to do about the dependency it brings in future. However, the debate in press and Parliament suggests cracks in the smooth surface.

Postscript:

On 14 May 2010 four upstream states, Rwanda, Ethiopia, Uganda and Tanzania signed their own Nile Agreement, giving Egypt and Sudan a year's ultimatum for signing on. Egypt's Water Minister furiously claimed his government would take 'whatever states necessary' to protect its historic rights. http://www.upi.com/Science_News/Resource-Wars/2010/05/20/Egypt-rails-against-new-Nile-treaty/UPI-25881274369502/; last accessed 22 May 2010. It is too early to assess the geopolitical impact of this surprise move.

3

RESISTING THE TURKISH PAX AQUARUM? THE ILISU DAM DISPUTE AS A MULTI-LEVEL STRUGGLE

> 'I appreciate their fears,' [Turkish President Özal said in 1992] 'but we will not harm them. To the contrary, Turkey will more than make up for the water shortage. I have tried to convince Iraq and Syria of our positive intentions.'

3.1 Introduction

Both the Euphrates and Tigris rivers have great extremes between their highest and lowest flow levels,[1] bringing risk of both drought and floods. The mortal fear of floods in Mesopotamia, the 'land between the rivers', is expressed in the Gilgamesh epos and the biblical deluge. Downstreamers are normally the first to shield themselves from flooding and develop the flatter valley lands, and Iraq is no exception. But the region is also drought-prone, inciting the impoundment of water in large dams. When midstream Syria started developing the Euphrates, the two countries just stopped short of a violent clash over water in 1976. But the two downstream countries have shared a concern ever since upstream Turkey embarked on its mega-multi-dam project to control the floodwaters on the Euphrates and Tigris rivers and develop its poor southeast in the late 1970s. With the launch of the Greater Anatolia Project, Turkey has truly been on a collision course with both neighbours. Like the Nile, the basin has frequently been presented as a prime candidate for 'water wars' (Bulloch and Darwish, 1993; Starr and Stoll, 1998; De Villiers, 1999).

The present study investigates water *securitisation* and *politicisation* in the Euphrates-Tigris basin. Given its importance to state building and integration, hydraulic development is a prime candidate for securitising moves, that is,

Figure 3.1: ***Map of Turkey***

being portrayed as so essential for national survival that it is non-negotiable and legitimises extreme measures (Buzan *et al.*, 1998). Debate, dissent and alternatives are foreclosed, so that 'normal' political processes cannot take place.

Is the Euphrates basin indeed prone to anarchic, dog-eat-dog conflict, or, is there a question of cooperation? Three different answers to this last question emerge from the literature: One voice sees no order at all:

- 'There is no cooperation whatsoever . . . a Hobbesian state of nature . . . there is no sign that the chaos is ever going to end' (Kalpakian, 2004: 89).

Others however take a contrary view:

- Turkey pacified the region, resulting in a *pax aquarum* (Kolars and Mitchell, 1991). Marwa Daoudy (2005) contends that Turkey is the undisputed basin leader (hegemon). Turkey's dominance is such that it can 'do whatever it likes' with the water, as then President Demirel famously stated in 1992 (Kalpakian, 2004).
- A cooperative regime has been formed under American hegemony, as Ayşegül Kibaroğlu claims (1996 and pers. comm. 2006).

The chapter will argue that the three narratives can be reconciled by taking a multi-layered approach.

Meanwhile, a politicisation process appears to have taken place over the Ilısu dam. Since 1983, several Turkish mega-dams for irrigation and hydroelectricity were built over both neighbours' objections. For a breathtaking moment at the turn of the century, however, the construction of the Ilısu dam, the first GAP (*Güneydoğu Anadolu Projesi*) dam on the river Tigris, seemed to constitute a break

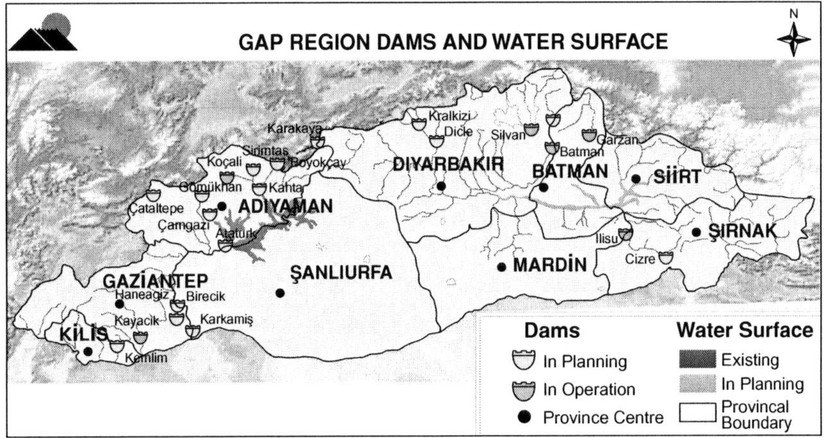

Figure 3.2: ***Overview of GAP dams***

in the pattern. The flooding of villages to make room for the Ilısu dam reservoir, including the historically important town of Hasankeyf, exposed the projected dam to resistance from a coalition of local, basin and international NGO groups who managed to stop the flow of external funding of the dam in 2001/2002.

What opened up the possibility to *politicise* the Ilısu Dam and its flooding, and how successful was it? The chapter is structured as follows.

Section 3.2 explores how Turkey, as a former empire, learned to be 'first among equals' in a 'rough neighbourhood', which, according to Aydın (2003), plagues Turkey with an 'insecurity complex'. Does this legitimise claims to exceptionalism at home and abroad, known as 'securitising moves'? (Buzan et al., 1998). Section 3.3 sketches the genesis of Turkish hydraulic development and discusses its relevance as a domestic 'concept of control' with respect to Southeast Anatolia. Section 3.4 analyses if such moves for closure have happened in Euphrates hydropolitics, and what effect they had on decision-making and resistance to the dam projects. Section 3.5 shows that institutional change (privatisation of the water sector) with a view to accessing international funds gave NGOs a look-in to attack construction companies and especially their financial guarantors. It focuses on the politicisation of the Ilısu hydropower project, structuring the analysis with the help of Buzan's security domains. It will especially zoom in on the way the campaign played out in Britain. Section 3.6 evaluates a discussion of the elements of the theory and their application to the case study. The paper concludes with an assessment of the usefulness of multiple chessboard analysis of hegemony.

3.2 Life After Empire

Turkish politics cannot really be grasped without taking the state's imperial legacy into account. Just like the Serbian trauma over their 1389 defeat (at the hands of the Turks) still informed late-twentieth-century passions over Kosovo, the memory of the giant Ottoman empire tends to dominate the political rhetoric in present-day Turkey. Some Turkish politicians have never abandoned the aspiration – at least in political discourse – to regain past glories of the Ottoman Empire (ca. 1299–1922), which led one Turkish president, Turgut Özal, to proclaim that 'the 21st century will be the Turkish century . . . from the Adriatic to the Chinese Wall' (quoted in Zürcher, 1998). In turn, Syria and Iraq have not forgotten they were once under Ottoman tutelage.

In 1920 the defeated Sultan signed the treaty of Sevres, which lobotomised the Ottoman Empire, leaving a small heartland around Ankara in central Anatolia, ceding West Anatolia and Thrace to European powers, creating Armenian and Kurdish states and putting Istanbul and the Turkish Straits under international control (Drorian, 2005).

The revolutionary Young Turks and their 'people's army' forced the last Sultan, Mehmet VI, to abdicate in November 1922, which put an end to the Ottoman empire, and established a secular, European-oriented republic with a strong role for the military. Turkish territory remained miniaturised: the Fertile Crescent (Iraq, Syria, Lebanon, Palestine and Jordan) became a Franco-British mandate, northern Mesopotamia fell to Britain and except for Thrace all European territories had to be ceded. Turkey became a state without external territories, but the new republican government managed to negotiate in the Lausanne Treaty of 24 July 1923 that the minorities did not gain independence and international control was rescinded. According to Drorian, the existential threat posed by Sevres continues to be an obsession for the present-day government, which explains distrust of European conditionality for Turkish accession to the EU and the insistence on unity, nationalism and secularism (Drorian, 2005: 259).

A guiding slogan of the Turkish republic in 1923 has been 'Peace at home, peace abroad'. The next two sections will look at Turkey's foreign and domestic politics, respectively, after which it will be explored how the two are linked by hydropolitics.

3.2.1 Turkey's Foreign Policy: Playing the Field

Rather than a has-been, post-Ottoman Turkey manifested itself as a regional player. Turkey is historically very well placed at the crossroads between Southeast Europe, the Middle East and Central Asia.

Aydın (2003) however sees a worried soul beneath the bullish exterior. Aydın claims Turkey is in a perennial regional 'insecurity complex', a permanent sense of feeling unsafe. In his analysis, being situated in a 'rough neighbourhood' explains Turkey's eagerness to exercise domestic and external control, and a prominent role for the military sector.

One of Turkey's worries is Iraq (Aydın, 2001, fn). Especially after his invasion of Kuwait, Saddam's territorial aspirations had been an ongoing cause for concern for the Turkish state (Aydın, 2003) and Turkey lent logistic support to the allied invasion of Iraq in 1991. However, Turkey preferred some overture with the Iraqis, as it occasionally needed them to grant rights to 'hot pursuit' of Kurdish separatists on Iraqi territory.

Saddam's hydraulic strategies against opposition were rather more radical than Turkey's. Saddam had a 'Third River' dug to connect the Euphrates and Tigris and develop its soils. This conveniently required the drainage of the wetlands between Euphrates and Tigris where the rebellious Marsh Arab population lived, the Ma'adan. While Saddam Hussein's marsh drainage strategy became an international news story, it is less well known that he apparently planned flooding Kurdish separatists in the north, the Iraq Kurd Federation. According to Middle East Watch, the Kurds were uprooted from the countryside with an estimated 40 chemical attacks (most notoriously on Halabya), fleeing but trapped by security forces in so-called Anfal campaigns. Farmland and trees were destroyed, villages bulldozed or dynamited, and it was planned to flood large areas of the Kurdish-inhabited areas by raising and breaking barrages.[2] An electricity embargo against Iraq's northern provinces threatened water supply until Turkey started supplying electricity to that region in 1994 (Jongerden, 1994).

Turkish 'neo-Ottomanists', such as President Özal, had always resented the loss of the Northern Iraqi region. Mosul and Kirkuk are rich in oil, and the population there is largely Turkoman. While the Turkish Army has emphasised the sanctity of Republican borders, Özal voiced the claim to the province of Mosul after Iraq's Gulf War defeat in 1991 – a *faux pas* he was forced to retract quickly.[3]

Turkish–Iraq relations have been pragmatic. Saddam's Iraq reportedly found it useful to provide logistic support to the Kurdish Workers' Party (PKK) in Turkey to weaken the Turks, while Iraq also cooperated with Turkey to control the PKK in northern Iraq, where they might ally with Iraq's own Kurdish separatists. Turkey also reportedly refused to block the Euphrates in 1991, despite allied requests to do so, arguing that 'water is life' and therefore it will not use water as a military instrument. While Ankara allowed the allied forces to use Diyarbakir, a key Kurdish-majority city in Southeast Anatolia, as a base for its war on Saddam in 1991, Turkey no longer allowed its territory to be used as an allied airbase in the 2003 war on Iraq.

Turkey manages to make much political capital out of its geographical location. It connects three macro-regions: Europe, Central Asia and the Middle East, a geopolitical nexus that virtually ensures NATO backing. Turkey has been a long-time member and cornerstone of NATO, and was one of the top three recipients of American foreign aid until the war against Saddam (after which Iraq entered the top three).

Turkey has also made considerable concessions to Europe to keep the door open to membership of the European Union of which it would, at a stroke, become the largest member. Converting Abdullah Öcalan's death penalty into a life sentence is only one of many European demands for reform Turkey swallowed whole. After the capture of Saddam Hussein, Turkey immediately declared its intention to respect the boundaries of Iraq, despite its territorial claims on oil-rich Mosul and Kirkuk. Realising that European membership would mean the obligation to accede to existing European water legislation (see also Hermans, 2005), Turkey commissioned a Dutch consultancy, Grontmij, to make a study of Europe-compliant integrated water resource management of a river it shares with Greece and Bulgaria.

Finally, the collapse of the Soviet empire has not freed Turkey from rivalry with Russia but opened up avenues for Turkey to exert influence in the Turkic countries in Central Asia – a 'pax Turkicana'.[4] While Iran can count on Armenia as its ally, Turkey has cultural bonds with the four Turkish-speaking states of Central Asia: Kazakhstan, Kyrgyzstan, Turkmenistan, and Uzbekistan. As the Americans would rather not see expansion of the Iranian sphere of influence, they back Turkish inroads in the region. '(T)here is . . . no local great power in the multipolar Middle East complex. It is also a region in which Ankara, interestingly, acts in a more unilateral fashion, and "dares" more than in the other regions' (Kazan, 2005).

In this regional context it is very helpful for Turkey that its territory is located upstream on the rivers Euphrates and Tigris, and (together with Lebanon, which has not succeeded in reaping the benefits of its natural advantage) is the only water-rich country in the region. Its geographical location at the headwaters of the Euphrates and Tigris, the main sources of freshwater of its most troublesome neighbours, Syria and Iraq, is extremely convenient to Turkey. Whether intentional or not, the control of water for development in its bold Southeastern Anatolia Project also meant control of water vis-à-vis its downstream neighbours. An unmistakable effect of the intensive damming of the two rivers is that, in principle, it enables the Turkish to turn the tap on or off.

By 1990 the GAP scheme had expanded to 22 dam projects (80 dams) and 19 hydropower schemes (involving 66 hydropower stations) on both Euphrates and Tigris,[5] providing irrigation for 1.9 million ha and investment in health, education, finance and transportation to modernise a traditional agricultural society in a region twice the size of Belgium (Balat, 2003).

Regional Water Trade?

It was noted above that in the geopolitical lay of the land, Turkey is very well endowed with water and premium location. While its upstream position and infrastructural development lends the country the position to control the 'tap' on its downstream neighbours, its enviable position as a water-rich state in a water-poor region as well as the (relative) political stability to exploit and deliver its water wealth also enables hydro-diplomacy with other states. The Turks recognise the significant potential for political gain in water exports – even though they have at times great difficulty providing water and sanitation for their own mega-cities.

In 1987 Turkey proposed a twin Peace Pipeline, at a cost of US$20 billion (1987 dollars) to provide water for the whole region: eastward to Saudi Arabia and westward to Israel and Palestine, which was universally rejected. While subsequently plans for a mini- and mini-mini-pipeline were developed,[6] none of these initiatives caught on. With an eye on the hot and dry Central Asian region, Turkey has also made a water offer to this region (Hillel, 1994) and proposed a water-for-electricity swap with Greece.

While these initiatives remained largely unsuccessful, the water trade pitch appeared to be working decidedly better when Turkey signed a military cooperation pact with Israel in 1996. Israel expressed a keen interest in water deliveries from the Manavgat estuary, close to Antalya. Annoying both Arab neighbours and domestic fundamentalists, Turkey signed an agreement in early 2004 to transport freshwater in giant, Norwegian-made nylon 'Medusa' bags by sea to Israel from the river Manavgat, with regular water supply foreseen from 2006 (Pamukcu, 2003). The experimental bags, however, had an annoying tendency to sink, so it was decided to transport the water in supertankers to Israel instead. But while Turkey was eager for a Public Relations success, Israel was slow to proceed with the contract. When in 2004, a deal was struck for the delivery of 50 million cubic metres (MCM) per year, no price or company was indicated (Gruen, 2004). Reported linkage politics, in which Turkey threatened to call off military orders and participation in GAP projects if Israel continued to tarry with the water contract (Kenon, 2003, Vidal, 2004), seemed to be borne out when both the water and arms deals fell apart in the same week in April 2006 (*Middle East Times*, 2006).

Finally, deliveries from the Anamur or Manavgat rivers to the occupied section of Cyprus, a semi-arid area with 200–600 mm rainfall, have likewise concerned water transfers by 10,000 m^3 'water balloons', launched in 1998 but considered uneconomic and prone to tearing, as well as underground pipelines. Large-scale structural water trade thus has not yet been in evidence (Biçak and Jenkins, 2000).

When the intended recipients of Turkish water ignored the offer or declined politely, they will have realised that 'gifts' also come with a degree of dependence and vulnerability in terms of water quality and quantity. Offering cooperation to domestic and external actors – the 'friendly face of power' – creates an obligation on the part of the accepting party. In their time, the ancient Greeks successfully employed the gift of a horse to fool the Trojans (who lived in what is currently northwest Turkey), who could not resist accepting, but in doing so, found themselves beleaguered from the inside. A sense of being at the mercy of others' unpredictable wiles can make some actors wary, or even paranoid.

3.2.2 Domestic Policy: Hydraulic Development

Like in many other hydraulic states, Turkey's development trajectory was state-led and authoritarian. In 1931 Republican Turkey instated a Kemalist form of etatism as a third way between capitalism and socialism – the 'strong state' took off. Until long after the Second World War Turkey was a one-party state and the army has often seemed to exercise *de facto* control – as the Turkish saying goes, other countries may have an army, but in Turkey the army has a country. This prevents political adventurism but also can be a brake on democratisation and reform (Aydın, 2003). The antagonism of democratic politics does not sit well with the military's ideals of unity and 'promotion of the state' (Drorian, 2005).

The hydraulic imperative for the development of its hinterland can be seen as a political project to weld together feudal and modernising (industrialising) forces into a historic national compromise. Swyngedouw (1999, 2007) sketches how Spain, after losing its empire, regenerated itself by 'colonising' its water resources in a hydraulic mission, while securing its international position by allying itself with the North Atlantic Treaty Organization (NATO). The story for post-Ottoman Turkey appears to look remarkably similar. The towering figure of Kemal Atatürk played a crucial role in the new strategy. In the 1930s Atatürk, father of the Turks, envisaged diverting the Euphrates and Tigris to the drier west of Turkey. This plan gave way to a development vision modelled on the river Dniepr development scheme and echoing the Tennessee Valley Authority. The American hydraulic plan for an integrated regional development project to develop the region out of economic depression proved a model approach to developing one's way out of economic depression, spawning similar projects in Jordan (Trottier, 1999), the Mekong (Bakker, 1999), Helmand Valley in Afghanistan (Cullather, 2002) and elsewhere.

An aspiration for autarky and exportable food and electricity nourished Turkey's internal regulation and resource colonisation drive. Turkey may be poor in oil and gas, which necessitates imports from Libya and Saudi Arabia, but the country is very well endowed with other raw materials. Resource development, whether by institutional or technical intervention, could play an important role in the quest to integrate the Turkish state. The GAP supported ambitions for a stronger export position to bring in currency in an often inflation-ridden and structurally shaky economy. The irrigation schemes could turn the region into a 'breadbasket' for the Middle East. In the 1970s, all three riparians had changed from food exporters to food importers, and all other Middle East countries are now massive net food importers. At the same time, Turkey's energy import bill skyrocketed due to OPEC's energy price hike as well as increasing demand. These economic reasons spurred Turkey to speed up the plan for Euphrates and Tigris development.

The GAP project promised to boost both food and energy security, understood as self-sufficiency. Annual hydroelectricity production from GAP will produce 22 per cent of Turkey's total energy generation with an installed capacity of 7,476 MW. Southeast Anatolia is dry (rainfall ranges between 470 and 830 mm) but rich in fertile soils. Irrigation enables the production of summer crops (cotton, maize, sesame and soybean), which so far was impossible in Southeast Anatolia. In all, the irrigation schemes are scheduled to develop a 2-million-hectare area, an area the collective size of the Benelux countries. The Euphrates is not particularly rich in fish, but this sector is also promoted, especially in the Atatürk dam reservoir.

After several big dams were built in the 1960s and 1970s (Keban, Karakaya dams), the scheme came to be conceived as an integrated development project in successive stages. After evaluating 22 different combinations of four dams of different heights, the State Hydraulic Works department, DSI, had presented the Lower Firat (Euphrates) plan in 1970 to bring irrigation and low-cost energy to the surrounding plains between what are now the Keban and Atatürk dams. In 1977, the Lower Firat plan was integrated into a package with all other schemes in these regions, seven hydropower and irrigation schemes on the Euphrates and six on the Tigris, by the name of GAP. In 1983 construction of the project's centerpiece, the Atatürk Dam, started.

Given the large outlay and uncertainties involved, the GAP Master Plan of 1989 recommended to scale back GAP to priority projects (Brismar, 2002), but at the same time continued its radical reorientation towards a regional people-focussed rather than water-oriented development project It sought to propel the region, seen as backward, in terms of education, agricultural practices, gender relations, environmental conditions and participation.

In 1995 the GAP was again evaluated, this time against sustainable development criteria, which led to a joint programme with UNDP, 'Sustainable Development Programme in the GAP Region', an umbrella project of 29 projects. It sought to promote community participation and advance the role of women for sustainable regional development (quoted in Brismar, 2002).

Glowing press releases call attention to tremendous export boosts (in cotton and grain) that appear to have been induced by GAP.[7] The project is meeting all its hydroelectrical goals, benefiting urban and industrial interests and has brought good road infrastructure to the region. However, while the expansion of energy production progresses impressively, the development of irrigable lands is lagging, so that there have been employment opportunities for skilled workers from the west rather than for unskilled, semi-literate and often poor labour from the southeast, which could intensify disparities in income distribution and further exacerbate social tensions that the project was intended to ameliorate (McDowall, 1996: 434–5). Moreover, *ağas* (latifundists), helped by a liberal shift in Turkish national politics under politicians like Inönü, blocked much intended land reform and may well be the ones to reap the benefits of agrarian development (Mutlu, 1996), as they are much better placed in having their land titles recognised. Thirty-eight per cent in the region do not own land, while compensation for flooding tended to be given to landowners rather than sharecroppers. 'A few individuals with good party connections have succeeded in getting the state to allocate large tracts of land to them' (Barkey and Fuller, 1998: 190). Since a World Bank-induced water reform law was rushed through in 1994, irrigation associations have been created, charged with operation and maintenance of the irrigation infrastructure. While this meant to improve participatory management, it leaves great scope for local elites who already have access to dominate the process. To represent user groups or vote, you need a minimum amount of land, which effectively bars landless from having a voice and being trained in irrigation techniques (Harris, 2002).

Moreover, the war against the PKK since 1984 (see Section 3.2.3) also has its effects on the position of the *ağas* in Southeast Anatolia. The below section delves deeper into the Kurdish issue.

3.2.3 Incorporating the Kurds?

When the French and English laid down the current Turkish boundaries at San Remo in 1920 – blithely ignoring natural boundaries and denying the Kurds the nation-state they had been promised earlier – they laid the basis for many current resource conflicts in the region. Both Turkey and Iraq (as well as Iran, Syria and the former Soviet Union) have a sizeable Kurdish minority whose elites have not forgotten Kurdish aspirations for independence.

Like many states that harbour diverse ethnic groups within their borders, the Turkish state competes for legitimacy with centrifugal actors that have the power to supply vital social services and/or identity. In the context of nation-(re)building, the early 1920s continued the intensive homogenisation of the Turkish populations, including a massive exchange of ethnic and religious minorities as a consequence of fights with Armenia (1917) and Greece (1921–22). The First Turkish Republic, proclaimed on 23 October 1923, was defined as an indivisible, unitary Turkish state in which the Kurds formally did not even exist[8] – only as 'mountain Turks' or 'Eastern Turks' (*doğulu*).

Kemal Atatürk's relations with the Kurdish population started well, as several tribal chiefs had supported Atatürk's Young Turks to 'roll back' British and French domination of Turkish policy, as well as the influence of Christians, Greeks and Armenians. But when the 1920 Treaty of Sevres turned out to include an independent Armenian/Kurdish state in the East, relations turned sour.

As a fragmented ethnicity, the Kurds historically had not organised politically as a nation-state, but seized on the chance of self-rule. The Young Turks however made sure the promise of an independent state was erased from the Treaty of Lausanne. In 1924 Kurdish schools and organisations were outlawed. Now that the dream of independence fell through, the Kurds resisted 'horizontal integration' by an assimilative Kemalist republic, staging several uprisings such as the Sheikh Said rebellion in 1925, Bayoum in 1929 and in 1938 in Alevi-dominated Dersim (Tencili). The Kemalist republican leadership, in turn, regarded their particularism, but also their aversion to secularism as a threat to Turkish unity. This key plank of the Kemalist scaffolding was enforced in a (recently relaxed) curb on Kurdish identity, language and culture, seeking the cultural homogenisation (Turkification) of an imagined 'Kurdistan'. Atatürk's successor Inönü (a Kurd by birth) responded to the uprisings with mass deportation (Jongerden et al., 1997).

When the resolutely secular Kurdish Workers' Party arrived on the scene claiming to represent the Kurdish cause in the early 1980s, they did not command an obvious following. Although Turkish and Arabic groups are also significant in the area, Kurdish groups dominate the GAP region. But Southeast Anatolia is a patchwork quilt of landowners and landless, often groups of nomadic origin which various Ottoman rulers tried to sedentarise with varying success since the seventeenth century. Socially organised along tribal lines in *ashirets* (sing. *ashiret*, a kind of clan) (Erhan, 1997), Kurdish identity is by no means socially cohesive or culturally unified.

The PKK, however, began as a Marxist-Leninist party which, in true Leninist fashion, saw itself as the uncompromising front guard. In 1984, as construction works for the Atatürk Dam got under way, the PKK staged violent attacks on military but also civilian targets. The guerrilla war also included attacks on the Atatürk dam, the works for which had commenced a year earlier. Reportedly, 1,100 vehicles and pieces of working machinery were destroyed (Williams, 2003). While the PKK did not manage to stop construction works, slowing down development and the need for army protection inevitably drove up the costs of the project.

These attacks gave a face, if an ugly one, to the culturally fragmented and socially incohesive Kurds. While the Turkish state competed for allegiance and control with the PKK in the Kurdish-dominated areas, it reduced the domestic war from a multitude of contradictory identities to 'friend' and 'foe'. The uprising sparked a muscular response from the Turkish armed forces as well as paramilitary death squads (revealed in a parliamentary investigation in 1996). Both the Turkish Army and the PKK targeted the villages with intimidation, the former to smoke out insurgents from villages and forests, the latter to ensure allegiance to their cause. When the army appointed armed 'village guards', these were often left with an impossible choice: if they refused, they were suspected of PKK sympathies, but if they later proposed to step down, PKK would be unforgiving. The PKK asserted Kurdish unity by force and intimidation, making criticism and defection a capital offence

President Özal however saw the GAP project as an opportunity to integrate the Kurdish minority with economic incentives. Özal claimed to be part-Kurdish himself. Ending the military dictatorship, he came to power as Prime Minister in 1983 and President in 1989 on a platform of political and economic liberalisation, easing the authoritarian legislation by enacting Kurd-friendlier legislation in 1991, and accepting the European Court of Human Rights and anti-torture legislation (Jacoby, 2005).

When Turgut Özal became President in 1989, his vision – one of integrating the Southeast through hydraulic development – was reflected in the programme's expansion beyond agriculture and energy.

The GAP infrastructural plan thus also served a political ideal. Like the TVA model became a weapon in the fight against communism in the Cold War, modernising the 'backward' Southeast was also hoped to counter the allure of Islamism for the poor in a constitutionally secular state. Even today, the average income in Ankara is still many times that of Southeast Anatolia. The idea was that once wealth came to the Southeast, the locals would be less likely to provide sanctuary to the Kurdish Workers' Party. Economic development should also attract Turks from other regions in the Kurdish-inhabited regions. Hydropowered development seemed a peaceful way to integrate ('de-other') the poor Southeast, to prevent immiseration and secessionist and Islamic fundamentalist drives.

In Turkey, landowners, industry and army could subscribe to a hydraulic mission. But from the early 1990s on, GAP dams officially became an instrument in the 'fight against terrorism' (Özok, 2005). The war against Iraq had left Saddam untouched, but created a Kurdish zone in the north which gave the PKK a springboard for its attacks. Turkey's war with the PKK continued, but so did Kurdish support for its increasingly nationalist rather than Marxist ideology. Kurdish parties in the Turkish parliament were forced to denounce the PKK, or closed down if they did not. Özal however saw the continuing war as an obstacle to Turkey's regional ambitions; apparently in 1993 Özal, the PKK and other Kurdish leaders seemed close to coming to an understanding along the lines of a federation, and the PKK felt strong enough to call a unilateral ceasefire to end the *intifada* (Jongerden et al., 1997). But then the President passed away, and his successor Demirel chose to reinforce the violence against insurgents.

> Ankara has continued to devote enormous human and material resources to this conflict which costs approximately 3 percent of Turkey's GNP [Gross National Product] ($12.5 billion in 1994) and for which military expenses absorb 45 percent of the national budget and some 250,000 troops and other security forces. (Galetti, 1999)

The Turkish army employed a slash-and-burn-tactic to root out settlements suspected of collaborating with the militant PKK. The 'soft power' of hydraulic development was thus underpinned by the deployment of 'hard power' in a campaign to crush separatism (*repression* strategy), exposing Turkey to the criticism of treating Southeast Anatolia like a *de facto* military occupation zone.

As we saw in the conceptual introduction, securitisation of an issue-area or domain may serve as an expedient political strategy to add weight to the mobilisation of resources, while pushing out the political process of deliberation and choice. This mutually hardened stance stands in the way of the vision of peaceful integration President Özal had harboured. Both aspects of the strategy caused mass displacement. Caught between a rock and a hard place, tens of thousands fled the area to the big cities: Diyarnakir, Ankara, or left for Western Europe, but it is hard to say how villagers themselves felt about the GAP.

3.2.4 Downstream Fear of Floods

The Turkish hydraulic mission does not only impact on the country's relations with the Southeast, but also those with downstream neighbours. While the Turkish state asserted riparian rights in the absence of a basin treaty (Brismar, 2002), downstream states loudly complained that GAP is a water control strategy using physical control of the flow for political gain.

Downstream states usually develop water infrastructure earlier than upstreamers, and the Euphrates is no exception. Flood control of course brings many benefits: regulated water supply, agrarian and industrial development and control of territory. But especially in Iraq, rivers have historically brought flood distress and inspired Great Flood accounts like Gilgamesh as well as the biblical deluge recounted in the book of Genesis. This especially concerns the river Tigris: snowmelt from the Taurus and, via its Zap tributaries, the Zagros Mountains add their waters, often causing destructive flooding.

In ancient Mesopotamia, the spring floods were a source of acute fear each year; in recent times the 1954 flood raised the Tigris by 65 cm and ravaged the capital, Baghad. In response, Iraq built the ar-Ramadi and Sāmarrā barrages in the 1950s, to divert the floodwaters into Lake Habbaniyah and the Tharthar depression in central Iraq. Even larger works were carried out on the Tigris tributaries Zap and Diyala to tame the Tigris, though the last major Tigris flood is as recent as 1988.

Second off the block in building dams was Syria, which is upstream to Iraq on the Euphrates (Syria only has 44 km of the Tigris). The Cold War provided an opportunity for Syria to get its Tabqa (or at-Thawrah) Dam built between 1966 and 1973. This reduced flood risk for Iraq, but also the much-needed irrigation water and silt (and, less welcome, salt). Moreover, Syria filled its Tabqa dam reservoir only briefly after Turkey filled its Keban dam in a particularly dry year (Bari, 1977). Iraq claimed the dam's impoundment adversely affected 3 million

Iraqi farmers (Starr, 1991). As a result, in 1975, armed forces of both countries were mobilised at the border. The Arab League had to mediate.

Ever since Syria and Iraq's wings of the Ba'ath ('Renaissance') party split, relations between the two countries have been notoriously bad, and the 1975 clash was the closest the Euphrates riparian has come to violence over water. However, a common cause against a third party can make enemies temporarily set aside their differences and create a joint front. The GAP mega-project provides the occasion for downstreamers to join forces and deliver fierce protests and threats to Turkey each time a dam is announced.

If all the present dams in the catchment were to be closed all at the same time, the entire volume of the rivers could now be stored many times over. The fact that Turkey, in principle, has the ability to cut off Euphrates water for six months – however impractical that would be for Turkey – has been a source of acute discomfort for downstream countries. But while the 'water wars' literature sees resource scarcity as the driver for warfare, water is not particularly scarce in the Euphrates-Tigris catchment. Malin Falkenmark's 'water barrier' is a rule of thumb that postulates that a country that has less than 1,800 m^3 per person per year is water-stressed and less than 1,000 is water-poor. Turkey and Syria are nearing the 1,800 zone, Iraq is still way above that.

It is often claimed that, since 1970, the flow leaving the Turkish borders has diminished by half. Frequently, a GAP-induced 40 per cent reduction is predicted for Syria and up to 80 per cent less for Iraq; although this latter figure would be a cumulative effect of Turkish and Syrian dam projects (estimates differ, see e.g. Shapland, 1997). There are reports that two smaller Syrian rivers have run dry as a result of the reduced influx. But more important than the real impact is the *potential* to give the water tap a twist in either direction. This argument has repeatedly been voiced for the Euphrates.[9] Most of the mega-dams have so far been realised on the Euphrates (in Turkish: Firat): until recently, Turkey has laid relatively limited claim to its sister river, the Tigris (Dicle).

The final series of GAP dams will significantly enclose the river Tigris however. The *Ilısu* storage lake, just outside Dargecit, about 45 km from the Syrian border, will have a total storage capacity of just under 10.5 billion cubic metres and an operating capacity of 7.5 billion m^3. Normally, that would leave a buffer capacity of 3 billion cubic metres. As the average annual inflow of the Tigris is 15 billion m^3 the reservoir will account for half the total annual flow.[10] Opponents fear that the combined spare active storage capacity would enable a malevolent Turkey to arrest the river influx for some additional months, such that not a drop of Tigris water would flow into Syria and Iraq (Berne Declaration, 1999). While the majority of the catchment is in Iraq, where the two rivers merge and drain into the Persian Gulf through the Shatt al-Arab (disputed by Iran), the river receives 95 per cent of its precipitation within

Turkish territory, and the artesian springs just across the Syrian border are fed by rain infiltrated into Turkish soil before it works its way down to Syria.[11] But contrary to the Euphrates, Tigris tributaries also flow into Iraq, so Iraq is not wholly dependent on that river (Beaumont, 1998) The reduced amount of freshwater allowed to pass the border, however, would impair the diluting capacity to purify the wastewater flowing from the region's major cities and agricultural return flow. Baghdad, for its part, fears its flow to be contaminated by agricultural chemicals and pesticides. Another worry is that coarse sediment deposits may increase downstream flood levels (Williams and Associates, 2001).

Not just the closing but also the sudden opening of the floodgates would be disastrous. While admittedly rare, the water weapon has been known to be deployed in the basin. In 689 BC Sennacherib of Assyria dammed the Euphrates upstream from Baghdad, only to destroy it after sufficient water had assembled behind the dam. The sudden flood wave flooded the Mesopotamian capital and won Sennacherib the day (Gleick, 1993). According to a Pentagon statement, Iraq itself used strategic flooding of the Tigris to stop Iranian advances in the 1980s and indeed there were fears that the river would be used as a defence against the allied invasion in 2003 (CNN, 2003). A dam can even break accidentally: half a million citizens in Mosul and Baghdad are potentially at risk from a flood wave if a dam at Mosul should break. The dam on the Tigris, built in 1984, was 'fundamentally flawed' to begin with because it is built on unstable bedrock. Currently it is in a crumbling state according to the US Corps of Engineers and, according to the Special Inspector General for Iraq Reconstruction (SIGIR), inexpertly repaired in an American project (*Independent,* 8 August 2007). Such knowledge, apparently kept quiet so as not to cause a panic, teaches the downstream riparians some realism.

The impounding of the storage lake for the huge *Atatürk Dam* had created an alliance of convenience between Syria and Iraq. When Syria joined the anti-Saddam coalition in the Gulf War, the truce with Iraq fell apart and the two countries, officially, have not been on speaking terms since. But after a five-day meeting in 1996 the states decided jointly to dispatch threatening letters to companies involved in building the Birecik dam. When the Ilısu dam, a hydropower and irrigation project near Dargecit, 45 km from the Syrian border, and its smaller sister dam, Cizre (46 m in height, 240 MW in capacity) were mooted, Syria and Iraq again joined forces sending protest letters to funders and, especially after Turkey concluded an alliance with the Arabs' arch enemy, Israel, in 1997, mobilising the Arab League against the GAP. Turkey's upstream development caused the downstream riparians to be sufficiently 'realist' to agree in 1996 on a percentage distribution of whatever Turkey leaves them: 42 per cent for Syria and 58 per cent for Iraq.

The historic flow before Turkey started its project is calculated at about 1,000 cubic metres per second (m^3/s) at the border with Syria. The Arab states argue that since there are three states sharing the river's flow, each is entitled to one-third, giving the two Arab states a total of around 667 m^3/s (Gruen, 2004). Turkey could not agree with that amount, but signed a protocol with Syria in 1987 promising to release an average of 500 m^3/s, about half the river flow, across the Turkish/Syrian border, and has not flagrantly defaulted. The first major test was 1991, in which Turkey filled Lake Atatürk. This was a low-flow year anyway, but Turkey did supplement the balance later to honour its obligation. The Birecik dam was filled in another dry period, 1999 until 2001. When 2000 carried an extremely low flow of 75 m^3/s, Turkey made endeavours to let through 400 m^3 (Brismar, 2002). The Director of the General Directorate of State Hydraulic Works stoically commented one year later: 'I cannot make the rain' (quoted in Zawahri, 2008).

Turkey can thus claim to have acted in good faith not to harm downstream interests. GAP's downstream opponents especially criticise Turkey's perceived arrogance in positing its self-interest as the regional common good without conferring with its neighbours. In 1989, during the trilateral Joint Technical Committee called by Turkey, the two downstreamers had pleaded with Turkey to fill the Atatürk Dam without stopping the river. The Turks used the technical basin committee meetings as a way to inform the others rather than to negotiate, and declared the decision was final and non-negotiable: the flow would be arrested for about a month (Zawahri, 2008). Turkey proposed its neighbours basin-wide development, yet in 1990 President Özal claimed the entire Euphrates-Tigris basin a single Turkish river, pulling off the dazzling feat of declaring sovereignty over the entire basin in the name of *integrated management*. This way, Turkey resisted internationalisation of the water issue, as the water would be safest in Turkish hands. The co-riparians' attitude did not help things. While Turkey's neighbours indeed derive benefits from river regulation, it was politically unwise to admit this, and both countries kept making complaints and demands for more water.

Iraq and Syria claimed a breach of international law and riparian water rights. Due to the weakness of international water law, Turkey could (along with China and Burundi) refuse signing the 1997 UN treaty on non-navigable watercourses, claiming the treaty grants downstream states excessive rights – if it also does nothing for its international PR.[12] The downstream protest is not a particularly strong hand, though. With some stretch of the imagination, a breach of a 1946 Turco-Syrian treaty stipulating consultation between riparians could be invoked[13] as well as a Turkish-Iraqi Protocol signed that same year, which allowed Iraq to construct hydrological infrastructure and meteorological stations along the rivers inside Turkey 'to prevent downriver flooding and, thus, benefit Iraq' (El-Fadel et al., 2002).

International law provides only cold comfort for water plaintiffs – there are no widely shared and enforced principles governing international rivers. Iraq may insist on the international law doctrine of absolute territorial integrity, stipulating that no riparian is allowed to impair the quality and quantity of the water resources flowing within its territory. But Turkey can, with equal vigour, juxtapose the doctrine of unlimited territorial sovereignty, also known as the Harmon doctrine: each state can treat the water within its boundaries any which way it likes.

The Kurdish Card

As a downstreamer to Turkey, Syria protests against each new Turkish-built dam, complaining of failed harvests and interrupted water services in Damascus as a result of interrupted and reduced flows. Moreover, Syria itself has many historic issues with Turkey, including the loss of the province of Alexandretta (or, from a Turkish perspective, Hatay), which was given to Turkey by its French colonial rulers. Downstream Syria has long betted on the Kurdish card, allowing the Kurdish militants to train in the Syrian-occupied Biqa'a valley in Lebanon, as well as the extreme leftist Turkish urban guerrilla Devsol and other groups. When Turkey protested, Syria moved the Kurds to northern Iran, and when in early 1996 Turkey intercepted five Iranian lorries carrying arms, which Turkey claims were destined for the PKK, another diplomatic row ensued.

The line was toed when on 5 October 1998 Turkish troops were mobilised at the Syrian border in Hatay, and President Demirel told Syria to disband the camps, warning it would 'take any measures it deemed necessary' and refused to meet Egyptian President Hosni Mubarak, who had offered mediation between Syria and Turkey.[14] Still, Mubarak's effort paid off: when Syria arrested five PKK activists and expelled Abdullah Öcalan, this signposted the end of the Kurdish lever. The two countries signed the so-called Adana Protocol, and started to explore cooperation, including technical exchange of Turkish GAP and Syrian GOLD (General Organization for Land Development) project staff. To the chagrin of the Turkish government, though, the Kurdish issue keeps figuring prominently in international debates over hydraulic projects. International activists picked up on these issues and, as we shall see in Section 3.3, found a point of entrance to put the Kurdish-hydraulic link on the agenda in the late 1990s: funding dams.

3.3 The Dispute over Ilısu

3.3.1 Water Privatisation: A Window of Opportunity?

The international overlay on regional security dynamics is notable where project funding is concerned. To fund such an enormous project, a continuous stream of funds is needed. Finding external money for the GAP project has been a problem for the Turkish government. From day one a key external player, the World Bank (IBRD), has been unwilling to support a regionally controversial dam. This section looks into the institutional transition Turkey made in the 1990s to access international funds, in spite of World Bank objections to the dam. For this, Turkey needed to project a vision of GAP bringing mutual hydraulic benefit to an international audience. Instead, privatisation was the prelude to a heated internationalised dispute over the Izmit and Birecik dams and, more recently and intensely, Ilısu Dam, the first major Turkish dam on the Tigris.

As by far the most important donor to the region, the World Bank has proved highly effective in shaping economic policies in recipient states. Its veto on regionally sensitive projects can kill off a controversial water project for a considerable time.[15] Also, the Bank would now like to see water-intensive agriculture curbed in favour of industry and urban supply. However, in denying its flow of funds, the Bank proves unable to kill off a major project when the initiator is determined enough to find funds elsewhere. Although the World Bank formally decided not to fund GAP projects in 1984, the Turks apparently never even formally applied for Bank backing, sensing the Bank would show itself highly sensitive to protestations on the part of co-riparians Syria and Iraq.

The GAP project thus started on a self-contained basis. But an inflation-ridden economy groaned under the development effort, soon coupled with the cost of military engagement with the PKK. The lack of multilateral cooperation made itself felt in ever more painful ways when, in the early nineties, projects started to fall behind schedule further and further. More and more, the GAP seemed to look like the famed 'white elephant': the costly development project that never materialises. The fact that, after a temporary lull, the final stage of the Greater Anatolia Project has now gathered steam again is due to a radical institutional move: privatisation. As early as in 1987 the means to fund the *Izmit dam* had run out. Izmit is close to Turkey's capital metropolis, Istanbul, and the project was to provide water for homes and industry. At the instigation of President Özal, a private consortium was created, Izmit Su, to complete the works. Stockholders are the municipality of Izmit, the Japanese conglomerates Sumitomo and Mitsui, Thames Water of Britain and two local companies, Gama and Guris. Funders were British, German and Japanese. Thames Water was contracted under a 'build, operate and transfer' scheme to run the utility for 15 years before returning it to the municipality of Izmit.

The Government Audit Department, Sayistay, issued a detailed report in 1999–2000 saying that, from beginning to end, 'the project was full of violations of laws.' In 2002, after the contract expired, the Turkish Court of Accounts found irregularities in the contract that made the water too expensive.[16]

A key cost factor of project development involved the fee of Turkish lawyers struggling to legally enable the project. While private investment was possible under the 1984 Build-Operate-Transfer law, the legislative frame and infrastructure were simply not in place. While privatisation had been advocated by several Turkish governments since the 1950s, it is hardly compatible with the prevailing dirigisme. Privatisation means an important erosion in the state's primacy over public services. The privatisation law, opposed by the secular and religious right, was finally pushed through parliament in November 1994 by Tansu Ciller, well-timed to coincide with an important Galatasaray–Barcelona football match keeping many MPs glued to the TV screen (Zürcher, 1998). As a result, the Izmit project (dam, storage lake, sewage works and water utility) was ready to go on stream ten years after its abortive start.

Faced with an acute shortage of project funds for the remainder of the GAP project, Turkey needed to co-opt the global jet stream of liberalisation and privatisation in the water sector. As we shall see in the next section, however, privatisation exposed donors and guarantors to activist NGO strategy, calling them to account for their corporate governance practice. The Birecik and Ilısu dams were the logical targets for this thrust.

3.3.2 Locating the Ethics Gap: Export Credits vs. Human Rights

Given the ritualistic aspect of mudslinging every time a new dam comes on stream, the controversies over Birecik and Ilısu are unsurprising. But the privatisation in the Turkish water sector has brought new actors into play. Until 1994 conflicts over the Euphrates and Tigris remained within a neat Realist framework of rivalry between states as unitary actors. DSI decision-making on the Ilısu dam likewise appears to have been made in 'closed' mode: the ten alternative dam sites were not subjected to outside scrutiny[17] and competition – the hydroelectricity dam was put to tender for Build-Operate-Transfer but when no 'suitable' bid emerged, the project was awarded to a consortium (Cerem, 2006).

The privatisation of the Turkish water sector brought new transnational actors into play: transnational companies (TNCs), but also hot on their heels, international non-governmental organisations (INGOs) as transnational political actors. The campaign over the human rights situation in the Southeast and the opposition from co-riparians targeted the Achilles heel of a project of this size and scale: funding.

Private	TNCs: ABB, Balfour Beatty, Sulzer Hydro, Skanska and Impreglo; major banks back it up
Public	Governments; donor governments insure export (political) risk
Civil society	NGOs and INGOs: start campaigning

Table 3.1: ***Actor groups involved in Turkish dam politics***

For construction companies, the projects do not just provide opportunity, but for several of them they provide much-needed economic security: long-term income in a competitive market. However, participation in GAP also carried considerable economic and political risk for them – not just by investing in a controversial project in a country that was effectively still at war with itself, but also the potential loss of its hardware or people due to attack. An investment in Turkey's Southeast carries considerable physical, political and economic risk and international companies are loath to carry all that risk themselves. Given the securitised status of the project area, an export credit is no luxury. Governments of countries where civil engineering is an important export sector have so far turned out surprisingly eager to provide export credits. The contractors sought to alleviate this risk by securing export credits from their governments – from the export credit agencies (ECAs) of Austria, Germany, Italy, Japan, Portugal, Sweden, Switzerland, the UK and the USA in the summer of 1998.

Export credits were needed to secure the participation of British construction company Balfour Beatty, another important international player which had been approached by the construction giant ABB to subcontract the civil engineering works, while ABB would take care of the electrical engineering and Sulzer Escher Wyss to lead the construction consortium to realise the dam, the storage lake and hydropower station – further enterprises involved are Impreglio (Italy), Skanska (Sweden) and the Turkish companies Nurol, Kiska and Tekfen. The six turbines and generators will have a total capacity of 1,200 MW and an average productivity of 3,800 GWh per year.

The international private involvement exposed the companies and their governmental backers to angry Syrian letters and writs against foreign investors and constructors involved in GAP. Syria repeatedly claimed Turkish interventions damaged Syrian agriculture and water supply. Thus, when Ilısu was approved, Syria filed compensation claims from constructing and funding companies, including Chase Manhattan Bank, and threatened to blacklist/boycott them until a trilateral agreement was signed. Such downstream vocal resistance greets the start of any new Turkish dam project and thus was perhaps expected, but the guaranteeing governments had not counted on the GAP uniting Syria and Iraq and NGOs in an alliance of convenience over human rights.

3.4 Cultural Heritage: The Flooding of Belkis and Hasankeyf

As the funding for Ilısu dam became a news item, the *Bireck* dam, just north of the Syrian border also continued to be targeted. Started in April 1996 and completed in 2002, its reservoir necessitated the flooding of the 2000-year-old ancient Roman city of Zeugma in 2000. Labelling Zeugma a 'second Pompeii', opponents not just saw this flooding as a tragedy for local history but also for the world's cultural heritage. The GAP administration played down the issue noting that the city centre and hundreds of historic villas remain untouched: 'Turkey has so many [historic] resources that a single one cannot matter' when the cradle of civilization gives way to a new kind of civilization (GAP Administration quoted in Shoup, 2006).[18] An indignant editorial on the Birecik flooding in the *New York Times* was reprinted in Turkey and triggered a petition from Turkish archaeologists and architects. A stunning mosaic was salvaged after a $5 million donation from American billionaire David Packard (Shoup, 2006). It is not that the Turks have no sense of history. Turkey has sought to salvage the cultural richness in thousands of important archaeological sites in Anatolia threatened by dam construction. But 4–6,500 people in Belkis village and others in Sanliurfa, Gaziantep and Adiyaman provinces were not treated with equal care: they were displaced to make room for Birecik.

For the *Ilısu* hydropower project, the lower reaches of the coastal town of Hasankeyf (Hisn Kaifã), 36 km from Batman, 203 km east of Diyarbakir, will need to disappear to make the Turkish dream a reality. Eighty-one other heritage sites are similarly facing inundation, including several holy Muslim and Christian holy sites that are still in use today. Said to be a late Assyrian settlement dating back from the seventh century BC and a node of the Silk Road in the Middle Ages, Hasankeyf is known as the 'Efes (the Ephesus of the New Testament) of the East'.[19] It occupied a strategic position as a fortified castle, controlling the caravan route from Diyarbakir to Mosul in Iraq. But because the whole region is so rich in historic architecture (Diyarbakir, Mardin, Kıziltepe), Hasankeyf did not command much interest until a French historian published on it in the 1940s (Meinecke, 1996).

Hasankeyf has long been a neglected, crumbling open-air 'museum' with remnants of many civilisations. In 1969 a study of Hasankeyf was made and in 1978 Turkey's Culture Ministry pledged full archaeological protection to the town. In 1981 the site was listed among 22 declared first-class cultural heritage sites. The year before, however, in 1980, an international consortium had been commissioned to draw up a feasibility report for the Ilısu hydroelectricity project and in 1982 the Ilısu dam plan was ready, which included the submersion of Hasankeyf.

Naturally, Hasankeyf's countless caves were first to disappear under reservoir level. The biggest stone bridge of the Middle Ages built by the Seljuks and the tomb of Zeynel Bey will be next to go under (Sener, 2004). Other threatened heritages are the first minting factory, the medieval Koc and Sultan Süleyman mosques. In 1998 the Hydraulic State Works (DSI), which comes under the Ministry of Mining and Natural Resources, contracted archaeologists from TACDAM (Centre for Research and Assessment of Historic Environment) at Middle East Technology University, Ankara, to study the transferability of Hasankeyf's cultural heritage. According to Ronayne (2005), DSI cancelled its contract with TACDAM over 'corruption and incompetence'.

Almost US$1 million is now spent to restore the most attractive (seaside) part of it for tourism, and US$100 million will now be set aside for moving the most important cultural monuments.[20] But archaeologists point out that while Hasankeyf is in the spotlight, the dam will submerge 280 other historic places, including several holy Muslim and Christian holy sites that are still in use today. Only a few have been researched (Shoup, 2006).

Although the mayor of Hasankeyf moved into a limestone cave in protest against their inundation, the cave dwellers of Zagora had already been resettled in the 1970s (Outshoorn, 2006), but the present-day citizens of Hasankeyf town showed themselves unwilling to move. The BBC noted that 'many of the Kurds say that Hasankeyf is their last stand, the last remnant of what is left of any Kurdish identity and dignity'.[21] Journalists collected dramatic quotes such as 'My family has been living here for 450 years . . . they want to extinguish the culture of a thousand years for the sake of one burning light bulb' (in Shoup, 2006). Balfour Beatty director Sloane, however, noted that Hasankeyf was abandoned after the First World War and only reoccupied in the 1960s (quoted in Shoup, 2006).

International Protest

An ongoing campaign against large infrastructural projects had become successful in the 1990s. Local protest against dams like Arun in Nepal and Narmada (Bidaseca, 2004) was amplified to a global audience by an international NGO lobby, making large donors increasingly uneasy about funding. In fact, when a Swiss consortium won the Ilısu contract in 1996, it not only found the Berne Declaration (*Erklärung von Bern*) breathing down its neck, but a well-orchestrated protest on the part of a European NGO coalition.

The Bundesrat, to which the Swiss central bank USB is accountable, justified its export risk guarantee go-ahead for 470 million Swiss francs with a view to new Swiss jobs (1,200 full-time man-years) (Bosshard, 1999), Turkish development, and Turkish promises to look into expected negative side effects including forced resettlements, conflict over water rights with the downstream riparians, threatened cultural heritage and malaria vectors associated with stagnant water in a storage lake. The Swiss government in 1998 attached to its export credit (also covering a project in Ankara) the condition that an independent monitoring mechanism would be established.

Casting the GAP flooding and resettlement as a human rights violation struck a chord in Europe, leading to parliamentary questions in Germany and Switzerland. Nevertheless, by 1999 the anti-Turkish dam campaign so far had not achieved the hoped-for resonance. Birecik had acquired international export credit without much trouble, and it looked like Ilısu would get the same easy ride. The British Department of Trade and Industry (DTI) was 'minded' to issue a £200 million export credit to the project leader, Turkey's State Hydraulic

Works department (DSI) in 1999. Bemusingly, DTI's Export Credit Guarantee Department (ECGD), which governs export credits, was ready to defend the project as a fine example of its ethical policy, claiming it would contribute to Middle East peace (*Guardian*, 1 March 1999). But the agency had failed to confer with the Foreign and Commonwealth Office (FCO) about the diplomatic consequences of such a decision.

However, British water companies were especially vulnerable to negative publicity, Biwater having been embroiled in scandal over the Pergau Dam in Malaysia, and Balfour Beatty in the Lesotho Highlands Project, both over corruption (1998). Thames Water's BOT contract for Izmit had raised questions and watchdog organisations, such as PSIRU at Greenwich University in London, duly noted that the Export Credit Guarantee Department still had no ethical or environmental code governing those guarantees (it developed Business Principles in 2000).[22]

In Britain the Ilısu Dam Campaign was spearheaded by Friends of the Earth, for whom the project looked a choice opportunity to mobilise its political clout. Opposing the Ilısu dam as a symbol of unethical British investment, Friends of the Earth and the Kurdish Human Rights Project (KHRP) may have judged the general public to be increasingly blasé over issues of *environmental* quality[23] and *cultural* heritage, which had not grabbed many headlines of late. Likewise, NGOs are unlikely ever to be able to win the day claiming the dams are not *economic*. By recasting the issue as a *human rights* issue, they could play at a concern which to many people is an absolute, existential value at the individual and group level. The repression of Kurdish identity as a way of extending Turkish control was played by the coalition against the Ilısu dam on a *human* as well as *cultural* rights platform. This proved instrumental in strengthening the international anti-GAP coalition on a platform that also drew on environmental issues.

The opponents' discourse was at times heavy-handed. Activist archaeologist Maggie Ronayne of Trinity College in Galway, Ireland, called the project a weapon of 'mass cultural destruction' while George Monbiot, environmental journalist with the British *Guardian* newspaper and Visiting Professor at Bristol University, talked of 'ethnic cleansing' (Monbiot, 1999) echoed by Turkish human rights organisation Göc-Der: 'If you cut down a tree or kill a culture, that's war' (quoted in Shoup, 2006: 250).

The left-leaning British media proved very willing to lend their front pages to a more emotive frame. While Turkey and the UK foreign office advanced the project as promoting regional peace, NGO and sympathetic environmental writers like Fred Pearce and George Monbiot made it sound plausible that the project in fact would spark a 'water war' between the basin (see also KHRP, 2005). A water war proved a much more effective discursive 'spin' than cultural, ecological or economic arguments. When the flak became too vehement, the Trade and Industry minister, Brian Wilson, sought to reassure worried Liberal

Democrats in the House of Commons that no final decision had been taken. The affair was painful to the Labour government which sought to set itself apart from its Conservative predecessor, which some four years before was embarrassed by a big dam project in Malaysia.[24]

When questions were raised in the House of Commons, claiming the Ilısu's 'security implications' could extend far beyond Turkey's borders, and could affect British security interests as a member of NATO and Turkey's future in the EU,[25] the Blair government decided to wash its hands off the project. Hamilton (2003) argues that the desire not to upset regional power balances may well have incited British withdrawal from Ilısu.

Project Shelved?

Activists no doubt hoped that stricter conditions from project backers would mean the end of the project. Turkey however went along with opening up the project to international and local scrutiny and environmental accountability. This promoted an already ongoing project redefinition process. While GAP started in the late 1970 with the intention of reforming the socio-economic situation in the most underdeveloped Turkish region, the project's objectives have broadened quite a lot in response to recurring criticism. In 1989, the Turkish government commissioned a Turkish-Japanese consortium to draw up a GAP Master Plan and established the Southeastern Anatolia Project Regional Development Administration (GAP-RDA). Headed by the eloquent American-trained engineer Olcay Ünver, many 'enlightened' modifications were made, including socio-economic, environmental, educational and participatory facilities. Representative reforms included the establishment of Water Users Associations with farmer representation and decentralisation of decision-making to mayoral level. GAP administration prides itself on having turned around from a 'hydraulic mission-age' blueprint to a leading example of participatory integrated water resource management, what it calls a 'human centred development project'. GAP as a socially responsible, integrated water management project (Kibaroğlu, 2002) evidenced another 'passive revolution'[26] in response to prevailing donor demands at the global level, echoing emerging norms of 'good governance'. In spring 2000 GAP, in response to many criticisms, was reviewed again (GAP-RDA, 2001). The GAP Master Plan was the outcome of a 'participatory planning process', involving groups in such specific fields as rural development plans, social planning, economic planning, environment and infrastructure (GAP-RDA, 2001: 22). Consequently, the project won a Millennium Award from the International Water Research Association.

In this light, donor conditions such as a new Resettlement Action Plan (RAP) and an Environmental Impact Assessment (EIA) by Environmental Resources

Management (ERM) as part of the Project Implementation Plan must have seemed minor irritants. In Turkey, an EIA is only mandatory for plans drawn up after 1993, Ilısu escaped this obligation. But after the protests, an EIA got to be drafted in 2001 (Ilısu Engineering Group, 2001). The RAP was drawn up by Turkish consultants SEMOL following World Bank guidelines (Morvaridi, 1999). However, project and resettlement information is not made available in Kurdish, and communication relied on word-of-mouth.

In July 2001, the UK Government Export Credit Guarantee Department made the decision whether to provide £160 million backing for the project contingent on 'public comment' on the Environmental Impact Assessment report. The EIA procedure did not help to secure access to credit guarantees for Ilısu, as one foreign partner after the other backed out. Skanska had already withdrawn in 2000, while ABB – which was leaving the hydroelectricity sector anyway – had ceded its involvement to French company Alstom. Together with Balfour Beatty, Impreglio withdrew in 2001 after their export credit backers backed out. In 2002, the main financial partner, Swiss UBS, decided to pull out too, after which funding for the project was as good as dead.[27]

The strong international response to the 'water war' argument is surprising as 2001/2002 was a period of thawing Turkey's relations with both the Kurds and downstream neighbours. After 1998, the mood among the basin riparians had changed perceptibly towards conciliation or peaceful coexistence. Relations between Syria and Turkey improved dramatically after the extradition of PKK leader Öcalan. This heralded what seems to be a more constructive era in which military and economic agreements were initiated between Turkey and Syria (MacQuarrie, 2004). In 2001, the GAP and the Syrian development project, GOLD, signed a GAP-GOLD agreement (Kibaroğlu, 2002). In 2002 the two countries shared a Training and Expertise exercise (Protocol of 2002) and embarked on 'Track-Two' water cooperation initiatives initiated by former GAP boss Olcay Ünver, which seems to evidence that Turkey is willing to consult with its downstream neighbours. Also the PKK scaled down violent hostilities (until 2003), which raised hopes of lifting the state of emergency in the region.

The international backers pulling out only compounded Turkish financial worries, as the country faced another budget crisis in 2001, which made it difficult to go ahead with the envisaged expansion of the GAP programme. Still, the Turkish government was not letting go of its dam like that, and found new European partners who also could not turn such a large, attractive construction project down. After several years of standstill and studies for improvement, the Ilısu Dam project was quietly resurrected in 2005, when a new 14-member consortium including German, Swiss and Austrian companies formed. Alstom (formerly part of ABB) again became involved, while Cengiz, Celikler and Lider Nurol are Turkish partners.

Continued Protest

So far, reforms have failed to win friends downstream. The restart on the Tigris seems to have contributed to a recent rapprochement between Syria and Iraq on the Euphrates:

> In 2005 Iraqis and Syrians agreed to exert joint efforts to make Turkey fulfil [sic] earlier obligations regarding water allocation on the Euphrates, exchange information on hydrology and climatic changes. Syria consented to release more water for additional electricity production in Iraq. (Mirkasymov, 2006)

The World Bank proved a perhaps unexpected ally for the anti-GAP coalition in lifting the resettlement issue on the international agenda. The alliance scored two important victories by enlisting World Bank experts to write critical reports of the resettlement plan. In 2000, Ayşe Kudat, a Turkish sociologist who had worked for the Bank, had written a critical report on resettlement (Kudat, 2000). In July 2006, just before the restart of construction works, the Swiss NGO, Berne Declaration, scored another coup when they got the famous World Bank sociologist, Michael Cernea, to write a critical assessment of the new Resettlement Action Plan for Ilısu as updated by State Hydraulic Works (DSÍ) and the worrying record of earlier GAP resettlement (Cernea, 2006). That same month, at a low point in European–Turkish access negotiations, the European Court of Human Rights agreed in July 2006 to hear an application against the dam lodged by archaeologists, journalists and lawyers united in the Hasankeyf Volunteers Association, who say Hasankeyf must be preserved in its natural state.[28]

Turkish professionals also voiced criticism.[29] Local and international NGOs are keeping a close watch on proceedings, notably the Kurdish Human Rights Association, Friends of the Earth and German NGO WEED, which produces a critical weekly Ilısu update (www.Ilısu.org.uk). The international campaign against Ilısu has been revived, again concentrating on the flooding of Hasankeyf.

Two weeks before Turkish and Syrian academics presented the non-governmental 'Track-Two' initiative for closer cooperation at the Stockholm Water Week, construction began in August 2006 on Ilısu, if protested by 8,000 people including leaders of two political parties. Muharrem Dogan of The Motherland Party (ANAVATAN) proposed to lower the height of the dam to save part of the flooded area (470 instead of 510 m). However, the Minister for what is now the merged department of Culture and Tourism, Atilla Koc, made it clear that Hasankeyf would not be saved: 'Hasankeyf is already gone, it's been erased from history', while DSI General Director Eroğlu opined: 'this dam should have been built 30 years ago' (quoted by Shoup, 2006: 245). The Turkish government has taken out a US$1.2 billion loan for the dam.[30]

That same month, a Swiss delegation visited the site to verify Turkey was complying with international standards before it would guarantee the US$250 million loan. In February 2007, Turkey apparently issued a warning that all contracts would be called off if Germany, Switzerland and Austria refused to issue export guarantees. This is considerable money: the consortium leader, Andritz, for instance would take EUR 230 million. But the European backers stuck to their guns: despite Turkish leaders seeking to persuade German Chancellor Merkel, the three countries gave Turkey a 90-day deadline for meeting standards in December 2008.[31] The guarantors ultimately pulled out in 2009. The completion of the dam, slated to come on stream in 2014, is therefore far from certain but still, not all is lost; two Turkish banks have recently stepped in.

It is notable that the 'water war' argument has fallen out of fashion, though even in 1999 the claim was, to say the least, dubious. The mood between the riparians became more conciliatory after the clash of 1998. After the US President started Syria, the Turkish and Syrian leaders started paying mutual visits in 2004, during which President Bashir Assad was assured that Syria could make further use of the Tigris. A free-trade agreement between the two countries was signed and the year 2005 saw the establishment of the Euphrates-Tigris Initiative for Cooperation (ETIC). The initiative aimed to promote cooperation for technical, social and economic development within the river system (Dinar, 2009) and included a group of scholars and professionals from Turkey, Syria and Iraq. Turkey started meeting to discuss an increased Syrian share in Euphrates water, while a remarkable Iraqi volte-face on Ilısu on the Tigris in 2008 saw all three countries indicating much greater willingness to cooperate. Iraq's Water Minister, Rasheed, reportedly told Turkey's Environment and Forestry Minister Veysel Eroğlu, former DSI chief, that he wants the dam to be built as fast as possible (Yavuz, 2008).

The Turkish government's outlook on the project and its role in Turkey's security position appears to be changing, as part of an overall shift from 'hard' to 'soft' power in its foreign policy (Oğuzlu 2007). Its leader, Tayyip Erdoğan, misses no opportunity to court Kurdish voters, align with regional Muslim solidarities and annoy Israel. Israel, it was claimed during the Fifth World Water Forum session in Istanbul in March 2009, has put pressure on Turkey to give more water to Syria, to ease the pressure on itself in its own water negotiations with Syria on the river Jordan.

It has been widely rumoured that Turkey will now try to complete the dam with Chinese support. But the government appears to contemplate diversifying its options outside hydropower, too. The ruling AKP party has become deeply interested in nuclear power as an alternative to hydropower, and went ahead with a tender for a nuclear plant at Akkuyu in late 2008, despite only one bidder actually stepping forward.[32] This puts the government's commitment to the continuation of the final leg of GAP in fresh perspective. The hydropolitical sands appear to be shifting.

3.5 Discussion

3.5.1 Basin Regime: Nothing Ever Changes?

While I have argued that Turkey's water strategy is bound up with its political strategy, the word 'strategy' itself may be reading too much into a chain of events. Despite the war moves, the Euphrates tussle has often essentially proved to be political manoeuvring. In this sense, in spite of the apparent anarchy, a kind of regime, in the sense of patterned, predictable state behaviour (Puchala and Hopkins, 1987) can be said to be in place. The public posturing and linkage politics around GAP displays a strongly ritualistic pattern of near-wars followed by near- or placeholder agreements. For this, Turkey has basically kept pursuing the same multi-chessboard strategy at home and in the world, unperturbed by the changed dynamics around the 'balance-of-weakness' in the region.

The Turks are investing great effort into trying to convince others that this state of affairs is just, legitimate, even that their actions were clearly in the interests of the downstream actors as well. The Tigris is more flood-prone than the Euphrates – snowmelt in March can cause torrential flooding in April, the harvest month, which necessitated early diking, canalisation and diversion works in Iraq.[33] The Turkish dams regulate the hydrological regime so that they not only cushion the impact of floods but also improve the timing of the river regime to coincide with downstream agricultural needs. Dams will provide a cushion against droughts and premature flooding. Several dams are 'post-bay' dams to even out fluctuations upstream. Better timing would lead to more productive *downstream* farming as well. As Bilen (1997) notes, massive hydropower, while in itself not a consumptive use of water, limits irrigation and guarantees a downstream flow. This state of affairs creates a stability of expectations which can be seen as an *international public good* – though downstream neighbours do not usually like to see it this way. Indeed, as Kibaroğlu shows, throughout the GAP the states have worked together rather more than NGO material would lead us to believe. Technical teams on the Euphrates-Tigris have met on and off, despite recurring political threats of military action, a pragmatic acceptance of the *faits accomplis* on the part of the downstream neighbours.

The snag is, of course, that until recently Turkey has frequently denied its neighbours any real say in the regulatory decisions. In that sense, Turkey is exercising *de facto* dominance in a context of de jure equality. As a result, Turkish regulatory decisions, such as the occasional arrest of the flow to impound reservoirs, have been perceived as unilateral and self-serving. Given the stability of expectations Turkey's primacy procures for the basin, Turkish hegemony may not be all bad for Syria, but the Syrians object to Turkey setting the terms. Even as coriparian relations thawed, Iraq and, especially, Syria have made repeated, almost ritual threats (invariably answered by equally virulent language from Turkey) and used downstream strategies to counter Turkey's actions.

Overall, the recent initiatives seem to demonstrate a move towards a 'positive-sum' rather than distributive (zero-sum) power play. In this respect I agree to a degree with Ayşegül Kibaroğlu (1996, 2002) who, if based on slightly different reasoning, has argued there are unmistakable signs of *regime formation* in the Euphrates-Tigris. However, while there seems to be a movement from Realist going-it-alone to forms of cooperation, this new stable equilibrium remains within the context of hegemonic power relations. The Syrian government, having exhausted the leverage the Kurdish card procured them, has had to resign to Turkish primacy – since there is hardly a question of equal power relations between the partners. If cooperation becomes more structural, as seems to be the case, Syria and Iraq lose their leeway for making strong stances.

As Daoudy (2005) notes, the new internationally hegemonic discourse is all about benefit sharing. This would presume the exercise of collective power ('positive-sum') instead of distributive (and divisive) power, a radical change of scene. Now that cooperation is on the agenda, Syria finds itself in a dilemma. Both Turkey and Syria benefit from a stability of expectations but if cooperation becomes more structural, as seems to be the case, Syria loses its leeway for making strong stances. While there seems to be a movement from the realist going-it-alone to forms of cooperation, this new stable equilibrium remains within a context of hegemonic power relations at the global level. The fact that the Fifth Water Forum (as well as many other international conferences) was held in Istanbul in 2009 appears to bear testimony that the international community is accepting Turkey's position as a 'Middle Power'.

Securitisation and the State of Exceptionalism?

Turkey has sought to enhance its national security since the 1920s by laying great stress on *cultural* identity and integrity (the unitary state) as well as economic development (self-actualisation and opportunity-seeking), which, in turn, provides the government with greater legitimacy (*political* security). In crucial decisions, however, the government takes a backseat to the army, which sees itself as a guarantor of the Turkish national interest as a secular, modern state. After the 1960 coup d'état, the National Security Council (*Milli Güvenlik Kurulu*, MGK) was established in 1961, which consists of the President, the Prime Minister, the head of intelligence, the army Chief of Staffs and commanders of the military branches (Jongerden, 1994) and can overrule the government in issues of National Security. Until 2001, the Constitution required civilian authorities to prioritise its recommendations (Drorian, 2005: 264).

Turkey has NATO's second largest army, which sees as its role to safeguard both external and internal security (Drorian, 2005: 262). Atatürk saw the army as the guardian of the ideals of the Turkish nation (ibid. 263).

Type	Military	Socio-Cultural	Environmental
Turkey's move	GAP is a peace project	Humanitarian project; Turkish integration	Project enhances environment in barren regions
Opposition countermove	Project precipitates war	Human rights offence; project is part of Kurdish suppression	Project destroys environment; brings health hazards

Table 3.2: ***Discursive framing moves and countermoves in different security domains***

At home, Turkey has pursued a mix of coercive and consent-oriented *control* moves – carrots and sticks. The hydraulic developmental strategy however has not been successful in co-opting the Kurdish Southeast, and the GAP has become associated with domestic war. The violent clashes with the PKK put Southeast Anatolia under a regime of exceptionalism (the state of emergency). Dams have thus been planned and built in this securitised context, and therefore moved the decision-making process out of political debate. This elevated the Greater Anatolia Project beyond the realm of debate and backed it up with exceptional action – in Buzan et al.'s (1998) terms, the project became 'securitised'.

After Öcalan's extradition in 1998, relations with the Kurds seemed to herald a 'desecuritised' era in the basin (Table 3.1). Radical reforms of the GAP project suggest a shift away from the 'hydraulic mission', making the project more palatable to funders. But when Kurdish incursions restarted in 2003, military response continued. The Turkish stance on the Kurds therefore remains two-pronged.

While securitisation excludes all alternatives, politicisation opens up the closure. An alliance of convenience saw its chance when Turkey's pressing funding problem was partly 'solved' by liberalising the water sector. Turkey's military must have dreaded ceding a degree of (temporary) loss of state autonomy over water resources to international companies (political insecurity). In the Ilısu controversy each actor group mounted different types of security strategies at different levels. An astute international campaign sought to get international backers to pull out of the Ilısu dam. For this they used heavy verbal artillery: to them, the dam constituted a human rights violation and environmental and cultural disaster.

The Ilısu case is an interesting example of active domain linkage. Having generated little resonance with economic or environmental arguments, the opposition to GAP made more successful discursive moves into the cultural and military domains. In each of these domains, moves and countermoves were made looking to dominate it (Table 3.1). Sensing the change in international mood, the Turkish initiators pictured the project as essentially *humanitarian* and ecologically sound, that is, it sought to defeat the opposition in the same security domain. Likewise, while Turkish and British governments portrayed Ilısu as a project promoting peace, protesters presented the doom scenario of 'water wars'. It should be noted that in 2001, the water war argument on the Euphrates-Tigris had surprising *international* resonance, despite the dramatically improved relations between Turkey and Syria and little evidence of worsening Turkish relations with Iraq. This shifted the debate in Europe into a different, military league, away from Turkish-initiated 'peace discourse' of stability and shared benefits. Whatever the rationale, the move was relatively successful: the backers pulled out under pressure of a threat to their reputation.

Thus, security speech acts on all sides can be said to have played an important role in the ritual dances around dams. Successfully countering security with other absolutes, each camp could overrule the other's claim to monopoly on exceptionalism. So, in order to improve the political strategy, it seems the different domains have indeed been linked or relinked to domains where a more successful outcome was anticipated.

3.5.2 Multi-Level Games and Frames

Turkey continues to pursue its water objectives at a considerable price. Internationally, the controversy over the GAP has proved bad international public relations (reputation), not improving its chances of EU membership, and landed Turkey on the brink of war with Syria on several occasions. Also, the project has deprived Turkey of international funding; burdening a stressed economy with spiralling project costs. Political actors in all basin states operate within the limits of the possible in the power-political arena, and that power horizon still favours Turkish leadership. Turkey's international acts seem to be aimed at maintaining its role of a regional superpower, straddling Europe, the Middle East and Turkic Central Asia, for which it competes with Iran, Russia and, more recently, China. Rather than using an aggressive expansion strategy, Turkey bides its time and seeks to extend its spheres of influence (realpolitik), in the strong belief that this will benefit all concerned – benefiting the public good. Alliances with Israel and the USA underpin its regional power position.

Playing simultaneous games on multiple chessboards is a slow process with many repeated offensive and defensive (often merely symbolic) moves. While basin relations are now quiet under the American aegis, the last lap of GAP is still not safe from NGO attack, now under the umbrella of Save Hasankeyf. Turkish gains in co-opting Syria and regime change in Iraq have made international

NGO opposition to Ilısu in 2006 less likely to succeed than in 1999–2001, and the 'water war' discourse groundless.

It is unclear what Iraqis will do in the current anarchic situation, but we can expect Iraq will be too self-absorbed to grumble very much over dams in the coming years. American dominance in the Middle East is expressed in extensive economic and military aid to Israel, Turkey and Egypt. The USA enlisting Syria and Turkey in the first war on Iraq quashed any hopes of a cooperative basin regime, and established a *de facto* protectorate over Iraq. The Americans could thus operate in the region as a patron and/or policeman, but cannot without qualification be credited with regime promotion (Coskun, 2005).[34]

While Zawahri (2008) has good reason to doubt whether you can speak of 'cooperation' when no actor adjusts their behaviour for mutual benefit, the three countries have maintained an enduring minimal regime at basin scale, in the sense of stable expectations with primacy on the part of Turkey. Turkey's 'peace abroad' has been what Wolf (1998) has called 'unstable peace' built on a degree of brinksmanship, but things get solved by high-level negotiation rather than violence. Since 1998 there has been a move towards more basin cooperation.

Despite the water-based regional development strategy and repression of Kurdish insurgency, 'peace at home' has not quite arrived in the southeast; while the PKK continues its campaigns, the GAP can be expected to continue to be realised within a securitised context.

This chapter has pictured the power play over the management of the Euphrates-Tigris constellation as a layer cake of struggles at different levels (over global, regional, river basin and state rule) which impinge on each other. The implication of such an analysis would be that while hydraulic conflicts notably play out at the domestic and basin levels, they are also subject to the dynamics of global political economy and geopolitics. The layers in the cake are permeable, they interact with each other. As illustrated by the Ilısu case, this interplay offered a niche in a securitised environment to politicise an issue.

4

DEATH OF THE MEGA-PROJECTS? THE CONTROVERSY OVER FLOOD ACTION PLAN 20, BANGLADESH

Operation successful, the patient died. (Bangladeshi consultant on FAP-20)

4.1 Introduction

In the age-old South Asian cosmology, the river feeds, the river destroys in an endless cycle of death and regeneration. Whoever wants to control the river, attempts to control the Mother Goddess and play God over life and death. Nevertheless, this is what the initiators of the Flood Action Plan sought to do in Bangladesh after the floods of 1987 and 1988: to prevent flood destruction for good.

Flood Action Plan 20 (FAP-20), also known as the Compartmentalisation Pilot Project[1] was the Plan's flagship project, a Dutch-initiated experiment in participatory flood management in North-Central Bangladesh. The compartmentalisation of polders, enabling the controlled drainage of monsoon water, was conceived as an innovative and participatory compromise between 'wet' and 'dry' flood management (ISPAN, 1992; Faaland et al., 1995; Final CPP final report, 2000). The drainage between compartments was to be managed by user committees.

According to its eventual Technical Assistance Project Proform (TAPP) laid down in 1993, FAP-20 was intended to establish feasible, achievable and sustainable water management systems. While straightforward in engineering terms (Shamunnay, 1996), its operation brought with it a host of socio-economic, environmental and institutional issues which unexpectedly politicised the project.

As Geof Wood (1997) notes, 'with a centrally important natural resource determining so many other features of life [. . .] it would be surprising if there was no controversy'. The surprising thing about the conflict over FAP-20, however, is that a local movement against a fairly small project managed to create a global stir. The coordinating World Bank faced busloads of angry women in Dhaka shouting 'Break the dams!' and 'Stop FAP! Grow forests!'[2] The protesters were decrying the project's negative impact on the landless and fisherfolk in the project area and dwellers of the adjoining areas, which led to occasional violence. The European Greens organised a protest conference against FAP as a whole, in so doing mobilising international opinion against the scheme. Donors started to pull out in 1994, which almost led to the project's discontinuation after 1995. Disagreement over both the technical (compartmentalisation) and institutional (participation) element of FAP-20 led to several reformulations of the programme.

The case study seeks to understand why and how this happened by analysing hegemonic problem frames and counter-frames, securitising moves and countermoves to change the 'flood frames' of risk and responsibility. It zooms in on the 'felicity' of security frames and counter-frames shaping controversies on flood management with their intended audience. Because of the strong overlay of international development aid on the domestic scene (Section 4.2), the conflict over FAP-20 was played out as much at the international as the national level. After sketching the tense Bangladeshi political context in Section 4.3 and the project selection process in Section 4.4, Section 4.5 explains the intended participatory structure and experience with participation in FAP, after which the focus turns to unintended 'participation': the strategy of resistance and politicisation alternatives which, I will argue, had striking 'dramaturgic' content. In 1995, the project was at a crossroads. Section 4.6 describes the events and changes introduced in the second phase of FAP, and how the project fared in the flood of 1998. In closing, Section 4.7 contrasts the image of FAP as a mega-project to stop floods 'forever' with FAP as a programme of studies, as it is now sometimes represented.

4.2 FAP: 'Birth of a Mega-Project?'

4.2.1 Physical Context

Bangladesh is situated in the most active river delta in the world and has the highest density of rivers per capita. The country is the gift of the three main rivers: Brahmaputra-Jamuna, the largest river in the Himalayan system (extending into Tibet and Nepal), the Ganges and the Padma or Padda. The three combine before draining into the Bay of Bengal. In 1987 and 1988, Bangladesh experienced two truly devastating floods, the latter hitting the country especially hard as the peaks of the three major rivers synchronised within a two-week

Date	Event	
Autumn 1987, 1988	Major flood events in Bangladesh	4.2
1989	London donor conference; selection of FAP-20; presidential approval *BARC report against Green Revolution technologies*	4.2
1990, Oct	Final draft of project proposal FAP-20 (original TAPP July 1990)	
1991	FAP-20 inception report	
1992	Euroconsult contracted; public consultation	4.4.3
1993	FPCO's Guidelines for People's Participation	
1993	*FAP protests in Tangail and Dhaka* leading to - Dutch IOV inspection team reports - Dutch/German donor review mission advises to shore up FAP 20-Sirajganj - FAP TAPP being recast (June 1993)	4.5
1994	*BELA lawsuit against FAP-20* Donors starting to reconsider	4.5.4, 4, 7
1995, May	- Dutch mid-term evaluation team recommends continuation with different consultants - UNDP (Faaland) report 'Flood and Water Management: Towards a public debate'	4.6.3
1995, Oct	- CPP (FAP-20) Reformulation Mission Report - Change of main consultant	
1996	German ODA Minister visits, shores up funding in March, requests Inception report for 2nd phase	4.6.3
1997	Dutch ODA Minister visits	4.6.3
1998	Century flood hits Bangladesh (see 5.7.4). Absence of famine	4.6.4
2000	End of project; Final report released – but not the underlying studies	4.6.4

Table 4.1: ***FAP Project history and rationale. (Countermoves are italicised)***

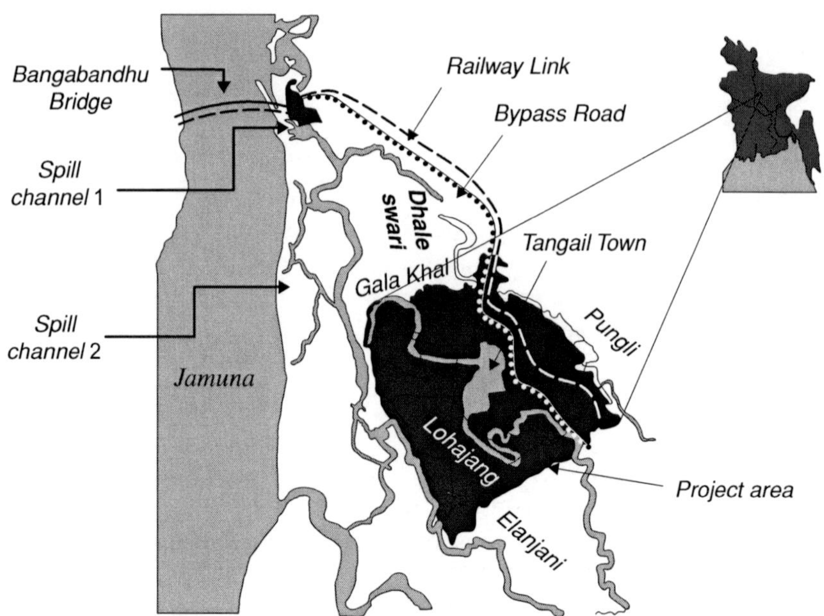

Figure 4.1: **Location of Tangail and Dhaleswari closure**

period. The discharge of the Brahmaputra-Jamuna, on average 19,000 m^3/s, approached 100,000 m^3/s in 1987/88 – compare this to the 12,600 m^3/s River Rhine peak as it reached the Netherlands in early 1995! The 1988 flood, a one-in-a-hundred-year event, put 60 per cent of the country under water for two weeks, damaging 7.2 million homes, affecting 45 million people and causing '2300 immediate deaths' (Wood, 1999).

Bangladesh has a very low gradient. Over 90 per cent is alluvial lowland (Raqub Ahmed in Gain 1998). The North Central Area, where Tangail and the capital Dhaka are located, is very flat, between 18 and 4 m above sea level (except the Madhupur Tract). Thus, as soon as the flood stage is reached, enormous tracts of land are flooded. This brings irrigation and sediment, but also erodes alluvial soils. Riverbank dwellers are plagued by riverbank erosion, especially in the monsoon (wet) season, which runs from June until October, accounting for 90 per cent of inflow. The soft soils are highly unsuitable for building structures, which makes 'the cost of building groins [*sic*] and revetments [. . .] very high' (Khalequzzaman, 1994).

An example is the Jamuna Right Bank Embankment (RBE), an extensive levee built in 1960 to stabilise the river Jamuna, whose width averages 10 km. The embankment broke in 1987–88. Sudden bank erosion, worsened by human-induced erosion to enlarge living space, displaces huge numbers of residents to *char land* (unstable islands), *khas* (state-owned) land and to the cities, notably Dhaka, intensifying urbanisation.

Geologically, the Tangail area, along the Jamuna, has been formed by faulting and tilting. Floods also carved out the landscape: the Brahmaputra-Jamuna, for example, has shifted westward by 100 km in the past 200 years and can cut a 30–50 m deep channel in one flood event. Morphological processes can give rise to opening and closing of tributaries, such as a shift of the Jamuna into the Dhaleswari offtake. Other offtakes are silted up such that upstream discharge is almost zero. This dynamic of opening and closing channels proved a vital factor for the survival of FAP-20 in 1995, as will be explained later on. The FAP-20 area is bounded by the Dhaleswari and Elanjani rivers in the west, Pungli in the east and Louhajang and Gala *khal* (channel) in the north; the south boundary is an existing road between Silimpur and Karatia. Climate is dominated by monsoon winds: a cold and dry Northeast monsoon rains from November to February, while a Southwest monsoon (June to October) brings heavy rainfall. While pre-monsoon rains fall in March, April and May, flooding in the Jamuna and its tributaries results from a long monsoon rainfall season and snowmelt from the Himalayas. More important at times is the local rainfall in the Dhaleswari and Old Brahmaputra, both meandering smaller rivers that rapidly run drier in the winter season as rainfall tapers off. Backgrounded by the problems posed by the flood (*kharif*) season, in which *aman* rice is produced, is the *post-monsoon* season, when all local rivers are just drains fed by excess irrigation water and groundwater – no new water comes in to replenish the flow. Especially the end of the dry (*rabi*) season, April–May, brings problematic droughts every three to four years (CPP Interim Report 1995, Annex 6). According to Boyce (1990), too little water is a greater threat for the area's 250,000 people (living in 202 villages) than too much.

The growth in agricultural production in this area has come from irrigated (groundwater-fed) winter crops rather than from monsoon crops fed by surface water. In light of these extremes, farmers tend to try and diversify their plots between different land elevations to avoid losing harvests to peak flooding or droughts (van Koppen, 1998).

Amid the many mishaps striking Bangladesh and other developing countries every year, the reason why this particular hazard reached the top of the international agenda seems fortuitous. According to Chowdhury (1992), what spurred the Bangladeshi president, General Ershad, to initiate a flood protection scheme for Dhaka and project order was the fact that the 1988 flood, unusually, affected the well-to-do in the capital, Dhaka: the American Embassy, the model towns and army cantonment as well as his own home. Mme Danielle Mitterrand, the then French president's wife and well known for her interest in social causes, happened to visit Dhaka and Tangail with an international media entourage, and, shocked at the damage, raised the issue with her husband, who in turn was eager to raise France's profile in the world as a benefactor (Boyce, 1990).

No.	Name of FAP Project	Funding Agencies	(Committed $ mn)	(Spent Approx. March 1996)
1	Brahmaputra Right Embankment Strengthening	IDA	3.36	3.36
2	Northwest Regional Study	UK, Japan	4.60	4.60
3	North Central Regional Study	EU, France	3.56	3.56
3.1	Jamalpur Priority Project	EU, France	2.85	2.85
4	South West Area Water Resources and Management Study	ADB, UNDP	3.83	3.83
5	South East Regional Study	DA, UNDP	2.20	2.20
6	North East Regional Study	Canada	14.60	11.99
7	Cyclone Protection Project	EU, IDA	1.00	1.00
8A	Greater Dhaka Protection Project	Japan	3.00	3.00
8B	Dhaka Integrated Flood Protection Project	ADB	0.57	0.57
9A	Secondary Towns Integrated Flood Protection Project	ADB	0.55	0.55
9B	Meghna River Bank Protection Short Term Study	IDA	1.15	1.15
10	Flood Forecasting and Warning Project	UNDP, Japan	5.70	3.50
11	Disaster Preparedness Programme	UNDP	1.10	1.10

Table 4.2: ***Flood Action Plan Subprojects***

No.	Name of FAP Project	Funding Agencies	(Committed $ mn)	(Spent Approx. March 1996)
12	FCD/I Agriculture Study	UK, Japan	1.60	1.60
13	Operation and Maintenance Study (Phase-I)	UK, Japan	0.60	0.60
14	Flood Response Study	USA	0.92	0.92
15	Land Acquisition and Resettlement Study	Sweden	0.40	0.40
16	Environmental Study	USA	4.04	4.00
17	Fisheries Study and Pilot Project (Phase-I)	UK	3.40	3.40
18	Topographic Mapping	Finland, France, Switzerland, Germany	6.71	6.50
19	Geographic Information System	USA	4.36	4.35
20	Compartmentalisation Pilot Project	Netherlands, Germany	17.09	11.84
21/22	Bank Protection, River Training and AFPM Pilot Project	Germany, France	40.00	19.41
23	Flood Proofing Pilot Project	USA	0.30	0.30
24	River Survey Programme	EU	14.70	10.90
25	Flood Modelling and Management Project	Denmark, France, Netherlands, UK	4.39	4.39
26	Institutional Development Programme	UNDP, France	3.60	3.40

Table 4.2 ***(continued)***

Mitterrand promoted the idea of putting an end to floods in Bangladesh – *for good* – at the G7 conference in Paris in July 1989. The G7 duly paved the way for the Flood Action Plan and endorsed the World Bank/GoB Flood Action programme, presented in December 1989 during a specially convened donor conference in London, where donors conducted a 'bidding war' (interview, Dutch consultant) between themselves. The political will to fund flood protection schemes triggered no less than eight flood studies, which will be discussed in the next section. The resulting package of 26 projects was tabled in London. While the World Bank did not fund any of the ensuing flood studies, it volunteered to coordinate between the donor efforts. Other donors were the Asian Development Bank, UNDP, the USA, European Union, the UK, Germany, France, Netherlands, Sweden, Finland, Canada, Switzerland, Denmark and Japan – 15 in all. Norway decided not to support the FAP but funded a very critical study on FAP by the radical, Sussex-trained Bangladeshi activist-sociologist, Shapan Adnan (Adnan, 1991, 1992; Hanchett, 1997).

The Dutch government accepted responsibility for three projects: FAP-20, FAP-5b (the Meghna Estuary Study) and FAP-25 (the Flood Monitoring and Management Project) – the latter co-supported by Denmark, France and the UK. According to Dutch interviewees, enthusiasm in The Hague was not great; it was the Dutch Embassy in Dhaka that persuaded a reluctant Dutch government to take up FAP-20 as a way to demonstrate Dutch prowess in water and people management. The Dutch must have been relieved that the Germans (KfW) showed a keen interest to participate in FAP-20. Their original agreement to work on a 50–50 basis later became 2-to-1: Germany shouldered EUR 20 million and the Dutch EUR 10 million, while the Bangladeshi counterpart contribution amounted to EUR 2.8 million (Kreditanstalt für Wiederaufbau, 2004). This brought in German Lahmeyer as a consultant next to Euroconsult, the main contractor for the Netherlands. Lahmeyer also provided the (Dutch) team leader, Armand Evers, as from 1994.

The next sections sketch how tremendous international overlay impinged on the framing of the floods in terms of cause and cure (selection of alternatives). For this it is important to delve briefly into the domestic and international patronage relations governing Bangladesh, which explain how dependence relations play out both within and outside the country.

4.2.2 The Sociopolitical Context

Domestic Patronage: Neo-Patrimonialism

Bangladeshi society is highly fragmented – as it were, compartmentalised (Kemp, 2004). There are 'few overarching social loyalties that can provide the social glue needed to develop [. . .] social and political organisations' (Kochanek, 1993). Kochanek identifies the weakness of political institutions, an authoritarian and unresponsive bureaucratic culture and highly fictionalised political parties as reasons why there is no real threat to a deeply ingrained patron–client system mediating access to and influence on the highly centralised political system (ibid.). Right from independence, the liberator of the realm, Mujib-ur-Rahman, instated a spoils system creating a culture of personal gain (Chatterjee et al., 2006). The bureaucratic culture is very top-down oriented, training of the civil service is very general, one's ascent within the civil service is mostly based on one' s length of tenure or political affiliation rather than merit, and public office is strongly personalised and 'politicised' (Chatterjee et al., 2006).

Bangladesh has a vibrant civil society, evidenced by an impressive number (some 20,000) of NGOs. They are often crisis-driven, but quickly adapt to new topical challenges with creative reformulation of their acronyms. Several go back to the late 1960s, and only later were 'discovered' by foreign organisations as targets for funding. They tend to be established by the educated middle class with good connections in the power elite (Rahman, n.d.). Indeed, NGOs tend to mirror patron-client politics; people follow leaders and look where the money goes. Thus, while awareness about FAP-20 was raised by an intellectual elite organised in NGOs such as BARC and BCAS, it could be expected that many people were following local patrons (NGO leaders) when anti-FAP protest reached the grassroots.

The systemic legitimacy of the Bangladeshi government is still very low. While an independent study shows the poor have great faith in the ability of government to see to their needs (Ali and Hossain, 2006) the interviews suggest that the political sector is universally held in low esteem, even by high-level public servants. This is in no small measure due to the tendency for politicians to be in it for the money. Rents obtained from development can be redistributed by legal and illegal means, thus providing the power base for domestic patronage. Politics and aid in Bangladesh are a means of personal enrichment through sanctioned corruption. While corruption and clientelism are also widespread in other case study countries, Bangladesh beats almost anyone, ranking 156th out of 163 countries in Transparency International's Corruption Perception Index 2006. Corruption played a part in subsequent external interventions to reform water agencies.

As Clarence Maloney put it, '[P]ayoff is the lifeblood of the country' (cited in Kochanek, 1993).[3] Each externally funded development project quite openly deducts a percentage for the ruling party (ibid.). Business co-opts politics such that loans are routinely forgiven and labour rights practically non-existent (the 'commercialisation of power', see Kochanek (2000)).

Securitised Decision in a Politicised Society

FAP began life in a securitised context: a centralised dictatorship, which claimed to create law and order in an unstable, deeply politicised society. Each and every single development project needed President Ershad's signature. While the floods legitimised radical measures, the absence of routine political context made FAP likely to remain undebated after the immediate memory of the flood had faded.

While Bangladesh returned to formal democracy in 1990, the FAP issue was only debated in a parliamentary subcommittee after the Dutch government insisted on it, feeling 'any controversial subject of such major importance must get 'legitimacy' from Parliament'.[4] Meanwhile, elections continue to be contested and governments systematically undermined by the opposition. A fundamental lack of mutual legitimacy between the parties originates in a dispute about heroes and villains in and prior to the War of Liberation. Until this day, political disputes are dominated by conflicts over definitions and symbols of ethnicity (Bengali vs. Bangladeshi), socialism vs. the private sector, secularism vs. Islam, and democracy vs. a presidential system (Kochanek, 1993). Mudslinging, inducing socio-economic paralysis through *hartals* (general strikes) and endemic political violence between parties is rife. *Jatiya Sangsad* (Parliament) has played a marginal role.

The Bangladeshi judiciary has a better standing than Parliament (Kochanek, 2000), but Bangladesh has not succeeded in separating the judiciary from the executive. Judges often have links to senior politicians and lower courts are 'venal' (Roberts and Fagernäs, 2004). This makes it hard for the Supreme Court to contravene the party in power. Also, the legal regime is not very well developed, and competing claims to land ownership can be made with different agencies (Wood, 1995). As the rate of adult literacy is low: 41 per cent of those over 15 (UNDP, 2003), people are at the mercy of the *literati*. The politics of obstruction and disruption dominates normal political strategy and also pervades university life. Political killings of student (*chhatra*) leaders are the order of the day, stifling academic life. When I was visiting Bangladesh in late 2000, a student (*chhatra*) leader on his way to his physiotherapist was killed by adversaries in Gulshan New Town. The ubiquity of private security forces underscores the tense climate (author's observations, 2000).

As the Government of Bangladesh has proved unwilling to cede much control to allow administrative decentralisation and economic liberalisation, local government and the market sector continue to be weak. Patronage extends to the business sector and consultancies; debts are seldom repaid. Industrialisation has been state-led and the state is extremely reluctant to loosen its grip on the economy (Kochanek, 2000).

Unhelpfully, local politics proves as troubled as national politics. Like Egypt, Bangladesh is a textbook example of what Weber has labelled 'patrimonialism', a form of traditional domination where the ruler, supported by an administrative staff and military forces, treats the realm as his personal property, handing out privileges and favours (Islam, 2006).

Given this culture, it is not surprising that the key water institute in Bangladesh has a bad name for corruption and clientelism – but NGOs are not exempt from these charges, either.

The key actor in Bangladesh's water management is the public works department, the Bangladesh Water Development Board (BWDB). The Board, a semi-autonomous public agency under the administrative control of the Ministry of Water Resources, emerged in 1971 from the division of the East Pakistan Water and Power Development Authority (EPWAPDA) and split into separate water and power divisions in 1972.

The Board derives its legitimacy from erecting large structural works and technical expertise. There is an increasing trend on the part of the donors for development projects to involve *NGOs* to promote development. In the Netherlands this has been institutionalised through co-financing institutions, which distribute official development assistance (ODA) money through private channels. Of those, ICCO (Interchurch Cooperation Organization) and NOVIB (now Oxfam Novib)[5] are the largest active in Bangladesh. The funding obtained from those co-financing organisations to a crucial degree enabled Bangladesh NGOs to voice their point internationally. In FAP-20 there was likewise an allocated place for NGOs, notably the Grameen Bank, famous for introducing micro-credit to the poor.

Yet, when FAP-20 commenced, the BWDB and the NGOs enjoyed very low mutual legitimacy. NGOs accused the BWDB of pilferage and corruption, and of being unable to listen to 'the people', given their dismissal of the protests. The Dhaka NGO Shamunnay, for example, characterised the BWDB's culture as 'secretive, arrogant and "exclusive"' (Shamunnay, 1996: 81).

From the perspective of engineers, NGOs lack the necessary expertise in water management, and engineers are keen to point out their less successful forays into water management. Lack of expertise is a major delegitimiser in the eyes of the engineering/consultancy community.[6]

A negative mutual image thrives on mutual isolation and indeed, in 1993 NGOs and the Government of Bangladesh (GoB) were not talking (IOV, 1993). For their part, several Dutch consultants I talked to in late 2000 were happy to level criticism at *both* NGOs and the GoB. A Dutch consultant interviewee labelled Adnan Shapan, the NGO sociologist-activist, as a 'nincompoop' and a 'pest' and the BWDB as 'hopelessly corrupt'. Another Dutch consultant noted that when BWDB engineers turn up at all, they are 'arrogant and give orders'. In the context of the latter, several interviewees feel too much money was thrown at Bangladesh without tangible results. A third Dutch consultant advocated cutting aid funds by a third, to force more rational spending on the part of the Bangladeshis.

Power, expressed in 'fear or favours' (Kemp, 2004), spills over from the domestic to the transnational level. There is a strong suspicion that international contractors 'buy' key people in the Government of Bangladesh, who help them to new projects by which a highly competitive international construction sector can survive (in Smit, 1993, and interviews). This is especially worrying as contractors are in fact preparing Terms of Reference and national policies.[7] But why is Bangladesh so dependent on the foreign aid community? To understand how this is possible, we need to look at Bangladesh's position in the international arena.

External Patronage

As Ferguson (1994) has shown for Lesotho and Mitchell (1995) for Egypt, the 'facts' can be stacked such that a country seems to be badly in need of international development assistance – in spite of both these countries doing rather well economically. Bangladesh, for its part, has been internationally portrayed as the epitome of dependence on everything ever since it was born: on India, which surrounds it on three sides; on the regional rivers, 90 per cent of whose catchment is outside its territory, and ultimately on international aid. While, as we shall see, a quite different image of Bangladesh is possible, successive governments have done little to change the image of dependency, as the picture of Bangladesh as a helpless, hapless victim of circumstance, born in famine and floods continues to strike a chord with donors (Bradnock and Saunders, 2000). When global warming came on the global agenda, Bangladesh again was a natural candidate for global concern given its dense population – 'by the time global warming is likely to be well-established, Bangladesh may well have a population density five times that of the densest developed country, Netherlands' (Myers, 1995 quoted in Bate, 2001: 56). A dependent image, constantly at the mercy of others, makes it attractive for Bangladesh not to take responsibility and ownership of flood mitigation efforts, while creating an expectation of support that makes it impossible for donors to abandon the country. External donors[8] and recipients are locked in a Catch-22 that not only keeps Bangladesh in a state of dependence, but also sustains a redistributive corruption culture. The development projects bring in money and capacities absorbed by amazing adaptability of both the GoB and NGOs to international development fads. Bangladesh is thus the dependent 'downstream riparian' to an international flow of aid money. This international overlay is reflected in flood policy which, like the flood itself, is predominantly transnational (BELA Bulletin, 1999). The fact that the FAP project was so clearly donor-driven reinforced this sense of imposition and victimisation, as if the Bangladeshis had no say at all in the FAP affair. As a rule, donors bring in consultancies from their own country, and it is foreign consultancies who tend to draw up the Terms of Reference for new tendered projects, and the new national Water Policy document is drawn up by a UK consultancy, Halcrow, whose especially productive connections within Bangladesh government did not sit well with some interviewees.

Yet, while the GoB will not bite the hand that feeds, donors only dominate policies on a temporary (project) basis, so that the continuity of the domestic configuration may ultimately win out. Two key players, Kamal Siddiqi (FPCO, the project management) and Ainun Nishat (IUCN, the nature conservation NGO) insist they were involved in 'everything' (pers. comm., 2000). The next section provides more detail on the selection of alternatives leading up to FAP and FAP-20.

4.3 FAP-20 Selection: A Compromise between 'Dry' and 'Wet' Management

4.3.1 Oscillating Flood Management Regimes

Flood policy in Bangladesh can be said to have oscillated between a strong belief in flood control (zero floods) and a more cautious small-scale, living-with-the-floods approach (zero control) – a 'dry' and a 'wet' frame (ISPAN, 1992; Faaland et al., 1995).

The 'wet' approach appreciates that not all river floods are necessarily bad floods. *Barshas*, 'good floods', or 'inundations' (Nishat, n.d.[9]), are those generally perceived as doing more good than bad, supporting soil fertility, fish catch, navigation, ecosystems and groundwater recharge, and so on. They affect a fourth to a third of the land surface each year (Brammer, 1990). When inundation causes damage to property and crops, disrupts communication and brings harmful effects to human beings as well as to flora and fauna, however, they are *bannas/banyas*, 'bad floods'. Flood proofing fits with this 'wet' approach. The 'dry' attractor on the other hand seeks to control all floods, emphasising the negatives of flood: fatalities, mass destitution and displacement.

The '*wet vs. dry*' debate can also be read as a clash between two 'concepts of (water) control': it reflects a stand-off between a preponderance of government-supplied and owned flood control infrastructure (dry) and NGO-provided and privately owned tubewells for irrigation (wet). Large infrastructural works are easier to control, and also to cream off for *bakshish*, while tubewells are far more scattered.

In more recent years, a corresponding debate has emerged whether agricultural development should be *surface-water* or *groundwater* based. Rice constitutes on average 71 per cent of Bangladesh's agricultural output[10] and Dhaka and Tangail are in the highest producing areas. But should this production prioritise protected cultivation of rain-fed T(ransplanted) *Aman* rice supplemented by surface irrigation in summer or groundwater-fed *boro* winter rice? (Wood, 1999; for a flood and crop calendar, see Faisal and Parveen, 2004).

An argument favouring surface water is that the expected gains of groundwater irrigation are predicted to level off later in the twenty-first century (Faaland et al., 1995). Moreover, arsenic in groundwater may lead to fatalities when consumed over longer periods of time. This will mean a greater emphasis on flood control/controlled flooding. In the course of the chapter, we shall encounter more dimensions of those 'attractors' (Table 4.3).

The international overlay has historically played a key role in flood policies in Bangladesh and its predecessor, (East) Pakistan. How did donor preferences influence the oscillation between the two flood management attractors? When Bangladesh was still East Pakistan, the report by an American mission led by Krüg had recommended the establishment of EPWAPDA, the predecessor of BWDB, in 1959, and the Master Plan of 1964, an ambitious programme of 59 major structures, 6,000–7,000 km of dikes and 4,300 km of drainage channels, polders in the flood plains to protect crops from flooding and enable a Green Revolution. The Master Plan was drawn up in Pakistan and for Pakistan, while most BWDB engineers involved in FAP were trained in Pakistan (Pitman, 1994).

World Bank (International Bank for Reconstruction and Development) reviews conducted in 1966 and, upon Bangladeshi independence, in 1972 supported the aim to reach agricultural self-sufficiency. But the Bank wanted smaller-scale, quick-yielding projects, and promoted a programme for low-lift pumps and small-scale irrigation. In 1983 a UNDP-sponsored comprehensive Agriculture Sector Review led to a Water Sector Master Plan in 1986 which again prioritised for small-scale irrigation development in the safer dry season (Brammer, 1990).

While the impression often presents itself that *all* policy change in Bangladesh is donor-driven, some of the change in thinking was at least in part self-propelled. After the 1987 flood, BWDB released a fairly self-critical internal report, 'Floods in Bangladesh 1987', which suggested more heed should be given to knowledge. Also the original National Water Plan Phase I of 1986 showed a moderate approach to flood control. This however was drowned out by the 1987 and 1988 floods, which triggered a pendulum swing back to the 'control' paradigm. Pitman (1994) argues that the Bangladesh government saw the FAP as a way of 'revamping' the 1964 Master Plan, and in so doing regain control 'from what they saw as the unfortunate effects of privatisation of minor irrigation' (Pitman, 1994: 3).

After the democratic transition, the new government commissioned a Task Force, who in its four-part report (Task Force, 1991) recommended a moratorium on structural works. The report went unheeded. Even as FAP was modified, the perspective of water as a *problem* rather than a resource resonated with the GoB and lingered throughout FAP. The next section will go into this in further detail.

4.3.2 FAP Selection of Alternatives

The dictatorial, military conditions under which FAP was approved suggests a level of depoliticisation that does not bode well for a range of domestically

	Protection Paradigm	**Resilience Paradigm**
Type of Development	**Dry**	**Wet**
Governing approach	Control of water and people	Adaptivity and decentralised management
Technical approach	Barrages and embankments – 'structuralist'	Flood-proofing – 'adaptivist'
Preferred scale of intervention	Large	Small
Food security strategy	Foodgrain self-sufficiency	Diversification
Knowledge base	Science and expertise	Lay knowledge
Supporters	Land-owning farmers, industry, engineering and construction industry, the World Bank, and engineering consultants	Peasants, fishermen, country boat operators, NGOs, and sociologists
Key agricultural input	Surface water	Groundwater

Table 4.3: ***Contrasting concepts of flood control: different dimensions***

generated alternatives. Internationally, however, the donor scramble to release Bangladesh from flooding provided plenty to choose from. It led to a spread of eight international plans drawn up after the 1987 and 1988 floods, in a fascinating lead-up to the World Bank's final flood management package. The plans clearly reflect the two main flood management attractors ('wet' and 'dry') introduced above.

It emerges from interviews that the selection of alternatives was based on personal as well as technical considerations. From the French side, the economist Jacques Attali led a team of 30 experts to draw up a 'permanent solution' to flooding in Bangladesh. The French report, the *Pre-feasibility Study of Flood Control in Bangladesh*, sought fully-embanked flood prevention and industrialisation, following in the footsteps of the 1964 Master Plan drafted by the GoB together with IECO, an American consultancy. The floodwall programme sought to embank the rivers, similar to the Mississippi (Chowdhurry, 1992) putting in 3–4000 km of embankments, as much as had been built in the whole period up until then. It would have cost anything between US$5.2 and US$10.1 billion, with US$160–180 million in Operation and Maintenance costs each year 'in perpetuity' (Boyce, 1990: 421), presenting Bangladesh with a huge debt. Had the French proposal gone ahead, there would indeed have been the question of a 'mega-project', a technical fix to deal with an 'Act of God'.

In defiance of this 'dry' river domination and control approach, the Americans took the view that embankments constrain river discharge and are ultimately self-defeating, as they cause sediment aggradation of the river beds and increase flash flooding, so that continuous dredging and re-excavation is needed (Khalequzzaman, 1994). The US Army Corps of Engineers, the American counterpart of the Bangladesh Water Development Board, shifted from a technology-oriented to a behaviourist paradigm in the 1960s, which means trying to keep people out of the flood plain through stimuli (zoning) and education rather than trying to keep the river out. This would fit the government's domestic flood frame – as we saw, the government blames irresponsible settling. But as James and Pitman (1992) note, non-structural measures such as zoning are also unfeasible, for lack of flood-free land, among other aspects. You cannot travel for more than 5 miles in Bangladesh without encountering a surface water body. Densely packed poor households tend to live in the flood plain where land is cheapest. If flood plain dwellers were evicted from the flood plain, where would they go?

Therefore, Peter Rogers and David Seckler, key water management experts on the American team, saw river training (taming the floods) as technically and economically unfeasible, arguing instead that Bangladesh has not so much a flood problem but a *poverty* problem. The way to reduce flood vulnerability was to increase incomes through expanding irrigation. The study proposed an efficient flood warning system and took an integrated, pan-regional (South Asian) perspective to flood management. This made USAID's 'wetter' *Eastern Waters Study* (Rogers et al., 1989) arguably the most sustainable, environmentally aware and 'holistic' proposal out of the set (Shamunnay, 1996), and addressed the GoB's external 'flood frame' which lays blame at the doorstep of India and Nepal. However, a regional solution was also the most politically contentious, as it relied on Bangladeshi cooperation with India at a time when the regional superpower had just declined to extend its river-sharing agreement on the Ganges (Padma) with Bangladesh.

India dominates the regional, mutually interdependent *hydrosecurity complex* (Buzan, 1991; Lindholm, 1995), outnumbering its neighbours in terms of demographic, military and economic power. This permits the country to pursue a divide-and-rule strategy in the region, concluding agreements only when India wants to and only with one neighbour at a time (Crow, 1995). In 1974–75 India unilaterally built the Farakka dam to divert more water to its seaport Calcutta (West Bengal). Bangladesh, as the downstream riparian to three major rivers, of which it controls only 8–10 per cent, claims upstream infrastructure has had a severe impact on water extremes, exaggerating both flooding in the wet season and desiccation in the dry season.[11] Bangladeshi protest to the UN led to the aforementioned Indo-Bangladeshi treaty, but Bangladesh feels this nascent international *regime* still gives the country very little influence on Indian upstream decisions (ur-Rashid, 2005).[12] The US study was dismissed out of hand for being too friendly to India. A senior Bangladeshi expert questions the integrity of the team leader of the USAID study, calling him a 'liar'.[13]

Around the same time, the Japanese produced the *Report on Survey of Flood Control Planning in Bangladesh.* This plan was similarly sceptical of large structures, emphasising urban protection and flood forecasting instead. A Chinese study, which compared the Ganges and Brahmaputra to the Yangtze, has remained confidential, even to professor Ainun Nishat who was involved in it on the part of Bangladesh (Haggart, 1994). It is clear, however, that the Chinese, like the Americans, have abandoned the control orientation.

Three more bilateral regional studies were drafted in which Bangladeshi flood experts worked together with India, Nepal and Bhutan respectively.

Finally, the United Nations Development Programme (UNDP) facilitated a flood policy study and a flood preparedness study (UNDP, 1989), carried out by local and expatriate consultants. While it also advocated regional cooperation, the study was closer to the French study, recommending embankments and river training, but placed a heavy emphasis on controlled flooding which requires embankments, but with more regard for eventual drainage of trapped monsoon water. This emphasis led to an integrated flood control, irrigation and drainage (FCDI) approach being taken in about half the ensuing FAP projects.

The UNDP/GoB study came out on top: its Eleven Guiding Principles (UNDP, 1989) combined controlled flooding with nods at non-structural works and participation with river training and channelling as national flood policy precepts. The GoB enacted these Eleven Principles and in November 1989, the World Bank and GoB collated the French, UNDP, USAID and Japanese reports into a Flood Action Plan, with a strong bias towards the UNDP study. There was a significant modification though: while the original UNDP programme proposal was in the same order of magnitude as the French plan, costing US$7.5 billion, the total budget for FAP was soon whittled down to US$200 million.

About 10 per cent of this budget went to FAP-20, a project that for all practical purposes exported Dutch 'poldering' technology in both its social and infrastructural sense.

4.3.3 Compartmentalisation: Solution in Search of a Problem?

Like many other projects started under the FAP banner, FAP-20 would very probably have gone ahead with or without FAP (Nishat, quoted in Shamunnay, 1996). Both Dutch and Bangladeshi interviewees claim that even before FAP, it had been decided that Tangail, on the Jamuna's left bank, and Sirajganj on the right bank would be selected as sites for experimental compartmentalisation. The Project Identification Mission in 1989, which included members of the Flood Plan Coordination Organization (FPCO), created to oversee FAP) and the assisting international Panel of Experts (Adnan et al., 1991, 1992), merely formalised that earlier decision. The planned reinforcement of the Brahmaputra Right Bank Embankment (BRE) became FAP-21–22, taking up a full fifth of the FAP budget.

Compartmentalisation was proudly presented as a Dutch innovation. Indeed, the Dutch speakers at a conference I attended in Dhaka in November 2000, organised by (Dutch-funded) Dhaka environmental consultants EGIS and the GoB, did not cease to emphasise the Dutch self-image of providing world-class flood management expertise in its fight against water.

Dutch educational and technical assistance to Bangladesh goes back to its independence. Several key Bangladeshi players in FAP-20 have pursued part of their education in the Netherlands, either at IHE Delft or ISS The Hague. In the course of Dutch involvement in Bangladesh, it has been increasingly recognised that in a subsistence society it makes little sense to keep the water out at all costs. Instead, Professor Wybrand van Ellen of Delft, struck by the similarity of the Bangladesh Southwest (Khulna Jessore) to the flat and marshy Netherlands landscapes, developed the idea of compartmentalised polders with British flood experts Hugh Brammer and Jim Dampster. All three men were part of the Panel of Experts and the idea was more or less implemented as proposed in different FAP projects: in FAP-4 (Khulna Jessore), FAP-3.1 (Jamalpur) and FAP-20 (Tangail), in Central Bangladesh. The Tangail area was to be divided up into sub-compartments which were fitted with regulated inlets and outlets. As FAP-20 was an agricultural scheme, a sub-compartment comprising Tangail Town was originally not planned for but once created, proved the most popular flood defence intervention.

While full control seeks to minimise residual risk of damage in extreme events, a controlled flooding regime allows part of the area inside the embankment to flood at lower water levels. Inlets allow floods into the area for natural irrigation and fertilisation, and promote fish growth at required levels. Breaking polders up into different sub-compartments, using existing roads and bridges, would make it possible to fine-tune water management, flooding only those areas that need the water and retaining it for as long as its users need it before draining it to the river. This made it possible to bring in extra water in early monsoon, and shut excess water out in the high monsoon season. As the rice crop grows and water rises, higher levels can be allowed, while at the end of monsoon the inlet would be shut to allow drainage, so that post-monsoon crops can be planted early. The embankments surrounding a compartment would have to withstand most, but not all floods, so that a flood would inundate agricultural areas but not (or not much) the urban and industrial areas (Euroconsult/Lahmeyer, 1995).

FAP-20 not only sought to address the regulation of the flood for irrigation, but also the *drainage* aspect by rehabilitating canals. Tangail area, the FAP-20 site, may have the lowest rainfall of the country, but it is still a very considerable 1550 mm/year. In the FAP-20 area every few years the heavy September and October rainfall gives rise to run-off congestion. When rainfall is extensive, the area becomes saturated, local flooding takes place and drainage is insufficient.

Controlled flooding thus seemed a fair compromise between the 'structuralist' control school of thought and the 'adaptivist' living-with-the-floods people. Indeed, the technology itself was hardly revolutionary anymore for Bangladesh – it was tried in different Dutch projects (Wester and Bron, 1998) and also in the World Bank-funded Right Bank Embankment rehabilitation plan (World Bank, quoted in Boyce, 1990). Moreover, the Panel felt they had the perfect institutional solution to mobilise thousands of farmers to coordinate their preferences: the Dutch polder model.

4.3.4 Selection within FAP-20

The Dutch sought to move compartmentalisation beyond the expected success of the FAP-20 project alone. Its Terms of Reference see FAP-20 as a *demonstration* project: if the pilot project were found feasible, the concept would be replicated in other parts of the country and in so doing revolutionise flood management in Bangladesh and elsewhere. To validate the idea, a series of adjacent compartmentalisation projects along the Jamuna were to be tested.[14]

As we shall see, the 'flagship carrier' label has come back to haunt the project, while the comparative experiment was already compromised at an early stage. As FAP-20 was formulated, three areas were handpicked: Tangail, Sirajganj as well as Jamalpur, which was also the site of the FAP-3.1, one of the 'main studies' in FAP. Jamalpur was dropped quite early, but Sirajganj was in for several years. The original idea was to have compartmentalisation projects on both sides of the Jamuna, with the Sirajganj project site to be administered by

NGOs, and indeed Water User Groups helped identify sub-compartment sites in Siranjganj.

Sirajganj was eventually dropped before the project's inception, officially because the GoB did not produce a written intention to ensure the stability of the Brahmaputra Right Embankment, so that the locations might flood anyway should the Brahmaputra Right Embankment (BRE) break again. The Jamuna's energy has an eastward tendency so that the right bank was under much more pressure than the left bank. By comparison, the Tangail area is a sheltered area. The German donor also blames the lack of funds for the deselection (KfW, 2004).

Dropping Sirajganj, however, deprived the experiment of any 'control group' limiting the project to a pilot in Tangail. To discuss the *institutional* challenges of the compartmentalisation approach at some greater depth, the next section will go into a core element of FAP-20: participatory management.

4.4 FAP-20 Participation and Openness

4.4.1 Widening Public Involvement

> The government was talking about enacting a law to ensure people's participation. It was as if the government were saying: 'We will set up a committee headed by so-and-so who will tell you to participate.' We (USAID) almost fell off our chairs when the conference secretary responded to the idea [. . .] saying, 'We've decided that if participation is going to work, it has to be voluntary.' (Pitman, 1994)

While India and Bangladesh are formal democracies, South Asia has been plagued by 'antiparticipatory centralism' (SAARC, 1992). When FAP started at the turn of the nineties, *all project information was securitised.* As Keith Pitman, an American consultant, related in a USAID forum on participation: 'For example maps were restricted. Field engineers had to go to Dhaka, make a tracing of a map, and then go back to the project'. Information provision to the general public was likewise minimal in this early phase and the topic was undebatable: 'We could not talk' (Pitman, 1994).

This was supposed to change after the democratic transition, but 'many began to wonder whether the government was trying to keep information from them' (Hanchett, 1997: 281). The first review process for FAP in 1990 took place behind closed doors; only civil servants and the Panel of Experts could attend, with confidential minutes. A FAP consultant, sympathetic to the NGO position, leaked internal project memos, which information ended up in Shapan Adnan et al.'s 'offending' 1991 and 1992 FAP report funded by Norway (interview, Dutch consultant). However, things slowly improved when four annual conferences were held in Dhaka, the quite critical discussions of which were commendably recorded in (English-language) publications.

Only in 1992, on strong donor instigation, an open review of the Flood Action Plan was organised and a five-day meeting held at the Prime Minister's Office in Dhaka, which provided an opportunity for some 600 journalists, NGOs and critics to submit written questions (Hanchett, 1997). A proceedings of this Second Conference was published.

The third conference in 1993 was organised by the Bangladeshi government. Questions again had to be written down and thus could be ignored by the chief engineer (Pitman, 1994). The fourth of those conferences, however, was repeatedly delayed and its proceedings not widely published. As the Final Report notes, this was a critical moment as FPCO was supposed to be dissolved at the time. The UNDP subsequently distanced itself from the donor-GoB statement following it.[15]

While FAP has taken much criticism for failing to consult local stakeholders, in fairness it should be noted that FAP-20 was unique in the Flood Action Plan in seeking to address the institutional aspect head-on. Indeed, the identification report states that 'unless there is local participation from the outset, it is doubtful whether compartmentalisation will ever be practical and viable' (ODA, 1990).

Like compartmentalisation, the idea of 'institutional poldering' was not earth-shattering: elements of Dutch 'consensual democracy' have tentatively been tried in Bangladesh in the Dutch-funded Early Implementation Projects of the 1970s and 1980s. BWDB officials claim that informal consultation between engineers and recipient communities (notably landowners) have been going on for decades, and they must have thought they were doing the same thing here.

But in the case of FAP, the social engineering was to work differently: polder committees were to be formed with different stakeholder groups. FAP-20's concept of multi-stakeholder consultation did not make immediate sense to the Government of Bangladesh, the people of Tangail – and perhaps, if truth be told, not even to the Dutch consultants. Indeed, as the project ran on, the original idea was somewhat obscured from sight.

4.4.2 The Consultation on FAP-20

The history of participation sketched above indicates that the Bangladeshi government was not initially very minded to dialogue with local stakeholders in the context of FAP-20. The donors however insisted on it – apart from such noble considerations as democratic accountability, cost was a key factor as compartment management in the past had been extremely costly and ineffective.

The meaning of 'participation' changed considerably in the course of the Flood Action Plan, even in the early stages of formulation. In 1991 Euroconsult, the FAP-20 consultant, started a large consultation asking residents which water problems they encountered and what solutions they preferred. The original idea was for the people of Tangail to decide to which extent they wanted controlled flooding. Polls systematically show that people who are not protected would like to see embankments. One reason is that that increases their social standing (various interviews). Once embankments are in place, drainage problems appear and people will try to offload the excess water on others. During the project, according to a Bangladeshi consultant, some people asked for more structures. Similarly, it appears from FAP-3.1 (Jamalpur) that people inside embankments are generally happy for the embankments to be there. The embankments, then, could count on a support base among the farmers. In this respect, the NGOs seemed to have been disingenuous in opposing embankments full stop.

On the other hand, because of the existing (porous) horseshoe embankment, Tangail was already fairly safe from flooding, so that many stakeholders there were perhaps not too keen on more flood protection.

There was logic to the options put to stakeholders in the consultation exercise. During the lifetime of a compartment, requirements of different sectors may change, and popular demands follow a predictable pattern. Demands for flood protection are likely to increase as an area becomes more economically developed. The degree of protection itself also gives rise to socio-economic change, such as urbanisation, which in turn will give rise to different demands. Based on this reasoning, Dirk Frans, a sociologist with a background in engineering, devised four progressively drastic water management options, lending them a dynamic for the future:

A) Improved drainage
B) Option A + throated inlets to mitigate danger of additional flooding
C) Option B + gated inlets and extra development works to re-excavate *khals*
D) Full flood control (Kvaløy, 1994)

According to one Bangladeshi expert, FAP-20 was an institutional development project until the engineers took over (interview, Bangladesh consultant 2000). The engineers, it turned out, had a quite different view of participation. Social research of necessity takes longer and may yield 'undesired' results. While project initiators saw sociological research as a way of 'selling' a project on its intended beneficiaries, that is not what sociology is for (interview, Dutch consultant). Impatient with the time-consuming participation process, the Board started to keep an eye on the clock.

As a result, the Needs Assessment and Consultation were curtailed under time pressure. Interviews and the work of Adnan (1992) suggest that the outcome of the consultation might have something to do with it, too. The do-nothing and drainage options, which emerged as popular from the consultation, would require the least engineering effort. The Bangladeshi engineers had different ideas: they simply dismissed the do-nothing (or little) option, while the Dutch Embassy's First Secretary, a Wageningen-educated irrigation engineer, was away (interviews, Dutch consultants).[16] According to an internal memorandum leaked to RAS, 'Flood Protection is a government policy which was reiterated in the Eleven Guiding Principles of the Flood Action Plan . . . , the option of no flood control for Tangail need not be discussed with the people' (quoted in Adnan, 1992). In all, 53 water control structures were built in the FAP-20 area.

4.4.3 Testing the Polder Model in Tangail

The Eleventh Guiding Principle for FAP says: 'Encourage popular support by involving beneficiaries in the planning, design, and operation of flood control and drainage works' (GoB/UNDP, 1989). The FAP-20 project foresaw a form of participatory decision-making in the day-to-day management of the compartments, envisaged as the Bangladeshi version of the Dutch 'polder model', a consensual, egalitarian model of decision-making, predicated on the idea that if not everyone is on board in managing a polder, everybody may drown due to the obstruction of a minority.

In 1992–93 the consultant crafted a system of water management committees at compartment (CWMCs), sub-compartment (SCWMCs) and *chawk*-level (Water User Groups) after the Dutch *waterschappen*. Committees would perform operational tasks, conflict handling, drafting maintenance plans and make decisions on preferred gate settings.

One Water User Group member would liaise with project staff and local government (*Union Parishad*s) at sub-compartment level, while the CWMCs had Water Board staff and local personnel working for Central Government. These allocate specific seats to four interest groups:

- Users and project-affected persons (PAPs)
- NGOs
- (Central) government organisations
- Local government

The first group consisted of farmers, fishermen, women and landless[17] (Euroconsult/Lahmeyer et al., 1995).

In 1995, water user groups had been formed in three sub-compartments. De Graeff (n.d.) reports that in the first year of their existence, *chawk* committees took care of the new structures and resolved some conflicts between farmers and fishermen. Yet, after anti-FAP protests focusing on Tangail, which will be expounded later, the donors pressed the GoB to make a better job of participation and to involve more disciplines in FAP. Engineers however felt unease at the unscientific nature of public involvement in technical discussions on planning, but a consensus developed on local people being 'partners' of professionals.

As a result, the scope of participation broadened. At first, the Flood Plan Coordination Organization, in charge of FAP, thought it sufficient to consult with farmers only while 'taking into account' other interests (IOV, 1993) – which meant the fishermen were not taken very seriously. The Euroconsult system had allocated seats to farmers as a homogeneous group. In an earlier review, however, the World Bank had already noted and found that in poldering projects, farmers at different land heights had quite different views of the ideal water level. 'The need for organising farmers numbering in the tens of thousands to set up equitable polder operations is one of the great drawbacks of the polder technology for wet season agriculture'. The new type of participation developed duly differentiated between highland, midland and lowland farmers. Yet, according to an evaluation by Datta (Datta et al., 1997), who was also involved in the mid-term review, this new system was not well known to the stakeholders and rather ineffective. The Dutch development assistance inspectorate (IOV)'s report (1993) notes the legitimacy of the polder-style decision-making process is in doubt in light of a poorly informed population. This makes the population potentially more amenable to manipulation – both to donor, GoB and NGO arguments. A Donor Mission in 1997 found that sluice gates were operated in places by project staff rather than WUG representatives. By that time, 100 *chawk* committees and 15 sub-compartment committees had formed (Lewins and Robens, 2004).

The system also showed little sensitivity to the marked power differences within rural communities. Both donor and NGO conceptions of 'the people's wishes' therefore wanted a more careful approach. As Dirk Frans noted (interviewed in 2000), the people are not always right but neither are the engineers.

4.4.4 Operation and Maintenance: Who Repairs the Breaches?

Another interpretation of 'people's participation' in FAP-20 was their involvement in Operation and Maintenance. The project uniquely involved a component of 'people's O&M' making use of people's familiarity with such interventions. Groups of local people, Local Contracting Societies, both male and female, could be hired to work on the structures, which also circumvented institutionalised corruption percentages. Clearing out channels and repairing embankments is hard work of bad repute, and contracted work easily drives up cost. In FAP-20, landless workers and women erect and repair levees instead, at a fee.

Curiously, while the problem has been known at least since the 1970s, donors have not insisted on better O&M of the projects they funded. The 1993 Dutch Inspectorate's Mission, for example, explicitly recommends redirecting the donor efforts to O&M of existing projects, but this recommendation was not enforced (IOV, 1993). This seems to be the case for FAP-20 as well – while the Dutch donor maintains there was a considerable amount in the budget for O&M, nothing was actually happening on the ground in 2000.

As a result, no one will be motivated to remove silt clogging up offtakes or pay the sluice-gate operator after the project is over. When there are visible dangers, like when in 1995 the Jamuna broke through to create a new inlet for the Dhaleswari, people did not wait for the BWDB to repair the local embankment.

While the move to set up local contracting societies can be lauded as pro-poor, this approach frames 'participation' as a rather convenient way for BWDB to shed responsibility for Operation & Maintenance (O&M). But hiring people as labourers does not give them influence on the project and in this sense does not score high on any participation ladder. It is fair to say the establishment of these societies evidences an appreciation the experiential fact that, in light of the Water Board's poor O&M record, in practice '(t)he only ones who do O&M are the farmers themselves. In 9 out of 10 cases they are right.' Jennifer Duyne (1998) has pointed out many impressive and well-coordinated local flood management initiatives in Bangladesh. Some of those initiatives may in fact be less than spontaneous, but compelled by *zamindar*-type feudal arrangements for compulsory maintenance by sharecroppers. In pre-colonial times mud banks were erected, maintained by landlords who levied taxes on the population. Under British rule communities learned to wait for the government to mend breaches in embankments rather than display initiative. But BWDB is not known for solid operation and maintenance works on its 7,500 km of embankments unless there is question of a serious flood. Any available funds tend to be 'transferred to new capital projects' (Faaland et al., 1995).

According to the FPCO-produced *Guidelines for participation* (version 1994) responsibility for and ownership of any water structures was to remain in the hands of the state (Hanchett, 1997: 286). The struggle for space, however, is always present and eats away at the planning and implementation of projects. Embankments are eroded by stealth and drainage channels tend to be under-dimensioned. Local public action, so-called, 'public cuts' of unpopular embankments by 'anonymous demolition crews', prohibited under the Embankment & Drainage Act of 1952, thus remained illegal (Hanchett, 1997). A 'public cut' of course means that the drained water is offloaded on the next area, and the suspicion of a cut can lead to intense conflict. During the FAP-20 episode, public cuts were made, some of which were stopped by the authorities.

According to:	External Cause	Domestic Cause
Government	- India's Farakka Dam - Upstream tree felling - Act of Allah	People's irresponsible behaviour (settling in flood plains)
NGOs	- Upstream tree felling - Western carbon emission causing climate change	Government not taking responsibility

Table 4.4: ***Risk, responsibility and blame: who/what caused the floods?***

4.5 Challenging and Politicising FAP-20: Naming, Blaming and Reframing

4.5.1 Uncertainty, Politicisation and Blame

To properly address the flood, it makes sense to determine what causes it. But as Thompson and Warburton (1985) have shown, there is no consensus between analysts on what causes floods upstream in the Himalayas, and likewise there is no undisputed narrative on downstream floods in Bangladesh. Depending on whether you believe the World Bank, the government, NGOs or an indigenous movement, you get highly 'contradictory certainties' about what caused the problem. All these actors and their blame stories can have 'felicity' with the decision-making audience, and should therefore be taken seriously in the analysis. These uncertainties promote storylines that do bring apparent certainty in the face of uncertainty (van Eeten, 1997).

A closer look at 'blame stories' in Bangladesh, such as in Table 4.4, shows a contrast between floods as an 'Act of Man', which blames specific actors for the floods, and floods seen as an 'Act of Allah': *'Through the events He is showing His will and power against which they cannot and should not do anything'* (Schmuck 2000: 85). The fatalist approach to cause and cure is often attributed to the whole of Bangladesh, to the frustration of aid agencies, as it hampers flood pro-action and preparedness: 'It [natural calamity] has been a part of our life as it comes every year in one form or another', Prime Minister Khaleda Zia told the press in 1991. 'No one has control over natural calamities' (quoted in Dove, 1998: 51, 53). Wood (1999) on the other hand claims that the Bangladeshi government blamed tree felling in Nepal and sea level rise, presumably on a different occasion. Whichever the blame story, it exposed the government to NGO criticism that the government was avoiding responsibility for its people's flood vulnerability. The attribution of causality also conjures up the question, Who should take care of the problem? Given its dependent self-image, the Bangladeshi government

Problem Frame	Solution Frame	Proposed By	Participation
Natural hazard problem ('Act of God')	Technical fix	French[18]	Minimal public involvement
Development issue ('Act of Man')	Integrative approach and linking sectoral plans	Americans and Dutch	Broad consultation of the public
Human rights issue (project as problem)	No project; build on people's resilience	NGOs and some external consultants	Popular resistance to flood project

Table 4.5: ***Expanded set of flood problem frames***

tends to leave responsibility to outsiders. This reflects the *internal* mudslinging between the prime movers in the security debate, 'engineers' and 'sociologists', which was foregrounded in the politicisation of FAP-20. This at times made it difficult to make out what was 'really' going on.

Jesse Manuta (n.d.) identifies two flood 'master' problem frames depicting flood as a natural hazard or a development issue. One can visualise a continuum running from fatalist ('it can't be helped') to a control mindset ('we can handle everything'). Somewhere near the control side, the *developmentalist* frame puts great trust in Man to overcome natural hazards, if only the stakeholders are on board (people's participation) and sectoral plans are integrated (Manuta, n.d.). Underlying these problem frames are moves for securitisation, seeking to legitimise extraordinary intervention measures, but are not invulnerable to counter-securitisations. As we shall see below, we will need to expand Mantua's framework by a third frame and securitised referent: *human rights* (Table 4.5).

The Flood Action Plan programme was triggered by a dramatic event that had strong humanitarian appeal: images of death, suffering and destitution gave the G7 a popular platform to start from. The military rule under which the project began allowed the Flood Action Plan to be rushed through with little opposition or even communication with stakeholders – a 'securitised mode of decision-making'.

However, different discursive coalitions have sought to open up the dominant problem frame, away from physical security, and the governance set-up away from top-down intervention. In developing a counter-hegemonic alliance, the anti-FAP movement developed a counter-frame by aligning different discursive frames into a 'discursive alliance' (Hajer, 1995).

I will categorise these moves in terms of securitising moves. The approach to securitisation pursued here is highly interpretative, though, as the 'security' aspect was often only implicit, rather than explicit, while its usage in the donor literature was rather loose.[19]

As noted, the FAP could ride on a platform of national interest and international moral outrage at the loss of life and economic assets in the 1987/1988 disaster. Intriguingly, both FPCO and NGOs have since downplayed the number of victims in the 1988 floods, originally one of the major 'selling points' for the FAP.[20] Already at the inception of FAP the rationale had shifted from physical protection to the stabilisation of *food* production to feed a booming population (Hanchett, 1997: 280). The dominance of this irrigation aspect, however, was not well communicated, NGOs claimed. Instead, there was the question of a 'water management project' (Houscht, n.d.). In 1993, Tangail protesters still demanded physical security, calling for flood control priorities to be changed 'from producing rice to saving lives' (quoted in Haggart, 1994) but the national water authority took the view that given the relatively sheltered position of Tangail vis-à-vis the Jamuna, there was no concrete danger to Tangail lives. The anti-FAP NGO platform did not support the view either. 'Water is not our enemy but it is our resource', as Khushi Kabir, its chairwoman, summarised this stance in 1995.[21]

Only for urban and industrial areas complete *protection* – which was thought to be 'uncontroversial' (IOV, 1993) – would still be feasible. While the Dutch donors kept invoking the 'fight against the water' even in 2000 (EGIS, 2000), the project went ahead 'because of the greater national interest to Bangladesh' (*Daily Star,* 18-3-94). FAP-20 intended to provide *a secure environment for more risk-taking in food production* to help realise food security as well as economic advancement, rather than the need to save local lives or livelihoods. Despite highly fertile soils, Bangladesh has one of the lowest per hectare rice yields in the world (Boyce, 1990).

Any pretence of rural flood protection for Tangail was abandoned in favour of *controlled monsoon flooding* for agriculture.But the famines of 1943 and 1974 (when 30,000 people died) are clear in the minds of policymakers, such that food security is a key priority in each five-year plan. Not just food security but *food sovereignty* is very central to Bangladeshi policymaking. While Myers (1995) claims it is 'generally thought' that the country will become ever less able to feed itself, Bangladesh has over 90 per cent self-sufficiency in food.

Agricultural development based on Green Revolution technologies, notably high yielding varieties (HYV), is a cornerstone of five-year plans. The FAP aimed to increase the number of harvests per year, per hectare yield and the diversity of crops. Especially FAP-20 hinges on 'foodgrain security as the route for food and other kinds of security' (UNDP, 1995). *Environmental* concerns were raised from the start, but only became a core concern after preliminary results of FAP studies also showed adverse affects (Shamunnay, 1996). To established engineers, like Kamal Siddiqi (FPCO), the environment is synonymous to the resource base, so that he could not see why people would worry over the environment while they were going without food (Haggart, 1994).

At the turn of the 1990s, *poverty reduction* became the buzzword in programmes run by Western donor agencies and Bangladesh was a textbook example. Nearly half of Bangladesh's 133 million people live below the poverty line. It is the only country categorised as least developed with a population over 75 million (Islam, 2004).

Agricultural development, it was noted, did not necessarily alleviate poverty and might increase social inequality. The Dutch Inspection agency prided itself therefore on the fact that through FAP-20 the Netherlands had adjusted FAP policy towards a poverty alleviation orientation (IOV, 1993).

The dynamic driving force in Bangladesh is a booming *population* (despite a successful birth control programme) (Caldwell et al., 1999). Poverty alleviation, according to the Association of Bangladeshi Engineers, necessitates large-scale land reclamation and dam building (Association of Bangladeshi Engineers, 1995). Once the farmers increase their wealth, other sectors of society will start to benefit too.

The Bangladeshi leadership echoed the view that development was a way out of poverty: '(T)he recurrent problem of flooding inhibits [Bangladesh's] development potential and stands in the way of the economy taking off in real terms' (letter of the PM's secretary to the French government, 1994, cited in Haggart, 1994). But not only flooding was seen as a brake on development, so was resistance against FAP – Ross Wallace, the World Bank representative coordinating FAP from 1990, reportedly went out of his way to discredit the opposition as 'anti-development' and 'criminal' (Nicolassen, 1993).

How was the developmentalist discourse countered? This is the concern of the section hereafter.

4.5.2 Resistance to Developmentalism

Eleven days prior to the London donor conference starting FAP in 1989, the well-respected Bangladesh Agricultural Research Centre (BARC) issued a report (BARC, 1989) warning that introducing Green Revolution innovations such as HYVs of rice require more fertiliser, which, if indiscriminately applied, deprives soil of organic matter Since HYV seeds and inputs will need to be bought again and again, this can open a credit trap to cover the cost of seeds, fertiliser and pesticides. This can precipitate the 'debilitation of the local food security system' and the loss of *livelihood* resilience to withstand food crises (also noted by Wood

(1999) and others). The 'sanctioned discourse' of agricultural development, however, brooked no opposition: in response, key members of the discussion forum who drafted the BARC policy brief were 'strategically removed from office' (*FAP Monitor*, 1995; Chadwick and Datta, n.d.).

Funded by the Norwegian government, which had decided to stay outside FAP, Bangladeshi sociologist Shapan Adnan seconded BARC's political economy perspective, revealing that flood victims of 1987 and 1988 were mainly the landless poor who lacked clean drinking water and food, while the rich hardly suffered because of the bumper crops following the floods (Shapan Adnan 1991; also Clayton-Dalal et al., 1992). The Flood Action Plan only got under way because even the richer areas in Dhaka were affected.

Critical researchers contracted to work on various FAP studies sought to change the programme's problem definition. The social development and gender consultants Suzanne Hanchett and Mahbuba Nasreen, for example, claimed that the problem is not flood but economics (Hanchett and Nasreen, 1992). Concentrating on improving monsoon yield benefited landowners at the expense of sharecroppers and the landless fishers, widening socio-economic disparities.[22]

The promised 'secure environment' for Tangail in practice only meant security for landed farmers protected by the embankments and, if need be, musclemen. FAP-20 was feared to redistribute security between economic sectors and those providing for their livelihood inside and outside the system,[23] reinforced by inadequate compensation measures for harm to livelihoods.

> Flood control and irrigation create new land and enhance the value of existing land. [. . .] The value of land changes when it is protected from early flooding, or drained from water-logging, by embankments and canals – but only those landholders with land in the 'command' of such constructions will benefit. (Wood, 1994)

Such concerns begged the question: Why support the rice farmers anyway? Rice can be imported cheaply from the world market, and much more easily than fish (Faaland et al., 1995) – while fish is the only accessible source of food to the poorest. Bangladeshi governments have interpreted food security as autarky from the country's early beginnings (Faisal and Parveen, 2004), but it can also be framed otherwise: as developing an export base that brings in enough revenue to import food requirements (virtual water).

FAP's 'dry' development model encouraged the enclosure of *beels*, squeezing the area available to fishermen. It created openings for the capture of *khas* (holy land, commons) land by the violent enclosure of common-pool resources. The sluice-gate operators are not paid and the SC committees remain unfunded. Thus, despite the intended participatory mechanism, those with money to pay the operator, or alternatively to pay musclemen (*mastans*) to force a decision, are effectively in control. Physical insecurity due to police beatings as well as intimidation from hired hard men was depressingly regular (e.g. Ali et al., 1998). A FAP-20 team leader also reports physical attacks from local contractors (interview, Team Leader).

Three out of every four Bangladeshis (predominantly women) at the time were involved in (part-time) fishing (Faaland et al., 1995). Mitigating measures in the project, notably cultured fishing, benefited landowners but not the landless, who often are fishermen. Fish production is the main livelihood of the Hindu minority, which makes up 10–11 per cent of the population of Bangladesh. Hindus have been traditionally barred from owning land and therefore consigned to being fishers and eating fish for their basic protein intake. Their economic and food security therefore is crucially linked to the mode of livelihood, with few alternative livelihood opportunities. Cultured fisheries also require significant investment, again disadvantaging the poor.

The political economy makes livelihoods and resource conservation issues impossible to reconcile. A Bangladeshi project consultant noted a national trend for draining fish ponds until the last fingerling:

> What happened in June/July: we put in 2 fish passes. After 15 July all the gates of the periphery were open. But what happened: all fishermen came and put their net, they fished up everything. In '96 I put special police for them not to catch fish, to stop the catch from July – September. But we have no jurisdiction beyond my area, no jurisdiction outside the area. The local *parishad* should take authority; it must take care of that. Otherwise there will be no sustainability. (interview, Bangladeshi project manager, 2000)

The most vulnerable group, however, are the millions living on highly 'insecure, unprotected areas' (IOV, 1993) known as *chars,* near the FAP-20 area and elsewhere on the rivers. In Bangladesh, space is still at a premium, as evidenced most graphically by people living on these islands. Each year, the Brahmaputra alone makes 30,000 people homeless (Schmuck, 2000).

Those outside the project area indeed regarded the project with suspicion. According to local authorities, the lure of flood protection attracted 30,000 into the area within a few years, and land prices went up tenfold (KfW, 2004). But due to the project, those who remained outside were worse off than before (Euroconsult et al., 1995) and there were press reports of 'violent clashes between pro- and anti-FAP people in the locality' (*Independent*, 1995). Conflicts between insiders and outsiders to the project area came to a head after the Main Regulator was installed at Jugini. The BWDB-employed operator of the Main Regulator structure told me he often had to run for his life to avoid being beaten up by musclemen (interview, 2000).[24]

Those displaced by the Jamuna riverbank erosion, already among the poorest of the poor, had to move to *char* lands. JCDP, a Bhuapur NGO representing *char* dwellers, tried to file a case against FAP as a whole before the Second International Water Tribunal in Amsterdam in 1992, emboldened by the attention their protest against the Jamana Bridge had attracted.[25]

JCDP argued that the food security paradigm underlying FAP-20 (self-sufficiency in monsoon foodgrain) was an outdated one for two reasons:

(1) the biggest production advances are made not in the monsoon but winter season (*boro* crops), and
(2) 'food' only read as 'rice' neglects fish as a source of protein in people's basic food intake.

Bangladeshi NGOs played on their concerns by phrasing their case in 'conservationist' livelihoods discourse, championing the case of the fishermen. The title of the Bangladesh Centre for Advanced Studies' (BCAS) booklet on FAP, 'Rivers of Life' (Haggart, 1994), sums it up. In response to the criticisms, a new contingent of consultants was commissioned to take a closer look at biodiversity and fisheries and concluded that FAP had done little actual harm that has not been done elsewhere (e.g., De Graaf, 1999).

An international NGO-led discursive counter-alliance presented their case as a *human rights* and survival issue. Human rights derive from a securitisation of an existential threat, the transgression of a boundary (Pia and Diez, 2007). Articulation of a human right where none had been established laid bare the existence of a conflict. Sections 4.5.3 and 4.5.4 discuss how this frame played out in streets, lobbies and courts.

4.5.3 Staging Protest: Politicisation of FAP and FAP-20

> 'The Dutch are funny people. They give money to one group of people, then they give money to another to oppose what the first group is doing' (Prof. Ainun Nishat, EGIS/GoB conference talk, commenting on Dutch funding for critical Dutch NGO Both ENDS, 22 November 2000).

Initially, FAP was not a major issue with the major NGOs in Bangladesh itself (see also Adnan, 1992; Haggart, 1994) and the NGOs working in the area did not coordinate much among themselves (IOV, 1993).[26] The first anti-FAP protests were started by international NGOs in 1991. Only in 1992, the Bangladeshi NGO Proshika contributed a paper to the Rio environmental summit in 1992 and in 1993 an international flood coalition of European, American and Bangladeshi NGOs formed in Strasbourg (Stiles, 2002).

We have seen that Tangail as a project site was not selected by donors for its typicality of Bangladesh but rather its convenience. Likewise, interviewees note that NGOs perhaps did not single out the area for their protests wholly for its own merits but as a symbol that happened to be within easy reach from Dhaka. This made it feasible for Dhaka-based NGOs like Nijera Kori, a non-governmental organisation organised around activist Khushi Kabir, to mobilise and support local protest.

Thus in 1992–93, anti-FAP processions and rallies ensued in Tangail and Dhaka, which found surprising resonance in the national, but even more the international press and donor community. The 10,000 protesters mobilised were mainly women. Women's groups, such as Gram Unnayan Parishad (GUP), took a major role because of their vulnerability to land take, intimidation and unfair compensation (*Daily Star,* 1995; see also Kvaløy, 1994). Female-headed households are 35–40 per cent of all households and almost 25 per cent of all agricultural households (Hamid, cited in Hanchett, 1997; Akhter and Akhter, 1997). The Tangail protesters successfully reframed the security issue from a *national* economic development issue into a *local* human rights issue resonated in Europe and North America.[27]

The women's groups presented handwritten petitions in several villages, and played a pre-eminent role in street protests in Tangail and Dhaka. It cannot be ruled out that NGOs stage-managed these demonstrations by bussing Tangail citizens to Dhaka (Kvaløy, 1994: 39) – many of them being illiterate and clients to NGO services.[28] While the spontaneity of anti-FAP demonstrations can thus be debated, the demos did get the media attention sought. As Hajer (2005) notes, NGOs are well versed in the art of dramaturgy ('staging'). The manifestations were filmed and screened over the world. Through their excellent connections with international NGOs and donors, the Bangladeshi groups thus nourished an already effective international lobby that just grew and grew, casting doubts in the minds of the FAP consortium over the wisdom of investing in FAP. Banking on their existing extensive international network, the Bangladeshi NGOs developed a supporting alliance of NGOs and (Green) politicians in the West, which helped leverage interest and profile in Europe and the USA. The GoB did not improve things by threatening measures against involved NGOs and to invoke the Anti-Terrorism Act in Tangail in 1993.

In the Netherlands, parliamentarians had already asked questions about people's participation to the Minister in 1991. A corner was turned when in 1992 the Bangladesh People's Solidarity Centre (BPSC) sent a protest letter to the Dutch government. BPSC, ICCO, Both ENDS and other developmental NGOs coalesced and called on parliament to terminate Government of the

Netherlands support to FAP, which led to questions raised by liberal-of-the-right (VVD) Members of Parliament.

In Germany, AIO, a platform centring around anthropologist-activist Hanna Schmuck, lobbied the German government. An anti-FAP coalition formed in the European Parliament and a high-level lobby was created in the USA. NGOs helped the European Greens organise a conference in Strasbourg on 27 and 28 May 1993 (interestingly, this is not mentioned in the project's Final Report's chronology), which, the heavily criticised World Bank representative left in anger. In North America, the University of Texas teamed up with the International Rivers Network fuelling a high-power lobby calling for the withdrawal of US support (Mitchell, 1998).

In addition to social issues, FAP-20 was presented as an environmental disaster in the making. In itself, FAP-20 was not all that different from earlier (polder) projects carried out in Bangladesh for many years, with a view to alleviating the population pressure and creating productive land. In the 1970s and 1980s, land reclamation in the form of poldering mushroomed. However, Bangladesh had failed to emulate Dutch successes, in part due to lack of funds and resources to pay for powerful water pumps to discharge excess water. As a result, each polder (especially the low-lying areas within them) inevitably had to contend with drainage problems: both – the Meghna-Dhonagoda Irrigation Project (MDIP), whose dikes breached in 1987 and 1988, destroying crops and infrastructure, and the Dhaka-Narayanganj-Demra (DND) project, which saw inlets and outlets silting up and fields clogged up are fitting examples. Most famously, Beel Dakatia, which suffered so much that the soil became completely infertile in the 1980s, turning the area into a dust bowl, could be held up to the donors presenting a similar 'ecological disaster' scenario for FAP-20 with potential for 'desertification' (banglapedia.com, also Atiur Rahman, 1989).[29]

The successful international politicisation of FAP, rather than an actual 'disaster' like Beel Dakatia, must have been a surprise to all involved, not least the NGO community. Spreading horror scenarios for FAP-20 with great media savvy, the activists fed donor worries. Critical reports were now also issued by donors, who were already becoming increasingly jittery about whether they were 'doing the right thing' (Soussan, 1999). The successful NGO campaign against the Sarwar Sarovar (Narmada) dam in 1991 and the half-successful protest on behalf of the *char* people affected by the Jamuna Multi Purpose Bridge and FAP 3.1[30] had opened a window of opportunity to lobby a nervous World Bank, and the NGOs' obstructive power grew accordingly. Post-Narmada, donors became very circumspect about supporting an unpopular project. NGOs benefited from the willingness of some donors (Asian Development Bank and the Netherlands) to work with them, giving them a niche in the project, while they could at the same time side vociferously against the World Bank, who refused to engage with them (Stiles, 2002).[31] World Bank Secretary-General Wolfensohn reportedly said he did not want 'another Narmada'. This made FAP-20 a soft target for protesters.

4.5.4 See You in Court

In addition to street rallies and political lobbying, the FAP-20 project was fought in court on a human rights platform, with a smaller role for cultural heritage.[32]

Mohiuddin Farooque, the late founder and Secretary General of the Bangladesh Environmental Lawyers Association (BELA), a nationally active NGO, predicted massive unemployment, displacement of people, damage to the soil and fish habitat and creation of drainage problems (*Daily Star* Editorial, 27-4-1994). Questions were raised in Dutch Parliament about this lawsuit. Jan Pronk, the Minister of Overseas Development Assistance responded that it can take considerable time for a case to come through – lawsuits are dealt with in chronological order, and in September 1994, the time the case was filed, the Supreme Court was still dealing with 1988 cases (Rolloos, 1995).

The BELA, however, persisted and succeeded in changing the law to allow a group to litigate pro bono, i.e. on behalf of the community. The Appeals court indeed allowed him to fight the scheme on behalf of Tangail, despite not being personally affected. In this capacity he tried to stop the FAP-20 on the grounds of unconstitutionality on behalf of a Tangail citizen. Notably, in the end the Writ Bench of the High Court Division of the Supreme Court[33] ordered the government to prove that FAP-20 was in the people's interest – which the government declined to do. Despite declaring the project illegal, though, the court decided FAP-20 was too far down the line to consider stopping it.

BELA then litigated on behalf of claimants who felt wronged in the land acquisition process and seriously under-compensated for the loss of their land, taken for flood defence structures. It is an understatement to say that the system for compensation is not well developed. Only for externally funded projects are there compensation rules, but they tend to pertain to farmers only. Houscht (n.d.) notes that foreknowledge enabled landowners to build large houses on sites they knew were going to be needed for the project, expecting to make a killing in a compensation claim. Others however are not so lucky. In more recent projects, efforts are made to compensate fishermen, but the landless still get a raw deal. If paid out at all, compensation money is siphoned off by local elites. The Deputy Commissioner, the acting district head, tends to dole out much less money than claimed, and claimants need to make repeated trips to even obtain that money (Wood, 1999).[34]

4.6 FAP Part II: New (De)selection of Alternatives

We have seen that opponent moves for closure managed to reframe the problem definition, but not stop the project, which was about to move into its second phase in 1995. A series of natural events (4.6.1 and 4.6.4) and political developments (4.6.2 and 4.6.3) triggered yet more changes in the project's make-up.

4.6.1 Accidental Closure?

But by mid-1995, the FAP-20 project was suddenly hanging by a thread due to a dramatic physical event. The construction of the large Jamuna Multipurpose Bridge necessitated the closure in October 1994 of nearby river inlets of the Old Dhaleswari, which feeds the rivers Pungli and Dhaleswari, which, in turn, feed the upper areas of the Tangail (FAP-20 project) area, spanning 2,560 km^2. Hydraulic modelling revealed that this would reduce the level of the Dhaleswari river to fall by 40–50 cm and the Pungli by 100–110 cm (Hydraulic Modelling for Dhaleswari Mitigation Study – IMWBD, 1995). This would reduce flood risk, but also the benefits of irrigation and soil flushing in the area.

The Jamuna Multipurpose Bridge is a project of great symbolic, economic and political importance to Bangladesh – the bridge provides a shortcut for traffic across the Jamuna, as well as making Bangladesh an attractive transport link between two parts of India. The Bridge was an important bargaining chip for Bangladesh in sealing an agreement with India over the Ganges: in December 1996, Bangladesh obtained a hard-won bilateral 50–50 agreement with India over the river Ganges.[35] In a separate treaty, Bangladesh admitted Indian transport across its territory, which cuts the route for east-west transport for Indian businesses to the state of Assam. Interviewees (and also Waterbury, 1997) suggest the two treaties are closely linked.

But one branch of government apparently did not know what the other was planning: there had been no communications between the Roads Ministry, in charge of the Bridge, and BWDB or the FAP team. Some water was still coming from two minor spill channels, which due to increased hydraulic head developed a steeper gradient and had started to scour, and from the New Dhaleswari intake. But for all practical purposes, the closure would render FAP-20 practically meaningless.

On the initiative of FAP-20, the Ministry of Water Resources called an inter-ministerial committee representing all parties concerned. Between March and June 1995 the committee drafted a report proposing a new intake channel, 100 m in width, to be constructed in the next two years.

But on 8 July 1995, as a FAP-20 workshop report has it (Euroconsult et al., 1995: 64), 'Nature intervened' by way of a 'spontaneous breakthrough' of a stretch of riverbank south of the closure, which found its way into the (blocked, minor) First Spill channel. The water broke through from the Jamuna into the Dhaleswari taking several hundreds of houses with it in the process. Conspiracy theories abounded.[36]

Meanwhile, it was crunch time for FAP-20 at the decision-making level. By 1994 most FAP studies had been completed or aborted; only pilots like FAP-20 were due to continue. FPCO's evaluation of FAP in October 1994[37] had culminated in an extensive wish list for 65 projects to be implemented in the next 10 years. A full fifth of the budget for this programme would be taken up by a prospective Bangladeshi Farakka Dam on the Ganges – although Biswas and Uitto (2001) claim that it makes no sense to build a dam there, since Bangladesh is a delta. Bangladesh would indeed favour dam construction upstream in Nepal, but this would require a multilateral treaty, which India is not keen on.

The Association of Bangladeshi Engineers claimed with a textbook 'There is no alternative' (TINA)-type move for closure:

> . . . (d)ifferent study reports [unnamed in the document, JW] indicate that Bangladesh to feed her teeming millions in the future and meet other sectoral water needs has no other alternative but to go for barrages in the major rivers. (Association of Bangladeshi Engineers, 1995)

But most plans were shot down by a World Bank 'advisory memorandum' to FPCO. A revised version produced by FPCO and the Panel of Experts, known as the 'Water Strategy Paper', which appeared six months later, in March 1995, avoided any mention of the FAP and turned out to be a very different and much more modest five-year programme (Huq–Rahman, 1995). The Flood Action Plan was renamed the Bangladesh Water and Flood Management Strategy (GoB, 1995). Instead of new hydraulic structures, the paper aimed at the development of a national water plan, institutional strengthening and integrated water management, which now meant round-the-year water management.

To the great disappointment of the Association, the Water Strategy Paper 'tactfully denies the possibility of construction of barrage [*sic*] on the major rivers of the country' (Association of Bangladeshi Engineers, 1995). This, again, was an exaggeration: that document and the FAP-II budget still provided for a Bangladeshi Farakka Dam on the Ganges, to respond to the lost influx due to the Indian Farakka Dam.[38] This dam, however, has not been built so far.

A new donor conference held in December 1995 did not lead to concrete pledges, but recommended better stakeholder involvement in any water-management investment and activities, more sustainability and a national water management plan.

4.6.2 BWDB Hegemony under Fire

When the Flood Action Plan started, the idea of integrated water management was still way off the map. Bangladesh experiences river floods and rainwater floods inland, and tidal and storm-surge floods in the coastal zone. The Flood Action Plan only tackles river floods. Bangladesh had diverted all its resources on flood protection in flood-prone areas rather than treating floods as part of an annual cycle of flood and drought that affects the whole country.[39] While there was a water planning institute – the Water Resources Planning Organizaton (WARPO) – that could have taken a comprehensive view, the Government of Bangladesh and its donors chose to superimpose a Flood Protection Coordination Organisation to coordinate, supervise and monitor the FAP works. This consisted of experts seconded from the Ministry of Irrigation, Water Development and Flood Control. More than BWDB, the FPCO was exposed to external influences (pressures), causing the IOV report to exult that FAP was 'unprecedented' in the level of cooperation between donors and recipients (IOV, 1993). A *Panel* of local and international *experts*, mainly funded by the UNDP, was formed to lend advice. It was expanded in 1992 to incorporate a wider range of disciplines.

However, the BWDB did not easily adapt to the new winds blowing in the field of water management, planning and practice. It traded on its earlier successes in coastal management and has taken a long time to learn to live with criticism and adapt. Security, to the Board, lies in control, hierarchy and technical indicators, rather than initiative; making mistakes is punished, in other words: the culture is risk-averse, which is likely to stifle innovation. One recently retired BWDB engineer told me that the BWDB has a centralised, rigid rotation system with little institutional memory. Normally, no evaluation takes place of completed projects, as BWDB views itself as too short of resources for this (interview, December 2000). Indeed the Dutch ODA Inspectorate (IOV) report of 1993 had tersely noted, 'FPCO and BWDB have been short on learning capacity'. However, despite complaints on the part of senior and retired BWDB engineers I interviewed, who felt that after a golden age up until about 1975, quality has gone down, *esprit de corps* is very high.

The 1995 donor conference recommended structural reform of the water sector. The World Bank plan forced the BWDB to shed several thousand of its staff, and restructure to incorporate more disciplines. In 1995 FPCO merged with WARPO, which was originally set up to prepare the national water management strategy. In 2006 BWDB was 'twinned' with the Dutch public works department, which itself had gone through numerous downscaling reforms. 'They [BWDB] know if they don't change they are going to die' (interview, Bangladeshi consultant, 2000).

On the basis of new *Guidelines for participation* (version 2000), the BWDB now hoped to 'solve' its burden by trying to hand more projects over to a still weak local government. This gave momentum to the pendulum swing towards smaller, decentralised projects, boosting the role of the local government ministry, LGED. Upgraded from the Local Government Engineering Bureau in 1992, LGED's strength lies in small local projects, and it now increasingly competes with BWDB for funding.

4.6.3 Critical Donors

The changed donor climate had important consequences for FAP-20. Both donors sent Ministerial Missions (1995, 1996 and 1997) and at various instances questioned the wisdom of pushing ahead. Questions were again raised in the Dutch House of Commons about the lack of participatory opportunities. The liberal-conservative party VVD pointed at the minority opinion of one member of the ODA inspectorate's report (IOV) inspection team of 1993 who disagreed with the report's conclusion that the project should go ahead.

The donors were annoyed enough with the controversy over participation to dramatically swap consultancies after the mid-term report. Formally, the reasons for Euroconsult's replacement by Haskoning are 'confidential' – the report intimates that they are not flexible enough and also too costly (Schulte Nordholt et al., 1995). However, while those interviewees who brought up their experiences with the Dutch consultant were less than enthusiastic about Euroconsult's performance, a measure of scapegoating and personal politics was strongly implied (interview Dutch consultant, 2000). It is also noted that the mid-term evaluation report was not officially ratified by the donors (CPP Final report, 2000) and it was not agreed by the interviewees that the new consultant did much better than the former consultancy.

Presumably, in response to all the turmoil the project management radically changed its stance locally by 1995. In December 1994, an Information Centre was opened at Tangail. It made impressive efforts to inform the public and listen to its demands. Kamal Siddiqi and his team leaders frequently visited the area and held meetings to motivate people and listen to their views. The leadership also put in several accompanying measures, such as roads, which had not been part of the original plan and a structure of eight different gates in the regulator to regulate fish access. The project even issued an anthology of press reports on FAP called *The Press Speaks* (FPCO, September 1995) including some coverage of the BELA legal notice to stop FAP-20.

In 1995 FAP-20 still ranked as a priority project (FPCO, 1995). But the excitement with the donors had clearly waned as the project reached ever more troubled waters. After the Germans threatened to stop funding after the 1996 mission, yet another overhaul was instigated based on a reformulation mission (Knaub, 1996; Datta et al., 1997). This new system, worked out in 1997, created room for fishermen, landless and women, however, it still did not take account existing informal local problem-solving, binding arbitration councils consisting of village elders (*salish*) and preferring to superimpose a new system instead. The guidelines were later characterised as 'confusing' by the Dutch ODA Minister, Jan Pronk (Final Report, 2000).

4.6.4 The 1998 Flood and the Project Aftermath

Just when the momentum for FAP was clearly lost, Bangladesh experienced the 'flood of the century' in 1998. Like in 1988, over 2,000 people died, millions lost their homes. Despite the losses, flood response counts as a success because there was no famine, vindicating Sen's endowment theory. The flood also was a major test for FAP-20.

While the Embankment Management groups, established to maintain the structures for the long run, had been less than dynamic – too much trouble for too little gain – but as the project area's residents could see the water rising with their naked eye, they put in joint efforts to reinforce and raise the embankments. While outside the project area, the majority of the country found themselves 8 metre under water, FAP-20 remained a dry spot. In fact people interviewed by Chadwick et al. (2001) in Jugini, inside the project area, complained that the flow was too low, so that insufficient floodwater reached their paddy fields and (agricultural) pollution was insufficiently diluted. The area received an inflow from people from the Jamuna left bank, which was fast eroding, using their social network and squatting on *khas* (government) land.

Some participatory principles took hold in national policy. In the run-up to the NWMP, a large countrywide People's Participation project was carried out to inventory what kind of water problems people identified and what types of solutions they preferred – if, far from flawlessly. Thus lay knowledge now plays a role alongside expert knowledge. 'You can discuss [i.e. debate, JW] the methodology but the *concept* is accepted' (interview, Bangladeshi consultant).

In the end, UNDP's (1995) prediction that the 'apparent attempt to approve FAP and secure funding for some of its major components before [. . .] public debate, will cost Bangladesh dearly' was well observed, but one wonders if there is no question of post-rationalisation. Would the donors and UNDP have been so critical if NGOs had been less successful at mobilising the press and public opinion against FAP?

The goals evolved and goalposts moved quite significantly over time. The water management philosophy changed dramatically in the 11 short years between 1989 and 2000. The protest coalition's frame was successful in that the water paradigm shifted away from FCD/I (Flood Control, Drainage and Irrigation) and the importance of fisheries is now accepted in the National Water Management Plan of 2000. Participatory ideas were enshrined in that plan, new actors found a place within the regime, while others were restructured.

In 1995 it was admitted that one of the key objectives was already outdated – rather than quick disposal of monsoon water, retention for the dry season now became key. After the reformulation mission, the main criterion became whether compartmentalisation is a good investment for contemporary Bangladesh. This made the issue much more *economic* in nature, a benchmark it signally failed (CPP Final Report, 2000).

The *cost-benefit* analysis of the project itself elicited much scorn in my interviewees. The internal rate of return of a project is supposed to be 12 per cent. However, as a Bangladeshi consultant told me in 2000, the consultant who does not 'get' that figure will not get the job, and the only way of protesting an approach you dislike is to 'get' exactly 12.0 per cent. 'They cook up a certain benefit, increased production. They don't know if it brings those benefits' (interview, Bangladeshi consultant). A Bangladeshi NGO representative calls it 'eyewash' (Bangla NGO interview, 2000). No matter the cooking, for FAP-20 the Internal Rate of Return turned out dismal. The final project evaluation report (2000) somehow comes up with 3.1 per cent, which it judges to be 'hardly attractive'. After some re-accounting in which some project cost is reassigned to projects other than FAP-20 (as was done for the Jamuna Bridge), the IRR yields 7.3 per cent, which is still too low for the discounting benchmark. The Final Report pointedly asks whether 12 per cent is a reasonable discount rate standard for any water project and notes that the intangible value, delivery from 'fear of flooding', would itself justify many projects in developed countries. Yet it seems to undercut this point by noting the standard of protection is a rather modest 1:20 (CPP Final Report, 2000: main report). But as the FAP-20 team leader commented (interview, 2007) EUR 10 million for 10,000 ha (actually 13,305, see KfW, 2004) may sound like a lot, but the economic internal rate of return (EIRR) will never be impressive for any *pilot* project – had the concept been repeated, economies of scale might have been realised.

In 2000 an internal WARPO review decided FAP-20 was neither replicable nor sustainable (Latif, pers. comm., 2000). Given the experiences with FAP, no large river schemes are likely to be funded externally any time soon perhaps, unless an even bigger disaster strikes.

When I visited the project site in late 2000, any sign of donor presence had gone, the Tangail project information office was nearly abandoned, and any remaining business was taken care of by a diploma engineer rather than a university-trained civil engineer, and a local consultant who would be leaving after four months. Despite having been on the case for 18 months, the engineer did not seem to know anything about the project, and is looking forward to his retirement in 6 months (interview, consultant Tangail). Some funds were set aside for Operation and Maintenance, but nothing much was done with it (interview, Team Leader). 'Land grabbing' on the riverbank reportedly has further encroached and polluted the river, especially in Tangail Town.[40] This was confirmed by two Dutch thesis students staying in Tangail for four months in 2007, who reported that many of the 65 structures put in place (15–20 were never built) were in bad shape, with channels being filled in to build a house on. The committees had all disintegrated, apart from one committee near the Regulator, members of which freely admitted their committee was only for show when donors come to visit. Their interviews did support the view that the need to consult and work with local people has taken root in BWDB, in part due to the FAP experiences.

4.7 Compartmentalisation of Knowledge: FAP as a Programme of Studies

The final received wisdom is to present FAP as nothing more than a programme of studies. The objective of the Compartmentalisation Pilot Project (FAP-20) was to gather experience with the planning, construction and operation of compartments in the flood plain of the Jamuna River while taking the local water management, institutional and socio-economic conditions into account (KfW, 2004).

Since FAP has come to be seen as a research programme rather than an action programme, it makes sense to look into it as such in terms of knowledge generation and dissemination within the decision-making regime.[41] Those who saw FAP as a *study-based* exercise to find ways to minimise flood damages are not too unhappy with the outcomes. In the press (e.g. the *Daily Star* of 19 July 1995) and in interviews with Bangladeshi engineers, project leaders professed satisfaction that the project showed compartmentalisation could indeed be done. But as we saw earlier, an obsession with deadlines led to rushed implementation before proper needs assessment, modelling and data-gathering had been carried out, so that the cart was put before the horse.

Apart from compartmentalisation, other approaches such as flood-proofing were indeed studied in the Flood Action Plan as a whole and, as we saw, there was increasing room for a critical researcher approach as the project progressed, so that local knowledge and practices (Chadwick et al., 1998) become more widely known. So if, as Ericksen et al. (n.d.), claim,

> [t]he spirit of FAP is . . . to examine the advantages and disadvantages of a range of alternatives for dealing with the abnormal flood problem and to combine the best options for various locations across the country (my emphasis, J.W.),

we can conclude that the closure arrived at in the 1989 London conference was not absolute.

The research debunked some of the stronger claims made by opponents. NGOs claimed in front of the Dutch and German Development Ministers, Spranger and Pronk, that five or six villages in the FAP-20 area were turning into sand bowls. A political point had been scored, but when research on desertification was commissioned, 'we couldn't find anything' (interview, Bangladeshi researcher).

Interviewees contracted to do qualitative research felt they were pressured by their principals to skimp on their thoroughness by imposing impossible deadlines. Consultancies hiring them often had little truck with qualitative research associated with need assessments and researchers felt the end reports were sanitised to comply with donor and GoB wishes. All researchers I talked to felt uneasy about the fate of their findings, ranging from misrepresentation to suppression of findings (interviews, also Soussan, 1999). Over time, researchers and consultants learned to stipulate no interference with the result, or that their findings could be published in accessible form elsewhere.

4.8 Conclusion

Compartmentalisation is, in a metaphorical sense, a state of mind. It is to see things as separate from each other rather than related (Kemp, 2004). 'Despite subsequent attempts to rewrite its genesis' (Faaland et al., 1995) the emphasis and starting point for the Flood Action Plan was a Flood Control and Drainage (FCD) approach – a technical fix with well-intended participatory add-ons, but politicised by NGOs and local groups. While the compromise contained structural as well as non-structural aspects, the emphasis was on structures for agriculture.

The Flood Action Plan was the biggest riverine flood protection project ever proposed in Bangladesh. But it was scaled down well before it took off, and in 1995, only the compartmentalisation project continued. The intervention that became emblematic of the Flood Action Plan, FAP-20, affects an area of only 13,305 ha. FAP therefore was neither the 'mega-project' the French envisaged (Boyce, 1990) nor what its critics claimed it had become, or even a predominantly structural flood programme. In hindsight, it was beside the point for FAP critics to zero in on the supposed enormity of the technology – the embankments and compartmentalisation. The billion-dollar 'mega-project' Boyce had warned about in 1990 was scaled back to a US$200 million programme of studies for FAP as a whole. A number of low embankments that were already in place before FAP, collectively known as the 'Tangail Horseshoe' built in the 1960s under the World Food Programme, were strengthened and supplemented under FAP-20. But far too many structures were put in place (engineers now acknowledge this) that can clog up the channels, creating drainage problems. Moreover some structures failed, as did FAP-21, the heroic attempt to rehabilitate 225 km of the Brahmaputra Right Bank Embankment project.[42]

Significantly, FAP became emblematic of a much wider range of contests about state-society relations (representation) and Bangladesh-donor relations, state-market relations (privatisation) and the balance between agriculture and fisheries. Reforms and participatory initiatives were implemented but failed to improve the sustainability of the project beyond its completion date.

FAP was originally legitimised with reference to 'physical security' and resisted on a human rights platform. A concern with security (saving lives) was clearly the impetus behind FAP as a whole, but the nature of Bangladeshi life provides less clear-cut positions in the balance between protection and risk-taking than it does in the Netherlands, so that the 'fight against the floods' made less sense in a Bangladeshi context. Apart from some local demonstrators, FAP-20 did not rate as a physical security concern in the debate.

Indeed, the constituency of project beneficiaries changed dramatically in the course of the project. At the outset, the flood management objective benefited landholders, while apparently not excessively damaging other stakeholders. While Tangail Town was originally not provided for under FAP-20, in the end, there was a consensus among the local interviewees I spoke to that the main beneficiaries were the townspeople keeping dry feet rather than the farmers.

Both the river as threat (physical security) and human rights (vulnerability) were equivocal in Bangladesh, and had more immediate resonance with a European and American than a local audience. They also reinforced mutual stereotypes and antagonisms between 'engineers' and 'sociologists', strengthened by a lack of communication between them. The politicisation of the project forced a *rapprochement* between the two, which also catalysed more integrated thinking on water management and participation, which is now widely regarded as positive. The opposition to FAP managed to push a more 'integrated' problem definition by putting environmental and livelihood (fishing, cattle and groundwater) issues on the map. Protesters placed the 'development and participation for whom?' issue squarely on the agenda and successfully counter-securitised human rights by staging their protest in a media-friendly way.

The *discourse alliance* (Hajer, 1995) in the Bangladesh case, therefore, can be summarised as a combination of political fatalism and engineering dominance (control) for economic security, based on securitised food security, while the *counter-alliance* counter-securitised livelihoods, human rights and, ultimately, sovereignty.

Probably the most powerful element in the mix was the way the oppositional alliance within and outside Bangladesh managed to portray (frame) FAP as a whole as a most unwelcome external intervention – in which Bangladeshis were treated like guinea pigs in a laboratory experiment. For them, the flood plan was more like a 'protection racket' (after Tilly, 1985) than a help, as transferred technologies: compartmentalisation and poldering did not quite translate. The apparent similarities between Dutch and Bangladeshi landscape are gainsaid by the power of the Jamuna, which is rather greater than that of the Rhine, and the absence of an economic support base.[43] But apart from a manageable physical environment, compartmentalisation also depends on high standards of construction, O&M and a stable rule framework, which is sadly deficient in Bangladesh.

As a programme of action research FAP set out to kill perhaps too many flies with one swat. It provided a research opportunity to minutely chart the hydrological and socio-economic situation in a small area. Compartmentalisation and (the later conception of) participation proved more popular as an idea than their opponents would have it, but both compartmentalisation and participation were far from self-propelling. While in hindsight a great deal was learned, whether transferability of this information to the national scale was achieved or even possible is doubtful. The intention of the Government of Bangladesh to replicate findings came to nothing and there was limited use of results.

The success of the NGO lobby seems to have been due to its ability to provide a contrasting paradigm that struck a chord with the *Zeitgeist.* The opponents to FAP wisely concentrated on a human rights platform rather than 'living with the flood'. They would have a hard time defending 'living with the flood' in the light of the livelihood consequences of the 1988 flood. While they could successfully claim that post-flood years bring bumper harvests, the winners and losers from this bumper harvest are not the same people, as Houscht (n.d.) notes. 'Living with the flood' in Bangladesh is neither symbiotic nor conflict-free because of the many deaths and relocations floods bring.

As the concise history above has shown, it is not unthinkable the pendulum will swing the other way again. Until that pendulum swing, the grand ambition to eliminate floods forever has given way to an acceptance of uncertainty and institutional reform. When in 1998, the worst flood of the twentieth century,[44] the number of fatalities was lower than in 1988 (official figure: 1,050), this was attributed to investment in better flood preparedness (Ahmad et al., 1998) and, by some, to an improved food management system inspired by West Bengali economist Amartya Sen's (1981) theory of entitlements. This seemed to drive home the point that rivers are not the main problem and structures not the main solution.

When in 2004, around 600 people died in another bad flood, the water agenda had shifted to other concerns. It had been noted before that the Flood Action Plan only marginally addresses *cyclones*, which are the bigger killer by far. A cyclone hitting Chittagong in April 1991 claimed around 140,000 fatalities by drowning, deafeningly resonating the 1970 cyclone that took 200,000 lives. The number of fatalities claimed by floods is a relatively modest figure compared to cyclone fatalities, and with better management it can be significantly reduced – hence the new CPP: Cyclone Protection Project. Coastal protection and water contamination with arsenic are now seen as far bigger threats to popular well-being in Bangladesh.

Nevertheless, in 2006 the Asian Development Bank decided to follow up on its original Flood Action Plan project in the region of Khulna-Jessore, FAP 4, in the Southwest Area IWRM project. Many of the regional FAP reports were uncovered and original consultants like Dirk Frans were contacted. It seems that compartmentalisation is getting its second (or third) wind in this project, and this time 'water security' does feature in the project document.[45]

Glossary

Beel A low-lying depression in the flood plain that generally contains water throughout the year, a small lake or backswamp

Khal A natural channel, minor river or a tidal creek

Hartal General strike

Khas Commons, owned by the state or religious community

Mastan Thug, hired to beat people up

Thana The administrative unit of local government above the union level, consisting of three to ten *unions* (the lowest unit of government in Bangladesh)

5

THE MAASWERKEN PROJECT

FIXING A HOLE?

5.1 Introduction

The Dutch are famous the world over for draining and poldering marshes. So thorough were they that only 3 per cent of the country is still marshland. The developed land was defended with dikes and embankments. When a high-water event hit the southeast in 1993 and 1995, the Netherlands had not seen a riverine flood since 1926. The near-flooding of the river Maas (Meuse) served as a wake-up call for the southern province of Limburg. Dramatic pictures at Borgharen, where the Maas enters Dutch territory, incited national politicians to make bold promises: 1-in-250-year safety by 2005 and 100 per cent coverage of the whole Maas in 2015 (van Leeuwen et al., 2002).

The crisis event opened a window for special legislation in which everything seemed possible: special powers, unlimited resources, informal cooperation with citizens and a new lease on life for a languishing project, Maaswerken, to enhance the area's natural beauty by broadening and deepening the river, self-contained financially from the sale of gravel dug up from the riverbed. While the original project focussed on the Common (or Border) Maas area, the Southernmost stretch, which is a recognised site of great natural beauty, the plan developed into something much bigger after the flood of 1995.

The case study especially zooms in on what became a contentious issue: was flood defence really a security issue, and therefore eligible for urgent, special treatment, as the province of Limburg claimed?

This chapter sketches this debate as it traces the highs and lows of the Maaswerken plan from its conception in 1985 to its contractual formalisation

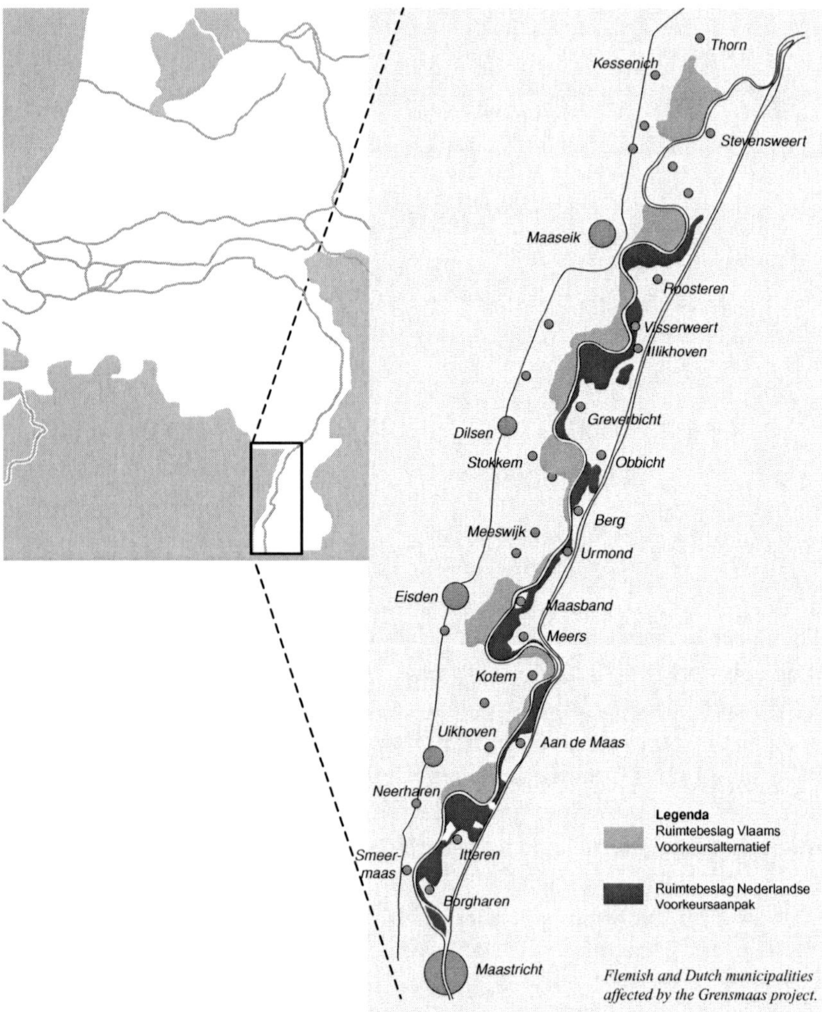

Figure 5.1: ***Location of the Grensmaas; river section shared by the Netherlands and Belgium. Both the Dutch and the Belgians have sometimes competing river plans. Dutch preferences for the Maas interventions are shown in dark shading, Belgian preferences in light grey***

dirty decisions were made that, however, cast a long shadow over the project's future, both under central (Sections 5.3 and 5.4) and provincial (Section 5.5) leadership. Section 5.3 discusses how the definition of security came to be played out in the context of the perennial struggle between Holland and Limburg, West and South, core and periphery. I will look at the various actors' legitimisation and delegitimisation strategies, which impinge on the definition (framing) and reframing of the problem.

5.2 How the Floods Saved the Maaswerken

5.2.1 Quarrying for Nature: An Uneasy Compromise

The Maas originates in northern France, near Nancy, and carves out a deep valley in France and Belgium before entering the Netherlands at Eijsden, where it is a natural border between the Netherlands and Belgium for 50 km. The Maas has 30 tributaries, some of which cross country borders, so that catchment, in fact, includes Luxembourg and a minor part of Germany. As the river changed its course in the past millennia, the Maas left a large fen in Central Limburg and as the earth crust rose, it caused the river to carve out new valleys, the older flood plain became what are now river terraces. As a consequence, the river is deeper than the hinterland, unlike the West Netherlands, so that floods do not cause damage beyond the area immediately bordering the river.

Given the area's low population (Grensmaas: 15,000 inhabitants in 1998), extensive agriculture (2,260 ha of agricultural land; MER Grensmaas, 1998) and relatively high altitude respective to sea level, there has not been an obvious need to dike up the river Maas in most areas down to Mook and Boxmeer. The Grensmaas, however, was fixed between 1860 and 1890 as a narrow trench of some 60 m width. As a result, the river speeded up and eroded the gravel riverbed.

By Dutch standards the Grensmaas has a steep drop – 45 cm per km – as it enters the Netherlands over 800 km from its source, after which the gradient flattens sharply, and the river loses its momentum. This stretch of the Maas, from Maastricht to Maasbracht, was originally a braided river, a system of gullies with natural gradients and low-lying islands which were frequently flooded. This is an unpredictable river stretch: the mean discharge, 230 m^3/s, is not a very informative figure. As the rain-fed Maas is prone to extremes, from flash floods of 3,100 m^3/s (in 1993) to zero, an effective flood warning system is no luxury (Duivenvoorden, 1997). The steep drop makes the Maas the only Dutch whitewater river, and badly suited to shipping. As ships can use a side channel, the Julianakanaal, the absence of navigation benefits the survival of rare fish species.

The Grensmaas (Border or Common Maas) forms the border with Belgium. The stretch following the Grensmaas is called the Zandmaas (Sandy Maas), because its slower flow promotes sand and silt, which are commercially not very interesting. By contrast, the faster-moving Grensmaas deposits gravel. Given these valuable gravel deposits, the otherwise scenic Maas has been exploited as an economic resource. Quarrying deepened the river, creating thousands of unsightly gravel pits in southern Limburg, filled up with water and used for pleasure boating (*Maasplassen*). Gravel digging also generates noise, dust pollution and heavy transport. Cracks in houses still evidence damage from the vibrations that come with digging. Together with nature organisations, citizens from the affected towns staged protests.

Meanwhile a greening of Dutch river management was taking place. Environmental conservationists started the fire, but were joined in 1980 by notable citizens protesting the damage dike reinforcement would do to the historic town of Bakel, Central Netherlands. This heralded a new era in river management in which acceptance of security measures could not be taken for granted. Environmental consciousness also affected within government, where 'green engineers' in the Departments of Agriculture and Public Works made their influence felt. The World Wildlife Fund's 'Living Rivers' (Helmer et al., 1992) report championed untamed, unconstrained rivers. Giving the river more space to braid and meander seemed an exciting perspective. Such visions inspired several 'green engineers' to take a fresh look at the Maas' potential to create 1,500 ha of natural values that could form part of a national ecological main structure linking habitats throughout the Netherlands.

The earliest ideas for a comprehensive, greener approach to the Maas valley date back from 1984. The concept of developing nature came from a group of driven civil servants from the Agriculture and Water Departments, in response to a contest set by the National Planning Agency. The underlying dilemma was that agriculture, still a powerful sector, is not a good basis for nature conservation, while just buying up land for straightforward conservation seems like a wasted opportunity. Quarrying seemed to offer promising opportunities for integrated regional development to create 'new nature' and improve 'spatial quality' (Klink, 1985, 1986; de Bruin, 1987; Stroming, 1990).

At the turn of the 1990s, the provincial government decided to phase out quarrying, bringing the hope for citizens to be rid of the nuisance after 70 years of excavations. To safeguard the future of the excavation, industry gravellers and the province concluded a voluntary agreement in 1990 to dig up 35 million tonnes more, designating the Maas valley as the final site for quarrying – the last profitable gravel site in the Netherlands. Limburg's Provincial Council issued its intention for a preliminary Environmental Impact Assessment (EIA) for a provincial excavation plan in November 1990. This EIA however was aborted due to NGO pressures for a more environmental approach (Teisman, 1995).

Combining gravel digging with environmental beautification seemed an elegant way out of a bad situation. Inspired by the French river Allier, which the plan's initiators liken to the look of the Maas in earlier times (Stroming, 1990), the project envisages an exciting natural stream with an interesting variety of habitats. Instead of fixing the riverbank, the original channel is broadened, which creates space to reduce the flood risk. The topsoil, which is commercially worthless, is used to fill the holes created by gravel digging. The Grensmaas river broadening project thus became a nature development project with an additional role for flood protection.

The intention to carry out the 'Maas valley project' was formalised between the Ministry of Agriculture, Nature and Fisheries, the Ministry of Transport and Public Works (Rijkswaterstaat), and the province of Limburg in November 1992, after which the Netherlands Economic Institute (NEI) and Twijnstra Gudde, a well-known Dutch consultancy, were commissioned to calculate the project's financial viability.

But the voluntary agreement gave rise to conspiracy theories about political deal-making to suit the gravellers. Due to the prior history of resource excavation in Limburg, public trust was already decidedly low. In the early 1990s the province of Limburg was plagued by political scandals over construction and gravel extraction. For example, in 1986 Aqua Terra, a shell company, bought and enclosed 8,000 ha of privatised lakes, arable land and campsites at less than EUR 3 million, which some provincial political parties considered an unlikely bargain. Moreover, the original 'green-for-gravel' deal had been promoted by a prominent mayor, Riem, who was later incriminated for taking kickbacks and having overly cosy relations with, among others, Panheel and Van den Biggelaar, two key gravel companies involved in the current project (Dohmen, 1996). This history was to haunt the Maas works for a long time to come.

5.2.2 The Flood Window (1995–97)

In response to the 1993 and 1995 high-water events, the outlook changed radically in Limburg. The 1993 flood led to the evacuation of 8,000 people and a financial damage assessed at the time at NLG 250 million, some EUR 122 million. While nobody died, the quick-onset floods caused considerable shock. Older generations were used to water nuisance, and would flood-proof their house. But new residents, especially those whose Limburg properties were second homes, were not so flood-aware. They found the flooding of their basement garages and fitted carpets unacceptable.

After that first flood, timed close to the May 1994 elections, national politicians and press flocked to Limburg, sharing the outrage that a flood could happen in this day and age, and promising compensation and security measures. True to Dutch form, an advisory commission for the Maas, named after its chairman, Boertien, was instated to examine what should be done. It favoured broadening and deepening the rivers to accommodate a large river volume rather than raising dikes (see Table 5.2), along with some adjustments in sewer piping and spatial planning.

It is at this point that a triad gravel-nature, development-security and the 'zero budget' precondition took centre stage. At that time, the potential for cost recovery by combining nature development and broadening the river through gravel extraction was perceived as a major selling point. Gravel extraction would double or triple the river channel's width and lower the flood plain over the 45 km Grensmaas stretch. After shallow gravel extraction for broadening and deepening the river, the Maas would be left to its own devices which, it was hoped, would create a varied, attractive form of wilderness.

The Boertien report claimed its preferred alternative ('2b') could be self-funding at no additional cost. Consultants interviewed in 2000 expressed strong doubts about this claim, though. An important factor in justifying a flood scheme is the damage avoided, inferred from the actual damage in past floods. One consultant doubted the damage assessment for 1993, and noted it was a mistaken assumption that the project would involve no extra costs for the project consortium other than for the economy as a whole. Finally, he noted, '2b' was the alternative marred by the greatest degree of uncertainty. While proponents promised a billion Dutch guilders (approx. EUR 440 million) in additional economic activity and a boost for tourism, no one could predict with any certainty whether the costs and benefits of the project would cancel out. This uncertainty was noted with some frequency in press and other interviews as well. Van Leeuwen et al. (2002), to cite one figure, quote a 10–25 per cent fluctuation in gravel revenue.

In the closing days of January 1995, however, the water again was at peak levels. Some 8,500 people left their homes while others braced themselves for the flood at home. Unlike the Rhine and Waal area in Gelderland, where 250,000 people were evacuated (see next chapter) the Maas did actually flood at Borgharen and Itteren (two parishes near Maastricht) and the cities of Venlo and Roermond further downstream.

Jolted by the public outrage, the Limburg authorities now expressed a far more favourable attitude to the Grensmaas project. The Provincial Council now was fully behind '2b' but demanded much faster project implementation than the projected 15–20 years, and wanted more money from the national government to realise this.

This was not as far-fetched as it may seem today. Despite the fact that no dikes breached and damage was much more limited than in late 1993, the national authorities really went all-out. A Delta Plan for the three main rivers, Maas, Rhine and Waal, was fast-tracked through Parliament and a series of temporary flood defences were planned along the main rivers.

Informal and Formal Governance

As a first, largely symbolic (Teisman, 1995) response to the high-water events, *kaden* were put into place under an emergency decision-making regime. *Kaden*, literally, quays, are earth embankments covered by impermeable clay. There are two types of *kaden*: revetments in residential areas and 'green embankments' for rural areas. These embankments were built around several flood-prone villages to provide protection against 50-year floods; the entire project is to bring this flood risk down to 250-year floods.

The emergency measures taken in the framework of the Deltaplan Grote Rivieren (DGR) enabled a fast-track process accompanied, it appears from the interviews, by a great deal of informality. To realise the crash programme, the DGR pushed aside all legal directives governing permits and exemptions. The Special Law governing the DGR, to remain in force until January 2001, bypassed all regulations, including the normally compulsory EIA (Dolfing, 1996a, b; Driessen and De Gier, 1997a). It extended the existing Expropriation Law which already provided for the 'immediate sequestration' of lands where no amicable settlement was possible: where a clear and present danger is applicable, restrictions can be declared inapplicable. It was feared that this would not hold once the danger had passed and the waters had receded, so these powers were extended. One need not have worried, though: out of the 600 cases where land was needed to enable the flood measures in Limburg; only two required formal impoundment, the rest of the cases were settled amicably. Social control to cooperate was high: no one wanted to be (seen to be) in the way of greater safety (Driessen and De Gier, 1997a).

Where residents started to worry about the loss of so-called LNC-values (landscape, nature and culture), which the Advisory Commission for the Maas prioritises, the *Raad van State* (Council of State) ruled that residents' interests (i.e. *dry feet*) *should* prevail.

Many stakeholders had other concerns at this time. They just demanded the fastest possible implementation and a higher safety standard. 'Everything was possible,' as one respondent puts it. Decisions were made on the hoof backed up by 'reparation laws': when the plans proved illegal or risky, reparation measures were rushed through, legalising facts on the ground. All this resulted in substantial changes in the programme of works being made, which were often at odds with zoning and environmental directives. After the 1993 floods, planning permission was effectively blocked. But in the general atmosphere of cooperation and informality, the drawings were frequently changed to accommodate local interests. A little-known but telling example emerging from the interviews concerns the soccer grounds at Borgharen. In the original plans, these grounds were not to be protected from the Maas – only the residential area would be ring-diked. Local developers however had set their sights on the grounds for a housing project, 170 properties in all. Once the football grounds fell within the protected area, the development remained safe – and so it went.

Under the DGR, the water management boards (*Waterschappen*) were charged with the implementation of the *kaden* programme, and given NLG 100 million (EUR 45.3) to do this. The Waterschappen are venerable, elected functional bodies, which exist in parallel to territorially based provincial government under different accountability patterns – initiated by farmers and monasteries as early as the thirteenth century, they operated separately from the public sector until they were incorporated in 1992. The boards hammered out the details of the *kade* plan in close consultation with local authorities and a heavy input on the part of the consultancies. These Waterschappen convened every conceivable action committee, took them round the area and inventoried everyone's wish lists, varying from people who did not want a *kade* in their front garden to a parish that did not want to be split in two by a *kade*.

In the process, the Waterschappen feel, much local knowledge was gained from citizens who knew a great deal about past Maas flood patterns. All in all, cooperation with local actors and contractors went, as two interviewees put it, 'perfectly'.

But things went a little too smooth for the provincial government's liking. A provincial interviewee noted:

> [F]ast-track decision-making has its risks too. The Zandmaas project is a 'calamity' project, which [fear of calamity] is always poor counsel. You will always be overtaken by new ideas. (interview, project leader)

The provincial authorities progressively pulled out of the informal consultations, fearing it would come to blows with the national authorities. Where the Waterschappen saw positive societal energies released by calamity legislation, others saw as a monster: the fast-tracking was condemned by the national Comptroller and the Council of State. For some in The Hague, the bunds episode was seen as another example of how things go out of hand when done the Limburg way (interviews). This has had its repercussions on the Maaswerken multi-project, which in future was to be far more tightly controlled from The Hague than the *kade*-raising operation.

It should be noted that within *Rijkswaterstaat,* several civil engineers actually advised against the *kaden* – preferring to adjust the resilience of residences to the river's variability, e.g. through flood-proofing of the most at-risk properties (van der Ven and van Dooren, 1998: 14). Flood-proofing, incidentally, could be another useful application for polluted sediment, which could be used for building mounds for raising houses (*terpen*) in new or existing locations for flood-proofing. Still, when confronted with this alternative, one interviewee, a noted expert, rebutted the idea (flood-proofing) on financial grounds: 'Raising a house costs NLG 100,000 (EUR 43,500) per house. Raising 14,000 houses would cost 1.4 billion (EUR 635 million).'[1]

As a result of the two high-water events, the flood protection element in the Maaswerken moved up to the top of the agenda which now consisted of four items (Table 5.1).

What?	**Where?**
Gravelling	Grensmaas
Flood defences	Grensmaas and Zandmaas
Nature development	Grensmaas (++) Zandmaas (+)
Shipping	Zandmaas and Juliana Channel

Table 5.1: ***Maaswerken in brief***

Security Policy and Normal Politics

In light of the security governance interest of the present study, the contrast between the Maaskaden and Maaswerken episodes (Table 5.2) is illustrative of the difference between security decision-making and normal politics.

What makes security decision-making so effective in getting things done? A first element has moral overtones. It seems that in these secularised days, disasters continue to have religious significance even for the secularised. The expression 'Act of God', which is still used in the insurance business, indicates that no one can be held responsible. However, the expression is also used by those in the engineering community who feel that a disaster is a punishment for human negligence. Like the ten plagues of Egypt, a flood disaster can be perceived to 'discipline and punish' a society such that it starts to make amends by adopting a pro-active attitude in the face of flood risk.

Taking a step back from this normative approach, there is a strong sense that disasters are exploited in the decision-making arena as windows of opportunity for bringing in a set of measures that was already waiting in the wings, bringing enough pressure to push preferred alternatives through. When there was a support base for a flood scheme, the beleaguered Grensmaas plan could be tabled and coupled (linked) with security provision simply because it was already there – Teisman (1995) calls this a 'clever solution'.

This perspective, so reminiscent of 'policy streams' or 'garbage can' theories of decision-making (Cohen, Simon and March, 1973), attracted a fair number of supporters in the water sector:

> The TAW [national Technical Advisory commission] thought that after the flood of 1993, the strength of the opposition to dike reinforcement would taper off. But soon the scene looked the same: the same resistance, more lawsuits (procedures), Thus the second high-water event was greeted with open arms, like a second chance. They went all-out, so the evacuation was logical. (interview, RWS senior engineer, 2005)

Maaskaden (1995–97/2001)	**Maaswerken (1997–2005)**
Triggered by calamity	Gradually developed by informal group
Emergency law: Delta Plan Great Rivers	Lack of clear-cut legal framework
Hard (if green) defences for protection	Combination of nature creation, flood protection and improved navigation
Waterschappen (water boards)	Public/private/NGO consortium
Fast-track procedure	Normal procedure
Polluted material disposed on no-questions-asked basis	Legally questionable disposal of polluted aggregates
Dispensation from Environment Impact Analysis (EIA)	EIA necessary
Informal participation	Formal participation
province pulls out	province takes the lead then backtracks
Openness	Self-imposed secrecy

Table 5.2: ***Striking differences between Maaskaden (fast-tracked emergency measures) and Maaswerken (post-emergency measures)***

At that stage of negotiation on the Maas works, another flood would not have gone amiss:

> In political terms, it would be a good thing if it would not take too long until the next flood. (Waterschap spokesman)[2]

While the Maaskaden were fast-tracked with special legislation, the Maaswerken project had to go the sluggish way of any other major infrastructural project. The flood some hoped for never came, but in 2000 as well as 2003 water again was pretty high. The mayor of Maastricht seized the opportunity to

Rounds	Goal Priority
I: Gravelling only	Ways of gravelling that minimise damage to natural values
II: Environmental motives come through	Grensmaas as nature development project with a gravelling element
III: Grensmaas in thrall of water nuisance	Nature conservation and security on an equal footing
IV: Part of Delta plan for the Great Rivers	Security dominates, environment is secondary and financial feasibility off the radar

Figure 5.2: ***Maaswerken project decision-making up trajectory to 1995: four rounds***

intervene in the debate. Procedures take too long, he claimed, the national government should do something about the structural flood risk in South Limburg.

> 'Had the water been only two feet higher, the Minister for Transport would have felt the need to rush plans for Maas security',
> said the Limburg Governor.
>
> 'It would be scandalous if a new floodwave were needed to get the money and get all parties in line.'
> Limburg Provincial councillor Vestjens[3]

It is easy to see what is so attractive about crisis decision-making. At the national level, where flood management had previously been unpopular, the mediagenic river floods triggered a fast-track for decision-making on the River Delta Plan (Dutch abbreviation: DGR). Amid a discourse of 'unacceptable social disruption', the central government took over in 1997.

5.3 Holland vs. Limburg, Rijkswaterstaat vs. Province

5.3.1 Reasserting Hegemony? Rijkswaterstaat Takes the Reins (1997)

> 'Could it be that Limburg is treated quite differently from the rest of the country?' (interview, provincial public officer)

When the Grensmaas project was mooted, the central government was involved in a process of decentralisation of its environmental and spatial planning policy. The project was presented as a nature development plan, and the province of Limburg was supposed to see to the implementation of, notably, Strategic Green-Area Projects (SGPs). The national river manager, Rijkswaterstaat, was

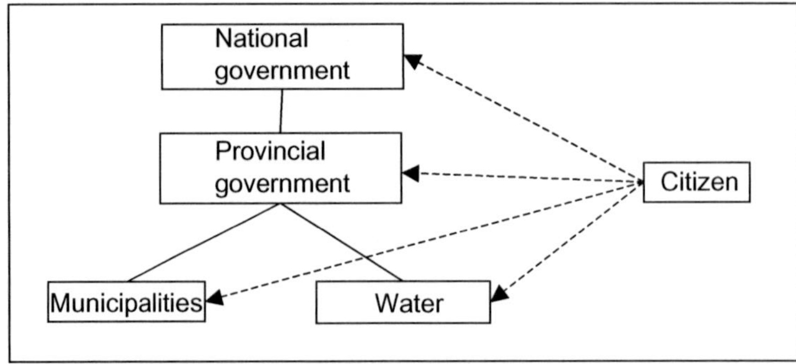

Figure 5.3: ***Institutional framework for water management in the Netherlands***

involved in a restructuring process itself, devolving many of its security tasks to *waterschappen*. The water department had been instated under the French occupation in 1798 to put an end to the long history of competitive diking between polder boards. The agency was said to have developed into a 'state within a state' when it was mandated to start a crash programme to deliver the nation from flooding after the 1953 coastal floods. But its defences had seen increasing opposition in favour of cultural and landscape values, and a steady greening of river management had de-emphasised the flood security aspect. Rijkswaterstaat had become a department like any other.

However, the high water events of 1993 and 1995 and the handling of the *kaden* changed all that. In 1997 RWS, which has by far the bigger budget and technological expertise in the water sector, took over as the pivotal actor in a make-or-break situation.

The EUR 340 million Grensmaas nature development scheme was linked with a EUR 900 million project for the downstream Zandmaas, a project to provide flood protection for a 148-kilometre stretch (Linne to Hedel), and the Maas route to improve navigation. A single Maas works consortium now organised the Grensmaas, Zandmaas and Maasroute works. The collective Maaswerken project organisation still had a tripartite constituency, with provincial authorities, Rijkswaterstaat and the Ministry for Agriculture, Nature Conservation and Food Quality. But the Maaswerken was now widely regarded locally as a Waterstaat project, not just by Limburgers but also by the Agriculture Ministry which at times formed coalitions with the Ministry of Housing, Spatial Planning and Environment (VROM) when they felt too outnumbered (interview, VROM 2000).

In the early stages of the Grensmaas project, protests were fairly muted. After the floods, Limburgers wanted the project badly and speedily. From

1997, however, when Rijkswaterstaat stepped in and made the Maaswerken a 'security-plus' project, protests from vocal locals – individuals, NGOs and municipalities – against the plans mounted.

The 'takeover' of the Maaswerken project by the national ministry in 1997 did not sit well with pockets of the Limburg population and politicians. The Maaswerken became a new arena in which old contrasts between 'Limburg' and 'Holland' were highlighted.

The province of Limburg has a distinct identity, which is bound up with its history. In 1830 Belgium seceded from the Netherlands, taking the provinces of Brabant and Limburg with it. The Dutch responded with military force, reclaiming much of the two provinces. In 1839 Belgium gained independence and in 1843 the right of trespass was agreed. However, (Dutch) Limburg has continued to feel culturally separated from the Netherlands (e.g. Osinga, 1997).

The feeling of being subjected to 'Hollanders' was reinforced by the fact that Limburg traditionally was the mining colony of the Netherlands. Coal, limestone, silica sand and gravel are only found in Limburg, and coal mining was a major employer in the first half of the twentieth century (van der Meulen et al., 2006).

When the mines closed, mass unemployment and poverty ensued. For decades, Limburg politicians demanded, and got, compensating measures. Limburg got its own university (the University of Maastricht) and the Central Bureau for Statistics (CBS) moved there, creating much-needed white-collar employment. Limburg lobbyists grew accustomed to having their way, which gave its image a bad taint:

> The perception of Limburg in The Hague is that of a merchant, the type that would sell their own mother. They always come [to The Hague] to see what they can get. (interview with Limburg administrator)

In the 1990s, however, things seemed to turn for the worse for Limburg. Some have linked this to the political change at the national level: the 'purple (red–blue coalition of socialists and liberals) politics' of the 1990s. Both in the national coalition government and in Limburg, the Christian Democrats (CDA) were no longer represented after a 70-year rule. Since CDA traditionally has a strong base in the province, the party had been most vocal in representing Limburg at the national level. In addition, the social-democrats and liberals had no roots in farming. By contrast, CDA traditionally represented the agricultural interest and saw nature development plans as a threat (interview).

The feeling that the Maaswerken, originally a Limburg-initiated project, was hijacked by 'Holland' and engineered by 'Holland' engineers seems important in understanding the politicisation, especially after 1997 when Rijkswaterstaat took control of the project. Some Limburgers' sense of being exploited is reflected in the statute of the local oppositional coalition BOM, which 'doesn't want any more Limburg land to be sacrificed to Holland roads.' Limburger Ria Dielissen said: 'I am not against a "safe" Maas and neither am I against nature development, but I am against [treating] Limburg as a colony'.[4]

Limburg interviewees professed annoyance that the province had to pay up for its own flood security, while the cost of flood protection elsewhere in the country comes out of the national treasury:

> In the West of the country, the House of Commons monitors the state of the dikes for each and every square foot of dike [but not here]. I can't really get my head around that.

This issue played out across political lines. As in the UK (see Chapter 8), the Maaswerken project provoked an intra-conservative debate: both the minister and the key provincial delegate represented that political party, but stood opposed on the flood issue. Regionally, the Maaswerken were supported by the same 'purple' coalition of socialists (PvdA) and 'conservative liberals' (VVD) coalition as that had formed at the national level.

One interview called the purple cabinet 'a Randstad government at the expense of Limburg.' Such sentiments allowed the centrist Christian Democrats, traditionally the largest party in Limburg, to present itself as the 'true' voice of the province.

But the Rijkswaterstaat initiative also raised expectations in Limburg.

> When it transpired that the Grensmaas might not be self-funding, the province didn't want to bear the brunt for that. At the same time, RWS said: the project is insufficiently directed, in the end the shortfall will be heaped on us. The [1997] policy agreement makes RWS responsible, financially as well. (Interview, Limburg administrator)

The Grensmaas had been bound to budget neutrality under the Advisory Commission on the Maas, which means the Limburgers were expected to pay for their own safety and nature development from gravel sale. But the Zandmaas of necessity needed to be funded differently – sand is not nearly so rewarding. This led liberal provincial councillor Math Vestjens[5], responsible for the project from the provincial side, mistakenly to believe The Hague was going to cough up the difference.

However, the national government did not see it that way. Leiss and Chociolko's (1995) axiomatic position that everyone will try to offload risk was much in evidence for a long stretch of negotiation time, when the cost issue was pushed back until the end of negotiations (interview, Ministry of Agriculture, March 2000).

By taking a non-negotiable zero-budget approach in the face of rising costs, all stakeholders entrenched themselves in an impossible bargaining position which endangered the integrity of the whole project. In fact, the demand for a balanced budget not only came from the government but also from the participating NGOs. Land in Limburg is owned by public (National Forestry Agency: a natural heritage NGO) and private (mineral extractors) organisations. As a public body, the forestry agency cannot invest venture capital in a risk-taking project, but the other two groups can and, unusually for an NGO, do participate. The NGO can only legitimate its participation by insisting on a 'neutral' budget, where costs and benefits cancel. Given the extreme unpredictability of costs and benefits, this has proved to be something of a political fiction. One interviewee reckoned the uncertainty about the economic proceeds of the gravel and sand extraction activities were '50 per cent'.

The water board president was a 'lone wolf' in this respect. Late 1997, the Public Works Minister upset the applecart by announcing that budget shortfalls forced her to postpone completion of all flood defence projects from 2005 to 2008. The Cabinet made NLG 560 million available for high-water defence on the Maas, but acknowledged this sum was not enough to realise a broad, integrated plan, as intended in the DGR. The Minister notes that the amount was the result of a 'political choice'. She tried to assuage public concern by pushing forward the flood defence aspect of the Grensmaas project, so that 70–80 per cent of flood protection goals would have been achieved by 2005. It soon transpired that this would be more likely realised in 2015 or 2017. The province of Limburg concluded this still meant additional financial risk and kicked the ball back into the central government's court.

When the new Vice-Minister for Water Affairs, Monique de Vries, offered some freedom to move budget from the Zandmaas to the Grensmaas budget, Provincial Councillor (Cllr) Vestjens refused the offer outright. Some money could be found in a roundabout way, though. Given the rising costs, nature organisations were taking a bigger share in the management of the areas. Also Natuurmonumenten rather than the gravellers was buying the 750 ha needed for implementing the Grensmaas plan with state subvention, as the Ministry of Agriculture subsidises any purchase for nature development.[6]

The haggling over the budget made it easy to background that the Maaswerken not only has a cost component, but an economic benefit side as well. Economic opportunity has been a powerful driver for altering the terms of the project – either expanding the protected area to include brownfield development area, or for compromising and subverting security standards.

The gravellers' consortium, Panheel Groep, considered the project as vital to its own economic survival (interview, gravellers 2000). The claim to the need for economic security for Panheel and to protect jobs for the region is delegitimised as 'overdone' by other actors, suggesting the support base for these 'partial interests' is far from universal. The project itself holds out great opportunity to others too – consultants, contractors and the shipping industry. News of a water project had stimulated speculative behaviour to raise the price of land due to be bought up in the interests of the project. Lingering annoyance over the handling of the Maasplassen (the gravel pits now used as boating lakes) was rekindled when Suytcote NV, a private player linked with the company that very cheaply acquired lands in 1986, resold it in 1996 to Limburg province at EUR 4.5 million, which immediately transferred them again to the nature organisation Natuurmonumenten and Limburgs Landschap, on condition that they could be used for temporary gravel storage. The Christian-Democrats in the provincial Council felt the province indirectly funded the Maas protection scheme by agreeing to questionable deals with Aqua Terra in 1986 and 1996:

> We are probably caught in a trap set by the Minister for Transport and Waterways, who herself has refused to pay up for the Maas lakes. Suytcote is a shell company; with the same director as Aqua Terra, the current owner, who picked them up for peanuts in the 1980s. Suytcote mysteriously arrived as a contender to pressure the authorities to buy the lakes, apparently to drive up the price. (*De Limburger*, 19 June 1999)

CDA also renewed lobbying efforts to develop the now-protected flood plain, which the improved standard of protection now enabled. There is always a strong push for revoking the tightened flood plain development rules for economic and housing needs.

A local interviewee feels, this is attributable to the image projected of the 'disaster site' by the national media. In the course of the 1990s, Borgharen became symbolic of the Dutch high-water events; the national news correspondent, Harmen Roeland, would always turn up in a raincoat and Wellingtons. The local respondent claims that the dramatic flood footage was in some cases stage-managed to create a more mediagenic image on national TV, damaging interests (interviewee 11).

It was the type of image that made then Transport and Waterways Minister Annemarie Jorritsma pledge 'safety for all by 2005'. In the next Cabinet (1998–2002) of the same political stripe, she went on to become Minister for Economic Affairs[7] and Vice Prime Minister. Promises made earlier could have backfired as the project ran into delay, not only putting her personal reputation at stake but that of her department as well.

A standard cost-benefit analysis was never really carried out. The Advisory Commission on the Maas had optimistically calculated a positive balance of

EUR 50 million. After 1995, a cost estimate of about EUR 225 million was made, only to be superseded by a calculation that went up to twice that figure. But most of all, a RWS spokesman said,

> it was a political decision in the *Zeitgeist*. There were many authorities in the field [in 1995] to look at the misery. Misery, emotion and stress cannot always be expressed in money terms. (*NRC*, 20 March 1999)

The cost-benefit ratio was already compromised by a systematic underestimation of the project cost and overestimation of benefits. In the view of one former project director, the eventual real cost usually turns out to be the original estimate multiplied by a factor 'pi' (π). Were this not the case, he feels, no major project would ever get started (interview, 2000). In this context, commercial interests have often overruled security interests. However, (indirect) benefits also accrued when new developments remained exempted from the ban on building in the flood plain. This leniency caused some at RWS to despair.[8] Such lenience can only affect the project's real *cost-benefit* equation.

A social cost-benefit analysis was commissioned by Bureau Maaswerken to be conducted by Maastricht University, but was never developed past the exploration stage. One salient reason was that it would not change the decision outcome anyway! (Mourits and Potten, 1998).

5.3.2 Security or Flood Defence? Risk and Responsibility Discourse

The stand-off between provincial and national government was to an important extent predicated on the definition (framing) of the problem to be solved in the Maas. The *security* issue provided the key battleground of exceptional-project legitimacy, in two respects: is Maaswerken a security or flood defence project, and are we talking about flood or high-water nuisance?

But while anthropologists claim that people in general dislike uncertainty (Sjöberg et al., 2004), political actors thrive on a degree of ambivalence and uncertainty (Trottier, 1999). Language games (rephrasing and reframing) can help them break a deadlock that would be hard to prise open otherwise. The semantic sliding scale on flood and high water (Figure 5.4) created ambiguity. Securitisation on the other hand eliminates ambiguity (Friis, 2000). Especially Limburg actors and the project organisation itself have made liberal use of the word '*security*' (*veiligheid,* e.g. in POL, June 2000) in a very broad sense. This could make all the difference as securitisation would merit fast-tracking and extra funding for the Maaswerken.

Civil engineers, on the other hand, like things precise and clear-cut. In Dutch water engineering parlance 'security' means 'the degree to which the security standard for water infrastructure is met' in most of the technical water

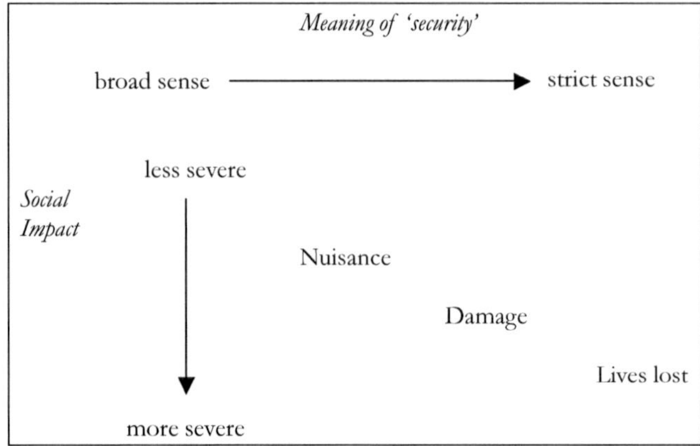

Figure 5.4: ***Semantic sliding scale of 'security' which comprises stricter (more severe) and looser interpretations of security***

management literature, such as the authoritative national Technical Advisory Group on Water Security (TAW, 1995). The referent of 'security' thus does not relate to people, but to the *stability of defence structures*. In this sense, the collapse of protection structures and soil instability can be ranked as physical threats – thus, it is quite correct to state that the security of the *kaden* should be a 1-in-250 standard, which means that they are not 'secure' when faced with a flood with a higher return period.

Engineers in consultancies were careful to point these distinctions out to me at the time. It seemed to irritate civil engineers that the Limburg actors continue to use the security discourse: 'There is continuous conceptual confusion. I am trying to make it clear there is a difference between [in]security and harm'.

This difference had attendant policy consequences in that the river reinforcements put in under the DGR were purposely not called 'dikes' but *kaden*. This label meant that they were not primary flood protection works, and as a consequence did not need to protect against inundations, but against 'nuisance' (interview, flood expert, 2005). This definition exempts the national government from responsibility. However, after a dispute with the *waterschappen*, the *kaden* were placed under the Flood Defence Act, so that they are a national responsibility and, by inference, come under national security.

Rijkswaterstaat's definition of security is much more restrictive than 'flood defence' – it is about life and death issues only. Limburg's comfortable position above sea level renders the security argument less convincing. To wit, no one has ever drowned in a Maas flooding (though the evacuation claimed a victim due to a sliding/skidding rescue truck), so it is not a security issue, strictly.

As it turned out, Limburg won a pyrrhic victory: the project won the security label, but lost the expected fast-tracking. Eventually, 'security' did find its way into the policy discourse with respect to the Maas, including Rijkswaterstaat, which now defines the Maaswerken project as

> a major infrastructural project aiming to improve security by changing the catchment [*stroomgebied*] of the river Maas in Limburg, North Brabant and Gelderland [my translation, JW].[9]

But there was a snag: by that time the philosophy of security had changed. As explained by the then liberal Vice-Minister, Schultz ten Haegen, in 2003, the Ministry cannot and does not want to guarantee 100 per cent security (Cleveringa Lezing, 2003). 'Improvement' was a good enough promise.

5.4 1998–2001: A Bumpy Ride

5.4.1 1998: Selection of Alternatives in the EIA

While local politicians played a part in the first round of Maas troubles, the most formidable opponent turned out to be the *MER-Commissie,* an independent expert committee called to approve the EIA document. The Common Maas and later Maaswerken projects were subject to an EIA, obligatory for major works. An 'unimaginable' amount of detail was collected. The EIA for the Grensmaas, weighing in at 7 kg and carried out by WL Delft Hydraulics, IWACO and CSO, took eight months to draft, and was well received (in 1996) by the MER-Commissie, the statutory body responsible for judging it. But for the Zandmaas, the EIA proved a major hurdle. The Zandmaas EIA report weighed in at 12.5 kg, the biggest such document ever published in the Netherlands, took four years to complete, and was rejected by the MER-Commissie for not being precise enough. One major criticism was that only one (old) computer model was used, ZWENDL. The EIA Commission advised the Minister for Transport and Waterways to re-research whether deepening and widening 'would make the Maas as safe as the province takes it to be'.[10] The revised figures show that the level of protection will be 1:40 rather than the agreed on 1:50.

A novelty, inspired by European law, was that the EIA was to be used for the design stage itself, not after it. The EIA obliges the initiator to bring in three different alternatives and subject them to public consultation. Originally, *four* alternatives were presented for the Maaswerken: a 'zero option' (do-nothing), an environment-friendly option, an economy-friendly option as well as combinations of these (Lamerichs, 1996) to be assessed and presented to the general public.

In addition to the four alternatives presented in 1998, an engineer called Martens presented a 'fifth variant', which he rated to be cheaper than the alternatives presented by Maaswerken: elongated plastic bags along the riverbanks. Filled up, they push up the water level to achieve the necessary draught for navigation, which will cause the groundwater level to go up as well. They would be complemented by 10-metre wide channels alongside the river that take less space than the planned 100-metre wide nature development corridors. A regional interviewee expected this to be dismissed on financial and technical grounds:

> They cost about three or four times as much per km. Reliability of sand and clay gets better over time, while plastic and concrete get worse over time.

To my knowledge, this fifth variant was not considered by the Maaswerken. This has not stopped the innovative technology from being tried elsewhere in Limburg for emergencies, if on a smaller scale.[11]

Eventually, stakeholder consultation was carried out with stakeholder groups and Flemish counterparts over *three* alternatives: apparently the zero option was dropped. The responses were collated into a Discussion Memorandum on the basis of which the final decision would be made.

However, by the time public information sessions were held, a pervasive feeling took hold that there was not much choice after all. This *early closure of alternatives* was in part attributable to cost overruns which provided a bias against the more expensive alternatives (various news clippings and interviewees). As the project faced increasing financial pressures, a final alternative was rushed through without any further consultation with stakeholders. It turned out that a pre-emptive deal had been struck to enable the Zandmaas pilot project involving a diversion trench at Lomm, implying the 'Combination Alternative' had already been selected while the Transport and Waterwys Vice-Minister was officially still working on the decision.

Five years before, Teisman, a professor of public management at Erasmus University Rotterdam, had already warned that funding would be a key risk to project survival. Foreseeable project implementation issues were indeed deferred indefinitely: distribution of responsibilities, costs and how to implement the project withoaut increasing the flood risk. This situation promised to present major risks to the survival of the project, which is strongly tied up with the logic of excavation economics. Gravellers will indeed start on the most profitable sites, foregoing the unprofitable ones – mandatory clustering of profitable and unprofitable sites would be required to ensure the exploitation of all project sites. In its 1993 feasibility study, NEI had already noted that gravel companies see their profit fall under the safe 20 per cent margin if they need to invest in clean-up measures. Also, the gravel market is deeply dependent on the rate of building activities and subject to heavy competition – by 1991, 60 per cent of gravel was already imported from Belgium (Teisman, 1995).

In 1998 the national government decided to deliberately under-permit aggregates extraction to promote alternative materials (Van der Meulen et al., 2006). As a consequence, in 1999 the province objected when Maaswerken asked for permission to start digging on six further locations, anticipating the Grensmaas plan, fearing the gravel companies would only sign up for the most remunerative locations. The Council of State in 2002 ruled the refusal was justified. This was a blow to the gravellers who wanted to start work straight away in anticipation of the project's kick-off.

Market and financial studies were carried out before and after the EIA but not during, and the gravel companies were not consulted for strategic reasons while experts in river hydrology, archaeology, toxicology, infrastructure, etc. were busy devising their best alternative. Perhaps inevitably, when the new option was presented, it soon turned out the numbers did not add up.

Other professional hole-diggers in the *socio-cultural domain* were also affected by the local misgivings. Under international treaties, new infrastructural projects must be surveyed for archeologically important sites. The Maaswerken diligently preserved 143 important sites.

While the importance of the heritage information is not disputed by local activists, the parish of Lomm, however, questioned the motives for the archaeological research carried out there for the pilot studies (Stassen, 2005). When the Maaswerken asked permission to dig 'trial trenches' there, it was feared the geological research benefits economic (gravel) interests rather than heritage conservation.

The river experts did not use the EIA as an evaluation tool but as a way to optimise the 'best' design. Uncertainties and dissimilarity of truth claims were overcome in true Dutch engineering tradition, by over-dimensioning the weak or unknown aspects in their constructs (Leenders, 2004: 154). Rather than make an integrated evaluation of different alternatives, compensating and mitigating measures were built in.

New uncertainties (climate change) and the rejection of the EIA undermined project support, but at the same time opened the door to new alternatives, widening the range of options to include retention (White, 1974).

Not Enough or Too Much Detail?

Above, it was noted that extensive consultation with stakeholders took place for the EIA. The Maaswerken Bureau went out of its way to answer to each and every question raised. No matter how far-fetched the objection, the experts were called in to win the argument.

> In the consultations with the public, there was this man, we call him Mr Fear-all, who started this thing about malaria. That makes the press. We contacted a health expert and it emerged you would need a level of salinity [in water] that's about ten times higher [than we have]. You have to counter that [objection] with rational arguments. (interview, project director)

While all involved were greatly impressed by the quantity and thoroughness of the information provided, the 'promotional' approach failed to convince all stakeholders of its impartiality. The data conveys the impression that the unease does not so much concern the promotional material as the wealth of information gathered. Two of my interviewees spontaneously expressed their amazement at the information *overload* brought in to justify the project, and importantly, the information overload upped the ante for any critical questions, which, it was easy to sense, would have to be of similar thoroughness inducing one municipality to hire a consultant for his expertise.

The Local Authority for Arcen and Velden felt bulldozed by information.[12]

> For each argument advanced by us you get three counterarguments from the public authorities. If you want to make a good showing you will have to spend hundreds of thousands of guilders on research.

As a counterbalance to the 'enormous PR machine' of Bureau Maaswerken bulldozing people with information the local authority hired Grontmij consultancy for 'objective research.'

Despite the wealth of information, some agrarian actors remained unconvinced by the information provided by the Maaswerken project organisation at the time. Damage to farms as a result of the Maas project has been calculated at the level of regions, not by plot. To be able to claim damages, agrarians will of course need to know what the 'threat' to their plots amounts to (*Limburger,* 8 June 1999).

While in 2000 a sense of pessimism and foreboding was notable, none of those interviewed actually doubted that the project would go ahead in some form. Sunk costs – economic, but also political commitments (reputation, legitimacy) – are strong project-sustaining forces in the Netherlands.

However, now that the EIA Commission and Comptroller had been assuaged, the troubles *really* started for the Maaswerken because of three legacies from the securitised time window:

- a scare over the 'bathtub effect' of *Maaskaden* (5.4.2),
- anti-trust litigation (5.5.2),
- a scandal over illegal discharge of polluted soil (5.5.3).

In 1999 and 2000, parliamentary questions were asked on safety, a sure sign of the issue's arrival in the national political arena. In 2001, disputes over competitive tendering and topsoil depositing caused expensive delays to the project and the environmentalists, gravellers and at one point the province, threatened to pull out of the project. Local groups and authorities devised a strategy and formed alliances with each other as well as external actors. It is this grassroots politicisation that I will now zoom in on.

5.4.2 *1999–2001: Politicisation of Flood Risk*

Protection or Peril? The Issue of Risk Displacement

The safety and risk displacement issue was the first controversy to make the headlines in 1999. New calculations revealed that the river widening would not realise the safety standard, and would therefore be supplemented by higher *kaden*. But the *kaden*, it appeared, would change a high-incidence, low-consequence *material* risk into a low-incidence, high-consequence *physical* risk in some areas.

The area protected by the *kaden* is like a bathtub (there is no spillway). Should the Maaskaden be overtopped in a 1:500 flood, there would be very little time for warning and evacuation and lives could be lost (van der Ven and van Dooren, 1997). This possibility unintentionally propels the project itself into quite a different security domain.

> 'Evacuation used to be done by vehicles when the water is still shallow, now you need boats. Which includes the cattle removal. And there's still barbed-wire fencing around the area' (resident, 2000).
>
> 'Should a *kade* fail, people could even be drowned who used to watch the water rise gradually' (Maaswerken spokesman).[13] 'It's the difference between ten soaked carpets and one drowned Limburg citizen' (interview, former RWS director, 2005).

When this hazard became public knowledge it caused a stir, leading to Parliamentary questions. The then Vice-Minister, Monique de Vries, admitted that the personal security of those in embanked areas may be endangered if timely evacuation is not realised.

Meanwhile an administrative debate went on in parallel about risk displacement across space rather than time: upstream–downstream equity at inter-provincial level. Due to the Maaswerken river intervention, a downstream rise of the water table in Brabant and Gelderland was predicted, necessitating additional retention, which would claim 10,000 to 20,000 ha to store 10 to 20 million m^3. In 1999, Waterschap De Maaskant in Noord-Brabant felt the Maas works could render its remit more unsafe. During the execution of the works the trajectory Boxmeer to Ravenstein would be temporarily less secure. As there is a large gas hub at Ravenstein feeding large parts of the Netherlands and Belgium, this situation might be important. The Waterschap therefore wanted the trajectory to be realised in the north-to-south direction rather than south to north. Brabant felt Limburg should solve its high-water nuisance problems within its own realm and even demanded a separate EIA for the retention basins in Brabant. This debate dragged on until 2005, when Brabant was given EUR 4.5 million to take measures to compensate for the consequences of the Maaswerken. Persistent local worries about project-induced damages in Limburg also resulted in a compensation deal in 2004.

5.4.3 2001: Renegotiation

Dutch political culture sets great store by inclusion and participation, and the project's management has aimed for a high degree of *consultation*. The 1995–97 'securitised' episode had opened up a window for a high degree of cooperative informal *public participation* – and hence, of 'co-ownership' – which included taking lay knowledge on board. As a consequence of the all-inclusive strategy, few could claim their voices had not been heard. During the EIA, stakeholders were again consulted, although as mentioned their influence on the choice was limited. After the EIA in 1998, however, there was little doubt that local people would hardly be involved in project implementation.

On 1 July 1999 the project partners signed a protocol, and by mid-2000 the private parties[14] officially formed the consortium Grensmaas. It gradually became clear that the scope of the project was going to be less extensive than planned for. As a more cost-effective alternative to widening and deepening the Maas in combination with nature development, it was now proposed to raise the *kaden* at Roermond, Venlo and Gennep as part of the Zandmaas.

The city of Venlo was particularly unhappy because the city would lose even more of its view on the Maas as a consequence of the raised *kaden*. Its municipality dismissed a dam planned right on the high road of Blerick as unacceptable. An alternative 'Maas corridor' plan, which Venlo developed with several municipalities, envisaged widening the river and nature development, complemented with removable *kaden*, for which Venlo would shoulder the bill of EUR 0.5 million. The Maaswerken however said it was simply too late in the day to amend the Maaswerken to include the corridor. In the end a compromise was worked out which, as first calculations showed, seemed to bring an even better safety effect than anticipated.

The lack of information and consultation in the lead-up to 2001 no doubt heightened public frustration and indignation at the political, NGO and community committee level, when the final Maaswerken plan was presented. The response was for people to 'participate' in the Longian sense (Long, 2002), sometimes cooperatively (coming up with alternatives), sometimes antagonistically – by filing petitions and appeals organising press-friendly protests. This issue will be expounded in the next section.

Revolt after the January 2001 Plan

The 1990 voluntary agreement between the province and the national government had laid down a cap of 35 million tonnes of gravel. That agreement had already been changed to 53 million tonnes in 1996. But even that agreement turned out to be rather elastic. In July 2000 it transpired that the gravellers would be allowed to dig up 55 million tonnes to fund the 1,000 ha of nature along the Common Maas. This Scope 2000 plan combined the Combination Alternatives with elements from other alternatives. On the basis of the EIA, a Provisional Design (*Voorlopig Ontwerpplan*) was prepared and released in late 2000.

Yet, the political solution found in 2001 differed substantially from any of the alternatives under discussion. The gravel consortium gained substantially: it was foreseen 66–70 million tonnes of gravel would be dug from the Maas valley – double the annual nationwide demand (van der Meulen et al., 2006: 167). The gravel industry also got an extra 200 ha, increasing the hectarage of the works on 15 digging locations by a third.

The farmers' organisation LLTB expressed anger about the loss of more agrarian soil due to the extra hectares set aside for digging and dredging. My Mook interviewee is not alone in feeling the order of priorities had been reversed: the green security project is there to legitimise gravel extraction, rather than the other way round. The Christian Democratic party, a consistent opponent to Maaswerken leading the 'digging holes' discourse, claiming it opened the door to 'unlimited' excavation, almost succeeded in vetoing the project in the Provincial Council, leading an ad hoc coalition of the Limburg regionalists PNL, the senior citizens party and two parties of the left. By vetoing the digging in Schipperskerk, a parish which had seen decades of gravel dredging, this meant a *de facto* veto on the Maaswerken, since there was no alternative location for the Schipperskerk site.

Nature organisations were unhappy that the nature development was greatly compromised and the 2001 compromise was clearly a bridge too far even for the conservationist Grensmaas consortium member, Natuurmonumenten. After consulting with the Limburgse Milieufederatie and Staatsbosbeheer they stopped all cooperation on the plan in 2001 and threatened to sue.

There were also successful local appeals against the trajectory of the *kaden* and two planned retention basins invited their fair share of resistance. On 25 June 2001 the Stichting tot Behoud Leefmilieu for Buggenum, Haelen, Born, and Nunheim filed a petition signed by 2,700 citizens to the public consultation procedure of the Maaswerken project on the draft EIA and draft provincial plan, which was originally due for 2003. The Heel and Haelen group feared that the Maaswerken's retention basin would set a precedent for inevitable future gravelling in the area west of the Lateral Channel. They feared excessive nuisance as well as tourists being scared off when the Koeweide harbour was used for transferring soil. On its initiative, Grontmij consultants were commissioned to research an alternative trajectory.

Further resistance came from Meerssen against gravelling in Bunde/Geulle. Meerssen sent three urgent letters to Bureau Maaswerken, one also signed by neighbouring Maastricht, Stein, Sudderen and Echt. Maaswerken was willing to look for alternatives for Bunde but not for Geulle and Voulwames.

Now Geulle has only 90 households, Voulwames 7. This small number did not deter citizens of Geulle and Voulwames to found an action committee, Stichting Leefbaar Geulle aan de Maas, in March 2001 with a well-designed and informative website. They felt their natural values in their areas will be 'sacrificed' for the Maaswerken.[15] Joining forces with other Maas organisations led to the foundation of the Samenwerkingsverband Organizaties en Bewoners Grensmaas (SOBG), which subsequently evolved into Bewoners Overleg Maas. BOM was a collective of local action committees throughout the region, to represent citizen and recreational interests in the Maas valley. BOM feels that the Maaswerken is first and foremost a project for extending employment opportunities for companies specialised in digging holes until 2015.

Another reason for joining forces was a report by the drinking water company that the Maaswerken plans would boost algae growth and as a consequence threaten drinking water. Dredging would release polluted particles from the riverbed which would end up in its own reservoir at Heel.

Jan van Eechoud, a retired chartered accountant from the tiny parish of Voulwames, became the spokesman for BOM. He vowed to put up a good fight: 'I expect the province and gravellers will come to an agreement, subject to an act of God (*force majeure*)'. In a supreme example of closure discourse he adds: 'Maybe we can provide that *force majeure*.'[16]

The logic of a large project demands that once a project has been decided on, you have to start planning on ever smaller details. The local opposition to the project, however, refused to argue with the project bureau on those details. While decision-makers are used to moving for closure at the general level, so they can start making decisions on ever more detailed, next stages of the project, civil-society opponents keep returning to the main decision. Each vertical bend denotes a point of *closure* and move to a more detailed (funnelled) level of decision-making.

In fact, even after the main decision was taken, quite a few alternative plans for the Maas have been tabled in the water community itself, not just by civil-society actors. This suggests closure was not made with sufficient support base, so that local civil society keeps putting spanners in the wheel. This suggests that the original decision has not sufficiently been recognised by its initiators as a political, wicked problem that has the potential to haunt the decision-makers forever.

5.5 Limburg Takes Over (2001–05)

5.5.1 Back to Informal Governance?

In response to the backlash generated by the plan of early 2001, the province of Limburg spotted a window of opportunity to reclaim the project and moved with great speed.[17] In this phase, the approach to communication and participation also saw radical change. Between July and November 2001 a new plan was drawn up, this time in closer consultation with stakeholders. Three *Gebiedscommissies* for the Grensmaas area[18] held their meetings in an informal atmosphere and in this spirit did not even draw up minutes – the Maaswerken site has minutes only from 2 November 2001. All (organised) stakeholders were welcome and could directly influence the agenda. This degree of informality was to spell more trouble for the Maaswerken in 2005 (pers. comm., consultant, 2005).

Not everybody could be expected to play along, though (Warner, 2006a). The *Vereniging Federatief Verband tegen Ontgrondingen* ('Anti-quarrying federation'), an environmental group in Born/Grevenbicht, had supported the 1998 plan for the Maaswerken, but sided against the new 2001 plan known as the *Basis* Plan. They felt games were being played with the Limburg citizens. While bilateral contacts continued, the Federation refused to sit on the Gebiedscommissie. Meanwhile, Lomm, the first targeted project site, were represented on the Gebiedscommissie, yet continued to fight the project in court in parallel to the multi-stakeholder negotiations.

The Basis Plan targeted gravel deposits outside the flood plain and no *plassen* inside the area and was rejected by several stakeholders, so that new negotiations were needed. The Final plan (*Eindplan*) was approved by the Limburg provincial authorities in December 2001. It allowed for less widening and put a gravel extraction limit at 50 million tonnes. Finally, implementation was planned in a much shorter time window. The Eindplan commanded broad support from PvdA, VVD, but also CDA and, eventually D66 (liberals of the left). PNL (regional party), the two left-wing parties, GroenLinks and SP, remained opposed, both because of what they saw as inordinate concessions to the gravel kings and because they feel that the Grensmasas required an international solution. To this, CDA and VVD raised the time argument: the longer the wait, the more investment in nature will be replaced by investment in *kaden* and more gravelling will be needed to balance the books. In fact in 2003, CDA proposed scrapping the nature development element in the Maaswerken plan. With funds getting in ever direr straits, 'all cards should be placed on security'.[19]

5.5.2 The Antitrust Issue

As noted, security decision-making excludes economic competition mechanisms, and invoking the complexity of the security project. Antitrust measures against consortia can only be avoided when the public partner can invoke an overriding 'higher interest'. Wolsink (2003) shows that the Dutch Public Works department, invoking this higher interest, has sought to avoid competitive tendering of infrastructural works by cutting up dikes into 5-kilometre segments. Recent Dutch 'anti-NIMBY' (Not In My Backyard) legislation aims to speed up and, in terms of the present analysis, 'close' the decision-making process.

In the same spirit, the province of Limburg had expected to be allowed to carry out both parts of the Maaswerken with pre-formed consortia. In anticipation, the province had hired a law firm to check whether competitive European tendering was needed. While the authorities had refused to disclose the outcome of the report,[20] on the basis of the outcomes they must have considered themselves in the clear.

However, when an ad hoc alliance invoked antitrust legislation in 2001, it forced the project consortium to justify itself in court. Both the municipality of Lomm and citizen platform Lomm Actief had appealed against the approval of a detention basin as part of the Maaswerken project. Digging a retention basin was all right with them if it enhanced security, they felt, but not to line the pockets of the local gravel digging industry. Together with Belgian gravellers who felt unduly excluded from tendering, Lomm Actief and individual members of other action committees started a European antitrust case.

The European Directive (93/37/EEC) stipulated that all projects worth over NLG 5 million (EUR 2.25 million) needed to open their tendering procedures to all European competitors. These rules are aimed at requiring minimum levels of transparency and establishing obligations to follow open procedures for awarding contracts, to facilitate fair competition between companies in all member states. These rules are also applicable to the tendering procedures for gravel extraction. The Maaswerken project leadership had filed an application for dispensation of antitrust rules with the Dutch antitrust regulator NMa in 1991. It argued that the complexity of the project warranted a consortium rather than open tendering. NMa begged to differ. The usual escape, splitting the works up into a great number of smaller works worth less than NLG 5 million, would make coordination so much more cumbersome.

The Dutch Department of Economic Affairs has tightened its antitrust enforcement such that it has already forced some extraction consortia to dissolve. In so doing, it complies with one of the cornerstones of the EU, the establishment of an open market, as vigourously pursued by the European Commissioner, the Dutch Liberal Frits Bolkestein.

However, the Dutch gravel extraction companies have tried to pre-empt the official procedures by buying land from provincial and local authorities in the gravel-rich parts of the Maas valley. By establishing property rights in the area, they avoid the risk of foreign gravel extraction companies getting the contract.

The Dutch government had granted the concession because the land is already owned by the excavators, who under Dutch law have the almost Maslowian-sounding right to 'self-realisation'. Under Dutch law, expropriation is not an option if the landowner is able to carry out the desired work, and gravel extraction companies can arguably carry out river widening measures. A private party takes care of the entire project implementation, including obtaining the relevant permits.[21] However, the European Commission did not consider this an overriding argument.

The Commission objected to both the Grensmaas consortium, and also the Zandmaas consortium DCM, composed of regional extractors. DCM, which the Maaswerken wanted to grant a concession to mine sand suitable for mortar production, already owned most of the 90 ha required. For the Dutch authorities, this meant that they were deprived of the chance to conclude a contract on better conditions.

Due to the successful mobilisation of the European competition authority, the process collapsed for over a year. The episode impelled D66 (liberals of the left), who had warned two years before about this problem, to urge the Maaswerken to prepare *alternatives* for the Grensmaas. The governor however felt that alternatives would give the European Commission the impression that Limburg had lost confidence in the Grensmaas plans.

In the end, compromise was struck that only polluted topsoil management should be tendered, while the 50 million tonnes of gravel excavation, as well as bridges and roads, could be carried out by the consortium. Parliamentary questions from D66 did not change the government's position. But while the deal settled the competition issue, the disposal of the polluted topsoil however turned out to be yet another problem for the project.

5.5.3 Finding, Filling, Fixing Ever New Holes – Topsoil and Budget

Topsoil pollution was another legacy of the 'securitised' Maaskaden episode. Next to creating a 'loophole' around economic competition, the Delta plan for the Great Rivers had overruled the need for environmental auditing. The DGR allowed 'class 4 material', heavily contaminated soil which normally would have to be disposed of at a controlled site, to be used as topsoil for the Maaskaden. After the return to normal politics, however, there was commotion over the use of toxic topsoil in *kaden*, Rijkswaterstaat and three provinces had presented 'active soil management' in 1998 as an innovative way of concentrating, isolating and displacing diffusely polluted sediments in the Maas flood plain, as well as the Rhine river branches. 'Clay screens' (now known as topsoil depots) were to be manufactured from unsaleable Maas topsoil, as a useful alternative to dumping them in gravel pits.

A scandal over the deposition of 180,000 m^3 of polluted soil dug up for broadening the river at Swalmen and Beesel in 2001 seriously compromised the project when the Purification Board (a type of Waterschap focusing on water quality) threatened legal action. The contract however freed the contractors of any responsibility, as national public agencies carrying out state law cannot be prosecuted for environmental offences, only investigated by parliament.[22] As a result, the Vice-Minister, Melanie Schultz, was formally liable for the damage, to her deep resentment.[23] The stored soil would need to be removed again at great cost – the costs of cleaning up the area are estimated at EUR 10–13 million. The provincial council chided the provincial administration, feeling there had been far too little control of the Maaswerken, especially when Cllr Vestjens failed to respond to any questions asked in the Provincial Council.

Meanwhile, spiralling project preparation costs had come under increasing attack as well.[24] The Maaswerken organisation has always claimed that the preparation costs had been comparatively low. The provincial government on the other hand claimed very expensive consultancies were contracted and its bureau overstaffed – many functions appeared to be staffed by a provincial and by a Waterstaat officer (pers. comm. RWS, 2007). It transpired the project office had spent EUR 140 million in preparation only: 80 million for the Zandmaas, 20 million for the Grensmaas, plus Limburg's 10 million investment in the preparation of the Eindplan.

The bureau was radically downsised, Maaswerken Director Joost Huurman was banned from speaking in public and the whole management team had to hand in their resignation. The new Maaswerken Director, L. Bijlsma, had to deal with the fallout over the topsoils. He predicted any new illegal practice coming to light for implementation of both projects to be the 'death stab' for the project. This made the project organisation extremely careful, even when environmental permission was granted in 2003 by Limburg and later reaffirmed by the Minister of Transport.

Pressures from the political sector were quite contradictory. After two high water-events in early 2002 and 2003, not all that comfortably withstood by the *kaden*, both politicians and activists called for speedy protection works. But the second half of 2003 saw petitions against the Grensmaas project presented to MPs (Helleman, 2005). The Maaswerken sat out the storms, as it waited to get the clean-up legally cleared – while critics claimed that they were in fact waiting for new legalisation that will ease the preconditions for managing polluted topsoil the Maaswerken way ('Active Soil Management'). The waiting however was not in vain – in 2005 word got out that according to European rules, lakes filled with topsoil are in fact waste dumps which need to be totally isolated and monitored. The topsoil issue had meanwhile been taken up to the Council of State.[25] The national government threatened to call off the whole project in case of a firm ruling. In that case a EUR 100 million compensation claim on the national government could be expected from the Maaswerken consortium. Public officials started to consider a Maaaswerken-*lite*.

Moreover, a two-year stand-off was to emerge in 2002 over the future Operation and Maintenance of the 40-kilometre stretch of *kaden* on the *Zandmaas*. A leaky water pipeline in Stein caused the dike along the Juliana (navigation) Channel at Stein to subside, requiring the evacuation of 500 people. The water boards refused to take such risks in future. Plus, who was going to foot the bill of an estimated EUR 12 million? During the negotiations, emotions were apparently so strong that at one point the province threatened to pull out. An independent commission, the Commission-Blom, forged an agreement. All *kaden* will fall under the 1995 Flood Defence Act, which means they are now a national responsibility. It also means they need to comply with the standards laid down in that act. The state will now have to carry the cost of replacing or resisting antiquated pipelines to ensure proper dike functioning.[26]

5.5.4 2002: New Gaps in Flood Defence

In addition to the shadow of the past, new information and legislation presented new hurdles for the Maaswerken project. Dark clouds gathered again when it transpired that the projected level of Maas protection was unlikely to be realised if climate scenarios were taken into account. RWS admitted in 2002 that both 1:50 for the *kaden* and 1:250 for the undiked Maas might not be attained, and that it had started the Integrated Maas Exploration (Imtegrale Maas Verkenningen), to look beyond 2015 for a 4,600 m^3/s discharge (Wesselink, 2007). To realise this ambitious goal, the cooperation of the Belgians would be badly needed. These explorations however were initially kept under wraps, as news about these explorations could be interpreted as the Maaswerken Bureau not having great faith in its own project.

The standards issue was relatively new for Limburg. In 1996 Dolfing could still note that in the *reglement GS*, a legal document for the provincial governors, there was no stated acceptable risk floor, that is, no desired level of protection. RWS used an informal standard for the Maas, but this is in terms of discharge: originally 3,800 m^3/s, but lowered in the early 1990s to 3,000. After the 1995 flood, the emergency *kaden* to be completed by 2002, were intended to meet a 1:50 standard.

Under the 1996 Flood Defence Act, 1:250 became a requirement within the *diked* areas in Limburg. The widened Maas channel, together with the recently erected *kaden* was deemed sufficient to guarantee dry feet on a 250-year basis – though legally the undiked areas did not fall within this protection level.

Even the adequacy of this normative standard of protection was already in dispute: Mook Local Authority felt 1 in 250 to be unacceptably low. Mook is situated in North-Limburg at the narrowest bottleneck. Any flood event has especially serious consequences for its Middelaar parish, which may find itself isolated. But it transpired that not all areas in Central Limburg were going to meet that 1-in-250 standard. The several redesigns made in the course of the project eroded the protection level in several places, both urban and non-urban.

5.5.5 2005 – A Viable Plan At Last?

On 23 June 2005, the project finally started, now with a projected cost of EUR 473 million, out of which 100 will be raised privately for digging two retention basins under 'self-realisation' rules.[27] On 1 July the POL (the Provincial Plan for

Limburg) was approved by the provincial authority. The way was finally cleared for the Maaswerken project.

However, the opponents do not let off. BOM took the case to court to try and quash the decision. It was unconvinced by the need for nature development. Aren't grazing cows as good for maintaining the lovely Limburg landscape as the Scottish wild cattle the environmentalists wanted to import? LNC (Landscape, Natural and Cultural) values[28] have strong links with people's sense of cultural identity, so that any new project perhaps predictably mobilised opponents using the discourse of rape and pillage when the memory of acute flooding wore out. While in 2006 the Council of State defeated all complaints so that the project could go ahead, the Federatief Verband demanded to stop the Maaswerken in light of pollution of the riverbed. This was rejected in 2007. But individual protests from residents who find the *kaden* going right through their back garden bring more delays, so that the new 2008 deadline for closing the gaps in Limburg's flood defence again is unlikely to be met.[29]

5.6 Conclusion

In his famous economic theory, Lord John Meynard Keynes (1936) proposes that the problem in a recession economy is not scarcity of resources but an inhibition to consume. Consumption will lead to more capital accumulation, more employment and more prosperity. Since it doesn't matter what the consumption is for, governments can boost the economy by spending their money on anything – even digging holes in the ground and filling them up again – rather than saving it up for the future.

A strategy of finding, fixing and filling holes, in a literal and figurative sense, also comes to mind when contemplating the somewhat dispiriting history of the Maaswerken plan – the river scheme that sought to strike a happy balance between flood defence, natural values and sand and gravel extraction. Many local stakeholders however continued to see the project in a different light: a *carte blanche* lifeline for the regional gravel-dredging industry by another name. Local voices claim that the project sought to re-establish the legitimacy of gravel and sand excavation, which had got a bad reputation in Limburg.

The formal project framing has been contested throughout the Maaswerken's history. Started as a nature development project, it turned out to require a discursive strategy of *securitisation* (framing an issue as a security issue) for its survival, changing the rationale for the project from a trade-off between nature creation and gravel extraction to a flood protection project with environmental and economic benefits. In essence, however, repeated politicisation pitted the two main problem frames – 'green security project' vs. 'quarrying project in disguise' against each other. This got worse in the course of time, since a contradictory set of project goals soon made the project run into financial difficulties even before it began, relying more and more on gravel digging to fill gaping financial holes. I tend to agree with Van der Meulen et al.'s (2006) analysis that the 'closed' nature of Maaswerken planning put the general public but also contractors in a reactive position. Nonetheless they fail to address the province's post-March 2001 efforts to do better on this count. In the disastrous year 2001, Limburg regained the lead in the Maaswerken, and can be credited with restoring confidence by closer consultation with stakeholders. Limburg could however not shake off its image of having sold out the province to gravel companies (Van Meurs, 1995). Even now the contract has finally been signed, it looks like this image will continue to haunt the Maaswerken project for years to come.

In the course of its history, security absolutes were thrown into the Maaswerken arena at almost every turn, and, interestingly, from a theoretical perspective, from every 'Buzan security domain'. Securitisation became an option in the aftermath of two critical water events. The high-water events of 1993 and 1995 were a window of opportunity to carry though a number of emergency measures that would otherwise be difficult to realise. The problems of these fast-track decisions were only becoming apparent in due course: raising *kaden*, dumping polluted soils, forming a consortium without tendering, it all caught up on the project: 'normal politics' involved difficult questions on antitrust, cost-effectiveness, environmental laws/EIA and participatory processes. Reframing the project as a security issue also reaffirmed the hegemonic position of Rijkswaterstaat, which had been on the decline in the 1980s and 1990s.

In many respects, however, the security momentum was lost early in the process, the Maaswerken became like any normal project and after one of its many crises, Limburg successfully reaffirmed its leading role in the project. Perhaps the shadow of the flood was not long enough to reap the benefits of security decision-making for the initiators. In the end, the project lost five years in overcoming a series of perhaps foreseeable crises.

6

PUBLIC PARTICIPATION IN EMERGENCY RIVER STORAGE IN THE OOIJ POLDER – A BRIDGE TOO FAR?

6.1 Introduction

Should (and can) central government work with local stakeholders to prepare for extreme flood events? Can you plan together with citizens what to do in the event of a surprise attack? In other words, can the governance arrangement be rearranged such that a type of *co-production* of flood security between government and civil society is possible?

The international aid community is currently promoting stakeholder involvement in planning for and response to extreme events.[1] They see local participation as integral to integrated flood governance. Not only relief experts and public managers should be in charge of calamity management, the affected population should also be consulted and updated, to allow for better awareness and preparedness. This calls for much better coordination between the public sector, the aid relief sector (often private or NGO) and locals.

Like public security, the institutional set-up for disaster management has long been geared to a top-down policy mode. As a matter of course, calamities are dealt with in a highly 'securitised' (Buzan et al., 1998), non-inclusive, manner, legitimised by the need to protect existential values. The logic of disaster *relief* is one of quick, emergency response, so that there tends to be little time for democratic debate. Still, the brunt of coping with disaster is still borne by local citizens rather than external or national disaster management experts (Kirschenbaum, 2004). Community-based (neighbourhood) organisations have the network and specific local knowledge to improve effective communication and help. It would therefore seem prudent to consult and involve stakeholders in decision-making on the type and modality of protection they should get when the next disaster strikes. Contemporary insights in disaster management emphasise the need for disaster *preparedness* which can be far more inclusive.

The present chapter sketches the changing governance arrangement for riverine flood control, considering the extent of local stakeholder access to calamity decision-making when planning for national extreme events (crises) in the Netherlands.

After the floods of 1995, the Dutch government made a radical break, moving from 'vertical' (dikes) to 'horizontal' (space claims) security provision. This compelled the Ministry to involve itself in the area of spatial planning and negotiating with citizens and local authorities. Does the move away from dikes bring a 'de-securitised' mode of governance – a move from 'vertical' (top-down) to more 'horizontal' decision-making? A case study of emergency flood storage in a polder on the river Waal, mooted in 2000, illustrates a clash between 'securitised' and 'non-securitised' mindsets vis-à-vis floods, notably between those who propagate public consultation in flood management and those who do not. It is discussed whether desecuritisation also necessarily means the (re)politicisation of security governance.

Section 6.2 will sketch the policy context as a backdrop for issues of community involvement in the 'integrated flood security chain'. It shows how security governance in the Netherlands and internationally has changed to an approach that seeks greater stakeholder involvement and preparedness, although it is noted that flood management has been lagging in this respect. Section 6.3 then outlines the history of the decision-making on flood storage to see how the decision to flood the Ooij polder in extreme events was taken, legitimised and resisted. Special attention will be paid to how the decision-making process produced foreclosure of alternative frames, and how alternatives proposed after the polder selection process fared. Section 6.3.3 investigates how the planning process was politicised, triggering a (discursive) 'logic of war' on the part of its opponents, who advanced a counter-frame contesting the sense in the government's 'solution'. I will then assess to which extent this politicisation affected the involvement and 'voice' of the local community in flood security provision. This leads to an analysis of what *kind* of civil-society involvement is meant when calls for participation are made (Section 6.4).

6.2 Towards a Different Model of Security Governance

In the Netherlands, calamity policy is a responsibility of the Home Office, while flood policy is the responsibility of the Public Works Department and water (polder) boards. The Home Office has pushed for integrated disaster management, and acted as coordinator for integrated security policy (Lünneman, 2003). In 1993 it published a whitepaper together with the Dutch departments of Social Security, Public Works, and Spatial Planning and Environment, calling for a more *integrated security policy*. 'Integrated' here means a coherent, coordinated set of instruments and policy measures to reduce insecurity. This coherence is operationalised as a 'security chain' consisting of *pro-action, prevention, conscientisation, preparation, response and relief/recovery.*

Who is to take care of this chain? The trend in the national government of the last decade has been a steady decentralisation and public involvement in risk and responsibility. The *Raad voor Maatschappelijke Ontwikkelingen* (RMO), an authoritative advisory body to the national government on social issues, has advocated a focus on the interaction between the public security provision system and self-organising capability of citizens. Local security, it is asserted, can only be provided if NGOs, companies and citizens assume responsibilities. While security provision is centrally planned and managed and implemented in a top-down manner, in practice, many other institutions need to be mobilised to respond to all kinds of threats to security, such as social workers and traffic regulators. These actors become rather more important if we extend the spectrum to earlier links in the security chain; hazard prevention, conscientisation and preparedness. If the wider civil society is well prepared for calamity, the response to an extreme event is much more effective and the 'impact' of an extreme event will be reduced. As we shall see in Chapter 8, private insurers take on a key role in Britain, and it is now debated in the Netherlands what role the insurance sector can play here. An insurable risk means floods are no longer seen as an 'Act of God' but rather as a risk people can influence by location and preventative measures.

The country's institutional set-up for flood management has historically presented an interesting hybrid of 'logic of war' (emergency politics) and 'logic of peace' (normal politics) security planning that might offer inroads for widening the actor base of the flood management regime (see Chapter 1). In the thirteenth century, long before there was any central government, farmers banded together to form the non-public, deliberative bodies, known as water (polder) boards, to pool resources for protection infrastructure, negotiating preferred drainage levels for groundwater and, more recently, guarantee water quality standards. The verb 'to polder' comes from the egalitarian process of bargaining and compromise in creating and managing polders. The water boards, whose number ran into thousands until quite recently, however competed with each other and not infrequently offloaded risk onto neighbouring boards creating hazardous situations. In 1798 the French occupying force established a national authority, Rijkswaterstaat, to ensure the security of the main river and the coast. While the polder boards continued to share responsibility for dike operation and upkeep, Rijkswaterstaat came to dominate security management, especially after calamities.

When flood security has become institutionalised in practice, there is no need to constantly make speech acts reminding the audience of the urgency of flood policy. In the Netherlands, conditioned by a perennial struggle with rivers

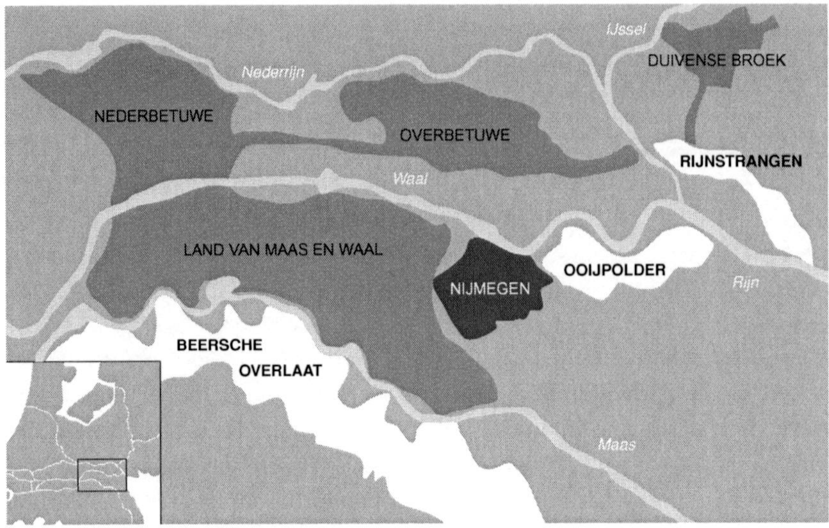

Figure 6.1: ***Areas in white are proposed flood storage polders***

and sea, even a relatively modest flood event is termed a 'disaster' and becomes *securitised* (Buzan et al., 1998). A grateful nation proudly stood by as the Public Works Department built the grand Delta Works after the 1953 sea flood. As Dicke (2001) explains, technological self-confidence, boosted by Dutch expertise in civil engineering, promoted a discourse of invulnerability. This confidence obviated the need to consult end users about flood management structures and decisions. As rivers were successfully contained, a political space for protests opened up only in the 1970s and 1980s, an alliance of environmentalists and

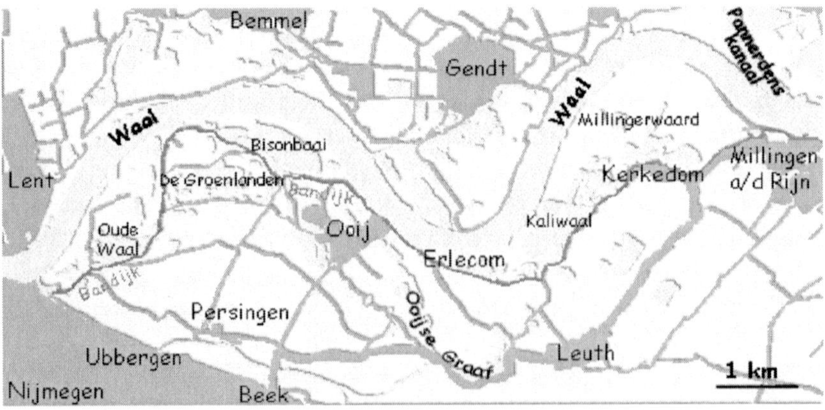

Figure 6.2: ***The Ooij polder***

local stakeholders who saw their dike houses and cultural landscape destroyed by dikes. In response, an era of greener engineering started (Disco, 2002).

The normative discharge had only just been lowered from 16,000 to 15,000 m^3/s in 1993 (Driessen and de Gier, 1997b) when the high-water events of December 1993 (Maas) and February 1995 (flood on the Maas, near-flood on the Waal and Rhine rivers) woke the country up to the 'residual flood risk' the rivers could still pose.

Dire predictions of more frequent and intense climate change-induced extreme events dented the sense of invulnerability, a new 'Delta Plan', this time for the Maas and Rhine rivers, was rushed through in emergency legislation (Chapter 6). The standard was raised to 16,000 m^3/s, while the water sector advocated 18,000. However, this did not change the general mood in the Waterways Department that dikes cannot be raised forever. In 1995, research started on 'failure factors' other than overtopping dikes, and a new, 'horizontal' flood defence strategy was sought: finding space for the rivers rather than constraining them even further.

The final straw that changed calamity policy, however, was not a flood but a *drought* inducing an unexpected dike shift near the town of Wilnis in 2003 that changed the acting Vice Minister's (Melanie Schultz van Haegen) mind. She turned round to the view that the government cannot promise 100 per cent security and that some calamity is inevitable. In this, she joins an internationally growing awareness amongst policymakers that all calamity cannot be averted (UNISDR, 2002). The liberal politician envisaged a process in which multiple actors *jointly* take care of the security cycle from sensible planning and flood prevention to flood response and compensation.

Thus, the water department belatedly accepted the implication of the 1993 integrated security chain memorandum it had co-signed. The study by Rosenthal and 't Hart (1998) shows flood response left much to be desired after the high-water events in 1993 and 1995. Since then, the Home Office's and Water Department's calamity policies became much more aligned. The decision-making circle on water management was widened to municipal planning departments, the housing department, traffic authorities, the fire brigade, etc. An integrated view of (spatial) planning, warning and evacuation systems for flood management as contemplated in the Netherlands would also invite a more participatory mode of decision-making for disaster management.

Coordination is not an easy task even between national ministries, let alone between central and local governments. The Ministries of Spatial Planning and Economic Affairs and provincial and local government usually do not perceive flood safety as the primary decision criterion, tend to lean on the Public Works Department to take care of flood defence, and have seen the 'standstill principle' on flood plain development as unnecessarily restrictive. Once a site receives extra flood protection, the temptation to build right behind that defence is considerable (the 'control dilemma', Immink, 2007). The moratorium on building in flood plains, put in place in 1995, was rescinded in 2005. The new role for the Public Works Department as one player among others implicates it has to be more assertive/aggressive in negotiations, and less of a protector-patron.

Chastened by opposition to its dike reinforcement projects in the 1980s and early 1990s, the Public Works Department sought cooperation with polder boards, provincial and local authorities, who were specifically asked to come up with ideas and initiative themselves for river management, which together were dubbed 'Room for the River'. The national government also decided not to put the new plan under emergency planning or to fast-track the decision-making process under a straightforward 'public planning procedure' (*Rijksprojectenprocedure*), but decided to pursue a *PKB* (*Planologische Kern Beslissing*). PKB is a lengthy planning procedure with much greater scope for participation and redress. The attitude to lower/level authorities and citizens thus looked a lot like the 'logic-of-peace' mode of security governance.

The following case study[2] describes an episode in which the modality of citizen involvement in decision-making on flood storage became a conflictive issue.

6.3 Controlled Flooding Revisited

Given the 'disaster status' that 1993 and 1995 were given in the media, many non-regional people, including Prince William Alexander, now seem to believe that the Rhine and its branches flooded in Gelderland in those years.[3] But for many local people, the traumatic aspect of events was that of leaving the area in panic, when 200,000 people were evacuated in the Central Netherlands. Until 1993, the Netherlands had thought itself invulnerable, so there was no calamity plan. After the near-flood in winter 1993, however, the responsible water board had an evacuation plan prepared in 1994. The peak discharge in early 1995 was actually lower than the 1993 peak, but now that there was a plan, there was something that could be used, which made it compelling to use it.

While it was still unclear that a disaster was imminent, there was great pressure to do something (interview, Public Works Department, regional director). Interviews suggest that Nijmegen Mayor d'Hondt and Gelderland's Provincial Governor Terlouw considered allowing the Overbetuwe region to flood, as it had already been abandoned by evacuated citizens, to save the downstream Alblasserwaard polder:

> . . . (T)he Alblasserwaard had not been evacuated while the (higher up) Bommelwaard had. When the Alblasserwaard dikes were on the verge of breaching, that request came up [from there]: please cut the dikes on the other side to save us. [. . .] I thought: in future that should not

> happen to us again. If you want to do something as radical as inundating a whole area with incredible levels of damage, you have to reflect on that, confer very well with the political sector and come well prepared to make a decision. (interview, former RWS director, 2005)[4]

The dikes were never cut, but the idea of inundation as a last-ditch escape was now on the agenda. After the 1995 event, the decision to widen rivers to make more space for flood waves had resulted in a series of proposed measures for bypasses, dike shifts and removals and river restoration along the Rhine and Meuse: the Room for the River programme. This involves structural changes along the Rhine, Waal, Merwede, IJssel and Maas rivers to enhance river capacity to cope with 16,000 m^3/s discharge on the Rhine, which is 3,500 m^3/s more than the highest river discharge ever (in 1926 – the 1993 and 1995 peaks were lower). Creating more space for floodwater by widening them and digging flood bypasses would mean taking land from and nuisance for private and civil-society actors.

As the deadline for the public presentation of the 'Room for the River' plans neared, however, two key worries emerged inside the ministry. First, at the close of the 1990s, flood experts started to worry about bigger floods. The 1994 Mississippi flood and worrying climate change scenarios begged the question: What to do if an unusual flood peak hits the Netherlands? It was clear that, even if all the Room for the River programme's measures were in place, this would not be able to cushion such an event. Experts started to project a 18,000 m^3/s peak scenario in light of climate change and upstream (German) works. Silva (2001) however claims that in 100 years' time, even a 19,000 m^3/s peak will indeed be possible.

Second, 'Room for the River' would generate an enormous amount of quarrying material (sand and clay), which the market might not be able to absorb (interview, *Room for the River* manager, 2005). Would it not be more sensible to concentrate intervention in a few rather than many locations?

Such considerations put the issue of planning for 'residual risk' of a 1-in-1250-year crisis event on the internal agenda of the Public Works Department. Thoughts turned to controlled flood storage – allowing excessive floodwater discharges to inundate 'calamity polders', which are sacrificed to save other areas.

This idea was presented in 2000 as the closing piece of a large-scale plan to widen rivers: Room for the River. It appears from interviews with the protagonists that they had hoped that the actual decision on the specifics would be delayed until after further study. But they had not counted on the political agenda of their political boss, the Vice-Minister for Water Management.

It should be noted that there is plenty of historical precedent for controlled flooding (drainage) in low-population polders or polder compartments. Controlled flooding/drainage was common historical practice in the Netherlands all through the ages, including in the Ooij polder area under scrutiny here. Overdiking (making your dike higher than your neighbours' dike) and 'public cuts' of a dike opposite yours to keep dry was usual. The Beerse Overlaat, the largest of the indicative calamity polders located in the province of Noord Brabant, only lost its function as an emergency flood diversion tool by the middle of the twentieth century.

The issue of where to direct excess flood water had been dormant for decades – as the last river floods had been in 1926 and 1947, there was little incentive for decision-making. But as we saw, it became pressing again in 1995. The word 'calamity polder'[5] was first mentioned in 1998 in the WL Delft study, *De Rijn op Termijn* (Dijkman et al., 1998) to denote a retention area between the dikes in downstream areas. Therefore, others, such as the national government, can step in to compensate them for their loss. After the commotion in 2000, the original coinage, 'calamity polder', was changed into 'emergency flood storage' (*noodoverloop*).

6.3.1 To Securitise or Not to Securitise the Flood?

Is emergency flood storage a calamity or a normal event? This is a key question, as it informs the mode of decision-making to be employed – the logic of war employed in life-and-death planning or routine democratic decision-making.

Several interviewees, including the environmental spokesman, were nostalgic about the time when all involved were of a similar mind, the Delta Act for the Great Rivers of 1995 fast-tracked mode of decision-making was uncontroversially carried through, paving the way for swift action. The office of the Dutch Institute of Civil Engineering is reportedly emblazoned with a parody of the Lord's Prayer: 'Give us our daily bread, and a flood every ten years'. Yet, as we have seen in the preceding chapter, such periods of closure for the sake of 'national unity' fall apart as the memory of the flood fades. Thus, by 2000, the momentum propelled by the 1995 event had dwindled and 'Room for the River' had to go through normal procedures.

Nevertheless, the emergency storage policy for extreme events added on to 'Room for the River' added a crisis element that made it a prime candidate for 'securitised' calamity planning. Reflecting on the public upheaval that the publication of controlled flooding in Gelderland was to generate, many at the Public Works Ministry wished they had kept the policy under their hats. 'Many of us thought: why didn't we just send a circular to responsible public officers in a plain brown envelope?' (pers. comm., RWS policy staffer, 2002).

Had they done so, the affected inhabitants might never have heard about the calamity plan. However, the Vice-Minister for Water decided to publicise it. The Vice-Ministry for Water had only been created in 1998. Before that, the Minister of Transport was responsible for water management. Because transport itself is a heavy portfolio, most Transport Ministers had been happy to leave water policy to their civil servants. One interviewee paraphrases his former boss, Transport Minister Annemarie Jorritsma, as saying: 'Your job [civil servant] is to come up with the solutions, my job is to get it past the House of Commons' (Interview, former RWS director, 2005).

But now that the new post of Vice-Minister for Water had been created, the politician occupying it, Monique de Vries, felt she needed to put herself and her policy on the map. As her policy adviser at the time puts it, there is a 'direct relationship between the column inches in the press and political support for one's policy in the House of Commons' (interview, policy aide, 2006). Little leeway could be gained for effective water policy and conveying a sense of urgency. Moreover, as a non-water expert she found herself in an isolated position within the Ministry. What interviewees call an institutional 'clay screen' seemed to seal De Vries and her aides off from the high-level public officers, who are seasoned, politically savvy water experts. The policy aide therefore advised her boss to 'make a noise' to get everyone's attention.

The Vice-Minister indeed decided to throw the cat among the pigeons. A choice moment for this was the presentation of the Room for the River policy document at Slot Loevestein castle on 29 February 2000. Many eyebrows were raised when the Room for the River document turned out to display maps of controlled flooding areas. Generally, decision-makers prefer vagueness, deciding the rough contours ('search areas') but leaving the actual designation of affected areas until later. Maps are so politically explosive because they concretise winners and losers, provoking people to oppose something to avert the worst. There was an uneasy precedent when in the province of Groningen, in the North of the country, 'search areas' for emergency rainwater storage were hashed on maps after a polder flooded with rainwater in 1998. Angry farmers occupied the Waterschapshuis to force a change of policy (pers. comm., former *Waterschap* staffer, 2004). The politician's pragmatic senior policy officers had not dissuaded the policy when they realised she was going to involve controlled flooding in the Loevestein document. Regional Public Works officers also claim the central office had also not bothered to inform the Arnhem branch of their Ministry (RWS interviewees).

6.3.2 Legitimising Emergency Flood Storage

After Vice-Minister De Vries had gone on the national news and the following current affairs programme, *Netwerk*, the hoped-for 'panic' was generated all right but there was a political risk in surprising stakeholders. While the Vice-Minister was prepared to shock her colleagues at the Ministry, she expressed surprise at the backlash outside the circles of government.

The first wave of protest in 2000 was instigated by provincial authorities and well-established (corporatist) civil-society organisations: the Chamber of Commerce, the Social Partners (i.e. employers and employees) of Gelderland, and farmers' unions. Immediately after they saw the indicative controlled flooding areas hashed on the map in the Room for the River document in 2000, they hired counter-expertise: a report from the same well-respected engineering consultancy that had mooted the idea of controlled flooding in the first place, WL Delft. The consultants predictably reported that controlled flooding in itself is a sound idea, but not in the locations and modalities it was proposed now.

The province of Gelderland was the first to question the underlying assumptions for emergency storage, notably the need to prepare for 18,000 m^3/s rather than 16,000. To support this doubt, the province of Gelderland had a report carried out with North Rhine Westphalia state in Germany and, in due course, support from the Public Works Department. The report found that 15,500 m^3/s could flow into Dutch territory in case of flooding in Germany. A highly theoretical superwave would bring 16,500 m^3/s. Only in case of no flooding in Germany whatsoever, that is, sky-high dikes in Germany, a maximum scenario of 18,700 m^3/s would be possible. Given the implausibility of such high dikes, Gelderland continued to stick with 16,000 m^3/s as a target for 'Room for the River' and remained opposed to emergency storage.

The Vice-Minister however was determined to explain the emergency storage policy to the stakeholders. Her communication expert at the time is a great fan of social learning and advised a dialogue to develop shared meaning in a one-to-one relationship with the citizens. The Minister thus treated controlled flooding like any other Room for the River project rather than seeing the deliberate flooding of an inhabited area as a 'securitisable' crisis policy. The envisaged interaction with citizens, however, was soon thwarted by senior policy advisers as well as a hegemonic ministerial policy culture that discourages too much communication between minister and citizens, or indeed minister and public servants. When a first bus ride across the 'backyards' was made, 'the coach soon filled with civil servants' (policy aide, 2006).

The Home Office meanwhile was not best pleased with the Water Vice-Minister's unexpected move, either. An internal memorandum indicates it did not oppose controlled flooding as a way to deal with residual risk, but saw the issue rapidly becoming unfit for discussion (*Minuut,* 2002). It asked its Minister, Remkes, to demand an explanation in the cabinet meeting (interview, Home Office, 2006). As a result, a commission was instated by Home Office and Water Department in 2001, to be headed by veteran liberal senator David Luteijn, to research the necessity of the policy measure and indicate suitable areas. Other pressing issues for the commission were the operation of such polders, compensation for flood-induced damage and public support base.

The commission took a year, in which seven technical studies were carried out. The commission could rely on an almost unlimited budget – the outlay eventually reached EUR 1 million.

Early Moves for Closure

True to Dutch style, the commission's membership had been selected on a good spread between political affiliations. It drew both on Luteijn's own vast network and veterans of earlier water committees. Technical experts were thin on the ground in the commission and some interviewees note with surprise that key functions like the two project secretaries and technical liaison were relatively junior career bureaucrats. The commission therefore had to rely on the supporting technical expert group.

The commission's president was quite clear on the assumptions with which he started his work. Crucially, he treated the '18,000 flood' and the need to do something about it as a given. He brooked no discussion. The exclusion of debate and alternatives is a core aspect of 'securitisation'. In his discussion of the Copenhagen School's concept of securitisation, M. Williams (2003) points out that visuals are as important as the written and spoken word in 'securitising' moves. Indeed, to impress the urgency of the task at hand on his fellow commissioners, Luteijn had a video animation shown, prepared by RIZA Lelystad, representing a disastrous flood event. This video drove home to key members that something needed to be done. Thus, while others (notably Professor Wybrand van Ellen) called for calm, taking a step back, doing nothing was not a viable option for the committee: 'if you do nothing, you will have to evacuate half a million citizens'. (NRC 2002)

Luteijn's 'move for closure' was to lead to a clash between 'converts' and 'doubters' within his advisory group. Since 1995, research had been on the way into uncertainties in dikes,[6] showing that many more 'failure factors' than overtopping dikes play a role in flooding – piping, dike systems interaction, and seven other factors (Silva, 2001). An official at Rijkswaterstaat Oost-Nederland (interviewed in 2005) recalled a furious row between those who accepted a degree of uncertainty and those who did not. The mayor of Duiven, a town in the designated Rijnstrangen area, part of a 'focus group' for the commission, likewise sought a hearing for the dissident view.

This debate however looked to be time-consuming, and Luteijn felt he had no time. Various interviewees describe Luteijn as an avuncular, 'quick and dirty, can-do' commission leader who delivers and had not time for distracting uncertainties, both in terms of rationale and of information uncertainties. Moreover, when the 'Purple' national governmental coalition (see Chapter 7) fell prematurely in early 2002, Luteijn decided to speed up the work to be able to present its report in time to set the agenda for the new Cabinet.

While the Vice-Minister's intention to interact with the polder came to nothing in 2000, Senator Luteijn certainly reached out to the region during the drafting of his report: he made three consultative rounds, organising consultation meetings with local government representatives, and 'intermediate organisations' of civil society – consumer associations, Chamber of Commerce, etc.

The most notable feature of the consultation process, however, was that the concerned 'grassroots actors' themselves were not consulted about the designation of their polder for floodwater storage. When interviewed by us in 2005, the commission's Chairman Luteijn declared security is simply 'too important' to extend discussion to citizen stakeholders. All this suggests controlled, 'crisis-mode' decision-making.

Site Selection: Lack of Space

The amount of water detained determines the amount of space needed to deal with top-end flood scenarios. Given the Netherlands' considerable population density (452 per km^2), it is not so easy to free up space for floodwater storage. The selection process reflects this quest for space.

In the Loevestein report, the indicative sites for flood storage were both up- and downstream. WL Delft's counter-report criticised the preliminary site selection, preferring a focus on the downstream Alblasserwaard and nearby polders on the lower part of the Rhine. But as the Luteijn Commission set to work, the lower Rhine disappeared from view, as the impact of flood storage in those polders was held to be much less than upstream areas. As the Ooij polder, a 3,300 ha area, came into view as a candidate for floodwater storage, the Luteijn Commission at first considered the whole of the Ooij and Duffelt for storage, which includes a German part, the Düffel. Historically, Kekerdom and Leuth have long belonged to Germany, Dutch and German farming organisations and businesses have social and commercial ties, and attend each other's annual meetings and New Year's functions. Gelderland meets with Nordrhein-Westfalen and riverine municipalities meet twice a year. For long-time residents, the binational space appears to be one unpartitioned reality (interviews 2005).

Like the Ooij's inhabitants, the river does not respect boundaries either so that inundation would also affect German territory. To explain the policy and assuage German fears, Public Works officers made well-appreciated visits to visited municipalities in Germany like Emmerich and Kleve – in fact rather more so than talking to their Dutch counterparts in the Ooij (interview, policy advisor, RWS Oost, 2005).

It appears that the integration of land, water and society required for Integrated Water Management (Mitchell, 1990; GWP, 2000) fell afoul of a classical clash between hydrological and administrative boundaries. Inundating German territory (Duffelt) would thus have international consequences, which would present a foreign-policy issue the government did not want to burn its fingers on. RWS could not or would not take measures that had trans-boundary effects. But it did not appear feasible to flood the Ooij only. Isolating German territory from impacts of actual Dutch controlled flooding would require a dike of 8–9 m' height running from the German–Dutch border up to Nijmegen to retain the water in case of a controlled flooding event (*Volkskrant* 2003). In 2002 the German state of North Rhine Westphalia announced it would build a dike itself if controlled flooding were to go ahead.

By concentrating on the Dutch side, the commission lost a sizeable chunk of the projected inundation capacity. The three areas that were finally selected (Ooij, Rijnstrangen and Beerse Overlaat – 90, 115 and 365 million m^3 respectively) cannot nearly handle as much water as originally intended.

6.3.3 Local Response to the Commission's Report

The Ooij's population is about 13,000, 10,000 of whom are concentrated in the town of Ubbergen en Beek. Many dwellers have lived in the polder for generations, but the region has also seen a steady trickle of 'imported' residents from the western conurbation and elsewhere, looking for peace and quiet in a rollicking landscape. These newcomers, it appears from the interviews, were not as prone to bowing to authority as the older residents were. The region has a history of activism against spatial plans. First in the 1970s, it resisted a plan to widen the bottleneck at Lent, a parish where the river Waal narrows from 1 km across to 450 m. This widening plan, to make space for shipping, was to eat into the polder. Then in the 1980s, a local platform resisted planned dike reinforcement.

However, the fact that the action committee was formed over two and a half years after the first public announcement of emergency flood storage plans and six months after the publication of Luteijn's report, indicates slow growth of civil opposition to the plans. Two out of three eventually selected areas put up scant resistance, while in the Ooij polder, resistance initially consisted of isolated protests. When it became clear in 2001 that the Luteijn Commission had a preference for the Ooij, the mayor of Ubbergen protested, but citizens appeared to wait and see. This changed when the local Rabobank, which had a very strong local client base, stepped in. It issued an leaflet voicing their alarm in May 2002, when the Luteijn report came out. In September, Nout van der Ven, a desktop publishing expert from the region, mobilised a small group which started to meet 'chaotically' in a local function room (local citizen, quoted in Roth, Warner and Winnubst, 2006: 118).Farmers had also caught wind of developments and placed straw dolls with slogans in high-visibility locations. Awareness had thus been raised, but without a clearly defined organisational focus, when the Rabobank organised their thematic annual meeting for its members in November, with David Luteijn (a member of the Rabobank's national board) as its special guest speaker.

Once the report was finalised, Luteijn was keen to present it in the region. He felt he had a strong hand, being able to give the region far-reaching guarantees for compensation of damage from emergency storage. He also came with a catchy metaphor; the calamity polders were like an 'air bag' to cushion the impact of a crash (Luteijn Commission, 2002).

Luteijn's presentation proved a real eye opener for the Ooij. After a tumultuous question-and-answer session speaker and audience clearly came away with a different assessment. While Luteijn, interviewed in 2005, claimed that the region was basically 'won over', Ooij citizens were so outraged about the plan that they decided to form an action platform. Unlike many other protest groups against water intervention, the protest became driven by well-to-do 'bourgeois' townspeople rather than farmer-led.

Water disasters are normally treated as an external security risk that you cannot influence. When a government itself decides to drain floodwater into a low-population polder, the external risk fully becomes an *internal* risk to the flood-affected citizens, i.e. a risk someone (the government) is responsible and accountable for. This brings a tension between the local and national interest.

Citizens of the Ooij polder did not fundamentally dispute that their area could be flooded in an extreme event to save others. 'We don't lie awake worrying that one day things may go wrong'. As the first area to be affected by a flood wave once the Rhine has crossed the German–Dutch border, the Ooij polder dwellers have more or less accepted that risk (interview, HWP spokesman, 2005). But they doubt the ethics of that decision. After all, in any (hydro-)social contract (Warner, 2000, 2004; Meissner and Turton, 2003), a government should protect its citizens, not put them at risk of drowning.

Prime target for the campaign was the new Vice-Minister, Melanie Schultz van Haegen. Upon taking office in 2001, the liberal politician had been led to believe by Luteijn and her policy advisors that the mood was right clear for controlled flooding. In taking office, Water DG Bert Keijts presented her with three options: shelve, look for a support base, or take action. The Vice-Minister opted for taking action (interview, retired policy adviser, 2006). The platform concluded she 'didn't get it' and saw her decision as a 'declaration of war' (Sanders quoted in *De Volkskrant,* 2003). From now on, the Vice-Minister was the 'enemy' and the platforms started looking for allies (interview, HWP spokesman, 2005). In terms of our analytical framework, the polder was effectively 'counter-securitised'.

While the camps were barely talking to each other, they sought to align others for their cause. The platform formed three working groups – communication, legal and technical. Inspired by a fundamental belief that floodwater should be quickly discharged rather than detained in a densely populated area, professor Wybrand van Ellen, a well-known retired Delft engineer who lived close to the area, made calculations for the technical group questioning the assumptions of the Luteijn Commission, such as the '18,000 flood' scenario. In so doing, he opened up the government's flood management frame. He found likely (the province of Gelderland) but also unlikely allies for this in the engineering community: the platform caught wind of a critical internal technical study underlying the Luteijn Commission's report completed in August 2003 by two well-respected consultancies, WL Delft and HKV Lijn in Water. The carefully worded report did not dispute the merits of controlled flooding, but claimed the plan for the Ooij was uneconomic and ineffective – or as one of the consultants later summarised it, 'weird'.[7] After the legal working group made a call on the *Wet Openbaarheid Bestuur* (Freedom of Information Act) on the part of the Hoogwaterplatform, the existence of the requested report was first denied, then it was 'mislaid' and the wrong document sent (interview, Hoogwater platform spokesman, 2005). Another critical advisory report was leaked to the *Trouw* newspaper in 2002.[8]

Meanwhile the communication group produced leaflets, a regular newsletter and a sophisticated, widely read website with links to all relevant reports (www.hoogwaterplatform.nl). It organised media exposure and a powerful political lobby. At the national level, the group bussed parliamentarians around the region to show the consequences of river storage in the polder. Local business made small donations to fund these activities.

Not only the platform made good use of the media, Ubbergen en Beek mayor Wilbers preceded the citizen platform in protesting the measure. During an interview platform leaders asserted he tried to steal their limelight. Together with nine other local authorities, five Dutch and four German, Ubbergen en Beek commissioned counter-expertise from Delft sociologist Enne de Boer. De Boer had already made a social impact assessment for the Water Department's *Bouwdienst* in 2000 and concluded it would be a hard sell. His 2003 report ridiculed the 'air bag' metaphors and the 18,000 m^3/s scenario, claiming that the German river banks will flood long before the river reaches the Low Countries, since current German efforts aim to control flooding at 14,600 m^3/s. In sum, the protests had become an (international) public-private-NGO partnership.

Range of Alternatives: Controlled or Uncontrolled Flooding?

Now that the solution frame was opened, what options for the Ooij were in the picture? The human agency aspect in controlled storage brought an operational uncertainty issue: when to open the floodgates. Experience in 1993 and 1995 suggests that when in doubt, mayors and engineers tend to make a decision, even if a premature one, rather than waiting and seeing (interview, retired RWS officer, 2005; van Meurs, 1995). But given the limited storage capacity of Dutch polders, opening them too early would mean missing out on any spare storage capacity for a second flood peak.

What about *un*controlled flood storage? Neither flood experts nor politicians liked this variety, but environmental groups such as the Gelderland Environmental Federation (GMF) saw new environmental opportunities from allowing the water to come when it comes. However as the Ooij polder became a more serious option, the local chapter started to feel uneasy about public support and the GMF dropped its support such that discussion of the option became taboo (Martinet, pers. comm., 2005). The Ooij platform's technical experts found that embanking towns like Kekerdom might raise the groundwater level such that the town would flood anyway, badly affecting residences for months. Thus, while economic damage would be significantly reduced (from EUR 650 million to 120 million in the Ooij, see Commissie Noodoverloopgebieden, 2002: 18), controlled flood storage would mean months of nuisance after the polder evacuees returned to their homes. A highly effective PR visual deployed against emergency flooding was a blown-up photo mock-up of Kekerdom, submerged. This striking visual made 'controlled flooding' seem barely preferable to 'uncontrolled flooding' – putting in bunds around the inhabited areas would make it more rather than less dangerous, displacing the risk.

While the Ooij platform did not bring radically different alternatives to the table, at least two other actors did in 2003. To the great annoyance of the Riverenland Waterschap, The Knooppunt Arnhem-Nijmegen (KAN), a regional collaborative alliance to promote the region between Arnhem and Nijmegen, commissioned a report from Haskoning consultants in Nijmegen to research eight options for water management. The consultants found for a chain of very small controlled flooding areas, similar to an initiative developed at the time in neighbouring North Rhine Westphalia. That same year the national forest conservation agency, Staatsbosbeheer, published its alternative in the report 'Lonkend Rivierenland' ('*Enticing fluvial area*', Staatsbosbeheer, 2003), proposing to dig a whole new bypass (green river) through the area. Neither report generated much interest.

Apotheosis

Meanwhile, the Commission and water department sought to sell the intervention to its intended audience. An internal memo (*Minuut*) from 2002 shows that the Public Works Department's communication desk categorised stakeholders view as 'friendly', 'neutral' and 'hostile' and strategised to convert the fence sitters. But as the Vice-Minister enjoyed maternity leave in 2003, the HWP's political lobbying effort at the national level began to reap success: a political deal saw the two largest parliamentary parties (Labour and the Christian Democrats) acting in tandem to move the money reserved for controlled flooding to supplement the budget for 'Room for the River', which expected a shortfall. Back from her leave, Vice-Minister Schultz concluded the race was lost and in April, well before the scheduled date, she presented the Cabinet's position that emergency flooding would be shelved, reduced to an option among others, due to cost-ineffectiveness and lack of sufficient public support.

In September that year the current affairs TV programme, *Netwerk*, suggested that the case might be reopened. The Vice-Minister was said to pressure the Nijmegen city authorities to agree with a controversial plan to widen the bottleneck at the north bank (at Lent), which was linked with a EUR 80–90 million national contribution to a new bridge over the river Waal. If this deal was off due to protest from Lent dwellers, reporters claimed, she would table the flood storage plans for the Ooij polder again. When this made the press, the Vice-Minister strenuously denied this textbook example of linkage politics, and had a bunch of flowers sent by courier to the platform chairman with a message that the controlled storage option was off the cards.

6.4 Discussion: Four Types of Participation

This chapter has explored a case of policymaking for extreme flood events. The interviews suggest that in view of the hitherto lacklustre profile of her newly created office, Water Vice-Minister De Vries decided, and was not discouraged by her public officers, to take the 'political road' to find a legitimacy base for a policy that was not yet in evidence within the bureaucracy. Her initial treatment of the policy in a *non-securitised* mode, however, was thwarted by that same bureaucracy. The Luteijn Commission, instated to defuse conflict and find a public support base, broadened the debate to intermediary organisations, but excluded affected citizens with a securitisation rationale – national security was too important to involve citizens – thus stirring rather than dousing the flames in the region.

The commission opted for early closure on controversial issues, and a promotional ('selling') policy vis-à-vis stakeholders once the report was finished. The upshot was that a polder whose citizens were at root understanding of its flood risk turned against the policy. Only when the platform failed to get a hearing and experts sympathetic with the Ooij inhabitants' case found many technical, legal and economic flaws with the plan to flood the Ooij, did controlled flooding really become a bridge too far for the polder people. The stakeholders in the area only really started to rebel when their technical advisors found that the plan was not sound (Table 6.1).

Participatory Security Matrix

The above case study has highlighted different modes of dealing with calamity. The emergency flood storage faced decision-makers with a problem: Are we to treat this in a closed, *security* mode or in an open, routine-planning mode? The

Time	Stakeholder Group	Strategy
March 2000 and 2003	- province, social partners - KAN	Counter-expertise
2002	Mayors	Counter-expertise and media
November 2002	- Rabo Bank - Citizen Platform	Counter-expertise, lobbying, media and information campaign
2003	National political parties	Parliamentarian motion
2001 and 2003	- Water experts in government - Experts and consultants	Counter-expertise and pressure

Table 6.1: ***Resistance to controlled flood storage: actors and their strategies***

ministerial flood managers' tendency was the former, but the Vice-Minister's initiative opened up the arena for *dialogue* with stakeholders. The upshot was a mix of both: behind-closed-doors expert deliberation plus a highly Dutch form of consultation of non-public stakeholders (civil society and private sector and local-level authority leaders), which however bypassed the policy-affected local population. Excluded stakeholders then decided on a counterattack, *politicising* the issue such that it became a parliamentary debate.

The case study suggests a greater range of modalities for (non-)participation than 'wartime' or 'peacetime' decision-making, with different degrees of actor involvement in considering policy alternatives. Figure 6.3, compiled and systematised by the author on the basis of various strands of literature, applies the modalities found to the present case study; arrows and numbers tracing the dispute's development through time. Let's take a look at each quadrant separately.

Until the past few decades, the standard response has been a 'securitised' crisis mode of high-level experts and managers in the security services – with slight exaggeration: while young and able-bodied soldiers took care of war, retired army and policemen took care of calamity response (Pearce, 2003). In principle, this modality could involve local people in calamity management without abandoning the 'logic of total war'. This 'mass emergency' logic, however, reduces citizens to not much more than soldiers. The active role of the citizen as

		Agreement on values **high..................low**	
		Threat not open to dispute	**Threat open to dispute**
Agreement on facts	**High**	Securitisation (foreclosing debate by speech act) *(0)* *mayor emergency chief, need-to-know top-down instruction for extreme event*	Open conflict, internalising antagonisms (power of argument) *open contest on security policy; mayors side with CBO 3*
	Low	Routinisation/Managerialism (foreclosing debate by risk management) *2* *consultation with intermediate organisations and local authorities, not with citizens*	Dialogue: (power of *better* argument) *1* *joint learning with local stakeholders*

Figure 6.3: ***How to counter calamity in a participatory way? A 'participatory security governance' matrix. Matrix axes based on Hisschemöller and Hoppe (1998). Arrows denote chronological development of Ooij episode***

a part of the state's security apparatus would mean a return to ancient Greece, where 'particular active responsibilities such as jury duty, or even the hoplite armies and the notion of "warrior citizens", made citizenship as much about responsibility as entitlement' (Muller, 2004).

Such mass mobilisation is unlikely in the Netherlands, but another aspect of normal emergency planning is reminiscent of planning for war: secrecy or information on a need-to-know basis. Sending mayors a 'plain brown envelope' with instructions for emergency flooding (interview, RWS officer, 2004) while keeping citizens in the dark would have been standard procedure in the past and therefore is indicated with the number zero in Figure 6.3.

An increasingly practised way for governments is no longer to treat risk and calamity management like a war but like a normal challenge we can handle rationally. A 'managerial' approach to risk (Aradau, 2001) 'defines down' threats that were previously constructed as extraordinary as normal and routine risks, unless they become 'disruptive of the social fabric'. This 'desecuritised' approach is more intricate, as the enemy (the river) is not external, it is now our friend, but needs to be kept in line. In this modality security governance becomes a public–private co-production. This 'participatory desecuritisation', however, does not preclude a depoliticised handling. The road chosen by the Luteijn Commission is most reminiscent of this 'managerial' approach: civil-society organisations were consulted in controlled focus-groups without veto power, but affected citizens were not.

In the wake of a flood wave, the analysis of the problem and the solution may be uncontroversial and a 'securitised' or 'managerial' solution may be accepted. But in the Ooij case, the flood had been more than five years ago, and both the analysis of the problem and the values leading to a solution turned out to be contested, not only with local stakeholder but also within the expert community. 'Wicked' (intractable) problems, where both values and facts are disputed or uncertain, cannot be solved by a political process only. They may require a mix of politics and technocracy (post-normal science). For such problems Hisschemöller and Hoppe (1998) recommend undertaking a signalling and social learning process first.

What Vice-Minister De Vries's aide professed to have in mind (as related during the Nijmegen book presentation session) was indeed a form of deliberative democracy. This approach aims to consult with stakeholders to enable social learning to arrive at a policy consensus on the basis of argumentation. A dialogue does not see actors as mere rational individualists, but as social beings who are aware of the interdependence with regard to the problem in hand, and are willing to deliberate for collective action (see also Röling and Woodhill, 2001). Deliberative democracy thus enables a *dialogue* on security itself. While a security speech act is a one-shot activity based on a fixed interest definition, a dialogue, in which participants' subject positions and preferences can change due to force of argument, which, in turn, could lead to different process outcomes (Sjursen, 2004).

In a multi-stakeholder platform (MSP) it is not the majority-plus-one that decides, but a process of consensus building between representatives of pre-identified identities (Dryzek, 2002). These identities may be 'public', 'private' and 'civil society' but also based on economic interests (farmers, industry and homeowners) or linguistic, ethnic or religious affiliations (Warner and Simpungwe, 2003). A multi-stakeholder platform for flood preparedness (Warner, Waalewijn and Hilhorst, 2002) does not solve problems, but can promote flood awareness, increase social capital and promote joint learning. While I have claimed elsewhere (Warner, 2006) that a tendency for Habermasians (e.g. Hemmati, 2002) to see an opposition between MSPs and politics is often spurious, there is still a 'residual risk' that MSPs lead to depoliticisation, to 'taming' both the issue and stakeholders (Currie Alder, 2007). Depoliticised handling of security means conflicts remain unaddressed and key stakeholders excluded. A consensus-oriented dialogue can kill the 'vibrant clash of democratic political positions' required for a 'well functioning democracy' (Mouffe, 2000).

The matrix makes it possible to trace chronologically the security governance choices made for extreme events. Seeking the front pages to boost her political profile, Vice-Minister De Vries decided to forego the 'plain brown envelope' option, i.e. security policy behind closed doors, assigned the top left corner as option *(0)*. The stakeholder dialogue for joint learning she appeared to favour (Phase *1* in the diagram), however, was swiftly prevented by her department and replaced by a commission which allowed a limited, controlled form of societal consultation to 'sell' the policy (*2*). The exclusion of the local stakeholders led to civic protest and indeed skilful *politicisation* of the issue (*3*). The opposition pictured the Vice-Minister as 'the enemy', conducted a 'knowledge guerrilla' unearthing an apparently classified document, undercut the assumptions of the Department's frame, and successfully counterposed a frame in which controlled flooding was the problem rather than the solution.

Due to the antagonism and polarisation inherent to politicisation, chances are that politicisation takes the form of hardened positions. However, if there is no *a priori* consensus on values, depoliticising real social tensions over an issue will only defer politicised confrontation. The analysis of the Ooij suggests that, given the basic willingness of local stakeholders, their positions were not immutable and a multi-stakeholder process of 'joint learning' might have opened alternatives rather than the politicisation that ensued. In this sense the road taken was a missed opportunity for hammering out a mutually acceptable deal, a mode of safety governance in which Hilhorst's three domains of knowledge and action (experts, managers and locals, see Chapter 1) could act in step. It proves difficult for central government to be less controlling and for citizens to break an ingrained culture of relying on government for its security. However, other Room for the River experiences, show that citizens' initiatives are not restricted but can also bring alternatives to proposed interventions (Roth and Winnubst, 2007).

In light of a perceptibly more concerted effort in shaping calamity policy between Public Works Department and the Home Office, the latter of which is more used to dialogue and bargaining, a greater role for citizens in future calamity policies cannot be ruled out. But the title of the current state-funded research into 'limits to participation' ('Living With Water' Project no. 008), might be a pointer that the Dutch government is wary of ceding too much space.[9]

7

THE JUBILEE RIVER

FLOOD ALLEVIATION OR FLOOD CREATION SCHEME?

7.1 Introduction

Resigned local citizen: 'We like Venice . . . ' (interview, 2000)

The floods of July 2007 brought shock and disruption to large parts of England. Not only properties, cars and trees were affected, a water treatment failed so that half a million people went without clean water. But while flooding caused traffic chaos on the M4 motorway at Maidenhead, the town itself escaped thanks to the Thames flood relief channel, the Jubilee River. Though small by international comparison, the flood relief channel was the biggest and most expensive riverine flood relief scheme to date in the UK.[1] Apart from its environmental benefits and technological daring, the project sought to be socially responsible by engaging citizens to participate in its decision-making.

The Jubilee River project was a tangible result of a vision of greener, more participatory and especially more integrated water management for the Thames imagined by John Gardiner and colleagues, with the National River Authority, Thames Region, a precursor of today's Environment Agency (Gardiner, 1988).

Despite a public enquiry, a lawsuit and Parliamentary questions, Gardiner could still claim at the turn of the century that the project was 'uncontroversial' (pers. comm. Gardiner, 2000). However, the Jubilee River became subject to more controversy and technical investigation in 2003 after parishes downstream to Maidenhead (Datchet, Old Windsor, Wraysbury, Horton and Staines) experienced appreciable flood damage. This raised the issue whether the flooding at Datchet was the consequence of an 'Act of God', of irresponsibility of building in the flood plain, or of human failure on the part of the planners of the Jubilee River.

The present chapter pits three competing *problem frames* in flood management against each other: flooding as the problem, flood plain development as the problem, and the project itself as the problem. Different blame and remedy stories clashed, based on different flood, river and risk management paradigms.

The chapter starts with a review of the changing frames in river and flood management as identified in the UK literature (Sections 7.2 and 7.3). Against this backdrop, Section 7.4 traces the selection of the preferred option and objections and alternatives tabled by opponents. A project that challenges a dominant paradigm (frame) has to clear a great number of hurdles (Section 7.4.2). Section 7.5 looks into the strategies to co-opt or confront opponent stakeholders. It examines how successful the initiative for a participatory process has turned out in the light of conflicts with various stakeholders which necessitated various changes and led to a Public Inquiry in 1992. Section 7.6 goes into the recurring floods in 1998, 2000 and especially 2003, which tested the flood diversion channel and led to acrimony between flood managers and stakeholders.

The case study is based on an extensive archival review of published and unpublished project and policy documents, some 15 interviews with senior project and policy staff of the Environment Agency (EA) and MAFF (now DEFRA), the Internal Drainage Board, Buckinghamshire county, Taplow parish, Eton College, English Nature, multiple conversations with Flood Hazard Research Centre staff at Enfield, as well as exchanges by electronic mail with Maidenhead citizens and project consultants, mainly in 2000 and 2001. Interviewee selection was the result of snowballing. Apart from project documentation, the search draws on grey project literature kindly made available to me by John Gardiner in 2000.

7.2 Risk and Responsibility at the Interface of Water and Space

7.2.1 Naming, Framing and Blaming

To understand actors' positions in a dispute, one has to understand their *problem frames*. 'The frames held by actors determine what they see as being in their interest, and therefore, what interests they see as conflicting' (Schön and Rein, 1994: 29). Frames mobilise the values against which 'risks' and policy 'problems' are judged to exist. Ambiguity and indeterminacy is reduced by *naming* things within a certain frame, to contextualise the issue. 'Naming' (labelling) of problem elements influences the range of alternatives that will be examined. It is within a frame that problems are judged and synthesised. Framing is defined as 'selecting and highlighting some facets of events or issues, and making connections among them so as to promote a particular interpretation, evaluation, and/or solution' (Schön and Rein, 1994).

The act of 'naming' can make an issue political: it explicitly identifies a culprit causing a loss, it attributes an undesirable effect to an undesirable cause. Some issues become embroiled over the allocation of blame and the distribution of power, while others appear to be tolerated within norms of social values and trust (Tansey and O'Riordan, 1999: 72). The naming of 'foreign elements' and ascribing blame to them for mishaps is a political act. 'Blaming' refers to who or what is held responsible for the problem or perceived threat. In the domain of risk and security, such 'blaming' is especially salient when it concerns existential 'survival issues' (Buzan et al., 1998).

The conception of risk and responsibility underlying different risk frames brings different expectations and prescriptions of what government and citizens are expected to do to reduce flood risk, that is, the governance arrangement. This section will inventory the frames of risk and responsibility in water management, river management and disaster management, as identified in the literature: who and what caused the risk and who is responsible for remedying it? These frames will be the context for an analysis of the discursive moves made by the main actors in the debate on the Jubilee River. Risk is politicised when someone is felt to be to blame (Douglas, 1994). The stand-offs between planners, developers, citizens and EA can be seen as 'blaming' narratives (Section 7.6.3).

7.2.2 Frame Change: Looking for a Niche

Hegemonic frames provide stability in an issue-area. Change is bound to be incremental, will mostly take place within bureaucracies and companies (the socio-technical regime) and will eventually bring lock-in (closure) rather than radical paradigm shifts (e.g. Dosi, 1982). By contrast a major change in policy frames is marked by a broad public debate (Scrase and Sheate, 2005). What changes a dominant frame (policy paradigm)?

Out of the several available approaches to understanding policy change, a particularly appealing candidate is Punctuated Equilibrium Theory (Baumgartner, 1994), which suggests that crises and catalytic changes and focusing events are strong candidates to revolutionise dominant policy frames. Due to their strong psychological impact, flood events as 'windows of opportunity' fit the bill perfectly, and indeed Johnson et al. (2005) have shown that the floods of 1947, 1953 (coastal), and the river floods of 1998 and 2000 provided the impetus for policy change in British river management. However, this is not a hard and fast rule: as Scrase and Sheate (2005: 122) note, the landmark Drainage Act of 1930 was not impelled by a flood event, and as we shall see, neither was the creation of the Maidenhead, Windsor and Eton Flood Alleviation Scheme (MWEFAS), the later Jubilee Channel. Moreover, these policy changes were not accompanied by a meaningful change in the constellation of actors and rules that make up the policy regime governing an issue area.

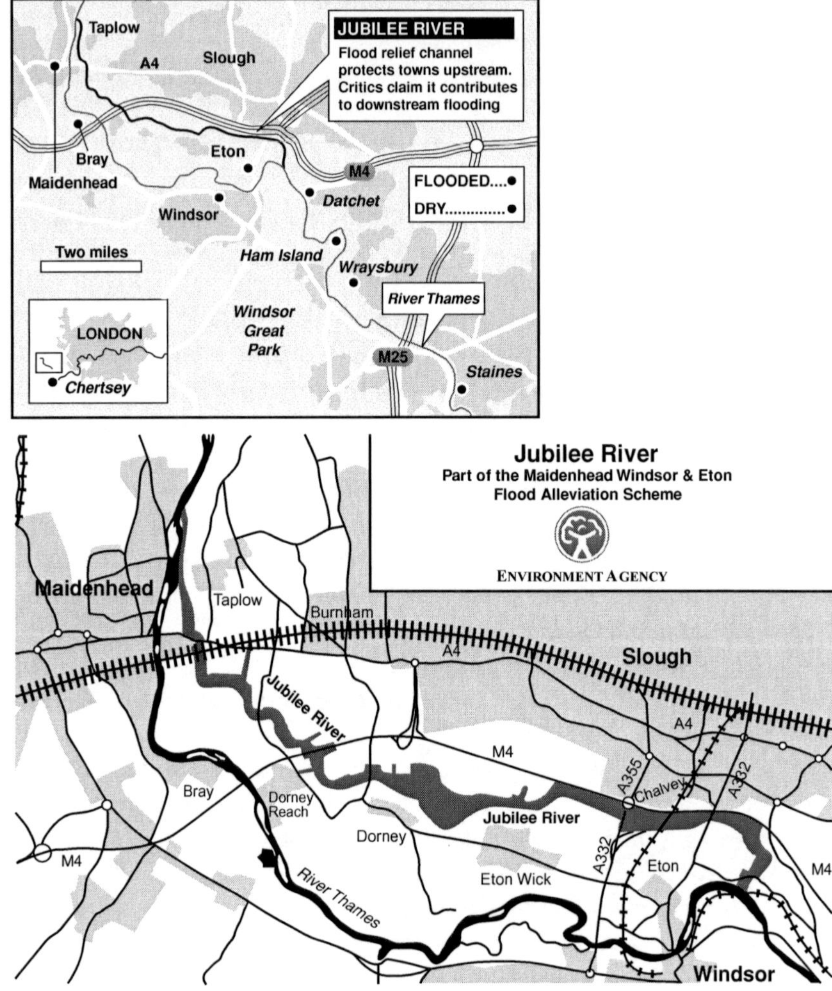

Figure 7.1: ***The Jubilee River project area***

I will therefore consider a different candidate analytical framework than 'focusing events' to understand policy transition. I will examine the MWEFAS, largely the brainchild of John Gardiner and his team at the National Rivers Authority, Thames Region (NRA–TR) and its underlying philosophy of green engineering and integrated river management, as seeking to fill an innovative *niche* within a multi-level perspective of transitions (see Box 7.1). The 'green engineering' approach generated a clash between different frames (paradigms) and may have been crucial in promoting substantial shifts in the flood management regime.

Box 7.1 Multi-Level Perspective on Transitions

Niche: denotes a space where individuals, based on existing knowledge and capabilities develop new technologies or concepts that are geared towards problems of existing regimes. Niches provide space for learning processes and development of social networks, which support innovations. Innovations generated at this level are usually radical.

The patchwork quilt of *socio-technical regime* accounts for stability of existing technological development. Regimes refer to rules of the game that enable and constrain activities within communities. Patterns may arise here in the form of path dependencies, whereby particular innovations are facilitated or constrained by existing networks, investments or regulations. If innovations are generated at the regime level, they are mainly incremental.

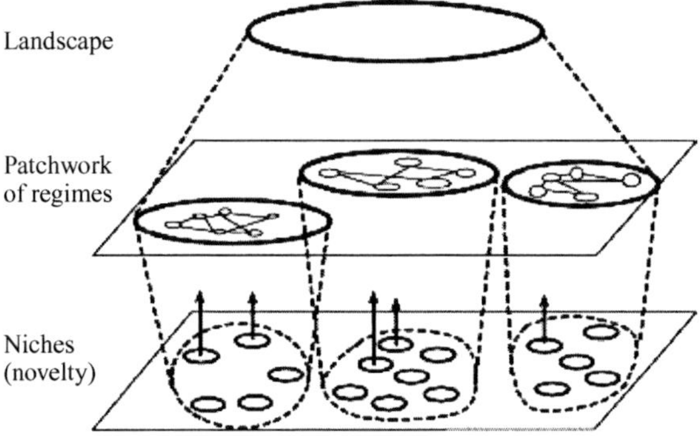

The *socio-technical landscape* encompasses the wider, 'harder' context of a regime in the form of board economic, demographic and (geo)political processes. The context of landscape is very difficult to change and if it does change, it takes much longer than in the case of regimes.

7.2.3 Paradigm Shifts in UK River Management – Changing (Master) Frames and Governance

It is a truism to state that the UK does not have a 'disaster culture': the myth that Britain is largely free from natural hazards persists (Bakker et al., 1999). As a result, citizens were not very aware of floods and other types of risks until the Easter Floods of 1998. When a flood happens, stakeholders perceive it as a freak event, display a pervasive attitude that floods are 'Acts of God' and rely on self-help rather than on government.

To make it onto the public policy agenda, a risk has to be perceived as a *public* risk. When people's desire for security has to be squared with the change and discomfort that inevitably accompanies an intervention that promises to provide protection, there is a tension. People seek security, but also stability and continuity ('ontological security'). Conservatives perceive risks as less dangerous than progressives (Lupton, 1999). In this dilemma, anxiety about flooding can translate as aversity to change, rather than aversity to risk. Thus, the Maidenhead flood scheme led to antagonism between liberal newcomers and change-averse residents who lived in the areas all their lives. An example of this conservationism is the concern for the integrity of the Green Belt, which has long been sacrosanct. The construction of the flood channel itself also counts as development of the Green Belt.

The untouchability of the Green Belt has increased market pressure on non-Green Belt land, in turn increasing flood risk (Norton, 1994: 41). Despite the ban on Green belt development, in practice, each year 2,400 acres of Green Belt are being developed. England's southeast is also the economic powerhouse of Great Britain. The ensuing housing boom is actively promoted by the urban-oriented Labour Government. This puts great strain on both drinking water resources and on space. The challenge is thus to balance growth and conservation, between urban sprawl and rural values.

A shift in emphasis from rural to urban is also perceptible in the changing philosophy underlying flood management. Tunstall, Johnson and Penning-Rowsell (2004) identify three phases in flood management strategy in the UK:

- Land drainage to ensure food security (1930s–1980s), aimed to protect fertile land.
- Flood defence (arterial drainage, 1980s and 1990s). This aims to protect people while working with the environment and reducing risk.
- Flood risk management (recent years), focusing on land use planning and development control. The 'risk-based approach' not only considers the probability of flooding, but also its impact (damage).

These phases can be seen as the expression of quite different (security) problem frames (Table 7.1). In Britain, Flood Defence Boards, originally known as Land Drainage Boards, are charged with improving land drainage for agriculture. After the First World War, *food security*, which underlies the first of the three phases, became a top priority. As late as 1977, 100,000 ha per year were drained with grant-aid and the Ministry of Agriculture supported a new drainage project to boost food production (Tapsell et al., 2005). In spite of persistent agricultural production surpluses since the 1980s, the agricultural sector retained a privileged position in Britain. The rise of nature conservationists, however, successfully took on landowning interests in the 1980s. In 1984, grants for low

Wave	Paradigm	Recipe	Management Focus
1	Unmanaged (pre-modern)	Live with floods	Coping
2	Protection	Control river behaviour	Risk management
3	Non-structural	Adjust human behaviour	People management
4	Integrated (holistic)	Mixed approach	Uncertainty management

Table 7.1: ***Green and Warner's (1999) typology indicates a chronology of four flood responses, governance to deal with risk and responsibility, each of these implies a threat and a remedy***

field drainage came to a stop (Scrase and Sheate 2005) and urban flood protection came to be prioritised. The coalition between urban and 'green' flood defence became the new dominant problem frame when the Maidenhead flood scheme was conceived in the mid-1980s. This formed the background of the green flood protection scheme.

Gardiner (1992) sketches a different story of three-stage development towards catchment management. An exploitation-led phase characterised by single or dual-purpose schemes gives way to integrated management as pollution starts to impact on the whole of society. The drive to improve *water quality* through pollution control[2] triggered more integrated modes of river management paradigm creating opportunities for water *quantity* (flood) management – a structural (re)linkage of previously isolated domains. It was to take until 1992 for the National Rivers Authority to start drawing up catchment plans – still well before the European Water Framework Directive of 2000. Catchment plans were in fact oriented at sub-basins, so that a larger river like the Thames has six river section plans. 'There are flooding problems along the whole length of the river Thames, but it was considered impossible to solve the problems along the whole length in one go.'[3] The MWEFAS was thus considered a first step (niche) for this (with 182 more to follow) towards the a 'whole-catchment' approach (the third stage in Gardiner's chain) for the Thames, with the hope of following it up with a downstream extension, a channel running between Datchet, Chertsey, Staines and Beaconsfield. The present chapter assesses how far he got with this striving.

In the process, the case of Maidenhead, a prosperous commuting town for professionals working in London, provides an interesting interface between the new rich and the landed rural classes. The traditional countryside dwellers saw the channel as a distortion of an otherwise most agreeable landscape for the benefit of the newly rich.

The MWEFAS project was born out of a desire to move from traditional incidental flood defence engineering (hard structures, straightening rivers and draining wetlands, Green and Warner's 'second wave' (see Table 7.1), to a more environmental and integrated form of *river management*, the 'fourth wave') combined with a stronger control on flood plain occupation behaviour – the third wave.

7.3 Planning Between a Rock and a Hard Place

'You build houses in the floodplain of a river . . . that is bound to have some effect.' (Maidenhead official, 2000)

This section explains the planning set-up of flood and flood plain management in Britain. Some public speakers would contend this is a contradiction in terms: the British 'just do not do planning' (FHRC consultant). Flooding, as a case in point, has been attributed to poor planning of riverside areas. However, it seems fairer to say that while there are plenty of plans, river planning guidelines have not been enforced very much.

Despite calls for 'Joined-Up Government'; the British organisational scene also remains characterised by very loose coupling between agencies. Two interviewees claimed a lack of inter-organisational communication and cooperation to be an aspect of the individualistic British culture. 'We don't *want* to communicate' (EA consultant). Relations between central and local government have been especially difficult. The Thatcher administration (1979–1990) has sought to erode the powers of local government and transfer them to a public–private structure, which was only partly rescinded by Labour (Jouvé, 2005).

Nevertheless, there is a decision-making structure, which will be rendered here in highly simplified form.

The *Ministry of Agriculture, Fisheries and Food* (MAFF, now DEFRA) can be said to dominate the decision-making regime: any plans initiated by the *EA* and *Local Authorities* need to be accepted by the Ministry (Werritty, 2006). In practice, MAFF considers the 257 *Internal Drainage Boards* (agricultural land), the EA (main river), and 400 Local Authorities (non-main river) as its operating agencies,[4] and does not appreciate the Environment Agency initiating its own policies (Ingen-Housz 2007).

MAFF, the EA and local councils make up *Regional Flood Defence Committees*, deciding on and implementing flood defence and drainage works in low-lying areas. There is some overlap of responsibilities in this system.[5]

Central government	- MAFF/DEFRA - DETR (Department of the Environment, Transport and the Regions)
Local government	- Local authorities (boroughs and counties)
	- The EA (previously NRA)
Private sector	- The (land) development industry

Table 7.2: ***Key actors in the UK flood regime***

Obviously, these main actors represent different interests vis-à-vis flood (plain) management. Local Authorities of towns have tended to promote flood plain development to raise municipal revenue, while the EA now seeks to stop any development of the flood plain.

Constraining the river to protect population concentrations in urban areas may well displace the problem to rural areas, while Internal Drainage Boards traditionally defend their agricultural mandate rather than built-up areas (Penning-Rowsell et al., 1987).[6] While the central government has various 'central mechanisms and default powers', intervention is politically risky. Central government has only scant idea how local government planning works. Central government is therefore content to leave flood plain policy to local authorities. This caused it not to intervene, despite a deadlock between local authorities and water managers (Norton 1994), playing out their strategies in the ever-contentious interface of water and space: local flood plain management.

Another key national player in flood governance are the private insurers. In 1961, in an act of what the *Economist* has called 'obsessive avoidance of risk', the British government 'offloaded the burden of compensating damage of victims of flood damage' (*Economist,* 2006). The public–private gentlemen's agreement means that the state takes care of flood defences, while the private companies – for fear of nationalisation – agreed to provide cover no matter what the risk, except if continual, regular flooding was unavoidable (Huber, 2004). The UK government does not take any responsibility in protecting citizens from floods (Scares and Sheate, 2005) nor in compensating for losses. However, if a flood happens, it is the flood victims who carry the can, as the insurance fee for the area will go up (Crichton, 2002).

After the 1947 floods, flood plain development risk had briefly become a significant *risk frame*: the Chief Engineer of the Thames Conservancy (created in 1857) called for planned zones along the river in which development was banned. Proposed measures were quite radical: 'When any property in the flood plain came up for sale, [he said] the County Council should buy it and demolish it. This was not popular and the idea soon died the death' (Martin, 2005). Development on the urban fringe west of London after the Second World War was thus carried through against Thames Conservancy advice. Urbanisation exacerbated run-off volumes and speeds and encroached on the flood plain. During this epoch, attempts at comprehensive planning developed largely in a vacuum – planners and developers mutually ignored each other. While post-Second World War, land conservation has been paramount, agriculture and mineral extraction have largely been exempted from land-use planning. Local authorities must have a plan but the law is not very specific on what this plan should cover. An environmental consciousness on the negative impacts of drainage on wildlife emerged in the 1960s, but the Nature Conservancy Council was understaffed compared to the drainage authorities. MAFF appointees had a strong voice on the local and regional Land Drainage Committees (Scrase and Sheate, 2005: 126–7).

Until the 1980s, flood plain policy remained liberal. Government Circular No. 17/82, for example, called for Water Authorities to adopt a 'positive' approach when considering proposals for infilling of the flood plain. Small developments and domestic extensions were not referred to Thames Water for comment. The emphasis changed to minimising the number of people and buildings at risk to flooding to preventing the impedance of flow and loss of flood storage capacity.

The original Thames Conservancy had meanwhile become the Thames Water Authority in 1974, to become the National Rivers Authority, Thames Region in 1989. The National Rivers Administration–Thames Region (NRA–TR) started with an enhanced environmental mandate after the Land Drainage Improvement Works (Assessment of Environmental Effects) Regulations of 1988. Annoyed at the laxness of flood plain controls, it decided to show a firmer hand vis-à-vis the developers and local authorities. Thames Water's River Division started to strengthen its planning liaison team by including experienced planning professionals of the Royal Town Planning Institute to take a 'tough negotiating stance' with developers from 1988 (Gardiner, 1996), the year the Maidenhead scheme was approved. The NRA was well aware that its flood defence initiatives did *not* respond to a widespread public demand, and it was to take until the turn of the century that development control was on the agenda again. Because of agency underfunding and tight deadlines for appeals, Local Planning Authorities (LPAs) are easily outfoxed by developers. But it is not only developers that need persuading to limit flood plain encroachment. Local Authorities have great discretion in setting flood plain policies and as a result some authorities are far stricter than others. The water authority is a statutory consultee in LPAs, but the environmental authority's guidance is overruled in a great many cases (Crichton, 2005).

The authority's say has been eroded by institutional reform. The Thatcher administration (1979–1990) sought to erode the powers of local government and transfer them to a public–private structure, which was only partly rescinded by Labour (Jouvé, 2005). The privatisation of the water sector pushed through in the 1989 Water Act split Thames Water into a commercial water supplier and a quasi-governmental National Rivers Authority (NRA). This separation proved extremely disruptive to those left behind in the public sector.[7] The multiple reorganisations left their mark on the continuity of the archives, impairing institutional learning and loss of institutional memory. Due to the rushed division of the assets, records have proved irretrievable. During my visit to Reading in 2000 I observed that the EA there only had a few files left from before 1990. New developments are seldom communicated to those who stayed behind and established lines of communications broken down. Commercial sensitivity makes information harder to come by, as gleaned from two EA interviewees:

> 'You have to find your way round the system. If I try phoning Thames Water and they try to block me, I call a friend within TW to put me through.'
>
> 'The bit you're dealing with doesn't pass on information to the bit that isn't privatised.'

In 1995, the NRA was again split up and reformed, the next in a long succession of overhauls. The new agency-to-be was intended as a one-stop shop for business to overcome an 'administrative nightmare' as well as a strong counterpart for the European Environmental Agency (Cullingworth & Nadin, 1997). Created under the Environment Act of 1995 out of the NRA and other environmental agencies, the EA has a general supervisory duty over all flood defence matters, as implemented by the Flood Defence Committees, but only has largely *permissive* powers over land drainage and flood defence works on main river and only some regulatory control over non-main rivers. The Ministry of Agriculture retained control of new works through its allocation of grants.

The EA, inherited a beleaguered position from the NRA. The agency was nearly privatised in 1994, while its budget was immediately halved by the Conservative government of the day. While the EA had high ambitions for its role as flood protector, it started out with little mandate and financial leeway to do so.

7.4 Site Selection and Justification

7.4.1 Looking for Opportunities: Why Maidenhead?

As the scheme had to be a flagship, a success on the way to something bigger, the choice to locate the flood scheme in the Borough of Windsor and Maidenhead seems far from accidental. Because of the experimental nature of the scheme, a site was selected for which there was sufficient historical flood information as well as a foreseeable positive cost-benefit ratio. The section hereafter looks at the debate over how that ratio should be calculated, after which the protection standard is discussed.

The River Thames rises in Gloucestershire and flows east. When it reaches Maidenhead, it reaches a bottleneck: the natural channel only has a capacity for 275 cumecs – above that level, the banks will overflow and a flood will occur. Upstream of Oxford, some areas are therefore substantially flooded during relatively minor events. During floods, the River Thames overtops its western bank at Maidenhead, Cookham and Bray. After the big flood of 1947, lesser floods in 1970 and 1990 continued to cause minor damages. The February 1990 flood lasted 14 days, affected 520 properties in Maidenhead and entered 40 of them (www.jubilee-river.co.uk), so a popular support base was anticipated in Maidenhead, especially since the number of at-risk properties had grown: from 1,560 in 1947 to 3,303 in 1989 (by 1998 there were 5,000).[8]

Opponents have pointed out that these houses should not be in the flood-prone zone anyway. The stance on the part of the Borough of Windsor and Maidenhead on planning has been less than firm. The borough judged that the zoning regulation after 1947 would cause the area to become derelict and thus destroy its amenities. Maidenhead's local authority sought to strike a balance between limiting the number of people at risk from flooding and foregoing the benefits of development. The 'town map' of 1953 and Review Town Map of 1965 became the point of reference: it is the only document on which decision-making could be based until the 1978 flood plain policy (Norton 1994: 26). Constructions that would encourage developments in the vicinity and in turn radically alter the character of the area were refused. Maidenhead will permit development in the 1947 flood plain (1-in-50 to 1-in-60-year flood) but not the 1974 flood plain (1:5). It controls residential development in the flood plain. Since 1947, Maidenhead Council planners have allowed the construction of over 3,000 dwellings on the flood plain. Approval of planning applications was not even-handed.

Having found that, along the length of the Thames, areas were flood-prone, in 1983, a study of the Thames was carried out with a view to developing an integrated Catchment Management Plan (CMP) to ensure drainage would be subject to source control and balancing of the various water-related interests (Gardiner, 1992). Seeking to integrate structural, environmental and socioeconomic aspects, the study is rated as an early example of multidisciplinary research to identify optimum design and routing for a multifunctional land-use project. As there was an extensive flood record of Maidenhead flood levels, the town was a promising first candidate for an intervention scheme on the Thames. In 1981, the Thames Water Authority appointed an engineering consultancy, Lewin, Fryer and Partners, to study options for the relief of flooding in Maidenhead.

On 26 January 1989 the Regional Land Drainage Committee (RLDC) agreed to allow a flood alleviation project at Maidenhead and to investigate the optimum level of protection and flood alleviation works for Windsor and Eton. The mainstay of the project is an 11.6 km bypass designed on the eastern bank of the Thames, leaving the river at Taplow Mill, upstream of Boulter's Lock at North Maidenhead and rejoining the river downstream at Black Potts viaduct (Windsor), to ease the peak flow at Maidenhead in a 1-in-65-year flood. The 'River' is in fact a traditional trapezoidal channel, with a bottom width of about 30 m, and since the slopes are 1:1.5, the channel is 45 m wide at the top. There is a 300 mm freeboard to accommodate bank level fluctuations (Atkins Closure report, 2007). To give the channel a 'natural' look, the river is unlined, divides around islands and has natural river banks and reed beds to recreate habitats lost to past land drainage works and channel improvements and the local Thames corridor. According to the National Rivers Agency/Environment Agency, these works had turned the project site into a 'relatively ecologically uninteresting area'. MWEFAS envisaged the creation of new green spaces: a wetland, providing reed beds, nesting boxes, pools, beaches, etc. to attract a wide diversity of birds, amphibians and insects, plus an ecological study area. Walks, picnic areas and bird-watching and fishing sites are incorporated. A cycle path along the river leads all the way to Heathrow.

The Maidenhead channel was designed to carry 215 cumecs (42 per cent of Thames flood flow) during a 1-in-65-year event – the remainder would be carried by the Thames and the west bank channels. In addition, the scheme comprises a flood wall at Cookham and defences at North Maidenhead. The Thames flood of 1947, the greatest flood in centuries, had caused great damage in Maidenhead, with 2,000 houses inundated. When in 1954 Maidenhead was flooded again, however, this was due to two local channels overtopping their banks: the Maidenhead Ditch (the main flood route through Maidenhead) and The Cut, rather than the River Thames. In the 1960s these streams were widened so as to reduce flood incidence to 1-in-10 to 1-in-20. The MWEFAS scheme included the rehabilitation of the silted-up Ditch to provide a flood capacity of 15 m^3/s.

7.4.2 Clearing Hurdles

The Community Charge

It would be too bold to maintain that the Jubilee River was built just because there was money available, as some interviewees have claimed. However, there is much to be said for the theory that it took full advantage of existing institutional opportunities.

Funding for the Jubilee River primarily came from two sources: the Agriculture Ministry's grant-in-aid and the Local Authority *community charge*. It is mainly townspeople who pay the charge, as the rate only goes on properties; farmland is zero-rated. This system means that affluent areas can raise far greater sums for flood protection than poor regions.

This mechanism rewards schemes in wealthy (financially secure) areas, where the value of assets to be protected is likely to be high. As the regions in practice have to pay for their own flood defence, the richest regions can afford the 'best' defences, while the most flood-prone areas tend to be among the poorest.

In Southeast England, 6 million people live in flood-prone areas. The development of flood plain land has more than doubled in the past 50 years, so that exposure to floods on the Thames is growing fast. The lower the elevation at which people live, the more flood-prone they are, and since flood plain land is cheaper, this land is often developed for social housing (Crichton, 2005). As a result, the poor are more at risk from flooding than the affluent. The vulnerability school of disaster studies home in on such systemic inequalities as poverty and marginalisation, which explains why people have little alternative but to live in flood plains, in spite of obvious vulnerability to flood hazard (Blaikie et al., 1994; Pelling, 2003). But in the case of Maidenhead, with an average income 15 per cent above the national average, it is the affluent who knowingly take the risk of living by the water (interview, consultant). Maidenhead is only 35 miles west of London, and commuting to the capital by rail or road is reasonably easy. Successful professionals working in London have bought properties in the attractive area on the river. The affluence of the area was not lost on newspapers reporting on the 1990 floods. They spoke of 'showbiz people and eccentrics' and 'expensive boats mooring alongside' during the evacuation of 1990. According to one news report, the Maidonians fleeing the flood looked 'like women leaving a ball'.[9] People in the region have no problem conceding that MWEFAS is a project for the affluent that could not have happened in upstream Wales, despite Wales being more flood-prone.

MAFF Grant-in-aid: Disputed Cost-Benefit Analysis

In addition to the community charge, the Ministry of Agriculture, Food and Fisheries (MAFF) can give grant-in-aid for capital works for flood protection. In principle, the Ministry's contribution would be limited in the relatively rich Southeast, where MAFF contributes 15 per cent of the value of capital project (elsewhere in England and Wales this figure may run up to 75 per cent). Still, given the relative constraints of the EA resources, MAFF's contribution was very important to the project.

Originally, the cost of the combined scheme at a 1-in-55-year flood protection standard was estimated at £36.3 million and to provide benefits of about £41.7 million giving a benefit cost ratio of 1.15 to 1 (internal NRA memo, 16 February 1989). These figures soon were to be revised upwards.[10]

The UK's Ministry of Agriculture (MAFF, now DEFRA) is populated by engineers and economists (Bakker et al., n.d.) and economic justification has been the only criteria in MAFF's 'decision rule' for funding flood schemes (Crichton, 2002). A healthy cost-benefit ratio coupled with a punishing discount rate for the lifespan of the project – required by the Treasury – proved a major hurdle to have the MWEFAS accepted and funded. MAFF took a strongly tangibles-oriented stance, only accepting cost-benefit analysis as a viable funding criterion.[11] Since everything depended on the economic viability of the project, the choice of methodology to arrive at the numbers was crucial.

The NRA wanted to develop a different scoring system with due regard for indirect costs (such as costs of disruption to traffic and emergency services to cope with a flood) and socio-economic values. For example, people need medical care and run a greater risk of dying from stress after a flood. This brings direct medical costs, which are not often counted but also indirect social costs.

The Agency was especially interested in the success of the MWEFAS scheme as it would open the door to a follow-up, Datchet-to-Wraysbury flood scheme, further down the river as part of an integrated Thames protection plan. Therefore, it welcomed a method that would boost the 'benefits' side of the CBA. This could be done in two ways: by increasing the tangible (material) benefits, e.g. by higher assessment of property values, or by involving intangible (immaterial) costs, such as psychological and environmental damage – not counting the cost of social disruption when a major traffic corridor such as the M4 is flooded (www.jubilee-river.com quoting NRA, 1992b).[12]

In 1990, the NRA commissioned the Flood Hazard Research Centre, Middlesex University, whose flood manuals form the basis of flood damage assessment in the UK to calculate that ratio for MWEFAS. Gardner had worked for years with the Centre's Director, Professor Edmund Penning-Rowsell, and in 1995 was to become a professor at Middlesex University.

FHRC researchers (e.g., Parker, 1983) had long argued that non-monetary (non-tangible) aspects such as disruption, trauma of displacement may be as crucial as monetary values. FHRC findings for the Maidenhead scheme (Penning-Rowsell et al., 2005) underscored this earlier work. Apart from this, the brunt of this work concerned flooding from sewers (Green, 1988) and salt water (Parker et al., 1983). The debate over the quantification of environmental damage complicates the equation even more. The FHRC calculation did not rule out that 200 per cent could be the more realistic figure.

To reflect the greater affluence of the residents of 'upmarket' (Norton, 1994) Maidenhead, Eton and Windsor compared to the southeast average, a 'Maidenhead factor' was introduced. This inflated the value of assets to be protected and, as a consequence, the benefits of the scheme. This was significant since the first calculated benefit-cost ratio had not been impressive to start with: At first it was assessed at 1.21:1 but the 'Maidenhead factor' boosted the figure to 1.41:1, which the Environmental Agency called a 'very robust figure' (EA, Oxford visit, 1998). However, inclusion of recreation and amenity benefits were disputed by the *Treasury,* reducing the cost-benefit ratio to a less convincing 1:1.07. The cost at that time was assessed at £45 million, the damage prevented over its lifetime as calculated at £50 million.

Environmentalists argue that monetisation of social and environmental values don't hold water, as other types of values are at issue. There is no commensurability between the two (Espeland, 1998). Scrase and Sheate (2005: 118) for example consider cost-benefit analysis part of the 'naturalised' flood frame: 'in flood defence policy few people ever question the application of cost-benefit analysis, which is essentially a test for national economic efficiency, in a context that was once framed as one of unpredictable and local risks.'

But the water agency was in no position to defy the quantitative frame. The political nature of the calculations caused opinions over the way the calculations should be done to be widely divergent. The assignment was perceived by a MAFF interviewee as a 'numbers-fiddling' exercise to promote the scheme (interview, DEFRA, 2000). However, while other interviewees called the MAFF policy officer a 'dinosaur', the FHRC numbers also failed to satisfy the NRA: 'in 1990, the flood in Maidenhead, our figures were quite a lot higher than the Middlesex Uni assessment' (interview, EA, 1999).

Only after the floods of 1998, the intangibles camp scored a victory after the Agricultural Select Committee urged to include social and environmental values in the economic justification. The outcomes of these evaluations however remain subject to much dispute, given the necessarily subjective way these costs and benefits are calculated. After the 2003 floods the MWEFAS numbers were 'reassessed'.[13]

NPV and CVA. Apart from disputes over the values included in cost-benefit analysis (CBA), the discussion was complicated by studies using different methods of calculation. Other commonly practised ways of evaluating flood investments ex-ante include the Economic Internal Rate of Return (EIRR) practiced in FAP-20 (Chapter 4) and Net Present Value (NPV). FHRC commissioned Nigel Arnell from the Institute for Hydrology to do a run to determine the Net Present Value of the future 50-year benefit of the scheme. Arnell concluded that there was a 66 per cent probability that a 50-year benefit would be less than the scheme costs, placed at the time at £26.68 million – in other words, a 34 per cent chance of cost recovery (Arnell, 1988).

These measures however do not take social benefit perception into account. Another consultant, Jan Brooks, carried out a Contingency Valuation study into the value of the scheme to the local community. This brings out non-market values, since the trauma from evacuation and invasion of the private sphere may well be very different from actual market values of damaged goods and properties. 'The questionnaire yielded a £3 million benefit. MAFF threw that out completely' (interview, consultant).

Proceeds from Gravel?

Given that the Thames has a gravel bed, how about paying for the scheme from gravel proceeds? As profits from gravel can be anything between 40 and 60p to £1 per tonne, potential profits from an expected 3.5 million tonnes would be substantial. One observer even charged that gravel proceeds were the main driver for the Maidenhead project (Clearhill, 1994). But prior rights to land sold by the EA would eat into the EA's proceeds: the landowners can claim royalties, which makes it hard for the Agency to derive any profit from the sale. Indeed, when disputing the Valuation Office's decision that the minerals extracted from the river were rateable (taxable) as a commercial operation on the basis that it does not make a profit on mineral sales, this Valuation Tribunal decision saved the Agency half a million pounds in rates.[14] Still, an economic risk was that the project was in competition with Eton College's rowing course, which would produce 4.5 million tonnes in 11 years for a 'contracted market that is already fully supplied'. Unlike in the Netherlands case, gravel royalties were eventually not included in the benefits but showed up as 'negative costs'.[15]

7.5 Selection of Alternatives

The need to arrive at a favourable cost structure limited the number of feasible river management alternatives for flood defence, but still left open a range of possibilities for selection. For example, there is no a priori reason why there should be a channel. The present section looks at the selection process.

The Thames is a rain river in a rainy area – average rainfall at Bray (Borough of Maidenhead) over the 18 years leading up to 1997 was 735.4 mm. Floods tend to be the flash flood-type.[16] Moreover, the Thames is highly regulated, with a sequence of weirs along its length, which increases the speed of flow.

Possible technical options to reduce flood risk on the Thames are upstream storage, protective banks, dredging or a relief channel (Venables, 2005). *Upstream storage* to detain the 1947 peak, 500 m^3/s, would require a detention area of 720,000,000 m^2, an area the size of Oxfordshire. The embankments along the length of the river are minor. *Flood banks* up to 2 m high were considered but it was realised landscaping would be a major problem and raised water levels would lead to increased groundwater levels leading to further flooding.

River deepening and widening, the 'apparently simple options' (Fryer, 1999), would encounter environmental but also social hurdles, as it would require the removal of several islands. *Dredging* between Reading and Teddington (where the Tidal Thames starts) to allow for navigation also contributes to the drainage of floodwaters, but after 1997, dredging up 100,000 tonnes of aggregate a year was stopped. This was done in the full expectation that the new relief channel, the Jubilee River, would take care of the flood risk at a stroke – though as we shall see, it did not.

A channel option was deemed most acceptable from an environmental standpoint.[17] Yet, in the selection process, at first the EA seemed willing to consider *non*-structural approaches to Maidenhead flood defence, such as flood-proofing. This was a relatively new idea in an environment where flood infrastructure is the norm.[18] The Flood Hazard Research Centre was commissioned to look into (cheaper) alternatives, which effectively implied a non-structural approach: flood-proofing of each individual property, constructing bunds around each neighbourhood and around the main built-up areas. While their alternative would be substantially cheaper in capital cost than the £83.5 million of the prevailing option at the time, the authors grant that non-structural measures entail other social requirements: individual effort (sandbags and flood-proofing of buildings) and more community support for their maximum effect (Penning-Rowsell et al., 1987). Also, continuous information and education is required, which may be costly. The 'non-structural' report was never formalised and summarily dismissed for 'arriving too late', although 'cold feet' on the part of the project initiators may also have played a part (interview, EA officer, Reading).

How did the National Rivers Authority, the forerunner of the EA, come up with this particular channel? In all, no less than 29 alternative scheme elements with 492 possible combinations of channel routes were considered (Fryer, 1999).

The NRA commissioned Lewin & Fryer (now part of Black and Veatch) to select 10 alternatives. Given the weight of economic considerations, the channel should follow the shortest route, and limit the number of structures (Eton College presentation by J. Gardiner and G. Fryer, 1998). The last and cheapest alternative out of the ten was selected in 1987. While the report provides technical and economic reasons (practicability and cost) to justify this option, a consultant admits that 'potential solutions came into your mind *conditioned* by the strategic views of the NRA' (MWEFAS consultant) on east-bank (or north bank: Venables, 2005) channel. For a time, a west-bank channel through the centre of Maidenhead was favoured, a section that was currently 'extremely unattractive' and, unlike the east bank variant, mostly contained gravel (Lewin and Fryer note to Gardiner, 12 April 1988). Residents in Taplow and Dorney, which would be affected by the channel works, were in favour of this alternative, but objections from the National Trust and cost factors counted against it.

7.5.1 Standard of Protection (SoP): How Safe is Safe Enough?

Underlying the cost-benefit ratio for the Maidenhead scheme was the extent to which the scheme would reduce the return period of damaging flood from the local 5-year return period, which the EA deemed 'unacceptable'. The eventually selected scheme was to a still modest 1-in-55-year standard. Any protection level under 1:75 may be too low even to qualify for insurance (Crichton, 2005) – flood protection standards in the UK are uniformly set at 1 in 100. In Scotland, flood defence grants are not given for anything under 1:100. The Maidenhead scheme was never going to meet that standard, either.

While these could be brushed aside as technical debates, the more pressing psychological problem is the acceptance of residual risk by the project beneficiaries. When project leader Colin Martin admitted – in conformity with EA policy – that the 'possibility of floods [is] not entirely ruled out', Alistar Forsyth of Taplow, then parish chairman, expressed horror: 'There was never, ever any suggestion that it [the scheme] would *not* eliminate flooding in the Maidenhead area' (emphasis added). Such a zero-tolerance perspective of flood risk has an impact on the risk and responsibility issue, which will be discussed at the end of the chapter.

The Second Channel

John Gardiner's vision was to connect planned gravel developments on the Thames such that they did not just result in a bypass for Windsor, Eton and Maidenhead but also further down for Datchet, Wraysbury, Staines and Chertsey (DWSC). His view was that the 'quality and quantity of a catchment's water environment is determined by land use'. While the MWEFAS scheme had 'nothing to say about the management of the floodplain' (Gardiner, 1996), the Datchet extension would become the UK's first flood plain management plan (FMP) (*Imperial Engineer,* 2005). A flood study for these areas was carried out in 1992.[19]

While most options for this stretch involved channels of various lengths, a fifth option proposed reprofiling a section of the Thames between Datchet and Wraysbury (see Table 7.3; Option 1). Digging out the riverbed by up to 1 m[20] would avoid the need to create a channel. MAFF, expected to contribute 15 per cent to project costs, proved reticent to spend this money for either project unless there was overwhelming support. The DWSC stretch failed to clear the cost-benefit hurdle: 'all the options turned out to be marginal. In the end it never happened, the benefit-cost ratio was not there, it was below 1.' (interview, consultant)

Here, too, public hearings were held, which attracted few stakeholders. As we shall see below, this stance also summed up the role distribution on the MWEFAS scheme. This caused a lot of modifications to the original alternative.

<table>
<tr><th>Option</th><th>Works</th><th>SoP</th><th>Problem</th></tr>
<tr><td>1</td><td>Major reprofiling of River Thames with no diversion channel</td><td>1: 18</td><td>Loss of ecology and impacts on aquatic biology, fisheries and water quality.</td></tr>
<tr><td>2</td><td>No works to the River Thames with (~40 m) diversion channel</td><td>1: 20</td><td rowspan="4">Need for landfill removal; impacts on groundwater quality.</td></tr>
<tr><td>3</td><td>Minimum works to the Thames with medium channel (~50 m)</td><td>1: 40</td></tr>
<tr><td>4</td><td>Significant works to the Thames with major channel (~60 m)</td><td>1: 65</td></tr>
<tr><td>5</td><td>Extensive works to the Thames with extensive channel (~70–80 m)</td><td>1: 100</td></tr>
</table>

Table 7.3: ***The five options for the proposed Datchet channel***

7.5.2 Convincing Local Stakeholders: No Taxation without Consultation

> 'Look, I've got a lot to do, let the engineers tell us what the options are and we'll say what we want.' (local fisherman, 1992)

Let us now look into the participatory process for the MWEFAS and try to explain how the project came to be conflictive from the start – despite the EA's best efforts to be inclusive and open. This was not self-evident: Tunstall and Green (2003) call the planning process in Britain 'secretive' while Cosgrove and Petts (1990) warn that 'the link between water management and power remains unbroken.' Perhaps part-necessitated by the Agency and its predecessors' limited mandate and means, the idea for the MWEFAS was to enable a greater extent of prior *stakeholder consultation and openness.*

Due to the absence of a powerful mandate, Gardener's team realised the Agency needed an inclusive strategy to pull the project off. This section looks into the nature of this participatory process and seeks to explain how the project came to be politicised from the start, despite the EA's best efforts to be inclusive.

Gardiner's team sought to close the gap between experts and stakeholders by designing a public participation process.

What kind of participation was the NRA–EA seeking? As Arnstein's ladder shows (Table 7.4), there is rather a marked difference in power sharing depending on what form of participation you privilege.

Fordham (1998–99; quoting Sewell 1974) notes a degree of alienation between engineers and the general public, as it is engineers who define the problem and select the options. Traditionally, few stakeholders were consulted beforehand, so that if no one complains, decision-making can be swift. Projects were presented as a fait accompli package, so that NGOs and local citizens had to make a big noise in order to exert some influence. Since the 1980s, however, there are more statutory consultees for new projects such as Roads and Highways, and the Royal Society for the Protection of Birds and English Nature. From its instatement in 1989, the project team held five years of talks with the mandatory consultees such as the Royal Society for the Protection of Birds (RSPB) and English Heritage and other environmental and conservation groups. One result of this was that English Nature was contracted to oversee the tree-felling programme for MWEFAS, in light of the project's environmental ambitions. At the time, this process was lauded as progressive.

While the statutory stakeholder consultation rules prioritised intermediate civil-society groups, information sessions were held with local stakeholders as well. The fact that these hearings were held *before* any public enquiry was new to Britain, but several stakeholders nevertheless felt caught as they were consulted *after* the decision had already been taken. FHRC surveys found that stakeholders would like to be consulted on a number of options rather than just the one the project initiator prefers (Tunstall et al., 1994 quoted in Tunstall and Green, 2003).

Gardiner and his team however maintained that you 'cannot promote 101 alternatives [. . .] project development cannot be totally open, protocol has to be maintained. Professionalism, customer orientation and careful advertising sells a good product' (Gardiner, 1992). Thus, when a local survey of local attitudes towards the scheme was commissioned to Middlesex Polytechnic (now University),

> (t)he Environment Agency were very difficult about the questions we could ask. There are some very peculiar questions in there. We felt it was better social science if we asked them [= the respondents] about different options but they [the NRA] wanted to ask about the preferred option. But they got into trouble over this . . . as expected.' (interview, university researcher, 2001)

The survey showed that people did not share the NRA's view that the MWEFAS project area was neglected and in need of environmental

8 Citizen Control	Stakeholders handle the entire job of planning, policymaking and managing a programme.	Varying degrees of citizen power
7 Delegated Power	Citizens holding a clear majority of seats on committees with delegated powers to make decisions. Public now has the power to assure accountability of the programme to them.	
6 Partnership	Power is in fact redistributed through negotiation between citizens and power holders. Planning and decision-making responsibilities are shared, e.g. through joint committees.	
5 Placation	For example, co-option of handpicked 'worthies' onto committees. It allows citizens to advise or plan ad infinitum but retains for power holders the right to judge the legitimacy or feasibility of the advice.	Varying degrees of tokenism
4 Consultation	Attitude surveys, neighbourhood meetings and public enquiries.	
3 Informing	A first step to legitimate participation. But too frequently the emphasis is on a one-way flow of information. No channel for feedback.	
2 Therapy	Both are non-participatory. The aim is to 'cure' or educate the participants. The proposed plan is best and the job of participation is to achieve public support by public relations.	Non-participation
1 Manipulation		

Table 7.4: ***Arnstein's ladder of participation***

gentrification – they valued the landscape as it was. Nevertheless, the EA felt that the locals would be on their side if they recognised the extent of the threat. To sell flood protection you have to sell the idea of flood danger. 'Memories are short' (Gardiner, 1990) – therefore the project's public information documents constantly remind readers of it in its appeals for support. The EA's 1997 leaflets (*Protecting your homes*) emphasise the 50th anniversary of the 1947 flood almost as if it were a cause for celebration.

Significantly, after the 1998 floods John Gardner's colleagues at FHRC (where he had meanwhile been appointed professor) criticised this approach in their submission to the: 'it is [. . .] not the Agency's function to promote schemes but to determine whether any scheme is justified and to identify the best option available.'[21]

It should be noted that Gardiner's interpretation of 'promotion' has a wider scope than selling an innovation to the public. A project initiator has to invest heavily to persuade the planning committee at county level. This is no different for the EA, whose flood works affected the integrity of the Green Belt. Gardiner notes that while planning authorities are easily outfoxed by developers, the Agency has to play fair:

> The cost to promote schemes of this size is 10 per cent of the total cost before you even start. You need that amount to go through the planning process. *If you ask: where did we go wrong, this is it.*

If a developer starts it he puts in 2 identical applications. He negotiates with the council with one of them. If the council hasn't determined in 14 days it's a non-determined application. That effectively forces it into a public enquiry for DETR determination. Sometimes it's a public enquiry, sometimes it's a written representation, but for structures of this size it's a public enquiry.

It can get extended and extended forever. Either party can refer it to the Minister to call it in. Most Local Authorities don't like public enquiries – they have to foot their own bill. Planning applications get through because the LAs run out of money. It can take tens of thousands of pounds.

Meanwhile for the second application they talk to the local authority. For example Reading fought them twice for the detail, by the third one Reading Borough Council gave up. They reckoned it's gonna happen anyway, this is the best of a bad job.

We will encounter the regional planning authorities further down, as the planning application with Buckingham Council is discussed.

Clashes with Eton

So far, I have mentioned issues that could be solved by relatively minor accommodation. The NRA also had to contend with hardy and skilful adversaries who were not easily swayed. When the preferred channel option was selected (at that time it was still to protect Maidenhead only) and the general public consulted on the basis of the NRA's 'preferred outline scheme' in 1987, 'details such as the precise route were still under consideration' (Tunstall and Green, 2003: 42). Eton College was first off the block to send the EA back to the drawing board over the stretch of the canal that crossed its famous playing fields, known as Agar's Plough. It had to resite a dog kennel and save a prehistoric site there. Eton would not accept a £1 million drain under its 'hallowed' playing grounds, which necessitated a £8 million detour for the Maidenhead channel. The College was not swayed by the level of protection the channel would provide the college itself: Eton is situated in a more elevated area and therefore less flood-prone: 'we held out in 1947, so we'll hold out now' (interview Eton, 2000).

While *territory* (land take) at first glance seemed to be an issue with Eton, in fact the land take was much more framed in terms of scenic and cultural values of a history-laden area. Eton is part and parcel of the English national heritage, the college proudly claims it is older than the royal family. Its lofty heritage made its playing fields 'hallowed ground', where prime ministers had played rugby, and gave rise to the famous (if historically dubious) quote attributed to the Duke of Wellington: 'The battle of Waterloo was won on the playing fields of Eton.' To touch the playing fields was to touch the core of the college's identity.

Eton also did not accept the compulsory purchasing order (CPO), which forces a landowner to cede land to carry out public works. The college refused to abandon the rights to the land even temporarily, and was prepared to take its fight against the CPO up to the High Court, questioning the Minister's ability to confirm the Order. It would have taken an Act of Parliament to force Eton to comply.

Eton College cited loss of land value because of land 'held with'. In this context, the NRA–EA formally had a strong hand in the light of the strong land drainage tradition in the UK. The institutionalisation of drainage boards in the Land Drainage Act of 1930 facilitates compulsory land purchase for flood schemes such as MWEFAS. The relevant Environmental Authority has powers to acquire the freehold of land for the purpose of enhancing land drainage schemes. As a consequence,

> We had a CPO [Compulsory Purchasing Order] under our land drainage powers, confirmed by MAFF. Eton issued a direct challenge. We didn't want to use the freehold so we offered an easement. The inspector's representative looked at it in April. In June the solicitors looked at it for legal challenge. The Minister sat on it until March 1995 – approval, CPO confirmed. On the last day of the inquiry, Eton filed a formal legal objection saying that the document was flawed. The EA said

> the easement was sufficient as it gives EA all the problems. A CPO extinguishes all third-party land rights. You don't know they're there till someone remembers. Our barrister said Eton couldn't do it, their barrister said they could. Because of this the rest of the CPOs were also on hold on all other land. The 3rd counsel said it was too complex, it wouldn't stand up in law; basically unworkable. In April 1996 Eton agreed to buy the land by CPO then we would resell the land. (interview EA, Reading).

By way of compromise, Guy Roots, counsel for the National Rivers Authority, suggested splitting the scheme up into two schemes, one for the Maidenhead area, the other for Eton and Windsor 'as the more controversial route passed through the latter area. This would have the advantage that the whole scheme would not collapse if not given parliamentary approval'.[22] This alternative was dismissed and the College won the court case.[23]

More prosaic economic interests may have played a role here. Eton College planned a 150-feet, £10 million Olympic rowing channel,[24] which was to be built simultaneously with the Jubilee Channel. The gravel from two projects would flood the construction market with quarrying material and depress the fetching price. Because gravel disposal from two projects, MWEFAS and the rowing lake, would flood the market with gravel, a deal was struck that the Jubilee River would be dug first, and the Eton Rowing Scheme at Dorney after that, by the same consortium: Eton Aggregates, formed by four quarrying companies: Lafarge Redlands Aggregates Ltd., RMC, Tarmac and Summerleaze, 'an excellent example of cooperation within the quarrying industry for the benefit of the wider community'.[25]

However, relations between the NRA and Eton over MWEFAS remained strained when in 2001 Public Hearings were held over the newly adopted Planning Guidance (PPG 25), which laid down flood contours within planning for development was to be constrained. Eton expressed scepticism about the EA's ability to provide adequate information, citing the MWEFAS episode as evidence:

> I am afraid to tell you that in our recent dealings with them (the Agency), they have been less than helpful. The EA has consistently refused to release information about the effects of the Maidenhead scheme. They simply will not tell us what the flood levels will be when the scheme becomes operational. . . . I suspect that the EA may not have the available expertise or resources to properly undertake the role as anticipated in PPG 25. (Eton College, 2001, during the second consultation for PPG 25)

Parish Protest

The rowing lake issue brought in another player: Dorney Parish Council. The parish councillors were fighting a 'trench war' with Maidenhead's local authority as Eton College's Olympic rowing channel (Dorney Lake) was to be routed across the common in Eton Wick and Dorney. The Maidenhead scheme again would pass through Dorney Common. Two channels so near to each other seemed too much of a good thing in terms of nuisance from construction.

> We knew that the Dorney Common plan was unpopular but when we were only planning to protect Maidenhead there was *no other route* economically or environmentally viable. Extending the scheme to Windsor made it possible to rethink the whole route. (Jean Belcher, Thames Water, emphasis added)[26]

In response a new version of the flood diversion project was proposed, extending the Maidenhead (7,000 at-risk properties) to Eton and Windsor (8,000 more). This enabled the protection of a sum total of 15,000 at-risk properties. The window of opportunity resulting from the need to replan the channel also created an opening to address some complaints: The extended channel would 'not now skirt the southwest side of the village in full view of many residents' gardens as was originally feared' (ibid.).

Dorney was not the only parish councils displaying considerable activism. For *Taplow*, just upstream of Maidenhead where the MWEFAS channel begins, the struggle against the MWEFAS was part of a long 'fight' against various infrastructural schemes, such as an extension of the M4 motorway and a fifth runway for nearby Heathrow Airport.

Taplow parish council were among the 'hundreds' of local people voicing complaints which later led to a Public Inquiry of 1992. They were especially worried about Taplow's historic gardens. While floods are usually seen in quantity terms, they bring pollution into people's houses, too – 'The residents of Taplow do not want Maidenhead's dirty water'.

Parish councillors are volunteers. The 'tonnes' of evidence amassed by the EA made local stakeholders feel outgunned. Taplow faced a 'battery of lawyers' and a roomful of evidence, while it itself could only hire a very junior barrister.[27] But Taplow Council had its day when the Maidenhead flood scheme was first discussed in the House of Commons:

> A county councillor at Taplow Parish Council also acts on the Flood Development Committee so they had a little inside info about what was going on, and using that to wind everybody up. I think they overstepped it, lobbying their MP like crazy. [. . .] On 9 November, I went to the House of Commons. Every MP can start an adjournment debate at the

> end of a day. One name out of the hat can raise every subject he liked. Tim Smith (Cons) raised it. We had been primed so it wasn't wholly unexpected. He brought the audit office in to audit the scheme twice. It didn't seem nice at the time but it was quite nice later because we got a clean bill of health. (interview, Taplow Parish councillor)

Bucks County

The above protests reflect the issue of 'nuisance distribution': Dorney and Taplow parishes claimed the risks and benefits of the project were adversely skewed towards them. A similar issue emerged at county level. The flood relief channel is routed such that its bulk would end up in Buckinghamshire to save a population concentration in high-damage flood-prone areas in Berkshire. The county of Berkshire supported the project in the name of progress, while Buckinghamshire opposed it in the interest of landscape conservation.

Buckingham County voiced objections based on landscape values. Since it was the policy of Buckinghamshire County Council not to grant permission for the extraction of minerals in the area affected by the proposed flood relief channel, the County proved an important adversary. The council argued there was no pressing *need* for development in the Green Belt (interview, Buckingham Council officer). Bucks County could go along with a lesser scheme for Maidenhead, but worried about the impact on the landscape. The authority commissioned a consultancy to come up with smaller-scale alternatives which aimed to minimise impact on the landscape. In fact Taplow parish, too, fearing damage to its historic gardens, commissioned a report with a design for a smaller project. Both bids for a smaller scheme were dismissed by the Agency on practical grounds: 'If you want to do half the channel width, you don't have less land take' (interview, EA officer).

> Apart from the channel itself, there was lengthy controversy over the nuisance from and disposal and valuation of aggregates, especially gravel (in the benefit-cost section), which again opened up a choice between alternatives. The NRA had sought to pre-empt this issue by constructing most of the bridges over the channel before it was excavated, which made it possible to move excavated material along the channel and out onto major roads, 'rather than create congestion, nuisance and environmental damage along minor roads crossing the Scheme. (Venables, 2005)

A key issue was who was to transport the aggregate from there, by what means of transport. Strong contenders for the contract were ARC Southern (Greenways) proposing transport by railway line, which was thought to be more environmentally sound. Parliamentary questions (16 December 1998) urged Her Majesty's Government to look into this option. Yet the rail haulage option has seen strong opposition from Dorney and Marlow councillors. Dorney council, complaining of 'intolerable noise from haulage', went on to portray the EA as 'uncooperative and uncaring'. Yet team leader Colin Martin claims he had no complaints from the council (op. cit.), suggesting the parishes' bark was much worse than their bite. Although ARC had obtained planning permission for importing the minerals from the Scheme into their pit at Sutton Courtenay, Oxon, they did not get the contract after all. Nuttall's removal bid by *truck* turned out to be more cost-effective. A £1 million conveyor belt enables transport on the river Thames saving residents lorry nuisance.

The Public Enquiry

Given the limited mandate and low enforcement of flood plain development controls, it is not so surprising that the NRA–EA has placated stakeholders rather a lot, with a view to 'keeping the peace'. As illustrated by the above saga of Taplow and Eton the EA proved to be inclined, if sometimes under pressure, to take many local objections into account. Environmentalists were co-opted by modifications to facilitate badger traffic, provide for alternative bat roosts and the isolation of a contaminated area at Manor Farm.

The EA's project team was prepared to go quite a long way to obtain the planning application from the counties involved by negotiation with stakeholders. But in light of 'hundreds' of complaints the planning application was refused, and an appeal had to be made to the Secretary of State who 'called it in'.

The NRA had to organise a public enquiry before an Inspector of the Planning Inspectorate, held between 20 October and 17 December 1992 in Reading. The inspector called on to assess the Maidenhead scheme, David Bushby, was a MAFF appointee. Tunstall and Green (2003: 34) notice that public inquiries in other types of infrastructural project (e.g., roads and railways) in the UK have been formalities, 'no project has ever been turned down.' But in flood defence, earlier cases brought painful defeats, so the NRA knew it was not going to be an easy ride. In the UK, public enquiries have been dominated by the 'public interest' (as defined by the government) rather than an ideology of participation – government reckon most opponents to act in their own interests and see no need for publicly funded protest as found in the Netherlands. Stakeholder interest shown was far from overwhelming, though, enabling the public enquiry to be cut from 16 to 8 weeks.

The Inquiry brought several minor amendments to the scheme, as well as a firm promise that downstream Datchet would not be suffering from the channel, now that the MMWEFAS would be going ahead but the Datchet extension would not. It is indicative of the NRA's approach that it managed to persuade one of the project's fiercest critics, the independent Taplow parish councillor Ewan Larcombe, that the Enquiry might have been 'one-sided' but 'scrupulous and fair' (Larcombe, thamesweb posting, 29.03.04). After the Inquiry, the EA continued to make significant amendments, such as changing the timing of traffic lights to reduce traffic tailbacks due to the temporary M4 motorway diversion (*Maidenhead Advertiser*, 18 June 1999; interview Taplow Parish, 2001). Such amenities could come in handy as a bargaining chip: in case sand and gravel transport by lorry were not accepted, there was also not going to be a new roundabout for locals affected by the scheme.[28]

The only group left empty-handed seems to be boating enthusiasts, who expressed unhappiness with the limited navigability of the Thames river. No money could be found however to put locks in the weirs to make the Jubilee River navigable, which would be difficult anyway due to the varying channel depths (Venables, 2005).

7.5.3 The 1997 Review: Reopening the Frame One More Time

'11. Beware cost reductions that masquerade as value engineering' (Dodds and Venables, 2005)

In spite of all concessions to stakeholders, the MWEFAS project went through crunch time in 1997 when it was time to finalise the agreements for channel construction with the contractors. The negotiation of 'Contract 6' with the contractor, Balfour Beatty, in light of the project's spiralling costs had caused almost a full year's delay.[29] This quiet crisis (it did not reach the press and was not mentioned in any interview) came to light years later when MWEFAS project leader Colin Martin revealed the meeting to project critic Ewan Larcombe of Taplow. According to this information (Larcombe, 2005), Balfour Beatty proposed an alternative design. Along with five other cost-reducing modifications, such as a trapezoidal channel instead of a rectangular one, the contract included a 'value engineering' clause that promised further cost reduction. The EA, the Designers, and the Construction Contractors got together for a one-day 'Value Engineering Workshop' away from work, to discuss whether and how to change the design of the Jubilee River. This *opened up* the project frame rather drastically: a 'divergence' ideas phase included suggestions not to have a channel at all, or to build a large-diameter pipeline. A few weeks later, the Design Change Group whittled down the list of possibilities to about ten items. At a second meeting, technically viable and (expected) cost-saving alternatives were selected.

Thus, one may legitimately wonder if the Jubilee Channel, held up as an excellent example of the Royal Academy's sustainable engineering principles 2 ('innovate and be creative') and 3 ('seek a balanced solution'), had not sinned against principle 11 ('avoid cost cutting masquerading as Value Engineering').

Whatever the driver for this rethink, the new approach was to become controversial after the Thames flooded in 2003.

7.6 Floods At Last

7.6.1 The 1998 and 2000 Floods

> 'This is not a time to blame. If you are on the Titanic and you have hit an iceberg, you focus on getting everyone off before you shoot the captain' (Horton and Wraysbury councillor quoted in Terri Judd, 'You can't stop it, so you get your stuff out of the way', *The Independent*, 25 July 2007).

It was noted above that the EA often had to take recourse to sell the project to its intended beneficiaries, verbally and pictorially, to the floods of 1947 and 1974 (*Protecting your homes*, 1997). No one died in these floods; the level of 'threat' concerned shock and discomfort rather than danger. The 1990 floods helped put high water on the policy agenda but had smaller impact. This was only to change when the UK experienced a run of flood events at the turn of the century. Since major floods had not happened for five decades, the EA did not give this policy area the highest priority during the first few years of its existence. When the police, who were charged with flood warnings, unilaterally shed this task (Crichton, 2005), the EA felt compelled to take over the responsibility for flood warning in 1997, so it was understandably ill-prepared for the job when floods hit England at Easter, 1998. The flood warning did not reach many people it should have. The EA was subject to fierce criticism for the mismatch between those actually warned and those in need of a warning. In the 'Bye Report', the parliamentary Easter Floods Review Team lambasted the 'complicated, confusing for the public and regionally varying arrangements'.[30] Had the 1998 Easter Flood, in which five people were killed, been seen as national disaster, the ensuing public outrage could have empowered the Agency as a national flood managing institution.

Nevertheless, the Minister reacted to the Agricultural Select Committee's inquiry (House of Commons) into the 1998 floods by setting high-level targets that included a supervisory duty for the EA. According to Jean Venables, the Chairperson of the Thames IDB,

> [N]o one knew what it meant so nothing was done about it until recently. Now we're collecting information from other authorities to see what isn't done. Some didn't even know they had it [. . .] Defending properties is not a must-do – There is no legal responsibility; most of it [= flood protection] is permissive. No heads will be dismissed if we don't. (J. Venables pers. comm., 2000)[31]

In November and December 2000, heavy rains again caused floods in England, affecting some 10,000 homes. The MWEFAS channel had been excavated but not yet connected to the Thames so that the Channel could not be of much help in withstanding that year's winter floods. After these events, attitudes on risk and responsibility started to change rapidly (Johnson, Tunstall and Penning-Rowsell, 2005). The EA got its chance to be stricter on flood plain development. The precautionary principle (flood warning, self-help) and land use planning/development control were the core of the 'PPG 25' (Planning Policy Guideline) issued in 2001 in response to the Y2K floods (Tapsell et al., 2005). This guideline sought to restrict development of the flood plain inside the contours demarcated in the flood maps provided by the EA. Insurers take these flood maps as an indicator for the 'insurability' of properties. But short of a national disaster event it will be impossible to evict or buy out the people who already occupy the flood plain. PPG 25 will therefore likely only affect *new* developments.

Meanwhile, pressure for intervention mounted both from the private and civil-society sector. The insurers' umbrella organisation, ABI, put a moratorium on flood coverage until 2002, urging the government to review its commitment to flood protection, as the insurers could not 'keep subsidising' losses of this scale (some £200 million) (Huber, 2004). The ABI qualified its definition of what constitute 'exceptional circumstances', so that it does not have to provide cover for lack of 'sustainable defences'). The flood premiums would go up according to historic damage, shifting responsibility to homeowners (Huber, 2004). A 'flood tax' on properties was proposed, but eventually rejected.

This move forced the government to speed up its flood defence efforts at a time EA budgets were eroding. Disappointed citizens had expected much more of the EA in terms of structural defences and flood warning than it could muster, and – as we have seen – more than it was even mandated to provide. The discrepancy between governmental capabilities and citizen expectations, as well as a discrepancy between perceptions of who caused what, came to a head in 2003, when Datchet, Chertsey and Wraysbury suffered major flood nuisance.

7.6.2 The Channel's Inauguration and the 2003 Floods

By the time it opened in November 2001[32] the Jubilee River had cost £110 million. Consultants Lewin & Fryer, Nuttall and Balfour Beatty won plaudits for their 'soft engineering' approach, which was seen as the way forward in flood relief. The Royal Society of Engineers singled the project out for its Hambley medal in 1998; it won the ICE Award in 2002[33] and the Royal Town Planning Institute Award for Planning for the Natural Environment that same year.

Good press was also generated by a spectacular crossing under the M4 and the Western Region Railway (Walford, 1998). To enable traffic moving at all times, the culvert structure was frozen, then jacked underneath the bridge in 1999 to allow the river underneath a Victorian railway embankment. The preservation of another Victorian railway, Black Potts viaduct, which leads up to Windsor Castle, also attracted attention.

The costly modifications can be said to have been successful in public relations terms. Satisfaction with the resulting environmental enhancements seems high, as epitomised by one interviewee who had rejected the project first but proudly showed me round the project gushing about how nice everything looked.

But was the channel also ready to withstand the next high-water event? Because the channel is not lined with concrete, it depends on vegetation for river bank stability. It appears that bank vegetation had not yet settled as the Thames started to rise at the turn of 2003 (Venables, 2005). Over the New Year, signs of erosion started to show in the banks of the Jubilee River and the cycle path progressively fell into the stream. EA workmen carried out stabilisation works with bags and stones and inflow was temporarily reduced to 144 cusecs. The EA had closed the radial sluice gates at Taplow, as the waters started to rise in the biggest flood since the Great Flood of 1947. A 'Severe Flood Warning', denoting danger to life and property, was issued. On 4 January the sluice gates were opened again to prevent Maidenhead flooding. According to procedure,

> [t]he Jubilee River is operated when the flow in the River Thames at the Old Windsor Weir in Wraysbury exceeds 190 m^3/s. When that occurs 20 m^3/s is diverted to the Jubilee River. As the flow in the River Thames increases, the flow into the Jubilee River is increased in steps of 15 m^3/s.' (JMP report, 2003)

This allowed the water in the channel to rise at what the agency claims to be 'a very, very gradual rate'. Opponents claim, however, that the increase allowed the flood level at Windsor to rise to 320 cumecs (140 cumecs above the target flow) much too fast, and to contributing to flooding nearly 130 properties in Datchet downstream because the flood water travelled faster between Maidenhead and Datchet than the pre-Jubilee River and seems to have been a cause in breaching the bank of the local Myrke Ditch.

Thus, while 1,000 properties were saved – only one low-lying flat building in Maidenhead was affected – 128 were flooded 6 miles downstream in Datchet, a parish under the jurisdiction of Maidenhead and Windsor Borough. Chertsey, which falls under Runnymede Borough, also flooded, in part due to the (un-dredged) local river Bourne, a tributary of the Thames. In addition to downstreamers, the parishes of Marlow, Bourne End, Bisham and Cookham, just upstream from the Thames bifurcation, also blamed the Jubilee River or the floods (JMP, 2003) The local MP; Michael Trend, said: 'People who live upstream of the beginning of the scheme feel intuitively – I hope that this is not an urban myth – that there may have been a bottleneck effect', (Parliamentary question, 13 January 2003).

In response to the shock of being flooded, there were calls for a public inquiry, to clarify concerned questions about the effect of the Jubilee River. To the disappointment of downstream parishes but also Maidenhead council[34] the EA felt a new public enquiry would take too long and cost too much. Instead, the Agency instated an Independent Commission in January 2003, to be headed by a senior engineer, Clive Onions, to publish a report for three yet-to-be established FRAGs (Flood Relief Action Groups, now called Thames Flood Teams) which he was to chair. These FRAGs are made up of Local Authorities, Representatives from affected communities and other relevant Agencies. Two community action groups had meanwhile formed, The Upstream Group (TUG) and ThamesAwash. Together with the River Thames Society's Flood Committee they applied to join the FRAGs. Maidenhead's local authority rejected this, but accepted their participation via two Community Support Groups, to be chaired and represented on the FRAG by two Parish Councillors, appointed by the council.

The Onions report concluded that 'the flooding was [. . .] exacerbated by loss of the flood plain at Maidenhead, Dorney and Eton Wick and by the cessation of dredging since 1993 for economic and environmental reasons, which reduced the river capacity over time.'[35]

The EA also organised FRAG Open Days. During one of those 'road shows' at the Borough of Spelthorne,[36] the EA admitted the Datchet banks could also breach and need reinforcing. Ewan Larcombe (Chairman of Datchet Parish) questioned the openness of the FRAGs, feeling the Open Days were a cover-up. Larcombe called for the immediate closure of the channel by welding the gates.[37] Later, he insisted the Agency should seek full planning application for the repair works near Datchet. That same month there was still a concern that angry citizens of Wraysbury, 'decimated' by the 2003 flood, would disturb a council meeting about the issue. Further anger ensued when it became clear the next month that the 'independent' FRAGs chairman, Clive Onions, was in fact a senior associate of Arup consultants who were involved in the design of the Jubilee River subcontractor.[38]

The affected local authorities did not await the Onion reports. A report by JMP Consulting was commissioned by the Royal Borough of Windsor and Maidenhead together with Spelthorne, Elmbridge, and Runnymede Borough Councils (JMP, 2003). JMP concluded that rainfall in 2003 was significantly higher than in 2000, but not extreme – more such floods can be expected. When citizens of Spelthorne, Elmbridge and Runnymede were interviewed for the independent JMP report investigating the flooding of 2003, a great majority of the respondents blamed the Jubilee River. But JMP concluded that at most 10 per cent of the effect on Datchet can be attributed to the Jubilee River.

This finding did not rehabilitate the flood scheme, though. The most damning report was drafted by structural engineers from WS Atkins, environmental consultants. They found in 2004 that the Jubilee River's banks were too low and too steep, and that inappropriate materials were used.[39] Up to 700 m of embankment was 'A1', that is, in need of immediate replacement. Only 35 per cent were 'erosion-proof'. Also the report criticised the use of non-standard procedures which made response to floods unpredictable. To Atkins' surprise, a stilling basin (to dissipate energy from high waters) downstream of radial gates was missing at Taplow, the weir's apron came loose and almost all structures were found flawed.[40] It concluded that even at the best of times, the Jubilee River and the Thames can together carry just 325 m^3/s, 63 per cent of the original design specification. After completing the works, the channel will still be 10 per cent below design capacity. Yet Ian Tomes of the EA feels the agency has done all it can, short of starting a whole new project.[41]

The report also claimed the Lower Thames model for the Datchet-to-Wraybsury stretch was flawed and should have estimated downstream levels by 30 cm higher. 'The news has shattered our confidence in the entire scheme', commented Maidenhead local authority cabinet leader Mary-Rose Gliksten. No wonder, as a consequence of this embarrassing episode, the EA found itself compelled to review the flood contours which form the basis of PPG 25, reclassifying 'areas that it previously described as safe from flooding as being back in the floodplain' – which was bound to have restrictive effects on allowable planning permission in Maidenhead, notably in no-more-safe Cookham, and on flood insurance rates. It became clear that the 550 cumecs design capacity would not be realistic – especially while climate scenarios predict 20 per cent extra rainfall.

The Agency's initial reaction was still soothing: the EA had it be known that '[t]he Flood Relief Scheme is not a failure'.[42] Chris Birks, EA manager, responded to citizen complaints that it's a 'learning process' but 'you can't countenance going back to straight sided trapezoidal channels', meaning a return from soft engineering to hard engineering. However, in 2006 the Agency decided to concede defeat[43] and file a suit for damages. Given the complex management structure (some 30 consultants involved), it is not easy to assign liability to anyone, but the Agency decided to take their engineering consultants, Lewin and Fryer, to task.[44] The matter was settled with an out of court: Fryer & Partners will have to pay £2.75 million in damages.[45]

New Lease on Life for Integrated River Plan?

The flooding of Datchet and Wraysbury also reopened a window for John Gardiner's original vision of a second channel. EA promised to investigate the feasibility of the second channel down the Thames, as part of a new River Thames Strategic Flood Defence Initiative. The original five options for a 16-kilometre extension of the Jubilee Channel, tabled by Gardiner in 1992, were compared with a do-nothing and a do-minimum option.[46] But the cost of these options had meanwhile tripled (in 2004 sterling) and would now range from £92 million (river reprofiling) to 248 million (different lengths of channel) (Hansford, 2004: 5). The editor of Thamesweb believed DEFRA would rule the scheme out principally because not many people would be expected to die in the event of the Thames flooding and, secondly, that houses on the Thames do not qualify as belonging to the socially needy' (Thamesweb). Indeed, while options 2 to 5 were thought to be economic, the new report concluded that only a 'do-the-minimum option' would attract DEFRA funding in light of the Ministry's grant standards.[47] Indeed, the scheme was rejected on the basis of a low DEFRA priority score. In response, the Thames Flood Forum, a Berkshire flood action group, said it could cough up the £200 million needed for such a scheme itself.[48]

The momentum for the second channel project may have been sustained after the 2007 floods – the new Brown Government promised to spend a billion pounds a year on flood defence (by 2024). In response, Adam Afriyie, Conservative MP for Windsor, asked the Environment Minister, Hilary Benn, in Parliament (20 July), to reconsider the lower Thames scheme.[49] This was indeed done: in September 2009, the government launched a consultation about a new Lower Thames Flood Strategy, which proposes three diversion channels for the stretch between Datchet and Teddington (12,000 houses at 1:100 risk). Two thousand people participated in the consultation; ThamesAwash and other citizen groups however express old misgivings, reminding the EA that the design of the Jubilee River was changed after the consultation.[50]

The debate has interestingly backgrounded the fact that Datchet itself has done little to reduce its exposure to flood risk. While Datchet never actively promoted flood plain development, Neil and Parker (1988, see also Parker, 2000) had taken the Local Authority as well as the Department of Environment to task long before for poor recognition and awareness of the risks from flood plain development there. The town had been safe from floods since 1947, and simply taken this safety for granted until the sequence of floods at the turn of the twenty-first century.

7.6.3 Naming, Framing and Blaming

Going back to the MWEFAS now, we can summarise its story in terms of contrasting *risk narratives* (see also van Eeten, 1997). Protecting a well-to-do area made it possible to use the scheme as a choice opportunity to enhance the area's environmental quality while still expecting a good cost-benefit ratio. This facilitated a discursive alliance between flood protectors and environment conservationists. As noted, this was a clean break with the existing disaster culture in which citizens had to rely on self-help. Contrary to Leiss and Chociolko's claim (1995) that actors will always seek to offload responsibility for risks, the

Who Caused Floods	What Caused Floods	What Should be Done?	Who Should Act?
1. Act of God	Extreme weather event	Self-help Arterial drainage	Flood plain dwellers Catchment Board
2. Act of Man	Flood plain development	Restrict development	Developers and LPAs
3. Act of the EA	Flood defence scheme	Stop flood defence	Government

Table 7.5: ***Competing flood narratives***

Agency could see a clear benefit in assuming responsibility. Offering to 'protect your homes' raised expectations and responsibilities, which would also boost the Agency's standing and mandate in the policy regime.

In the 1980s, as in the 1930s, floods still seemed an 'Act of God' (Frame 1, Table 7.5) in a country without a disaster culture. But flood defence without a zoning policy works as an incentive to build more, which is contradictory with the long-running NRA ambition to curb encroachment on the flood plain. Real estate developers are keen to build in the flood plain, while the local authorities of Windsor and Maidenhead have not exactly discouraged it. The lax enforcement of development on the river meant the value of properties to be protected helped tip the balance in the cost-benefit analysis in favour of the project.

This confluence of interests did not fit the NRA–EA's preferred storyboard. In the NRA story, the developers are the sometimes ruthless villains who expose the citizenry to unnecessary flood risks (the 'dragon'). Some Local Planning Authorities aid and abet the flood by their lax attitude, allowing the Thames flood plain west of Oxford to be developed. In this story, only the NRA can deliver the good people of Maidenhead, Windsor and Eton from this risk, but only if the LPAs stop fuelling the 'dragon's' expansionist drive. So, from around 1988, a new problem frame arrived on the scene, in which developers and LPAs were blamed for exposing riverine towns to flood (Frame 2).

The *niche* it found to accompany the self-imposed protector role was green technology and openness (participation). The National Rivers Authority perceived a heightened environmental awareness and recognised that a social support for 'holistic' flood management projects required a shift from technology-centred 'monologue' to stakeholder 'dialogue'. The NRA–EA initiative to hold public meetings – an 'iterative process of explanation and listening'

(Gardiner, 1992) *before* protests were staged – was a marked step ahead in the UK context, if no clean break with the paradigm. But while the MWEFAS was ahead of its time in stakeholder consultation, 'promotion' and placation after the decision had already been taken formed the mainstay of the EA perspective on participation. The protests continued and led to a Public Inquiry.

To support their case, local protesters adduced a different problem frame altogether (Frame 3): it was not so much the flood risk as the flood scheme that threatened the citizens. They also took a very different view of the local cost-benefit ratio. The locals' ongoing counter-story sees the channel itself as a costly and ineffective monstrosity, despoliating the countryside and its historic and cultural values. What the EA saw as a neglected area, they saw as a thing of beauty (see also Tunstall et al., 1991). Several locals concede that infilling of the flood plain means increased risk, but the flood risk is something people have lived with for centuries, which makes them the unsung heroes who 'keep fighting the scheme'.[51]

When the Jubilee Channel plan was not extended, downstream stakeholders were worried that they would be more rather than less at risk in a flood event. They were promised in the 1992 Public Enquiry that they would not, but harboured doubts. When the EA's initial response to the 2003 flood, however, was to deny any problem in the structural design, their distrust in the Agency was vindicated. Seeing an 'imbalance of benefits and sacrifices' (see also Fordham, 1998/99) they voiced concerns like: 'Wraysbury pays council taxes to Maidenhead and does not want to be sacrificially flooded for Maidenhead's safety.'[52]

Technical experts concluded that the bypass can only have contributed up to 10 per cent to the extra flooding. Ironically, the Agency seemed to see the bank failure as an Act of God (problem Frame 1) and put in place structural, remedial measures. 'Open Days' continued the promotional approach, while reducing public participation by refusing a public enquiry. It took until 2004 for the EA to admit that most (but not all) of the initial allegations were correct, after which the agency decided to hold the structural engineers liable, effectively passing on the blame to its subcontractors. As an inhabitant of Windsor commented on the EA's insistence on blamelessness: 'I wish that someone would put their hand up and say sorry, we made a mistake, won't happen again' (*You and Yours* programme, BBC Radio 4, 10 October 2005).

We can conclude that the EA's increased role in flood protection created previously non-existent expectations, changing the flood governance scene in Britain. Speller and Twigger-Ross (2005) wryly observe that public risk communication with communities may have brought about a process of blaming the government when something goes wrong, which previously would have been dealt with through self-help in the absence of any state responsibility or duty for flood protection. The EA remains caught between rising demands for flood security and a shortfall of funds to supply it, although its flood budget is set to rise sharply in the aftermath of the 2007 floods.

The preferred way out for the Agency to handle flood governability seems to be a campaign for *flood acceptance*. A recent report notes that 'communities need to be helped to accept a certain level of flood risk, to accept that they need to share some of the responsibility, and to accept that by designing spaces to flood safety ecological benefits will also be increased' (Speller and Twigger-Ross, 2005). A 'tripartite partnership' between citizens, politicians and public servants would be an appropriate way of devolving power to citizens, 'sharing responsibility as well as rights to good environmental quality' as co-producers[53] (Skidmore et al., 2003). This would indicate a move toward a new *model of governance* (sharing responsibility), which has yet to crystallise. One step in this direction is the 'Making Space for Water' document released in 2005, which promises to adopt a holistic, 'risk-based' approach and promises to 'involve stakeholders at all levels of risk management' (DEFRA, 2005). It foresees Catchment Management Plans, longer planning horizons adopted, and EA will receive most of its funds in the form of grant-in-aid rather than from council taxes and IDB fees.

7.7 Conclusion

When I started investigating the Jubilee Channel, it struck me that so little seemed to have been said and published about it. Quizzed on this point in 2000, the project's initiator, John Gardiner, claimed to me this is because the scheme was 'non-controversial' and cites low turnout of consultation as circumstantial evidence. Given the largely successful bargaining during the planning stage sketched above, this assessment seemed obvious. A flexible attitude on the part of the initiators took away, or sailed around, many obstacles. But even at the time of the interview, 'non-controversial' seemed rather too rosy a view if we juxtapose an encouraging PR record with a High Court lawsuit, parliamentary questions and a call-in by the Minister of Agriculture.

The EA took a considerable financial and political risk by initiating the Maidenhead bypass. It was planned as a relief channel, and as such was legitimised as a green security-enhancing project. However, as floods in Maidenhead are widely seen as a nuisance for the rich and famous rather than a life-threatening issue in this area, any security strategy was bound to risk opposition by perceiving more harm than benefits from it. The weak position of its initiator, moreover, presented a number of procedural and funding risks to the survival of the project.

Perhaps this weak position necessitated the EA to make (too?) many concessions to maintain a support base. The Agency managed to sway or accommodate important opponents by re-routing the channel and providing additional amenities, arguably also in view of the symbolic value of a successful precedent for further projects. When the scheme did not deliver on its first test, the EA lost public confidence. The Borough of Windsor and Maidenhead remains the second most flood-prone area in the UK.[54] In response it developed a 'Building Trust with the Community' toolkit to turn the anger of flood-affected citizens into something more constructive.

The floods of 1998, 2000, 2003 and 2007 cumulatively appear to have punctuated an equilibrium. Still, while the EA's flood-related mandate has been enhanced and it is actively seeking new projects, it remains constrained by relatively limited budgets and a limited mandate. In this sense, the 'revolution' did not happen.

Has the MWEFAS project as an innovation revolutionised the flood management regime and socio-technical landscape? The Agency certainly secured the niche it sought for it. Its green engineering approach has certainly widened the scope of flood management options. An opportunity can take on the same urgency as a problem when the deadline is tight. The availability of money can be the driving force or accelerator for the project. This can be a 'use it or lose it' outcome of budget negotiations. It can be argued that the Maidenhead scheme would not have been possible, or experienced great difficulty without the availability of national funds and regional wealth. Once the decision has been taken, it is very hard to stop an infrastructural project, despite the spiralling cost.

A 'selling' rather than 'participatory' approach was opted for, which several stakeholders felt led to a foregone conclusion in the selection process. The consultation process, while rather flawed, was largely successful in persuading key stakeholders. Alternative options suggested by Taplow and Buckinghamshire County were discarded out of hand, while one developed by FHRC was never made public. Eton was more successful in 'bulldozing' significant changes in the plan invoking the sanctity of heritage. Stakeholders did not come forward with anything radically different. But while the project enhanced the EA's standing as an innovator, until the channel's collapse sent it back to square one, DEFRA is still dominant and has made it clear EA should concentrate on its operational role. The floods of 1998, 2000 and 2003 seem to have been more decisive in opening windows for reform in flood plain management and a review of the funding mechanism. The NRA thus appears to have lost some crucial battles but won the war: its vision of catchment management and flood plain management has arrived and established itself on the UK flood management scene. In that sense, John Gardiner can be satisfied.

8

THE POLITICS OF SIX RIVER INTERVENTIONS – A SYNTHESIS

'Security is not a number, it is a feeling.'
(Huib de Vriend, a professor of civil engineering at Delft University, cited in *Technisch Weekblad*, 27 January 2007)

8.1 Introduction

Because they instil primordial fears in people, floods have strong securitisation potential. Securitisation legitimises swift interventions in crisis mode and the control or exclusion of particular actors from the normal decision-making regime. What is more: successfully linking floods with security changes the domain, tilting the power constellation towards security professionals and cutting out the politics. It gives unusual powers over the environment, over people and procedure.

What does securitisation mean in flood management and how successful are securitising moves in river management? Does it strengthen or challenge the position of the leading actors, does it change the way things are done? Does it matter if the context was securitised before?

The past chapters have presented six cases, each varying in their physical and administrative context and technological intervention. The present chapter evaluates the six cases to see if and how security and risk talk influenced decision-making on river interventions, and if the flood or the flood project impacted on the decision-making regime. Following Balzacq (2005) it looks at agency, audience and context. A *hazard* approach sees hazards as forces of nature and seeks to prevent the hazard ever happening, so that society can worry about other

Disaster Narrative	**Security is About**	**Immediate Security Referent**
Hazard (Securitised)	Reducing probability	Dikes
Risk (Desecuritised)	Reducing probability × impact	Flood plain / polder
Vulnerability	Reducing probability × impact × vulnerability	Community

Table 8.1: ***Three disaster narratives***

things. It thus invites structural defences. A risk approach by contrast accepts that risks can happen in spite of the best efforts to prevent their incidence, and needs the cooperation of society to reduce the impact.

Section 8.2 first unpacks the key elements for securitisation analysis and categorises the different cases in which securitising moves were attempted according to a securitised or non-securitised *context* (8.3). Thereafter, the attention shifts to the *audience*. Sections 8.4 to 8.7 investigate if securitising moves were accepted for the sake of survival, or if they triggered resentment, rejection and resistance with the audience – intended target groups and uninvited interventions. Non-acceptance can be expressed in non-compliance, but also the politicisation (8.5), 'counter-securitisation' and even outright conflict (8.6).

Buzan et al. (1998: 72) predict that environmental securitisation will fail. Analogously, we may predict that declaring 'war on water' (flood *securitisation*) is likely to fail. How do water managers deal with this failure potential? Are they prepared to deal with water threats in a 'peace logic' (the everyday politics of decision-making)? Section 8.7 investigates what *desecuritised* (peace with water) flood management looks like, in terms of regime rules, participants and knowledge in project planning and implementation. Does this lead to normal politics or can desecuritised projects, like securitised projects, also trigger criticism and conflict and (re-)securitising moves?

The 'felicity' of a desecuritised logic will be analysed in light of the vulnerability narrative in disaster studies. The approach is sensitive to differential security outcomes, highlighting that not everyone is equally exposed to risk, but rather that the way the political economy is organised structurally exposes some groups more to risk than others – a *vulnerability* approach (8.8).

Section 8.9, finally, looks at the impact of flood and flood projects on the actors, rules and knowledge in the decision-making regime. The three narratives bring a layered perspective of regimes, showing that changes at surface may not evidence change at deeper power structures. A conclusion ends the chapter.

8.2 Securitisation Analysis: What is It?

Securitisation releases extraordinary resources and powers to counter the threat, exclude (discussion of) alternatives and dispel uncertainty and ambiguity, and trumps the debate by invoking existential, survival values, assigning the issue to the state as if by definition. Let us consider more fully what the defining steps and elements of securitisation are, and thus what steps are in order to analyse the case studies under scrutiny.

1. *Naming* a threat to a prized referent object (*protégé*), which may be material (homes) or immaterial (cultural values, holy sites). The declaration of a threat implies it has to be acted on urgently. If the threat is implicit or taboo, it is unlikely to trigger action.
2. *Framing* a threat: a theory of what caused the threat (blaming and claiming). Attribution theory teaches us that in case of complex causal relations, people seek to attribute agency and blame for risk and accidents to a single causal (f)actor, which then helps legitimise security measures. The source of the threat, the enemy, may be considered as external (upstreamers and polluting industries) or internal (irresponsible/deviant behaviour from within the community).

   It seems obvious that the enemy in a securitised flood is the river, inviting laying *blame* on someone or something for the high water event: God/Allah, climate change, upstream flood action, irresponsible settlement, and *claim* damages or remedial action.
3. Call for an unambiguous *remedy*, a (simple) solution for countering this threat. Attribution not only pertains to *causality* in hazards, but also to *remedies* – you still need a dose of 'magic' to contain risk: 'if we only do 'this, the problem will be solved'. Possible remedies are:

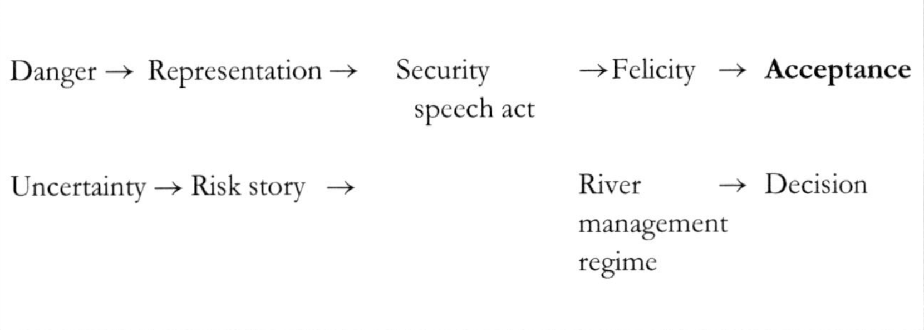

Figure 8.1: Conceptual model underlying this study

8.2.1 Context Matters: History and Overlay in Felicity

Thierry Balzacq (2005) has noted that security 'speech acts' are not unidirectional communications, but require *agency*, *audience* and *context*. A speech act only works because an audience approves and the context validates the (speech) act. Buzan et al. (1998) take *context* into account when they expect a security speech act to perform better if it refers to a recognised threat that people are familiar with. Securitisation can be institutionalised – you do not have to explicitly say 'security' all the time to trigger the desired response:

> [I]t is implicitly assumed that if we talk of *this* [. . .], we are by definition in the area of urgency: by saying 'defence' (or in Holland, 'dikes'), one has implicitly said security and priority. (Buzan et al., 1998: 27)

The case studies can be categorised according to context as follows:

- securitised and non-securitised states,
- securitised and non-securitised rivers.

- *Securitised context: the garrison state (Turkey and Egypt – Bangladesh until 1990)*

While the going definition of a 'crisis' normally would imply a short incidental peak on a longer time curve, securitisers in Egypt and Turkey have managed to stretch the operability of 'urgency' to quite extended periods. Political securitisation raises the barrier to desecuritising discourse even without the need for a discrete securitising event. Everything can potentially be a security issue, but it is for the state to decide this. As Wilkinson (2007) notes, such a situation makes it hard for social actors to make competing security speech acts.

- *Securitised river: recognised threat (Maas, Rhine – the Netherlands)*

In light of Buzan et al.'s remark on the impact of 'saying dikes', we would expect floods to be structurally securitised threats in the Netherlands, even if the governance context is not. The Netherlands lost many people and assets in past flood events, and until 2002 had civic 'dike armies' patrolling high water stages and only focussed on preventing floods, eliminating residual risk.

If the river threat is so institutionalised, a flood easily actualises 'sedimented' security (danger) responses in speech and practice. When the high-water event eventually comes, it is easily and 'felicitously' declared a crisis, and most proponents and opponents are agreed on the need to protect lives and assets, although they may differ about the way it should be done. The balance predictably tilts towards quick-and-dirty engineering – emergency embankments and river bank repairs – and crisis measures suspending normal rights and freedoms, such as zoning and expropriation. A flood securitisation thus successfully mobilises unbounded resources and a support base for countering future flood events.

- *Non-securitised context*

If the river is not normally seen as an enemy, as is the case in Britain and Bangladesh, the shock of a flood crisis could change this and impel emergency measures. Other security issues may strongly resonate, too, notably food.

8.3 When the Flood calls . . . Floods Get Securitised?

8.3.1 Six River Security Projects

Let us briefly recapitulate the six cases, organised by the above categorisation of context:

Egypt and Turkey – River Projects in Securitised States

While *Egypt* is the 'gift of the Nile', there would not seem to be a particular reason for Egypt to securitise Toshka, let alone for upstream Ethiopia to protest it. Egypt has achieved full *technical* closure of the Nile by building the Aswan Dam with a giant storage reservoir, Lake Nasser. However, every now and then bumper floods at times exceed the lake's capacity and required the construction of a spillway into the desert. Prepared not to waste a drop, the Egyptian government planned a giant project development, the Southern Valley scheme, to 'opportunitise' (Warner, 2004a) the flood years, that is, capitalise on the windfall flood years at whatever cost. The scheme would not only expand the currently constrained irrigable area but also create space to resettle millions of Egyptians currently living in the densely packed metropolis. Ethiopia saw it as a prior claim which would constrain its own security of future development and protested.

In *Turkey*, water is plentiful, and as an upstreamer, the country has no external river intervention to fear. The flood damage potential on the Tigris is mainly in the Iraqi delta, and has given rise to major infrastructural works there. The GAP dam project intended to bridge socio-economic divides between the bustling northwest and impoverished southeast. Having realised planned projects on the Euphrates, the Turkish government resolved to exploit and regulate the river Tigris. However, the Turks set their sights on the river for development of the resources for hydropower and irrigation as part of the Greater Anatolia Project (GAP). To create a reservoir adjoining the Ilısu Hydro-electric Power Plant (HEPP), effectively started in 2006, dozens of Kurdish villages including the historically significant town of Hasankeyf need to be 'manually flooded' and their inhabitants resettled.

Turkey sees the (induced) flooding of houses and heritage as a necessary stage in reviving the civilisation of Southeast Anatolia. But the citizens of Hasankeyf and other flooded villages saw it as the destruction of their home and heritage, while Kurdish rebels, moreover, saw it as a symbol of Turkish domination and made the river works a target for attack. As a consequence, Turkey's Southeast Anatolia region has remained under a state of exception since 1984. The reignited Kurdish uprising has ensured Turkish army presence in the Southeast region.

In Egypt and Turkey, full control of the rivers has not led to their demilitarisation and desecuritisation. On the one hand, drought imperilling energy and food security is still an issue, but also control of people, the strategic value of regional development and economic interests underpin a military role in the water sector. The river management projects are treated as national security because they are development projects set in the very regions that are subject to perceived originators of threats to national security – Upper Egypt and Southeast Anatolia.

It has been observed (Aydın, 2003 and others) that Turkey is existentially insecure due to a history of recurring wars and internal challenges. This has promoted coups d'état, declarations of the state of emergency and a strong role for the army. The securitised status of both project and political decision-making has foreclosed the scrutiny of project alternatives outside a select group. President Mubarak assures his subjects that multiple alternatives have been considered, and Turkey's State Hydraulic Works, DSÍ, studied ten alternative locations for the Ilısu Dam, several of which would have saved much or all of the historic city of Hasankeyf. As the Turkish project became a more integrated project, it gradually accommodated more complexity. In both cases, it is clear that they were not held up to public scrutiny before they eventually became politicised.

The Netherlands – Securitised Rivers in a Desecuritised State

While security concerns in the Netherlands had diminished in a largely flood-free epoch, two high-water events in 1993 and 1995 put flood risk back on the policy agenda. On the Maas, several locations flooded in both events. While no one drowned, the flood damage and shock of not being safe brought a sense of disaster which can be said to have rescued the Grensmaas project, an initiative by the province of Limburg. This plan for the Maas, developed in the 1980s, sought to combine nature development and flood protection by widening the river and creating natural embankments, funding the project with gravel extracted from the river (green for gravel).

While the Rhine did not flood, the consecutive water events, nevertheless, triggered 'panic politics': a preventive mass evacuation effort and emergency legislation in 1995. All of a sudden, security from flooding was the number one priority. The Netherlands took just two weeks to develop a Delta Plan for the Great Rivers and rush it through the Houses of Parliament and Council of

State. This plan authorised special powers to carry emergency measures on the Maas and Rhine for a two-year period, including the suspension of strict rules of accountability, participation and environmental regulation. The government put in emergency river dikes and a ten-year moratorium on construction in the flood plain. Significant informal influence on security decision-making was noticeable between 1995 and 1997.

An essential part of subsequent debate revolved around the question whether the flood issue was also a security issue in Limburg. When the Public Works Department, Rijkswaterstaat, took the reins of the project, Limburg had expected the river works to be adopted as a security issue, furnishing the balance needed for the project. However, RWS argued that Limburg is well above sea level with considerable space for a flood peak to disperse. In the end, the pro-security initiator, Limburg's provincial authority, won a pyrrhic victory: the legal security norm (a 1-in-250-year flood) was extended to undiked Limburg and the project went ahead, but without the hoped-for funds. This stripped the project of its more innovative and legitimating (or sweetening) features such as nature regeneration.

Fear of extreme events was also the rationale for the plan for controlled flood storage in the Ooij polder and two other polders launched in 2000. The idea was to inundate thinly populated areas to save more densely packed areas. The Vice-Minister initially decided not to securitise the decision-making, but to throw it out into the open. After provincial protest in Gelderland, the central government attempted to depoliticise the issue by instating an advisory committee. A wider range of civil society institutions were indeed involved in the commission's work. The security rationale convinced the committee members early on, but could not command the same felicity with local polder dwellers, who complained they were not consulted.

Bangladesh – Securitised Event in a Desecuritised–Desecuritising Context

As if devastating coastal cyclones in 1970, 1991 and 2007 were not enough, Bangladesh's rivers have not been kind on the country, either. The fatal coincidence of high water on the Brahmaputra-Jamuna and Ganges created two consecutive major floods in 1987 and 1988. The August and September 1988 flood claimed 2,000 fatalities and left millions homeless. President Ershad took emergency measures to protect the capital and to restore order. The mass human suffering incited French President François Mitterrand's resolve to stop the floods forever. The French rallied the G7 industrial countries around a Flood Action Plan for Bangladesh and proposed a US$5 billion mega-plan to embank all the three major rivers that besiege the country's flat territory (technical closure). The French discourse of delivering Bangladesh from floods justified dramatic structural solutions, to honour an implicit duty to protect Bangladesh rather than leave it to its fate. This securitising plan however lost out to the concept of polder compartmentalisation combined with flood-proofing measures, in keeping with the positive, life-giving aspect of flood risk; a partial desecuritisation of the river.

A flood risk assessment led to the deselection of two project areas, while the project's implementation stage was saved from discontinuation by a smaller flooding event. The Jamuna Multipurpose Bridge project started nearby had led to a blocked inlet feeding the FAP-20 area with water. An apparently spontaneous river breakthrough unblocked the inlet but also destroyed hundreds of dwellings. Yet when in 1998 another 'century flood' hit Bangladesh, FAP-20 showed its merits as a safe haven not just for Tangail but also attracting many refugees from outside the area.

Bangladesh's Flood Action Plan started under a dictatorship (political closure). The president had already declared a state of emergency for political reasons, providing little scope for dissent. This cleared many initial hurdles, as it obviated the need for democratic control. Thus, when a leading research NGO issued a critical report on flood management, this led to repressive measures against its directors. In 1990 Bangladesh reverted to a shaky multiparty democracy.

Technical as well as political setbacks repeatedly forced the initiators to change the project definition. A crucial factor was contested legitimacy. Local protest, coupled with a strong international NGO thrust, alerted donors to defects in the participatory structure and effects on the local socio-economic structure, based on communal land use. After local and international protests, the Bangladesh Water Development Board came round to dialoguing with the intended beneficiaries in 1995.

Britain – Flood Shock Event in Non-Securitised Context

Despite suffering its own 1953 sea flood event, in which hundreds died, the UK has no institutionalised securitisation of hazard: the government has no formal responsibility to safeguard citizens from floods; instead people are obliged to take out insurance to buy or build property. Flood security is not 'politicised' in Buzan et al.'s sense, and the Thames Conservancy and its successors unsuccessfully sought to securitise the flood plain by imposing development controls (keeping people away from the river). Local authorities, but also central governments facilitating a housing boom in the Southeast, showed weak opposition to the initiatives of flood plain developers.

The Agency also faced an uphill battle convincing public and civil-society stakeholders of the need for *flood defence.* It sought a role in providing security and protection ('Protecting your homes'), but wished to forsake hard defences in favour of environmental engineering: a flood bypass on the Thames with 'soft' river banks. This would promote a more integrated approach to river management and increase the natural values of what it pictured as an 'ecologically uninteresting' area. A truly integrated approach for the Thames, moreover, would require a second channel downstream from the first one. After a lengthy consultation process, a public enquiry and a revision of the project, the channel to protect Maidenhead, Eton and Windsor was built and opened in 2002.

By that time, pressure from insurers and public shock over repeated river floods had started to boost the legitimacy of public protection works. Unlike in the Netherlands, a minor flood event had come and gone in 1990 without greatly affecting the project. But three-year flood cycles (1998, 2000, 2003) ensured the issue remained on the political agenda. As the water rose in January 2003, the Jubilee River's natural embankment broke down and, among other factors, was locally believed to have contributed to flooding Datchet. In response, the Environment Agency put in emergency engineering works, denied any responsibility and dismissed calls for a public inquiry.[1] The aftermath of the flood dented confidence in soft engineering, but not in flood channels, and led to the decision to put the previously rejected channel extension back on to the agenda.

8.3.2 Windows for Securitisation: Solutions in Search of a Problem?

> Dominant advocacy coalitions attempt to define the problem and the solution together in one package . . . a solution [is] chosen first and the problem definition . . . fit into that. (Wolsink, 2003: 715)

The question starting this study off was whether flood events, or the projects to contain them, changed the policy scene (regime) through securitisation. The present study operationalised the actualisation of securitisation by considering what happens in a post-crisis mode of decision-making, a (natural or induced) high-water event. A crisis event reveals the social arrangements; the hegemonic discourses. A crisis simplifies the decision-making system as it copes with a potentially overwhelming challenge. This reconstituted crisis arena can 'punctuate' the reigning balance of power and its modus operandi, but also reinforce existing relationships.

On closer inspection the flood events rarely turned out to trigger new flood projects. It appears the projects were already there, looking for a niche to blossom. The FAP-20, Jubilee Channel, Maaswerken and Toshka case studies were all prepared *before* rather than after a major event. Although it was not possible for me to have inside information on decision-making on all the schemes, the available evidence suggests that, in most cases under scrutiny, the plan *preceded* the flood. In each of the projects, in addition to demand for security, there appear to be at least some 'supply' considerations at work beyond direct flood response when selecting them.

FAP-20 was already defined before 1987–88 floods and, according to interviewees, would very probably have gone ahead without the Flood Action Plan. Compartmentalisation gained prominence after the flood, though, as a workable compromise between the two competing paradigms of flood management: total control (hard structures), and living-with-the-flood (flexible response). While FAP-20 was the flagship, compartmentalisation was also a defining element in other FAP subprojects (such as FAP-3.1 in Jamalpur and FAP-4 in Khulna-Jessore). The floods however created a context in which the local Bangladeshi request for support could be articulated with security discourse on the global scene. From my interviews it was very notable that neither 'security' nor 'vulnerability' has much resonance in Bangladesh in relation to floods. But floods as threat resonated with donors used to speaking 'security' from floods and its lexical isotopes (defence, threat and fight against water): France, the Netherlands, now the Asian Development Bank. This provided an opportunity to develop an extensive programme of flood projects.

While the Jubilee Channel was of course built before the 2003 flood came along, the flood brought the second channel back for the downstream river section on the agenda which had been defeated on cost-benefit considerations in 1992. After another flood, in 2007, the second channel in some form appears to be making its comeback.

The Egyptian government needed several years of abundance to give the enormous Southern Valley project, lying in waiting since the late 1950s, a big push. Egypt's legitimisation, need for space and food security may be questioned by international scholars, Mitchell and Allan, but continues to be echoed in donor discourse.

In the Netherlands, the Border Maas (Grensmaas) nature restoration project languished until the flood came along. The floods provided a unique opportunity to save a nature development by hitching a ride with a 'dry feet' project; the gravel industry, who faced a ban on further quarrying, has strengthened its hand because its participation provides the economic rationale for the project.

Linking nature development with flood protection, gravel extraction and navigation together legitimised the hefty size of the intervention. The plan combined several interests and objectives, but without the flood protection aspect, it is doubtful that the project would have gone ahead in this form.

The story for the Ooij polder is slightly different: flood storage was a practice that had fallen into disuse in the Netherlands since the 1950s. When in the 1995 high-water event Gelderland was on the verge of an emergency inundation of the Ooij polder to save downstream polders, the plan to revive this practice emerged in 2000.

As for the Ilısu dam, there is no such clear event, although the energy crisis of the 1970s can be said to have been a significant help in legitimising an expensive hydroelectric plant.

Non-security innovations found a niche in the design of new projects when presented as flood control projects. From one perspective, greening the projects and 'making space' for the river was hoped to appease project-affected populations worried about the quality of their landscape or their access to monsoon water in each of the three 'wet' countries: river widening (NL), 'green' bypass (UK) and compartmentalisation (Bangladesh). On the other hand, the project itself saved or promoted non-security concerns such as environment and agricultural self-sufficiency and export, technology, the future of the gravel industry and the beautification of 'uninteresting' landscape. The power of flood defence can help something else to play hopscotch – a 'civilising mission' of regional human development as in Turkey and a new civilisation on the Nile or nature development in England and the Netherlands where project initiators sought to gentrify an 'impoverished' or 'visually uninteresting' landscape.

This finding is supported by a strand in the public administration literature that reveals that problems and solutions are not sequentially put on the agenda. Solutions may be waiting in the wings, spying the arena for an opportunity to make their way into the debate. The 'garbage can' (e.g. Cohen, March and Olsen, 1972) theory of decision-making predicts this – it visualises problems and solutions to be thrown into a garbage can where they can quite fortuitously meet. Kingdon (1984) sees windows of opportunity where problems, politics and policies are understood as three separate 'streams' which may come together when a particular 'window of opportunity' opens. But the meeting of streams in Kingdon's 'primeval soup' does not have to be accidental – the factors facilitating the window of opportunity can be helped along by key individuals ('policy entrepreneurs'), key events or *crises*. It may then well be that a solution (an alternative for flood management) has been waiting for a 'felicitous' problem to latch itself on to. All this would suggest that, rather than a problem in search of a solution, flood protection schemes may have been *solutions in search of* a problem. Unprompted, several interviewees voiced this assumption as well.

8.3.3 'Time Is On My Side'? The Shadow of the Future

Time may be the worst enemy of flood securitisation. No matter how 'structural' the state of emergency, there is inevitably an end to the sense of urgency that legitimises exceptionalism. While actual floods bring existential fears, these are often easily forgotten by those who were not badly affected. The post-flood drive and momentum quickly runs out (Huber (2004) gives it two years) if floods do not return and disrupt society. As attention shifts to other concerns, flood plain regulation is relaxed again and funding and handling of the project comes under scrutiny.

Popular acceptance of river regulation schemes thus cannot be taken for granted. As it is not easy to put flood management at the top of the agenda except just after a flood event, project initiators may feel that a carte blanche is needed to cut the red tape and get things done.

When the momentum for a river project starts to flag, it may be attempted to invoke a crisis, or adduce and invoke additional threats. As engineers who pray for a flood may not get it, other threats can be adduced to make the case for flood interventions. We saw terrorism as an additional security reason in Turkey and Egypt. Dutch and English river projects were legitimised by climate change-induced extreme flood scenarios. In the Netherlands, the possibility that floods *might* have caused great damage set in train measures like evacuation in 1995 and subsequent construction and regulation leading to the controlled flooding policy. When the emergency measures had run out, a programme of river widening interventions (Room for the River) was started. Worsening climate change predictions led to the upward revision of scenarios on the rivers Maas and, especially, Rhine. Water professionals started to worry: What if a never-experienced 18,000 m^3/s flood wave hits the Netherlands? This fear led policymakers to designate several polders for emergency flood storage with a view to saving more densely built up polders in 2000. In its promotional material for the Jubilee Channel, Britain's Environment Agency invoked the 1947 flood, but also dramatised the issue by invoking the horrors of the greenhouse effect, playing on latent fears in the project communication strategy. Thus the shadow of the past and the shadow of the future reinforced each other.

In Bangladesh, climate change did two things: it created a new 'culprit' outside the region, as it is Western CO_2 emissions that are believed to contribute most to climate change (Huq and Reid, 2004). But climate planning focussed on sea level rise rather than rainfall variability, shifting the focus from river flooding to coastal flooding and cyclones, focusing the discourse on sea level rise rather than on higher river flood stages.

It appears project initiators have three options to reduce the 'shadow of the future':

- to seek to extend or renew the security window through extra securitisation to keep up the momentum,
- to secure as many 'early wins' as possible while the emergency window is still open, or
- to take anticipatory action to accommodate the inevitable shadow of the desecuritised future.

This latter option might compromise the support base for securitised decision-making of the home audience. A solution may be a two-faced discursive strategy: a 'securitised' image of threat control is projected to the home audience, while the initiator in fact designs or implements the water management project with 'desecuritised', peacetime logic in mind – 'just in case', to prevent problems after the flood window closes.

Clearly, almost all the major problems the Maaswerken encountered since 1997 stem from decisions taken during the 'securitised' time window, without such anticipation. National and European accountability rules such as antitrust and environmental directives quashed regional security-induced consortium deals and exemptions from environmental controls after the floods.

8.4 Compliance with Securitisation: Felicity and Infelicity of Saying Security

> 'When a state actor makes a securitising move, it demands special powers to restore order, a temporary derogation from rules.'
>
> 'Responses can range from endorsement, passive acceptance and bargaining to non-compliance, resistance and conflict. Acceptance makes the difference between the effort (securitising move) and the success' (Stahl, 2007).

8.4.1 The Audience for Securitisation

Policy problems do not present themselves, they are framed. The framing already point at its solution. At the start of this chapter, the key security frame elements were defined as the risk itself (naming and labelling), imputed cause of risk (blaming and shaming) and preferred solution (remedy). All schemes were framed by at least one key actor as a defence or national security issue. The present section examines who needs to be convinced to make a successful securitising move.

The securitisation requires a felicitous convergence of enunciator, referent, object and audience bringing closure to a debate, to the policy agenda, or even to what can and cannot be talked about in society. Securitisation, as noted, is a call and response. While most of the projects in some way benefited from the flood window, all of the schemes got into trouble somewhere down the line. As large infrastructural projects can take decades to be realised, the consonance of the call and response needs to be sustained. A positive initial response from an audience ('let's do something about this!') does not guarantee successful legislation and implementation of the proposed remedy.

To assess the felicity of these moves we cannot measure the impact, but only note ex post that they did or did not generate public debate and resistance. A sure sign of successful securitisation is that critical voices are silenced or dismissed as irrelevant, that information remains classified, assumptions untested, blank cheques handed out and alternatives ignored. If it is untested, this can be seen as testimony to the strength of the securitisation.

Securitised projects never command a total consensus and can in principle be challenged. While flood protection is a powerful securitiser, the rationale leaves space for it to be discredited, its motives questioned, its implementation thwarted, and the procedure of selecting alternatives criticised by other stakeholders or non-compliance and civil disobedience. Especially when the immediacy is not overwhelming, stakeholders can find niches for advancing their doubts with relative ease: they locate, test and latch on a sore spot and secure it to question the need for securitised decision-making. Securitising agents will have to convince their audience they are acting in the latter's best interests, identifying with their feelings and needs (Balzacq, 2005).

Hilhorst identifies the following domains:

(a) The domain of *disaster governance*. In a securitised state, the state has great discretion over private rights and freedoms. The relevant audience may only appear to consist of a closed circle within the state apparatus, expected to control society and ensure its compliance. However, the case studies show even this isolated arena is not enough to control either the local or international levels. Where the local level is controlled, the superior level of decision-making may not cooperate, and where the national and international levels are aligned, the locals may revolt. Within the governance domain, the pivotal role of donors should be highlighted, whose support needs to be 'enrolled' indefinitely.

(b) The '*epistemic community*' of science and technology experts concretises the project with models, designs and evaluation studies. It may differ with the initiator on the need for securitisation and the assumptions underlying the flood (de)securitisation, but also with stakeholders on their 'real' risk. Experts are internationally mobile. Politicians who are experts in the water field (Christie and Hanlon, 2001) are exposed to their international peers. In democracies, they bridge the public, private (consultancy) and NGO sectors and may be mobile between the sectors. Scientific debate may support but also disagree with the securitising logic.

(c) The audience for securitisation involves the whole population, including those expected to accept the whole package of restrictions and sacrifices resulting from security decisions. Faced with a disaster, it is the local domain that bears the brunt of immediate coping and relief efforts (Kirschenbaum, 2004). Faced with acute insecurity, stakeholders are prepared to throw their lot in with an external security provider and willingly give up their autonomy. The modality in which order or safety is restored after a disaster event, however, may leave people feeling threatened in terms of their rights or identity. It may not accept the required sacrifices for the greater good if the project fails Balzacq's condition that the securitiser convinces the audience of acting in their best interests, feelings and needs.

Key 'audience' groups relevant to the present study are those identified in Hilhorst's (2003) three domains of knowledge and action. Each of these has a specific capacity to address hazard, and would ideally coordinate with each other to the hazard at hand. Yet, such coordination in flood response is not the norm, given the spectacular tales of ill-coordinated disaster response such as detailed by Christie and Hanlon (2001). Established practices (people speaking 'the same language' and working by similar protocols), within and between the domains, may obscure a clash between multiple perspectives of reality and interests. The alignment of the three (for accepting a securitisation or desecuritised network coordination) can be highly problematic, as they need to coordinate well to ensure disasters are adequately addressed.

Successful securitisation would align these domains in a consensus at one stroke. It appears from the Dutch case that the crash programme to build hard structures in Limburg encountered little controversy, even if it involved some hurried expropriation measures, and people enjoyed the informal access to security providers. Several Dutch interviewees were nostalgic about the immediate post-flood period, 1995–97 when everyone – flood managers, politicians, experts and local people – joined hands and could fast-track decisions. But even this apparently successful securitisation got into trouble after 1997.

Table 8.2 below lists five reasons why a securitising move might be resisted (from Gromes and Bonacker, 2007). In all cases (including Limburg, post-1997) part of the 'audience' did not condone the case for river securitisation. It appears that each of the three domains indeed played a leading role in the *non-securitisation* of one or the other project. After each point, it is indicated how this resonated in the case studies and which actor category contested. The case studies suggest some additions, captured in the 'other reasons' category.

8.5 Resistance: Non-Compliance, Politicisation and Conflict

In a European (liberal) context, any intrusion in freedoms needs to be legitimised to assure compliance. In liberal democracies citizens are imputed to comply with state rule because the law guarantees them protection. If they do not feel it protects them well enough, they do not feel bound by it (Boutellier, 2003). Coercion is the least effective way of ensuring durable compliance (Held, 1984).

In the event of a flood threat, emergency measures were accepted in the Netherlands. Despite the flood not happening on the Rhine, a majority of stakeholders claimed in a survey that they still felt mass evacuation was justified (*de Gelderlander, 2005*). On the Maas, Compulsory Purchasing Orders (CPO)

	Non/Securitising Move (Gromes and Bonacker, 2007)	**Applied to the Water Sector**	**Argument Advanced by**
1	The asserted existential threat never existed.	- The river is not dangerous - The river is not that dangerous - The extreme flood scenario is doubtful	- Ooij: epistemic community - Maas: donor (RWS)
2	The existential threat does not exist anymore.	- Food security is not an issue, as there is no water scarcity thanks to virtual water	- Egypt: (international) epistemic community
3	Ordinary measures suffice in order to respond to the existential threat.	- The river is a nuisance rather than a security issue - Special measures are not necessary	- Maas: river manager/donor - Thames: donor
4	Panic politics are not effective in addressing the threat.	- The strategy or project is not good enough - The intended plan will not do the trick. The river can't be tamed. There are limits to defence - It's better to adapt to the river than control it	Bangladesh, the Netherlands: local NGOs and (some) flood experts
5	The extraordinary measures avoid the existential threat but their side-costs are too high.	- Personal or social costs outpace benefits: project is the greater danger - Project costs are unsustainable - Technocratic approach - Project makes stakeholders more rather than less insecure (Collateral damage of fighting the flood too high) - Unwillingness to carry costs or sacrifice	Sacrifice: Local NGOs, epistemic community Costs: donors, epistemic community (all cases)
	Other reasons for resistance to securitisation.	- Other issues are more pressing - Distrust in motive or authority of initiator ('hero') or securitiser	UK, Bangladesh: Locals

Table 8.2: ***Non-securitisation applied to flood management in the six cases***

were accepted and the emergency structures, in the first two years after the high-water event, mostly uncontroversial. This makes for an interesting difference from Britain, where Eton resisted the CPO up to High Court, feeling there was no urgency for land take, however temporary. The Maas interviewees expressed satisfaction at the informal fine-tuning of the emergency *kaden* and did not complain that they were built without tendering.

8.5.1 Non-Compliance and 'Opportunitisation'

Actors who reject controls may resist directly, but also in subtle ways. The controls can spark 'deviant behaviour' (Bakker et al., 1999), that is, non-compliance with state laws and directives, undercutting institutional surveillance and control.

Spatial zoning reflects the behaviourist (institutionalist) approach to disasters; zoning measures and incentives 'teach' people to behave responsibly and anticipate disaster. It can consist of a total ban on development or the identification of risk contours linked to compensation coverage. This appears to be a losing proposition in flood plain, where enforcement is a particular weakness of flood policy and what is logical from a project perspective is not logical from a user perspective.

Whether because of the amenity value of living by the water, fertile soil, ease of access to waterways, low rent, or because other livelihoods are unavailable, the pressure to occupy the flood plain is relentless. While Bangladeshi politicians have blamed people for irresponsible settlement, there simply are no settlement controls that influence their settlement decisions. As FAP-20 was an experimental programme, it put in several more dikes than strictly needed, failing to anticipate the overwhelming need for space to live and till the land like before. Flood embankments claimed land used for dwellings, arable farming and cattle raising, which in Bangladesh is mainly done by women. The need for space was most clearly expressed in individual and collective erosion and 'public cuts' of dikes and clogging of drainage channels with new constructions.

While in Bangladesh people enjoy very few degrees of freedom in terms of location and livelihood, the Europeans in our case studies mostly accept risk because they can afford it (Loucks, 2006). Unlike Bangladesh, environmental 'bads' are not poorly distributed in the Netherlands, that is, socio-economic groups are equally exposed to risk. By contrast, environmental 'goods' are: If you can afford it, you can procure amenities not open to others, such as living on a scenic location by the water (interview, environmental policy expert, October 2007). Those who wish to settle in the flood plain in the Netherlands are not vulnerable, but privileged.

Just like a smokestack used to be a source of progress in 1960s Europe, an embankment in front of your house can be a source of social prestige in Bangladesh. In the European cases, however, nobody wanted an embankment in sight. The designation of the Ooij for controlled flooding was opposed, among other reasons, because it would make the region unsuitable for investment and cause property prices to fall. This meant that while demand for flood management intervention is voiced by property owners, opposition also comes from other property owners.

The phrase 'opportunitisation' (Warner, 2004a) may denote that, just like threats to survival, a development opportunity that seems too good to be true can bring actors to break away from normal rules and disregard rights. The pressure to develop the flood plain (or in Egypt the desert) is great and government-supported with a view to the overriding need for space for housing. Social and economic interest can override environmental and safety concerns. This can be done by state actors, but also by actors in society. In the Netherlands, the first step in de-constraining the river was a ban on flood plain development in 1995. But in Limburg I heard at least one story of emergency structures planners colluding with developers, moving a dike back further than planned to save more land for development.

In Britain, since 1947 river managers have been pressing for planning guidelines to 'make people behave better'. Each flood has spawned a call from the river manager for planning controls, but has been overruled by housing pressures (and economic opportunities) on the flood plain, accommodated by a persistently permissive flood plain development regime resented by the Environment Agency.

In Britain, this is different in metropolitans and London and between regions, but in Maidenhead the most flood-affected people court risk because they can afford to (interview, Winchester, 1999). This means risk-accepting behaviour and opposition to flood schemes. In Southeast England, local authorities and developers found ways to ignore or outwit planning regulations. There, and in Limburg local authorities have thus deliberately, if selectively, opened up the flood plain and allow building in low-lying polders, requiring citizens, civil society and local authorities to arrange security for the new dwellers.

8.5.2 Politicisation in a Securitised Context?

Political closure is achieved through invoking threats to national security and declaring a state of emergency, which has been in place since 1981 in Egypt and 1984 in Turkey. This makes every aspect of life a possible security issue. Since water is a strategic good for both countries, both Ilısu and Toshka river management projects were proclaimed 'national projects'. This makes opposition potentially treasonous and basin conflict potentially violent.

In Buzan et al.'s understanding of politicisation, an issue becomes subject to public debate and government takes responsibility for it (1998: 28). Domestically, political debate, even protest, is difficult to stage in a context where not only the project but all of society is securitised. Under the state of exception, rulers rely on the military and external protectors. But even authoritarian (totalitarian) states need to legitimise the state of exception they have imposed. Mega-projects may seek to procure this legitimacy. Wilkinson (2007) has noted that it is hard to 'speak security' in securitised environments. To start a debate in a securitised context, one has to make sure not to set oneself apart from the state's values. Does this hold for the two Middle East countries, Egypt and Turkey?

Domestically, out of the six cases, Egypt seems the most 'closed' on the political and technical continuum. The Egyptian press is infrastructurally controlled and public protest is not allowed. But even in the heavily securitised Egyptian environment, opposition Members of Parliament could seize on the downside of the river projects (corruption, favouritism and mismanagement). In Egypt, the expensive capture of excess floodwater gave critics a symbol to lambast other state projects as 'white elephants'. Despite the ruling National Democratic Party's firm grip on political life, it proved possible for opposition parties and scientists to expose what they see as a chimera, and despite the control of the press, the debate was reported in Egypt's biggest newspaper.

While domestic opposition could not make a strong stand in the securitised Turkish Soutehast at the turn of the millennium, an international coalition effectively politicised the issue. An oppositional international NGO coalition instigated a redefinition of hitherto ill-considered aspects of the project, notably the fate of adversely affected groups. The flooding of Hasankeyf gave opponents a dramatic image to latch on to and sharpen conditionality for bilateral loans. Export credit guarantees for the foreign contractors depended on donor state approval, so the INGO coalition targeted Export Credit Agencies (ECAs). When guarantors withdrew one by one, the Ilısu dam looked doomed.

8.5.3 Counter-Securitising Moves – Counter-Securitised Values

The way flood risk is managed can bring (unwanted) changes and create new risks. If a local community or NGO sees projects as threats to existential values, they may defend themselves against the project. Like states, they claim 'a right to use whatever means are necessary to block a threatening development' (Buzan et al., 1998: 21). This brings a different form of a 'defence (or security) dilemma': the presumably well-intentioned flood defence effort is framed by particular stakeholders as a vital threat, leading to mutual antagonism and, potentially, escalation, especially if they do not keep communication channels open.

In a securitised state, water projects are almost automatically securitised, but it is clear from interviews and project literature that flood managers in all non-securitised context also presumed that their intervention would be welcomed as a common interest. The *national security interest* was considered good enough reason not to discuss flood policy with local citizens in Ilısu and Toshka, but also, initially, the Ooij polder and Tangail. Initiators were happy to advertise the project, but not to open discussion that might call the project into question. In each case, however, the 'selling' approach opted for was not as successful as hoped for and in the Dutch, Turkish and Bangladeshi cases ran up against a successful counter-information campaign.

The Bangladesh project triggered unease with their region being used as a guinea pig area for an untested technology developed by Westerners fanning protests against the project. Several NGOs feared for local livelihoods being threatened by Green Revolution technologies introduced through FAP. Apparent BWDB indifference to the outcome of the consultation exercise failed to induce trust in the project or its initiators in an already antagonistic setting. This made the flood scheme a *human rights* issue in the non-European schemes while in Europe, cultural and landscape/natural values were securitised as at risk and untouchable.

All projects were pictured as a threat to the environment. (Note that in Britain, 'the environment' is also taken to include people's properties.) The river engineering projects in the Netherlands and England were a response to earlier environmental protest, claiming hard defences destroyed natural and landscape values, such as tree lines. 'Nature development' was presented as an economic compromise between security and environmentally sustainable engineering, with more natural banks, wetlands and Scottish cattle. But local protesters resisted developed nature, as they liked their more manicured cultural landscape just fine. Moreover, the modality to keep the project economic, gravelling, would bring nuisance and ugly pit holes and disturb peace and quiet.

In Britain, the Jubilee Channel was framed within an overarching city vs. countryside antagonism. Before the 2003 flood arrived, neighbouring parishes felt their peace and quiet, as well as their landscape and safety were sacrificed for Maidenhead, pictured as a commuter town for media types. The 'uninteresting' label the Environment Agency put on the Maidenhead area to legitimise its environmental enhancement in planning the channel was challenged by cultural heritage and landscape values defended by local stakeholders. They perceived the intervention as an (urban, centralising) intrusion of their territory and heritage values that do not need improving or sacrificing.

In each case, a peripheral area felt the need to defend its cultural integrity to an intervention. (I)NGOs and citizen platforms presented themselves as the defenders of this integrity. Citizens rejected their government's developmental ambitions with local water and space – feeling that neither their landscape nor their culture needed developing.

Health featured in both European and non-European cases. Stagnant water attracts parasites that bring diseases. Water storage projects in Bangladesh,

	Environmental	**Economic Values**	**Socio-cultural Rights**	**Human Rights**	**Political/ Military Security**
Threat	Degradation of landscape and natural values	Destruction of ecosystems	Resettlement	Safety	War
	Threat to livelihoods		Cultural assimilation threat to identity		
	Housing prices			Health	

Table 8.3: ***Counter-securitised values overlap sectors***

Egypt and Turkey were feared to promote the spread of *kala-azar*, malaria and bilharzia. Even in the temperate zone, on the Maas, a citizen worried about malaria but could be assured. But this was not what rallied opponents into a discourse coalition opening up a conflict frame.

The counter-securitised values are summarized in Table 8.3. Like securitisation, counter-securitisation has to resonate with its intended audience. It does not have to be followed up by extreme measures: threats and mobilisation can be enough to make the project initiator think twice, or to convince one's constituency that one has the eye on the ball.

Intense public debate (politicisation) is enough to signal the crumbling of a once successful securitising move. Politicisation in the sense of deliberation was expressed in parliamentary questions and political lobbying. Non-politicised negotiation won local stakeholders many placating concessions from project management. However, instead of debate, several conflicts escalated with minimum communication between the warring sides.

In all politicised cases, the discourse of crisis and catastrophe, survival and destruction resonated in the opponents' discourse. We may call this 'counter-securitisation' on behalf of civil society or other states.

Counter-securitising moves counter discursive closure with counter-closure, defending non-negotiable values against intervention. This polarisation triggers a threat–defence sequence quite similar to (attempted) securitisation, legitimising conflict, disobedience and, in the case of Turkey, violence.

Undercutting Assumptions: Alliances with the Epistemic Community

While fighting the values, protesters also sought to cast doubt on the knowledge supporting the projects. They co-opted or hired consultants in the expert community that doubted flood scenarios, showed up uncertainties, or provided alternatives. This had the additional strategic advantage of enlisting peers of initiating experts being able to speak the discourse of the initiators (x or non-x) rather than bringing local knowledge to bear (y-language).

'Blue engineering' initiatives were confronted by 'green engineering' but scant inclusion of local knowledge. In Bangladesh however the indigenous modes of land use and vulnerability reduction received increasing attention in the academic community in the course of FAP-20. In Turkey and Egypt, cultural heritage conservation issues rather than indigenous modes of water management attracted national and international academic interest.

Countervailing arguments were staged in settings for 'speaking truth to power' familiar to project leaders and policymakers: technical seminars, journal articles, letters to the editor in respected newspapers while at the same time, much more antagonistic civil protests were staged in the streets and town halls. The next section will analyse how the conflicts over river interventions escalated.

8.5.4 Conflicts and Coalitions

It is well known that an external enemy welds together a 'community of friends' inside the fences. A common enemy created a sense of community where there was none before, or where it was fragmented (see in this context also Harries and Borrows, 2006).

The fear of a flood threat or outrage over its realisation can also create a 'defining Other' (Ignatieff, 1993) where no clear community identity was visible before. A striking common element emerging in the case studies is an aversion to the river management project as a 'foreign body'. The reinforcement and escalation of antagonism over flood protection can be for reasons largely unrelated to the project as such.

The transition to democracy at the turn of the 1990s exposed the Bangladesh project to successful politicisation from a coalition of Bangladeshi and international NGOs. The way radical NGO campaigns are organised may bear a surprising resemblance to military mobilisation (Szerszynski, 2002: 55). In the desecuritised policy context of Bangladesh, England and the Netherlands, opponents took the form of local public protest and a sophisticated *information* and lobbying campaign. In each of those cases, opponents successfully mobilised the press and/or the political sector, and found a receptive constituency for their protests.

It takes two to turn a clash of interests into an open conflict. In Turkey and Bangladesh the government and donors pictured the opposition to projects as a threat (anti-development and against national security). A (piecemeal) 'logic of equivalence' built a common ground, a discourse coalition between actors that would not normally find themselves on the same side.

The anti-globalists enlisted a World Bank consultant to write a critical dam resettlement report, the Kurdish Human Rights Project worked with archaeologists over cultural heritage, while the threats of Iraq and Syria against dam funders underscored the anti-Ilısu NGO coalition's point that the project would lead to war rather than peace. In Britain, Turkey and the Netherlands, local authorities acted in tandem, if not always in perfect harmony, with the citizen platforms.

Bangladeshi NGOs had rarely taken an interest in water issues before, but found a common cause to tackle not just state but international interventionism, focusing especially on the Green Revolution technology introduced in the region through FAP. As a result, the project started with a stand-off between 'ignorant sociologists' and 'corrupt engineers who don't listen'. Male engineers were confronted by angry women in street protests in Tangail and Dhaka. The images were sent over to the Netherlands just in time to influence the parliamentary debate over FAP in the Netherlands. The World Bank, in turn, labelled the opposition 'anti-development'.

In Limburg, a logic of equivalence supported the conflict frame equating the Maaswerken with the greed of gravellers, the insensitivity of Delft engineers, the colonisation of Limburg by Holland, the wasteful project management and environmental pollution, the unfairness of 'desecuritising the Maas' and the 'purple' provincial and national authorities against a Catholic (Christian-democratic) political identity of civil society in the South Netherlands. From the point of view of the westerners, Limburg remained tainted with the brush of corruption and opportunism.

The citizen platform on the Maas, BOM, made alliances with Belgian gravellers to invoke European antitrust and environmental legislation to challenge the handling of aggregates, crucial to the financial viability of the project. This held back the project for a year.

Such antagonism is not evident from the Ooij case, which, however, did have a history of resistance to intervention, both expansionism from neighbouring Nijmegen and dike reinforcement works initiated by the water board backed by the Public Works Department. When the Ooij platform failed to get a hearing, it declared war on the Vice-Minister and her department. The feeling of acute distrust was apparently mutual: in the Ooij issue, an internal memo we retrieved suggests the Public Works Department similarly divided the stakeholder community on controlled flood storage into friends and enemies.

In both cases (if at very different scales and intensities) both protests were framed in terms of 'war' and 'struggle'.

8.5.5 The Crucial Importance of Felicity with Funders

So far, I have discussed the role of civil society and co-opted experts to trip a project up. One crucial actor has been underexposed: the project funder.

Apart from a regimented organisation and information campaign, the success of opposition can be ascribed to their targeting of the project funder. Donor compliance can make or break the project, and impose conditionalities. There are limits to anyone's blank cheque – the initiator of the case studies was never able to completely self-fund the flood project, it depended on the donor's values and assessment of the merits of the proposal.

The elasticity of budgets can be said to be a measure of the felicity of securitising the flood. Once the money runs out, funding becomes a test of the resolve of the government to continue spending whatever it takes to protect the country. When successfully legitimised (securitised), they may be pursued even at crippling cost – 'money is no object'.

It would not be immediately obvious that *funding* so often was to prove an Achilles heel for the project. A new, experimental mega-project is unlikely to have a good cost-benefit ratio. Large infrastructural development projects are seldom economic and invariably turn out to be far more expensive than budgeted for. When interviewed in 2000, a Maaswerken project leader only half-jokingly assessed normal budget overruns at a factor π (= 3.1415). This should not be fatal to successful 'opportunitisation', as repetition of the technology is expected to reap economies of scale and indirect benefits, including political prestige and technical reputation. In both the Thames and Brahmaputra projects, the idea was to select a relatively 'safe' project in terms of acceptable cost-benefit ratio and low risk of failure, with a view to replication elsewhere on the river. Both technical setbacks and protests put paid to that expectation, so that the logic of a series of channels (Thames) and compartmentalised polders (Brahmaputra) did not materialise and adjoining areas remained unprotected.

The Netherlands securitised rivers and Egypt's securitised political sector might be expected to have saved such projects despite the cost. When the Dutch Delta Works sea defences were planned in the Netherlands, the decision was made first – the cost-benefit analysis could come later (Smits et al., 2005). The Netherlands currently spends about 1 per cent of its state budget on flood defence, so that budget overruns would not put the Treasury under stress the way it did in Egypt and Turkey. Still cost turned out to be an insurmountable financial constraint in the Maaswerken negotiations. The cost issue was deferred until the end of negotiations. This procrastination however may have been a strategic mistake, as with the passing of time and no repetition of the event, the momentum provided by the flood window was faltering while the cost spiralled, cost recovery was a self-imposed inviolable bottom line. Peripheral Limburg relied on core 'Holland' for its funding. The Maaskaden (emergency flood defences) episode aligned with national emergency legislation. After 1997 the two sides, despite being project partners, did not see eye to eye over the 'security-ness' of river management on the Maas. When the local authorities of Limburg presented the Maaswerken as a security initiative, they ran up against a veto from the Public Works Department, who refused to disburse emergency money in 1997. Five years later, the Maas director had to leave, in part over the excessive administrative costs he was running.

In Britain river schemes had never been very large, and the overall cost of the Maidenhead project (£110 million and counting) has been much criticised by local stakeholders. MAFF had the power to decide the fate of the EA by insisting on cost-benefit criteria and eligibility criteria, especially a positive cost-benefit ratio, for the crucial 15 per cent grant-in-aid.

In two cases the financial aspect appears to have been an ex post legitimation so as *not* to fund or continue the project. In the Ooij, the securitiser had seemingly allocated the money to carry out the plan. The chairman of the platform did not win by questioning the project's morality as to how which is supposed to protect its citizens could propose to take a 1-in-1250 risk of drowning them, even if to save others. They won the battle when they located a report saying the project was not viable in cost/benefit terms, a point specifically singled out by the Vice-Minister when she announced shelving controlled flood storage.

Unlike the Netherlands, there was a serious national (rather than project-level) rather than self-imposed cash crisis to contemplate in Turkey and Egypt. This financial pinch opened a window for an ad hoc discourse coalition of co-riparians, NGOs and eventually parliamentarians in Turkey, and national political parties and press in Egypt, to target the project's lifeline: money.

To sustain disproportional outlay, a powerful donor is required who will keep furnishing money without strings attached. There appears to be a heavy overlay between different layers of the 'cake', between donors and recipients, core and periphery. A complicating factor for successful securitisation in the Dutch, Bangladeshi and Turkish case studies, then, is that the decision to securitise water is embedded in regimes at other scales, in which different rules may apply. The links brought in powerful 'audiences' that do not necessarily respond as hoped for, reducing the felicity of security mode for the river management project.

When these are aligned, it can help the states in legitimising their choices: an internationally hegemonic securitisation, the 'war on terror', justified local anti-terrorism measures (Turkey vs. PKK), international outrage over flooding justified large investments in the Flood Action Plan. But when the two spheres are moving out of sync, things look differently.

If the international context is *not securitised* non-emergency rules of competition and accountability apply on the international scene. But they proved rather elastic, given the need for donors to boast successful projects, and can use them to improve their position.

The Turkish and Bangladeshi projects had to parry the overlay of donors, who support the flood management effort but attached ability conditions to their support.

In the Bangladeshi projects, global outrage over the human toll of destructive floods legitimised an all-out effort to control the flood. The French proposed a control approach despite NGOs pointing out that both Dutch and local engineers had concluded the river will not be tamed. But flood control proposals were not accepted by the key donors, the USAID and UNDP. The US Corps of Engineers had discarded the control option decades ago. They opted instead for controlled flooding and flood-proofing. Donors also attached 'good governance' strings such as participation and a decent Internal Rate of Return. The economic rate of return (EIRR) however only appeared as a criterion in the evaluation after the project was closed. The Dutch Minister for Development Cooperation had allocated EUR 7 million more in 1994, despite a negative report from his inspection on economic merits. It appears that other donors had stronger concerns about financial viability than the Dutch, whose prestige as water experts was also at stake.

In the Turkish case, donors made export guarantees conditional on environmental and social conditions, such as an improved resettlement plan. International overlay splits the country in two (after Jacoby, 2005): there continues to be a schizophrenic tension between a securitised, peripheral Southeast concerned with military and economic control and the Kurds in Northern Iraq as closest concern, and a desecuritised, semi-democratised westernised centre (West Turkey) with European aspirations as an attractor, which enables it to impose principles of 'good governance' such as human rights and a de-emphasis of the Turkish army (Diez, 2000).

In Egypt, the national funding crisis can be expected to reduce the size of the, frankly, illusory Toshka project. But the Egyptians were in a better position to isolate themselves from the international overlay. They have indefinitely delayed the next phases of the project rather than depend on the outside world for the project's projected $90 billion budget. As there is no dramatic media-friendly focus of environmental or cultural damage either, this keeps the debate largely outside the scope of NGO and international critics.

8.5.6 Outcome of Securitisation, Non-securitisation and Counter-securitisation

All schemes under scrutiny here became subject to some securitising moves, but *closure* due to the flood itself was only pronounced in the Netherlands. All schemes also became subject to politicisation, despite three projects starting in a securitised political context, and attempts to include a degree of participation in the remaining projects. It was to be expected that the 'induced' inundation of Ilısu would elicit contest. But when I started the research project in 1998–99, I did not expect *all* schemes to get into trouble. By repoliticising flood policy, these claims also reopened the 'flood gates', i.e. undoing the closure to alternatives, compromises or even discontinuation of the project. The outcome in each case (except that the 'jury is still out' on Egypt) for initiators was to change, delay, shelve or prevent follow-up of the project or policy (Tables 8.3 and 8.4).

The security claims against the projects had an impact that may have surprised even its enunciators. The controversy over Ilısu hit the international press at a time when Turkish relations with both Syria and Iraq as well as the Kurdish population were improving. The claim that FAP-20 would create a dust bowl has not been borne out in practice.[2]

In Bangladesh, the Netherlands and the UK, the confrontation with opponents at national and international level meant the reformulations of the project and placating concessions, making the project more in line with 'living with the flood' concepts. The success the antagonists of the project managed to reap ranged from the shelving of the policy (Ooij), to the abortion of plans for replication (Bangladesh). Moreover, it secured the opponents a place at the table in future planning (cooptation).

Yet, despite the success of both non-securitising moves and counter-securitising protests, the projects did not disappear. The modalities of handling cultural and social concerns due to the Ilısu Dam may have been modified, but the dam and its reservoir are under construction as intended. Political and scientific misgivings have not changed Egypt's determination on colonising the Western Desert. Compartmentalisation was not immediately replicated, but found its way into later Asian Development Bank projects in Bangladesh. Controlled flood storage was shelved for the Ooij polder but its necessity appears in several reports from national planning councils (Pols et al., 2007; VROM-Raad, 2007) on the future of Dutch water management. The Maaswerken got new management and started work in 2005 and the Jubilee River has been repaired. While it is fair to conclude on the basis of the six cases that politicisation is inevitable, it is equally valid to note that once started, projects are unstoppable, whether securitised or not. The dogs barked, some bit, but the caravan moved on.

The hypothesis proposed in Chapter 1 assumed securitisation to be the norm. This turned out to be false: it appears from the analysis that the securitised and desecuritised 'spheres' are connected by spatial and temporal links, influence each other and to a degree depend on each other. This brings in a contextual understanding of how projects relate with the felicity of moves for closure: while a flood helps a project, protest hurts when it finds the funders' ear. The overlay of hegemonic de-securitisation, emphasising choice and rights, appears to defeat local securitisation necessity and exception. These links between the securitised locality/episode and desecuritised overlay invite the question what 'peacetime' decision-making on security issues looks like. As this is not a well-theorised area

Case Study	Hegemonic Actor	Project Initiator	Artefact	Securitised Context	Project Legitimisation	Opposition (discursive alliance)	Effect on Project
Egypt	President	President	Channel, irrigations scheme, new city, airport, etc.	State of emergency	Development and population pressure	Experts and domestic political parties	(Silence)
Turkey	DSI	DSI	HEPP dam	State of emergency	Development and terrorism	International and domestic NGOs	Delay, restart
Bangladesh	BWDB	Donor	FCD/I scheme	Dictatorship and flood aftermath	Safety and food security	International and domestic NGOs	No follow-up after project end
UK	MAFF	EA	Channel, part natural banks, part concreted	–	Safety and nature	Parish councils and county council	Second channel
NL–Maas	RWS	province of Limburg	*kaden*, widening, deepening	Flood aftermath	Safety, nature and shipping	Citizen platform and NGOs	Delay, restart
NL–Ooij	RWS	RWS	structures and sluice gates	Flood scenarios	Safety downstream	Citizen platform and experts	Shelved

Table 8.4: ***Outcome of politicisation for project***

in security studies, we will recall the precepts of 'peace logic' and draw parallels with security when making 'peace with the river'. After elaborating on this logic, we shall look into the politicisation of the 'peace logic'.

8.6 Peace with the River: The Challenges of River Desecuritisation

European water management has recently been witnessing a notable discursive shift from structural flood defence to a 'risk approach' and 'Room for the River' initiatives. The river is not frightening, it is now promoted as 'fun' in European projects such as *Freude am Fluss*. Since the above has shown that even in securitised contexts attempted securitisations were compromised, it is all the more relevant to take a closer look at the constitution of desecuritised water management. Below, it is assumed that the same obtains for the desecuritisation ('de-disasterisation') of high-water events.

If water is no longer considered an emergency issue by the key players, we would expect a situation where 'closures' are opened up: the state is no longer automatically the lead security actor, rights and freedoms cannot be shored up for the common good and acceptance of sacrifices is not self-evident. I will discuss each of those in the context of the case studies. It will appear that not only Bangladesh, Turkey and Egypt had trouble integrating these principles but also the Netherlands and Britain.

1. Reflexive Desecuritisation of the River

The current state of the art in disaster studies recognises that the way society is organised produces hazard in a complex interplay of natural and social forces (Parker, 2000; Hilhorst, 2003). This emerging 'holistic' paradigm (Green and Warner, 1999) sees hazard as mutuality, arising 'as a result of the social, economic and political order, which is transmitted through natural and semi-natural processes'. They are a function of the 'normal workings of society' (Parker, 2000). The way we control nature to handle water thus adds to our own vulnerability to floods. Unwise land use impedes run-off while dikes displace risk, increasing rather than decreasing vulnerability by raising dikes (Disco, 2002).

This 'internalises' agency in risks that were previously attributed to external agents. 'Reflexive modernisation' (Beck, 1992) suggests a smooth, anonymous process of 'adaptation' and 'adjustment'. It appears, however, that it was the politicisation of a closed security frame that brought different risk (security) conceptions to the table. In the 1970s and 1980s it became evident over the loss of cultural and environmental values due to flood defence led to the politicisation of sea and river defences, which in turn led to a national consultative commission proposing lower risk standards, green diking and alternatives to diking. Treating water as a friend, giving it space, and using 'green' technology for natural embankments as practiced in the UK and the Netherlands means to accept certain self-organising, 'chaotic' aspects of the river.

The newly acceptable freedom for the river is relative: it allows a greater degree of uncertainty, but within discrete limits. This became clear when the environmentalists initially advocated the 'ecological flooding' of polders in the Rhine basin. A flood is a great opportunity for environmental restoration.

When the Ooij polder was slated for flood storage, Gelderland's provincial environmentalist umbrella advocated *un-controlled* flooding. But the local chapter changed their minds about this 'let it flood' alternative when protests to uncontrolled flooding in the Ooij grew louder and their own houses would be affected. Total liberation of the river can rejuvenate natural systems, but also has the potential to necessitate destructive social adaptation. Even advocates of 'living with the flood' will accept the flood only up to a point.

More flexibility does not detract from the fact claims that Dutch engineers are still unprepared to accommodate a river's inherent instability and spontaneous vegetation (roughness). We do not like the river to take any space it likes. Man remains in control of the river (van Hemert, 1999).

Another limit to river management is the realisation that a rule or artefact that promises collective safety can invite unsafe behaviour. The safest dikes attract investment and settlement behind that dike, in spite of the residual risk of a breach which will then wreak more havoc in areas lulled into a false sense of security. The sea dikes protecting the west of the Netherlands are an extreme example of this: the defence system continues to be predominant in terms of protecting lives, assets and vital infrastructure, but has no evacuation plan (although the evacuation issue is now increasingly under discussion). Both in Limburg and Maidenhead, building defence structures legitimised and protected further construction in areas that previously had been set aside. This leads to the 'control paradox': a lock-in situation, where you seek to improve the safety of a system but end up more vulnerable as people feel safe and take more risks (Immink, 2007).

In the Dutch river areas the tendency has been to restore a liberal settlement policy on the river subject to public–private provision of safety measures. The already tolerated municipal leniency toward flood plain development in Limburg was sustained and vindicated when, after a 10-year moratorium, the Dutch lifted the ban on flood plain development in 2005 allowing innovative building in flood plains. Freeing up 15 locations – institutionalising risk acceptance – the Netherlands has replaced a ban on developing the flood plain by a bet on 'spatial quality'. Riverside land traditionally was a neglected area, a kind of wasteland. Making the riverside prettier by improving natural values could also attract investment to pay for beautification interventions.

Positive Shocks and Adaptation to Stress?

The 'water peace' narrative also evidences a belief in the salutary effect of (impending) crisis, which forces reflexivity and adaptivity to 'resource stress' and climate change. The theory of punctuated equilibrium in ecology, on which Baumgartner and Jones (1991) draw, points at the positive role of systemic shocks in changing the status quo (Gould and Eldredge, 1977). In the 'water peace' discourse, a system as a whole adapts – the whole transforms to a new 'steady state', more diversified, more scarcity conscious.

As we shall see in the third and fourth subsections, the reflexive turn involves participatory 'feedback' mechanisms that might democratise decisions impacting on security, with the potential to compensating and sharing the sacrifice. The fifth, on the other hand, introduces a 'vulnerability' approach, alerting us to structural causes of risk differentiation and the resulting limits to freedom for river and people.

2. Reframing Security as Risk

The realisation that the river cannot always be controlled is hard to take for control-oriented engineers. Yet, the Mississippi flood of 1994 in the USA, the failure of the Brahmaputra right bank embankment in Bangladesh and the high-water events of 1993 and 1995 in the Netherlands made it clear that there is always a possibility that the unthinkable flood can still happen despite the defences. The reflexive turn alluded to in Chapter 4 drove home the insight that human interventions may precipitate rather than reduce risk. A sense of 'ungovernability' and 'governance failures' became a focus of attention for a while in the late 1990s (e.g. Stoker, 1998).

To overcome the defeatism, a relabelling of problems has been notable in the environmental sector. Security is now known as risk (Giddens, 1999). A focus on risk means conceding defeat every now and then, but if well-prepared, risk does not have to have overwhelming consequences. In the past decade, the Netherlands has seen a clear shift from security, defined as the strength of the dikes, to the management of 'residual risk', which focuses on the impact of flood event on the territory behind the dikes as well as undiked flood plain.

Research into uncertainty has been going on since 1995 within the Public Works Department's research institute RIZA. But uncertainty proves politically unpalatable, it makes politicians and citizens feel insecure and engineers look incompetent (RIZA researcher interview, 2005). This appears to be no different in the UK, if we recall the Taplow parish councillor's outrage on discovering that the flood would not be fully and indefinitely contained by the Jubilee Channel.

In the Netherlands, a redefinition of uncertainty in protection as 'failure factors' sounds like certain knowledge, and is thus acceptable (interview, Silva, 2005). Currently the European Interreg programme funds the *Freude am Fluss* project (enjoyment of, or by, the river): living with the river rather than being afraid of the river. While the environmental trend was continued with the Room for the River approach, it was attempted to also make 'Space for people'. Below, we will discuss the consequences of this philosophy in more detail.

3. Regime Space for People? New Actors in River Governance:

While the river is constrained by dikes and channels, many can afford to ignore the challenge and leave it to the experts. Development controls reduce freedoms, but bring no responsibilities. A risk approach, however, requires the cooperation of many interdependent stakeholders. The switch to the risk approach seen in the European countries and for all practical purposes, Bangladesh, necessarily calls on civil-society compliance and cooperation more than a hazard approach, whether enforced through coercion or spontaneous coordination.

A challenge for water managers is to get the same things done under the peace logic of desecuritisation as you can do under securitisation. Being unafraid of the river is not necessarily reflected in the state being unafraid of people and people being unafraid of the state. To provide security river managers now have to clear a host of hurdles like cost-benefit analysis, openness, accountability, deliberation and development pressures.

A desecuritised approach to perceived dangers either means toleration of the threat or managing securitised issues in non-securitised ways, resisting them without violating normal rights and rules (Roe, 2004: 285). Non-state actors are expected to take direct responsibility for security provision, (by increasing coping capacity) or required to avoid aggravating the problem (reducing challenge).

The transformation from securitised to desecuritised decision-making brings a new political arrangement or arena (Huysmans, 1998a, b) with particular governance challenges. This arena transformation could, in principle, mean the emancipation of marginalised actors (Aradau, 2001) and democratisation of the process.

The trend under liberal Dutch Water Ministers not to treat the river as an enemy anymore has important consequences for the division of responsibilities. In the Netherlands, for example, protests against dike reinforcement had not only involved protest against vertical flood defence structures in the horizontal landscape, they also sided against technocratic, authoritarian interventions (van Hemert, 1999). Collaborative planning (Healey, 1997) promises better checks and balances, a balance of power that can act as a brake on ill-conceived projects and stimulate creativity (Wolsink, 2003).

Since 2003 the Public Works Department, together with the water boards, officially does not guarantee 100 per cent security. But who will take care of security now? As we saw, other actors in spatial planning are not necessarily willing to prioritise water security in their dealing and to relieve the Ministry of some responsibility. To avoid further free riding on its protection services, the Dutch water department was willing to lift its 10-year ban on flood plain development for occupation, on condition that a wider range of governance actors would take responsibilities in an Integrated Security Chain approach, from pro-action to rehabilitation. This means a *horizontal* (between national Ministries) as well as a *vertical* shift in sharing responsibilities (between the national and local levels).

Allowing multiple actors to participate in risk management as well as dialogue on planning, without the project getting mired, is a major challenge of river desecuritisation for a river manager. If dikes can break, one needs non-structural measures to cushion the impact. This requires cooperation on the part of those behind the dikes. Minimising damages can involve the cooperation of businesses and residents, who may have to move or adapt their mansions and be prepared to act when the flood comes (dike teams), accept occasional nuisance, and offer and take insurance against unreasonable loss. Initiators in each of the case studies organised different forms of *participation* consulting stakeholders at markedly different steps of Arnstein's ladder, and co-opting private and civil-society actors in *implementation*.

Thus, realisation of the Maas works was conceived by the provincial government as a consortium formed with private (gravel industry) as well as NGO parties (*Natuurmonumenten*) to ensure a balance of social, environmental and economic sustainability. The course the negotiations took between 1998 and 2001 indicates that these criteria clearly did not carry the same weight, especially when cost-benefit analysis became a key criterion due to the non-securitisation of the Maas.

The trend towards desecuritisation of the river in the Netherlands increasingly confronts the water regime with a spatial planning regime in which water security is not the core concern but has to compete with other interests (Immink, 2007). Spatial planning in the Netherlands has seen a tendency from social engineering to multi-actor social learning and network coordination. In the expert community this created legitimacy for the involvement of social scientists next to natural scientists (Immink, 2007). Not everyone starts on an equal footing: since natural values rarely bring in the economic gain that real estate does, developers begin with a head start. Space for the River easily translates as space for developers (de Boer, interview). Thus, a desecuritised regime creates the very situation for the Netherlands that has marred the EA's ambition of effective flood defence in England. In Limburg, the insistence on budget neutrality meant that environmental concerns increasingly gave way to gravelling proceeds to make the project economically viable. Both gravellers and environmentalists at various points threatened to leave the consortium. But the gravel industry could, and did, hold the project in a double bind as an economic survival issue: their non-cooperation would kill the project, while the failure of the project, so they claimed, would kill the aggregates sector and create unemployment. The environmentalists did not have the same veto power when they drew a line in the sand arguing natural values were put at risk.

4. Stakeholder Participation: 'Politicisation' Without the Politics?

How about involving the project-affected stakeholders in decision-making? We can look at this in terms of who can participate and to which extent, and if it had an effect on the *range of alternatives* considered.

It appears that while participatory structures are now experimented with in Turkey and Egypt, stakeholders had little or no influence on either project election or implementation. The next few paragraphs, therefore, will only discuss participation in Bangladesh, England and the Netherlands.

In the UK and Bangladesh flood schemes, project democratisation through public participation was part of the innovation, unprecedented in flood projects. Stakeholders were consulted about their preferences beforehand, while several NGOs were co-opted into the project preparation.

In Great Britain, the debate over the need for the project was curtailed with references to the 1947 floods. The publicised number of alternatives (492 !) is impressive, but the selection subject to strong NRA influence. The NRA commissioned research into a notable alternative on smaller-scale flood-proofing of neighbourhoods, which would have relied on much greater community awareness and involvement (Penning-Rowsell et al., 1989). The report remained unpublished and beyond competition. Institutional stakeholders did have more informal influence at the early stage when archaeology and historic values necessitated changing the routing of the channel. The subsequent public consultation rounds and subsequent public hearings in the 1990s led to many placating concessions in project implementation.

Opponents however developed and tabled alternative relief channel options, notably Taplow Parish Council and the County Council of Buckinghamshire. In contrast with the Dutch alternatives, these options consisted of different, mostly *smaller* versions of the same channel. All these new alternatives were, on the whole, rejected by the NRA.

In Bangladesh, the auspices for public consultation were initially bad. The selection between the eight FAP reports took place under a securitised political (dictatorship) context, outside the public view.

The later changes to the FAP-20 project were not a result of new alternatives being brought in, but of risk assessment as well as public upheaval. Two out of the three original project sites were dismissed after a cool assessment of natural risk – the structures being at high risk of being washed away. Out of the four options originally developed for public consultation, technical option for the Tangail site appears to have been 'steamrolled' by the BWDB, over the objections of the Dutch side and, NGOs claim, those of the local population.

The participatory exercise on alternatives for flood control was rushed through and its results ignored by the Bangladesh Water Development Board. However, after this troubled start the most far-reaching forms of participation of all schemes were tried by instituting a multi-stakeholder platform (MSP) structure for managing the sluice gates. The compartmentalisation project sought to democratise the distribution of the 'residual risk' from monsoon floods between stakeholders. The participation structure for FAP-20 was refined after the donors threatened to withdraw their support. The 'poldering' set-up, however, ran up against scepticism on the part of Bangladeshi project leaders. It can also be said to ignore and therefore institutionalise a social system marred by patriarchal, violent social relations.

Local involvement was extended to the participatory implementation (construction and Operation and Maintenance) phase, with local groups actively building embankments, hoping the project would be self-managed after the project's closure. This might have been given a warmer welcome if the local stakeholders had felt they had had a say in it and a budget to secure continued Operation and Maintenance after project end.

On the Rhine, a range of intermediary organisations were involved in the selection process of areas suitable for controlled flooding. Organised regional civil society and private sector umbrella organisations were consulted in focus-group settings but not locally affected social and economic interests. While similar to the Bangladeshi projects, it was not deemed opportune to consult affected stakeholders in the Ooij polder. Despite several platform participants having been involved in earlier protest against dike reinforcement pre-1993, Ooij dwellers considered dike raising as a preferable alternative to controlled flooding. This was dismissed by the Public Works Department as too expensive. Currently compartmentalisation is again considered as an option.

By the time the decision on alternatives on the Maaswerken was to be made, the momentum of flood securitisation had likewise run out. The Maas project thus had to comply with a legal (EU-induced) obligation to provide and consult the public on several alternatives. The public was duly consulted for the Environment Impact Analysis (EIA) on the Maas on their preferred options. The EIA was dismissed by the Dutch EIA evaluation commission for not considering some alternatives well enough. Time is money; and spiralling cost and economic strictures in the end forced a deviation from any of the previously proposed alternatives. This in turn led to the temporary departure of the environmentalist project partner from the project consortium and a severe dent in public confidence. After tough negotiations on project realisation, a variant outside these options was selected. When the project threatened to disintegrate, a range of stakeholders were consulted behind closed doors. Informal relations between stakeholders and provincial project initiators, which had chilled after the Public Works Department took over in 1997, were revived in March 2001 to break the project impasse. When a local action group successfully invoked European antitrust regulation, the project was again delayed. The provincial government initiators recognised the need to communicate much better and established productive relations with BOM, the regional citizen platform.

If we see public-initiated participation as an attempt to share control in process and outcome with stakeholders, all projects, then, prove definitely flawed. In each project, the initiators did not treat their project as a 'wicked problem', but as a technical challenge that needed to be 'sold' on stakeholders. In each case, however, the initiators framed the participatory process in a way that gave them a great deal of control, including the option of ignoring the outcome. The modality of public consultation chosen in each case presupposes a form of (participatory) negotiation that stripped participation of potential political edges. Both Bangladeshi and UK project initiators freely volunteered in interviews and writing (Gardiner, 1996) that theirs was a 'selling' approach, while the Dutch project approach in practice displayed the same strategy. This type of participation assumes that sensible people will respond to *reason* and agree with each other when confronted with 'the evidence'. The role of sociologists in FAP-20 appeared to prepare the ground for the right message.

In all flood management cases, the formal mode of participation offered was found wanting and too late in the process by some stakeholder groups. Directly affected stakeholder groups (local citizens in Hasankeyf and the Ooij polder) did not get a hearing: or chose to drop out of the (organised) participatory processes (*Federatief Verband tegen Ontgrondingen* in Limburg). The limited leverage the participants had made it attractive for stakeholder groups to opt out of the process, lobby influential decision-makers or attempt to cause a commotion in the press or donor community. Excluded actors and perspectives (they reasoned) could only find their way into the process through unplanned types of participation. 'Participation' can also be understood in its 'Longian' interpretation (Long, 2001): 'participation' does not only capture social compliance with externally organised processes with invited participants, but also spontaneous social engagement with a view to influencing its outcomes: protest, contest, obstruction and deviance.

But interestingly, various actors chose to cooperate and resist *at the same time*. This was encountered both in the international arena, on the Nile and Euphrates, where basin co-riparians were not consulted on the decision to build a mega-project on the river and predictably exerted pressure and threats at the political level. At the same time those same co-riparians participated in technical exchange and coordination meetings. In the other three projects, local groups likewise talked, formally or informally, with the project initiators while at the same time 'participating' by engaging in protest or political and legal contest, often breaching the vow of confidentiality. The issue of openness of information and communication is elaborated in the next section.

Information and Communication

While securitised decision-making invites secrecy and manipulation, desecuritised decision-making would be expected to be more transparent and accountable. An open exchange of information requires availability of project information in the audience's language with little trouble, in accessible language. In the cases under review, the degree of openness ranged from suppression of an EIA in Egypt and its delay in Bangladesh and Turkey, to a surfeit of information in the Maas and Thames projects.

Information itself may be withheld or even classified (securitised) invoking national security. A plethora of reasons can lie beneath non-sharing of information, from a desire to monopolise strategic knowledge, a sense of vulnerability down to sheer embarrassment because the information is incomplete, ill understood, disorganised, or inaccessible (observations by Van der Schans and Verhallen, pers. comm., 2003), which can breed distrust and hostility. In Bangladesh, researchers and consultants complained that important findings were whitewashed or suppressed. This meant alternative perspectives were suppressed or massaged.

Community platforms may be important as information brokers. Desecuritisation exposes a project to Right-to-know legislation (the Aarhus Convention: UN/ECE 1998, see Blaikie et al., 1994; Verhallen, 2007), which gives affected parties information that helps them position themselves, if not always with an eye on the common good. The itinerary of the transparency of the Flood Action Plan for Bangladesh is especially intriguing: a progressive information desecuritisation/dis-closure process started out with no information in Bangladesh on FAP; then public reports of meetings with ever widening groups, followed by a plethora of English-language studies that, however, according to the interviewees, were heavily edited. In the Ooij, the Platform managed to unearth a critical study underlying the advisory report on emergency flood storage, while in the Maas the absence of the minutes of the closed-door meetings with stakeholders during six hectic months in 2001, to salvage the Maaswerken plan, meant culpability before the Council of State for unlawful secrecy – or more precisely negligence for lack of process documentation.

When negotiations have to take place in a 'glass house', this makes it harder to reach tentative agreements. Early divulgence of plans for a river planning project that will involve a change in land use exposes project initiators to serious risks: it invites speculators to buy up land likely to be needed for the project, while early publication of 'search areas' also has invariably given rise to vocal protests, especially from farmers whose land *may* be project-affected.

5. Norm Differentiation

The shift from hazard to risk in the Netherlands means that different standards can be applied to areas with different population and asset densities. The calculation of required safety per area now explicitly introduces cost-benefit considerations in risk management, which can lead to a so-called 'norm differentiation'. Economic calculus means that areas with the same probability bring a higher impact in an area with many economic assets.

In the Netherlands, there always was an institutionalised difference between the level of protection between coast (1-in-10,000-year events), main river area (1 in 1250) and the diked-up part of Limburg (1 in 250). The best protected areas are those where most economic assets are hoarded. Within these three zones, however, the protection standards were supposed to be equal, although engineers knew better than that.[3] The eventual successful extension of the safety standard to all of Limburg fixed this, but by then the government had declared it was not going to guarantee it.

In Britain, the Association of British Insurers, ABI, warned in 2000 that from then on, premiums would be differentiated according to exposure and entire areas excluded from cover. This would shift responsibility wholly towards homeowners (Huber, 2004: 13). Insurers also tried to make the complicit government behave: The Association blamed government for more generally neglecting flood defence, that is, for not making the rivers behave.[4] But it also called for a stronger stance on flood plain occupation, that is: making people behave. To avoid paying higher premiums, citizens adapt their behaviour. This way, people's freedoms are still compromised – not by public policy, but by private risk management.

The (re)construction of risk has its winners and losers. The next section will bring in the vulnerability approach which attracted much attention in disaster studies in the 1980s and 1990s. The vulnerability approach notices that risk has its winners and losers, and that its causes may be systemic and institutionalised. This constitutes a consistent critique of the five tenets of 'water peace' just discussed.

In sum, the appreciation of the negative consequences of intervention and of the positive aspects of water for its amenity, landscape and natural values may lead to a 'greener' engineering approach and enable reframing of the hazard approach to a risk approach – from foreclosing any flood risk to resilient response. This opens up space for the consideration of alternative problem frames, alternative solutions and the involvement of alternative actors. Security is a co-production: local authorities, the market (private insurance and consultants) and civil society (watchdog NGOs, CBOs) take responsibilities, while international regimes also impinge on lower-level decisions. Security standards can be debated and negotiated, which can lead to norm differentiation in risk.

In practice, participation is limited, as decisions remain controlled by experts. These however rarely tend to be pleasant surprises to local stakeholders.

River management projects bring risk redistribution. A desecuritised approach relies on the coordinated coping capacities of the different stakeholder groups. While current writing on adaptivity and resilience tends to be concerned with the resilience of the system as a whole (e.g. a river basin), political ecologists would zoom in on how such adaptation affects different people in different ways. Below, I will zoom in on conflicts that are specifically related with the distribution of risk and vulnerability, alleged to result from desecuritised governance practice such as cost-benefit criteria. A 'vulnerability' or political ecology approach does not see these problems as incidental. Political ecologists see vulnerability to floods as conditioned by their systemic contexts, the workings of the political economy (Bryant and Bailey, 1997). The following section delves further into this.

8.7 Conflict Over Risk Distribution in 'Desecuritised' Projects

8.7.1 Counter-Blaming and Framing: Not Enough Protection

So far, we have encountered protests against flood schemes, claiming other values are more important than flood security. But much conflict on security projects was not directed against flood protection, but concerned the perceived sacrifices to protect others – *selectivity* in protection. As upstream flood works often increase downstream risk (Bakker, 2007), protest from downstreamers in Britain could be expected. But upstreamers (Ooij) made it clear they were not prepared to suffer nuisance and *increased* flood risk to guarantee the safety of lower-lying areas. The Ooij, an economically less developed but well-to-do area has to make space to save more developed areas downstream. The Ooij polder dwellers did not see why their protection should be less important than that of the neighbouring Overbetuwe and Alblasserwaard polders. For the citizens of Hasankeyf, where planned flooding of houses and heritage is a certainty rather than a 1-in-1250 contingency, there seems no local security benefit at all.

Projects in their 'desecuritised' phase, or those that never were securitised in the first place, are also exposed to criticism that the project does not protect people well enough. If anyone is imputed to have caused, precipitated or failed to prevent the flood, they are held to account for placing others at risk.[5] As Delft engineer Frans Klijn observes, if science and engineering do not release us from risk, it means floods are not considered natural disasters, but engineering failures. Thus, like securitising moves on the part of project initiators, a security threat was named and framed, attributions of cause and effect are made, blame placed and responsibility for the remedy identified in the local domain.

The Jubilee Channel was never really securitised, the project had to be realised without special pleading. The EA, moreover, could not boast the same credibility as its Dutch or Bangladeshi counterparts, while a source of blame was readily available. The Thames channel project got into real trouble when the project failed to withstand the flood. Residents in the downstream of Maidenhead saw hundreds of houses flooded in January 2003 and blamed the channel project itself rather than the weather event. They took the EA to task on this for imputed breaking of the safety promises to Datchet citizens made during the 1992 Public Inquiry. A strenuous denial of responsibility on the part of the river manager increased the antagonism between downstreamers and agency. A parish councillor blamed the 'value engineering', cost-reducing exercise, for compromising the security standard. When several consultant reports confirmed structural faults in the EA's 'green engineering' design, the Agency passed the blame on, litigating against its main subcontractors.

The blame discourse in these stories does not evidence a rejection of the initiator's security frame, but rather a call on the river manager to provide more protection. The implication of the way the complaints were framed was that if the collapsed 'green' banks of the Thames bypass had been constructed with good old-fashioned engineering, they would certainly have held. If the Ooij could be protected with compartmentalised dikes rather than flooded, people would feel a lot safer. On the Maas, residents of isolated properties outside the parishes to be embanked refused to be abandoned to make economies. The same sentiment is expressed in the non-acceptance of local residual risk (Taplow, Lomm): was the project not supposed to prevent *all* flood events?

These civil-society voices are joined by Dutch experts who argue for old fashioned dikes instead of investing in a 'medieval' (Boorsma, 1999) system of detention and calamity polders, and in Britain by structural engineers finding fault with the green embankments of the Maidenhead channel after the 2003 floods.

Conspiracy stories buttress insecurity stories: in interviews both Ooij and char dwellers outside Tangail claimed they heard explosions (Tangail) or saw army engineers preparing to explode a dike (Ooij) to provoke a breach in 1995. Such stories were never proved nor disproved, but evidenced the distrust in the state as protector.

8.7.2 Differential Vulnerability

The above has raised issues that may be tackled within a liberal 'water peace' paradigm. In this perspective, people have the choice to go and live in less hazardous locations and can mobilise the means and 'voice' to protest and negotiate compensation. But from a political ecology perspective, not everyone is in that position. Despite well-known hazard potential, many have no other choice but to settle in flood-prone areas. In Western countries, low-cost housing is more likely to be in flood plains. Bangladesh, for example, simply lacks the space to house people elsewhere, and the vulnerability school in disaster studies (spearheaded by Blaikie et al., 1994) reminds us that many marginalised people do not have a choice.

Environmental change, whether natural catastrophe- or human-induced, affects lives and livelihoods differentially. A vulnerability assessment predicts what may happen to a particular group exposed to a particular hazard (Cannon et al., n.d.). But for the most vulnerable in society, everyday subsistence is a hazard (see e.g. Allen, 2003). The flood itself may not make all that much difference in light of the myriad challenges, and the flood relief may not be much help. In fact, it may turn out to be another hazard.

Whether made under securitised or desecuritised circumstances, both floods and flood policies can significantly change the various different stakeholders' security positions, making some more secure and others less. Consequently, it can appear to stakeholders that not everyone's security is equally important. When flood defence structures (the cure) are seen as more damaging than the flood risk (the ailment), people feel more rather than less insecure. Not everyone has the same opportunity or desire to adapt. For some, security is scarce and seemingly zero-sum: more security for some means less security for others. Some settings are more likely to create risk and/or maximise impacts on exposed groups, instilling an acute sense of vulnerability and iniquity. The differentiation of benefits and costs seems to be built into their design with seemingly scant consideration for redressing the balance. A political ecology perspective can help us foreground the broader political struggles that the project is embedded in. Such a perspective does not see these disparities as accidental, but rather as the outcome of structural biases: the political economy of flood protection. A vulnerability approach focuses on local security and tends to script the affected stakeholders as victims. The analyst would therefore expect flood protection projects not to target the safety of the poor, except when the rich have also been hit. Above, we discussed security dilemmas and threats coming from an insecure state. Under non-security or desecuritised conditions, the state may withdraw to make more space for non-state actors and bring economic (cost-benefit) and social (participation) criteria.

In light of the constructivist approach taken in this study, the research has not expressly set out to investigate and assess the 'objective' distributive effects of flood protection schemes themselves but relied on the interpretations of actors and observers. As we have seen, the securitised projects were ultimately subject to 'desecuritised' governance criteria. For example, all desecuritised flood security projects were therefore ultimately expected to be legitimised in terms of *cost-benefit calculations*. This economic rationale promotes protection where the assets are, rather than a view that every life saved counts no matter at what costs, and excavation where the most valuable aggregates can be found, to balance the books for the project.

In Limburg, but also in part in Maidenhead, the amount of and proceeds (and VAT) from gravel that can be sold remained a crucial factor for the project's viability, which became acute when the initiators failed to have the project labelled a security project. The Grensmaas project's opponents argued they should not sacrifice the integrity of landscape for the profits of the gravelling and construction industry. The considerable concessions made to the gravel sector could be (and were) construed as another indignity inflicted on Limburg by the powers in The Hague.

Without such concessions, the river projects do not bring an acceptable *benefit-cost ratio* and people are (or may feel) left to their own devices. In Britain, where floods were never securitised at all and cost-benefit criteria appear unassailable, the government has reiterated people's 'own responsibility' in risk management. The points system underlying MAFF (now DEFRA) grant aid ensures the non-funding of trouble spots. For example, Tewkesbury flooded in 2007 but is unlikely to be protected in future as a result of the points system. Cost-benefit considerations precipitated the selection of Maidenhead over, for example, equally exposed and flood-prone areas on the Thames in Wales. To interviewed local critics, this made the Jubilee River scheme a project for the rich working in the media sector, the elite children educated at Eton and the royals at Windsor, while poorer areas are left behind.

The vulnerability perspective is especially poignant in Bangladesh. Bangladeshi critics had been quick to note in 1988 that General Ershad and the international community only sprang into action when the presidential palace and foreign embassies in uptown Gulshan New Town were hit and the helicopter pad in Tangail prevented Madame Mitterrand from landing there.

The donor's risk assessment involved in the selection of the Tangail scheme brought another perverse rationale: compartmentalisation might not work in a more flood-prone area, as the infrastructure washes away. Thus FAP-20 protected people who were already comfortably safe compared to the underprivileged *char* dwellers nearby. (In fairness, other Flood Action projects, notably FAP-3.1, have targeted the security of the *char* people.)

Food security, a strong legitimator of FAP-20, was predicated on green-revolution HYV rice varieties, reducing production risk for farmers. Project initiators kept an eye on the project's Internal Rate of Return. Boosting agricultural production (high yielding rice varieties) was so crucial, that landed farmers were privileged over landless fishermen and women. It strengthened *private property* which Lockeians seek to protect against state domination. The downside is that those without (registered) property or water rights are not (well) protected, as their assets do not feature in the calculations. The Tangailis of Central Bangladesh are used to working the *khas* (common land) and communal fishing. Fishermen and peasants saw the commons enclosed and saw no alternative livelihood opportunities. It legitimised the project enabling private enclosure of the commons (*beels*) driving Hindu fishermen, who are often already barred from landholding, away from their already very limited livelihood, increasing their overall vulnerability. While farmers were privileged over fishermen, townspeople benefited more than the countryside, even though it is in the rural area that the distribution effects of flood risks have the more immediate impact on livelihoods. Livelihoods, now seen as essential to human security (UNDP 1994), are thus not safe from either the securitised or desecuritised risk management practice.

In their official formulations, the Turkish and Egyptian projects specifically sought to *bridge* socio-economic gaps between centre and periphery, which would also stave off terrorism. Analysts such as McDowell (1996), however, have claimed most welfare benefits of the Turkish GAP accrue to the country's industrialised west rather than its impoverished southeast and perpetuates rather than redistributes feudal land tenure relations.

The colonisation (enclosure) of the Egyptian desert throws up a sharp contrast between the poverty of the resettled Nubians and Prince Talal's 100,000 ha plot. In response to criticism, the government has also promised smaller plots will be set aside for university graduates and small farmers. The question of how many *fellahin* might be persuaded to start again in such an inhospitable area is at least partly solved with a view to agricultural reform in Egypt, which asserted the property rights of (absentee) landlords. The state apparatus helped owners drive tenants off their lands, with the slums of Cairo or the 'greened desert' at Toshka as their only place of refuge to start again.

Societal and academic commentators have thus made pointed observations on the socio-economic effects that played a role in disputes over flood regulation projects, and the winners and losers emerging as a result.

However, the protests to differential security rarely came from underprivileged areas. The protest against the Jubilee River did not come from poor Welshmen who might demand similar protection, but from neighbouring middle class Taplow and Datchet. The Tangail protest movement had strong 'guidance' from national and international NGOs. In Limburg and the Ooij, organised protest came from well-educated town dwellers united in citizen platforms. These groups have the political access and resources to make a difference. Welshmen and Tangaili landless meanwhile fend for themselves.

State Retreat ?

The above approach has cast doubt on the benefits of public, let alone private, primacy in providing security to local actors. While 'desecuritisation' implies that 'securitisation' is always a possibility, the state may disengage from security, either because the danger is no longer an urgent worry (a-security: war has become unthinkable) or because society has found ways to tackle the issue without the national defence apparatus and national political involvement ('depoliticisation'). In Buzan et al.'s sense, floods do not have to be 'political' in that they are not a state concern: local communities and local or regional authorities may take care of their protection. Before 1798 in the Netherlands, 1958 in Bangladesh (East Pakistan) and 1995 in Britain, there was no central river manager bringing in flood protection structures. The trend (if less the practice) in the Netherlands discourse for about a decade has been to decentralise flood management.

The 'post-providential' (Ophir, 2004) state makes people more responsible for their own security. The idea is that by devolving power, taking their voice and capacities seriously and entering into partnerships, devolution can empower people. Making physical space for both the river *as well as people* requires the flexible, multifunctional use of space, such as amphibious housing, resilience and preparedness. This has opened a new phase in flood management, 'living with the flood', with a less prominent role of national flood managers.

Living with the flood is, of course, what Bangladeshi and other Asian communities have been doing all along. The 'vulnerability approach' finds that people have little to expect from the state and international organisations, and argue that rather than giving people relief and making them dependent on the international aid (economic protection) system, they should be given help in increasing coping capacities for coping with environmental hazard: reduction, preparedness. A 'sustainable livelihoods' (DFID, 1999) approach argues that people have social, environmental, political and financial capital at their disposal. Bangladeshis have learned not to depend on the state and rely on sometimes violent self-help in flood management. A World Bank-funded management devolution programme leaves them with the Operation and Maintenance of often substandard flood infrastructure. Still, in Tangail too, some residents called for physical protection by FAP-20 and appreciated hard structures in front of their houses, while thousands of outsiders migrated or fled into the polder in 1998. Bangladeshis are excellently attuned to the normal flood (*barshas*) but few are well equipped to stand the bad, century flood (*bannas*).

Self-management may be the highest form of participation on Arnstein's ladder of participation (1967), but Cuillier (quoted in Collins and Ison, 2006) notes that self-management can also be a form of *abandonment* if the government simply retracts its support with no compensating provisions and people do not feel safe on their own. Exclusion from national or international solidarity leaves the powerless to their own devices without consulting if non-securitisation resonates with their 'feelings, needs and interests'. Henri Giroux (2006) has called attention to the politics of 'disposability', a concept that appears to capture Egypt's 'politics of indifference' to the fate of the *fellahin* quite well. In the European countries, norm differentiation, liberalised flood plain management and selective insurance

Country	**Political Sector**	**River Management**	
	Securitisation: Political Closure	**Securitised: Technical Institutional Closure**	**Non-Securitised:**
Egypt	SoE since 1981	Nile diversion – politicised	Horizontal extension Demand management – politicisation
Turkey	SoE since 1979 War with PKK	Dam regulation Resettlement – conflictive	Regional development, Integrated Water Management – conflictive
Bangladesh	SoE until 1990, and after 2006	River training French plan 1989 – rejected	Controlled drainage Compartmentalisation – conflictive
NL–Ooij	Special River Law DGR 1995–1997	Mass evacuation – accepted	Emergency flood storage – conflictive
NL–Maas		Emergency structures – accepted	Retention River widening – conflictive
UK	None	CPO – failed	'Green' channel – conflictive

Table 8.5: ***Acceptance of securitised and non-securitised interventions***

coverage releases constraints on freedoms, but can also mean those who can afford it could lead to 'gated safety communities', protected enclaves on private mounds or behind private embankments.

Harries and Borrows (2006), associated with the UK's Environment Agency, argue that expecting people to help themselves in coping with the flood brings anxiety because people do not always have a clue how they are supposed to act. The 'risk management' approach underestimates how people deal with

	Conflict Over Protection	Conflict Over Intervention/Control
Egypt		
Turkey		Capture of commons
Bangladesh	Distribution: Inside vs. Outside project area; Residual risk	Capture of commons
NL–Ooij	*Kaden* Residual risk	Economic risk (investment ban)
NL–Maas	Embanking towns Residual risk Distribution: Upstream vs. Downstream	Despoliation of countryside
UK	Upstream vs. Downstream Residual risk Insurers reduce coverage	Despoliation of countryside

Table 8.6: ***Type of conflict over river management projects: too much control, too little protection***

fear. When people feel challenged by a risk they cannot control, one anxiety-managing strategy is denial. Risk communication and other risk management measures, other than issuing sandbags, raise anxiety without increasing a sense of protection. They advocate that a two-way communication between flood manager and residents about what people *can* do might help in case of a flood, in terms of the present study, empowering (bringing alternatives) rather than leaving them to self-help. In the West Netherlands the perspective is much more limited so that people quite rightly depend on the sea dikes (Warner, Meijerink and Needham, 2007). People cannot be expected to fend for themselves like that.

In a conceptual essay invited by the African Water Issues Research Unit (Warner, 2000a), I maintained that integrated water management requires an integrated society. In the current context I would maintain that an integrated water security also requires an integrated society. A fragmented society in which certain groups are excluded cannot easily reach coherent flood risk management.

Selective protection means the violent closure of the sphere of security and may bring us back to the 'pre-providential states' when elites instated containment zones to protect themselves or their clients and ward off sources of hazard (pestilence, pollution and deviance), meaning the abandonment of others exposed to hazard (Ophir, 2007). When this separation is no more functional and hazards affect the chosen few, environmental protective measures are taken.

8.8 Flood Events as Windows of Opportunity for Governance Regime Changes

The Punctuated Equilibrium approach (Section 1.2.3) predicts focusing events to break through established regime patterns. That approach is inspired by ecology, which teaches that ecosystems go through four phases of pioneering, colonisation, climax and decay. The last stage is marked by creative destruction. A favourite paleontological example is the creative destruction of a meteorite *wiping out the dinosaurs.*

Punctuated equilibrium theory suggests that flood events or projects can change the policy context. Did the floods wipe out the dinosaurs or did they adapt? In each of the 'hydrosecurity regimes' under review, a national 'hydrohegemon' could be identified – Rijkswaterstaat (RWS) in the Netherlands, the Bangladesh Water Development Board in Bangladesh, the Ministry of Agriculture (now DEFRA) in Britain, DSI in Turkey and the Presidency and army in Egypt. These leading agencies in their own way were in the process of downsizing and under pressure to redefine their roles as the project was mooted, giving other actors a possible look-in. How did the flood and conflict over projects affect the regime? Did they affect the role of the hegemon and the rules of the game, as Lowry (1998) maintains?

While an overall impact assessment is not possible on the basis of the data, I will draw preliminary inferences below with regard to openness and closure of the regime in terms of actors, roles/procedures and knowledge.

An emblematic event (Hajer, 1995) such as a declared *flood crisis* can indeed prove a short-lived window of opportunity for the river manager to have projects' plans and policies fast-tracked and the hegemonic position of the self-appointed national 'water defence force' strengthened. Such an event can generate the consensus that enables a cooperative regime to address common problems. Floods on the Rhine and Maas and elsewhere precipitated closer European cooperation on floods and the adoption of the European High Water Directive (European Parliament and Council, 2007). This, however, did not hold for Bangladesh, India and Nepal, a hydro-security system linked by three rivers and multiple disputes over borders and migration. On the Nile and Euphrates-Tigris basins, two cases of nearly averted war in 1998 may have improved relations between the riparians, allowing non-hegemons to make demands. But the more meaningful change may well be the influence of non-state actors on donors, including the international interaction of experts filtering down 'desecuritised' thinking.

At the domestic level, the flood security activism of Bangladesh's president, Ershad, after the 1988 flood did not silence his political opponents, who managed to have him deposed in 1990. The Toshka project enabled by the 'good flood' in Egypt brought parliamentary questions and even a *fatwa*, but mainly appears to generate indifference at home and abroad. Local government had been weak ever since Bangladesh became independent, but got a new lease on life as FAP progressed, such that the role of local government service, LGED, in water management increased dramatically. Public participation became enshrined in several national guidelines.

In the Netherlands, 'calling a crisis' after 1993 and especially 1995 enabled Rijkswaterstaat and *waterschappen* to take the reins – the evacuation plan for 200,000 on the Rhine and a Delta plan for the Great Rivers – despite the dubious evidence for such a 'crisis'. Nationally, authorities, experts and locals appear to have worked in concert to enable the quick construction of emergency dikes in Limburg until 1997. On the Maas, the (national) Public Works Department was seen as taking over the Grensmaas project and faced resistance from the provincial political parties, with a telling stand-off between provincial and national government in 1999 over a trial trench. The environmentalists dropped out when austerity measures impelled stepping up the economically more interesting aggregate excavation at the cost of environmental amenities.

The flood may also have precipitated the acceptance of an already initiated move from vertical to horizontal flood response, necessitating Rijkswaterstaat to take a different, more modest role in a 'polder governance' model of negotiation. This provided inroads for non-state and foreign agencies. On the Rhine, for example, regional actors accepted the initiative to take the lead in 'Making Space for the River', while the province of Gelderland's initiative, with the neighbouring German *Land* as partner, contested the 18,000 m^3/s scenario as hegemonic wisdom.

On the Rhine, the plan for controlled flooding had been hoped to boost the profile of the Water Vice-Minister and her Public Works Department, but was defeated in part by the department's own handling of the plan. Since then, ministerial restructuring and water policy decentralisation has continued.

The province of Limburg was the lead actor in the Grensmaas project. Post-flooding defence efforts first boosted the role of the *waterschappen* and the province, and co-opted both private-sector companies and major environmental NGOs in the Maaswerken consortium in 1997. Yet when the traditional security provider, Rijkswaterstaat, reassumed their lead role by taking the reins of the Maaswerken project, it refused contributing a 'security premium'. The province of Limburg challenged the definition of security maintained by the public works department, but lost. In 2001 when the project itself reached crisis point, Limburg regained the initiative and normalised consortium and stakeholder relations.

In Britain, the Maidenhead project was started by what was to become the Environment Agency, which launched its project proposal without a legitimising flood crisis. The Agency started from a weak position because of externally imposed change within the regime; NRA's transmogrification into the EA, and the privatisation of the water supply branch of the Thames, weakened rather than strengthened its role in the policy arena. The Agency sought to strengthen its position as a lead actor in flood policy and change the system of cost-benefit calculation. The analysis argues that a strategy predicated on environmental values was part and parcel of an ultimately fairly unsuccessful niche strategy to change the regime. Environmental and cultural heritage NGOs act as statutory consultees, but with limited interest in flood schemes. The EA challenged established regime rules, seeking to extend the accepted calculation of benefits in the cost-benefit analysis beyond lives and assets protected to include environmental and health damage forgone. In both cases, the challenger lost, and so far, nothing appears to have changed fundamentally (Huber, 2004; Scrase and Sheate, 2005). Two years after a flood, the Maidenhead flood alleviation scheme faced a public enquiry.

Yet, after repeated floods, the issue became an agenda fixture, making the EA's drive for more integrated flood management plans a policy reality. The Agency's mandate grew after the police abandoned its flood warning service, and after the insurance association threatened to withdraw cover after two costly floods if government did not pull its weight. The state appears to be taking a larger role, but EA's role in flood policy remains clearly subordinated to that of the Ministry of Agriculture, as reiterated in flood policy documents (Ingen-Housz, 2007).

The above are all pressures for change from within the policy regime. Was the regime challenged from the outside?

A window of opportunity for the opposition in Bangladesh was the gradual recognition within the technical community that the major rivers in this country cannot realistically be tamed dramatically. This realisation switched the focus of FAP discourse from saving the country from floods to integrated water resource management to meet multiple demands, rather than to rely on local knowledge and opponents' co-opted expert knowledge. This was possible as experts were not a united community.

Similarly, the Ooij platform, seeking to change the securitised mode and to challenge the assumptions underlying controlled flooding in their polder, enlisted a retired Delft professor and was supported by dissenters in the epistemic community who did not necessarily share their scepticism of the 18,000 m^3/s discharge scenarios, but were keen to discuss uncertainties.

To get a hearing, protestors in each case did not rely on their local knowledge only but enlisted water professionals and local and district authorities, while in Bangladesh and Turkey they benefited from the political skills of international NGOs. As the opposition reaped success, the ruling security coalition offered NGOs a place within the decision-making regime, which protesters then can accept or reject. Controversies over river infrastructure thus opened a window for opposition actors to become part of the governance regime.

In a political culture dominated by the politics of mutual delegitimation, Bangladeshi NGOs and engineers started out at loggerheads. NGO opponents of FAP(-20) had a tough battle on their hands to prove their mettle as flood management actors. As a result of their successful engagement, Bangladeshi NGOs found a mode of coexistence after the controversy over the Flood Action Plan (in which FAP-20 was a flashpoint that gave NGOs a look-in in the river management regime).

In Britain, Flood Risk Action Groups were established after the 2003 flood to involve citizens and local authorities more in flood preparedness. In the Netherlands, local civic action platforms gained inroads into the decision-making regime structure by joining regular talks with the Maaswerken project organisation and Gelderland respectively (*Waalweelde* project).

While NGOs were co-opted, not everyone agreed to be drawn into the regime. The anti-gravelling federation (*Federatief Verband tegen Ontgrondingen*) on the Maas, for example, took a 'non-participatory' stance. The role of an 'outsider' ensures the group not to compromise their principles, and legitimacy to continue to file administrative lawsuits and target the regional press.

Hegemonic Control?

In terms of Hilhorst's (2003) domains of knowledge and action, some opportunities have been created for better coordination between decision-makers, experts and local stakeholders. NGOs and local authorities thus found their way into the decision-making regime, widening the range of actors with the potential of improving feedback between state and society. However, it was noted the regime does not alter a structural selectivity in protection between actors and does not account structurally for the security of project-affected people. Taking a critical regime perspective, we can analyse what makes everything remain largely the same in terms of security control, despite obvious conflicts.

We have seen that in Turkey and Egypt, the hegemonic actor is faced with the challenge of how to maintain hegemonic control (*régie*) of political decision-making. Moving from one-party to multiparty rule without losing control of people. In a flood context, flood scheme initiators appear to have hoped they found ways of widening the *range of actors* in security provision and deliberation without needlessly endangering their control of the river. Project initiators in Bangladesh, Britain and the Netherlands must have believed the flood defence case was cut and dried, as they were invariably taken aback by the furore over the projects they started. They had assumed that the flood risk itself, expected benefits and a form of public consultation would be enough to legitimise the project. Protest thus brought defensive and placating responses. While a (semi)-caged river still instils fear, so apparently do non-state actors inspire fear in state agencies. Therefore, it is not only structurally securitised political environments in the Middle East that find it hard to communicate with local flood- and project-affected people about their security concerns, but also liberal democracies in Europe.

The present study yields that river management largely remains in the hands of technical experts, outside the political sphere. As Aradau (2001) notes, an increasingly practised way for governments is to treat risk and calamity management not like a war but like a normal, routine situation we can handle rationally. This 'managerialisation' treats risk like a technical problem, without great uncertainties. A 'risk' approach implies control and predictability enabling a rational calculation of means and ends (Fox, 1999). Popular participation then is required to incentivise stakeholders such that they do not increase risk (Aradau, 2001). Floyd (2007) therefore rightly dismisses Buzan et al.'s (1998) claim that desecuritisation leads to politicisation. Unease with more unobtrusive 'desecuritised' social controls as risk maps and risk profiling rarely inspires political protest. This, critical security scholars argue, gives the security establishment relatively free range.

If this reasoning is correct, a *transformation* of the political arena and emancipation of actors under desecuritised river management would seem to be wishful thinking.

8.9 Conclusion: How Does the Theory Illuminate Empirical Findings?

The analysis shows that a window of opportunity for securitisation never lasts very long in practice, no matter how structurally securitised the context. The window for securitisarion proves to be an undependable instrument of 'closure'. The window of opportunity for swift action closes and river schemes will eventually encounter either a serious challenge (polarisation and politicisation) or have to contend with the slow motion of 'routinised', everyday decision-making. Even in a political economy that routinely spends its way out of crises by investing in infrastructure, or in a permanently securitised context, initiators cannot count on unlimited budgets, legitimacy and compliance. All studied flood-related projects saw resistance and dramatic protest (rallies, parliamentary questions, high-profile lawsuits, walk-outs) suggesting local citizens felt their 'feelings, needs and interests' had been ill-served. Securitisation and desecuritisation have multiple audiences: experts and non-experts, decision-makers and decision-affected people. While we might concentrate on local stakeholders, flood managers, donors and experts are crucial to the successful completion or rejection of a flood defence scheme. The 'natural risk' of a flood and its distribution effects cannot be judged in isolation from the technical and administrative/governmental set-up, which bring their own risks parsed as threats or, as we have seen, opportunities.

While securitisation brought non-compliance and resistance, desecuritisation does not mean 'living with the river' is universally appreciated. It was noted in Chapter 5 on Bangladesh that a pendulum swing can be observed between *risk-acceptance and risk-aversion,* which drive *'wet'* and *'dry' phases.* Yet it was found above that aspects of water securitisation and desecuritisation, as it were 'conflict and cooperation with the river', can influence each other or even happen *at the same time* (see also Brouma, 2003; Davidsen, 2006; Mirumachi, pers. comm.). The above has thus described a practical dialectics between securitisation and desecuritisation with respect to floods, a stand-off between the special and normal politics. A 'water as politics' (political ecology) view of disasters challenging the two takes a similar view of the world as the hydro-hegemonic view of 'water wars'. This perspective, among other things, highlights that projects and protest can be symbolic: just like securitisation may be about something else than the professed threat, controversy over a flood project, then, is likely to be a focus for controversies about something else (territorial control, identity, historic grievances, etc.). To key actors, the Focusing Events may well be moments in a larger story of security and control, and opposition against its manifestations. The next and final chapter goes into this, and draws conclusions from the above findings for the body of constructivist security theory.

9

THE SECURITISATION OF FLOOD EVENTS

IMPLICATIONS FOR SECURITY ANALYSIS

> The argument is not about the reality of [. . .] dangers, but about how they are politicized [. . .] Starvation, blight and famine are perennial threats. It is a bad joke to take this analysis as hinting that the dangers are imaginary. (Douglas, 1994: 29)
>
> Emergencies demand rapid action . . . Presidents and prime ministers have to take action first and submit to questions later. But too much prerogative can be bad for democracy itself. (Ignatieff, 2004: 2)
>
> When there's a man overboard, you are not going to worry if it's a federal responsibility or a state responsibility' (New Orleans flood victim in *When the Levees Broke*, part 3, Dir.: Spike Lee)

9.1 Introduction

The preceding chapter by and large applied the conceptual framework of constructivist security studies, as developed by the 'Copenhagen School', to six empirical river management studies. The study set out to investigate the *roles 'security' and 'risk' discourse plays in (de)legitimising flood management projects, and how this affects the political and river management regime context.* It confirmed Buzan et al.'s prediction that environmental securitisation is rarely successful, except when the threat resonates with earlier threats. While security speech can change the arena, the study did not find much evidence for 'punctuating the equilibrium': regimes remained in place, new directions and actors in river governance manifesting themselves before the crisis returned when the crisis window closed.

However, the outcomes of the present study suggest that certain modifications and elaboration of the Copenhagen approach may be in order.

The present chapter will raise five issues:

1. We should not only attention to threats but also to the opportunity side of crises (9.2).
2. Research on security speech and practices should not only focus on elites, but also on societal actors (9.3).
3. Security speech and protest has a tendency to 'hijack' audience, which gives a false sense of consensus (9.4).
4. Neither securitisation nor politicisation is 'the problem' (9.5).
5. An integrated security approach may offer possibilities to impose conditions and accountability on security action (9.6).

9.2 Instrumentality of Security Speech: Crisis as Opportunity

In *The Rise and Fall of the Soviet Threat*, Alan Wolfe (1979) shows how the construction of such Cold War threats as the Missile Gap and other icons of the 'Red Scare' depended on domestic American political expediency. The analysis suggests that political and military elements benefited from the occasional dramatic representation of a threat, independent of its actual manifestation. In terms of the present research, the fear of Soviet power generated a *demand* for security in the United States that was met by a government willing to supply. Like any sensible supplier, they advertised (marketed) their wares by playing on the intended audience's needs and promises of effectively meeting them.

Demand for security in the face of hydrological hazard likewise appears to have a political seasonality in response to supply and demand. The awareness of risk and demand to be protected from harm is ever on the rise (Douglas and Wildavsky, 1983). While extreme floods are becoming more of a challenge due to a growing number of people settled in at-risk areas, but the demand for structural measures is also whipped up by climate change scenarios predicting intense floods and droughts. Whether in the case of the missiles or climate change, a degree of uncertainty about the future facilitates the invocation of vital threats.

The political response to risk is not always the search for a Teflon coating and/or diplomatic immunity (Hood, 2002, see also Leiss and Chociolko, 1994), but a willing supply side. Security provision can also be a livelihood or a political career In its most opportunistic sense, as Naomi Klein asserts, hazards are a business opportunity (Klein, 2007). But whether driven by greed, a concern for the safety of others or a sense of professional responsibility, the point remains that security services, civil engineers, insurers, mayors and humanitarian aid

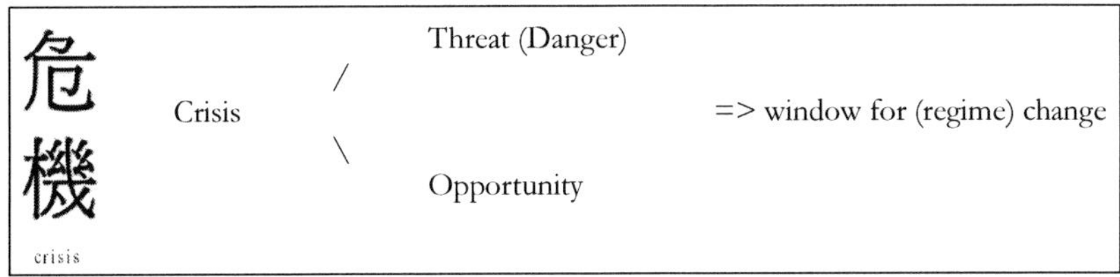

Figure 9.1: ***Chinese character for 'crisis' shows the two faces of crisis***

agencies are only too happy to promise prevention, protection and rehabilitation. As some will happily admit, they 'need' the occasional flood to keep up awareness and pressure on decision-makers.

A crisis is thus a contradictory animal, as shown most clearly in the Chinese character for 'crisis', which is a composite of two characters, 'threat' and 'opportunity' (Figure 9.1). A crisis represents danger, but it can also be a lucky break for some. Not only do floods bring fertilisation, ecological restoration or social capital, they bring a window of political opportunity – both for incumbents and challengers – to assert their legitimacy as providers of protection services.

For state actors, security can be instrumental in attaining ulterior goals – legitimacy, compliance, control over freedoms, resources and political standing within the bureaucracy. Huysmans (1998) even sees securitisation as

> . . . a technique of government which retrieves the ordering force of the fear of violent death by a mythical replay of the variations of the Hobbesian state of nature. It manufactures a sudden rupture in the routinized, everyday life by fabricating an existential threat which provokes experiences of the real possibility of violent death (Huysmans, 1992, quoted in Aradau, 2001).

Yet, the case studies have indicated security is not just the business of security professionals at central level. Regional and local authorities, experts, NGOs and community-based organisations take initiatives to protect their communities against floods, or as the case may be, against flood defence projects and policies. Decision-making theory suggests a linear process of agenda setting for solving a problem (Easton, 1965). But decision-makers and experts are not normally confronted by well-defined environmental problems; they frame them out of the complex mass of problem and solution elements, in so doing naming (attributing) culprits and remedies. The emerging dominant problem frame delimits the solution alternatives considered or excluded. Sometimes the problem itself is redefined (reframed) several times over until it gets 'solved' or otherwise disappears from the agenda.

A flood can be a window to promote existing security 'solutions', river schemes that were already lying in waiting. Securitisation and desecuritisation influence and reinforce each other through spatial and temporal linkages. The two appear to feed on each other, not just conceptually (Behnke, 2005) but also in the practice of flood governance.

Examples in the case studies abound. The need to divert overflow in Lake Nasser into the desert provided a window for Toshka. Compartmentalisation was already on the agenda when major floods ravaged Bangladesh in two consecutive years. A high-water event saved the province of Limburg's Grensmaas plan for river restoration. All researched flood schemes are more than just security infrastructure. Rather than quick technological fixes, they introduced more subtle ways of dealing with floodwater drainage (compartmentalisation and green river engineering) as well as extending the mandate by putting in measures to facilitate shipping (Maas), nature development and aquatic recreation (Maas and Thames), a vision of regional development (Turkey) or create a whole new civilisation (Toshka). The threat of flood insecurity allowed other, developmental and transformational policy preferences to play hopscotch on the back of security: they were 'security-plus' projects.

9.3 Can the Subaltern 'Do Security'?

Are political or academic 'authorities' the only actors who can do this trick? Buzan et al. (1998) state that securitisation has to come from a position of 'authority' – politicians, NGOs, experts, the media. This disadvantages those who cannot speak, for example illegal aliens (Hansen, 2000 quoted in Diez, 2000). This view however is contested: Litfin (1999), Aradau (2004) and others claim everyone can 'do security', even from an 'abject position'; the security-have-nots outside the nation can re-appropriate it for other purposes, for doing what they 'freely choose to do' (security as emancipation) (Aradau, 2004).

First, local actors mostly quietly look after their own security with or without projects, as they bear the brunt of hazards anyway (Kirschenbaum, 2004). Second, they can make intervening security actors lives difficult. Project implementation brings an interface (Long, 2001) between engineers and local citizens in which the latter may express a refusal to play and give rise to protests and active resistance from outside the elite. Vocal protests against project implementation in Tangail, Hasankeyf, Ubbergen and Taplow were such an embarrassment to project initiators that, given external support, they could not so easily be repressed.

Second, they can 'countersecuritise', that is, promote a security counter-frame that protects a non-negotiable value, legitimises extraordinary forms of protest and protection. For this, they can enlist more powerful actors, joining an existing discourse coalition or simply find themselves on the same side as others siding against the project. In the current study we saw the unlikeliest of bedfellows seeking to stop a project – Friends of the Earth, Trinity College, the World Bank and the state of Iraq all opposing the Turkish Ilısu Dam, anti-gravelling groups in Limburg siding with gravel companies from across the border and the European Union against the Maaswerken consortium.

This indicates that the support of certain 'members of the audience' is crucial to the success or defeat of security speech. The research project has identified crucial groups in that audience, as explained in more detail in the following section.

9.4 Selling the Security Story

9.4.1 Aligning Dispersed Audiences

Discourse is co-production: nobody can control discourse alone. A successful security discourse coalition, whether for or against a project, depends on the *context* and the *audience*. It takes a receptive audience to validate and 'instantiate' a securitising move. It was found that even in an authoritarian political system, the audience reaches far wider than the immediate *junta* membership. In each of the case studies the audience consisted of a mostly international network of disparate, occasionally overlapping groups that were not usually well coordinated among themselves. As will be argued below, the audience can be 'hijacked' and taken for granted, but it also has knowledge and agency. The present research identified (after Hilhorst, 2003) three core audiences who need to be aligned to counter a security challenge, and thus need to respond to the labelling of a situation as 'insecure' and in need of extraordinary measures: other decision-makers, notably:

- governance sector: decision-makers, funders, bureaucrats
- security experts: scientists and managers
- local response: the flood- and project-affected population

Governance Other actors in the risk governance sector also need to co-operate. Regional authorities need to give planning permission. Supranational directives contain norms that force accountability. Funding proved a particular Achilles heel for river management projects. Security discourse may well successfully command a 'blank cheque' for security measures in the regional or national arena, but requires others (donors) to stand surety for continued funding. As these operate in non-securitised contexts (or choose to invoke non-security norms), as they did in all the case studies except Egypt, they bring conditionalities that impair the sustainability of security measures.

Experts Security logic has customarily extended to the scientific community, where uncertainty only complicates the narrative and therefore is reasoned away into 'safety margins' (*waakhoogte*) and 'failure factors'. Securitisation does not allow ambiguity or uncertainty. In flood management, scientific uncertainty is 'tamed' by imposing safety margins, using stochastic tables based on historic flood data and extrapolation. But in each case, critics in the scientific community could be co-opted by protesters willing to challenge the assumptions of rivers schemes. While in the case of Bangladesh, academics championed local knowledge, opponents more frequently mobilised technical counter-expertise challenging river experts on their own terrain.

Local response Finally, a project intervenes in local lives. A project promises to protect local stakeholders, catering to a demand for security. If they had a traumatic flood or evacuation experience, they may well be willing to sacrifice a lot to ensure safety in the next event. In the Maaskaden episode, there were direct informal feedback mechanisms between project planners, implementers and affected population. In the other case studies, however, such intensive coordination has been very rare. The project-affected population is not coterminous with the intended beneficiaries. They tend to be background as an audience. So, where are they in the story? Are they (seen as) participants or silent witnesses?

9.4.2 Positioning, Blaming and Hijacking the Flood Security Arena

A great measure of policy uncertainty permits jumps (leaps of faith) in the security story, to make linear attributions that construct a neat security claim. These claims enable 'conflict entrepreneurs' (Friis, 2000) to bring together coalitions around a narrative that help forge an audience for a successful security speech act. By transforming the policy issue into a security arena with threat-defence sequence, this creates certainty and an action perspective. As a consequence, fence-sitters ('liminars') by their very existence are a threat to things, and are forced to become either 'us' or 'them'.

What kind of story does a securitising agent tell the audience? Flood securitisation is a story of a threat (the river) affecting a referent (lives and assets) and a remedy (infrastructure, zoning, etc.). The hero slays the dragon threatening the princess and as a thank-you gets to marry her.

The successful securitisation of the river, however, introduces another actor: it is also a direct (or indirect, Ohana, 2007) way of condemning Others. It is to discredit the opposition to security policy as the 'dragon's helper' – environmentalists, the deviance of greedy developers, lax local authorities, upstream interventions and climate change-inducing industries, whose behaviour presumably causes the danger to core values. 'Dissidents can be silenced most effectively when they are portrayed as aiding the enemy' (Dalby, 2000: 13). A contested security project in turn presents its opponents with an opportunity to position themselves as alternative heroes in the tale, with the project initiator as 'dragon's helper' (or 'lion unleasher') The present study not only found such stories for the Netherlands (after van Eeten, 1997) but also Bangladesh,

Turkey and Britain. The initial antagonism of the 'blue' and 'green' coalitions, 'engineers' and 'sociologists', 'intruders' and 'rebels' concerned a clash of two mirroring security stories delegitimising the opponent's values and narrative. The conflicting protagonists have reduced uncertainty by 'filling out the blanks' with a security story that creates certainty about, or unimportance of, the facts of the matter – and by not communicating with each other.

How about the 'princess', supposed to be protected? Labelling a group or the environment as threatened reconstructs the identity of this group as vulnerable victims. It was noted in Chapter 8 that local actors rarely feature in participatory designs for security schemes. It is not usual to interact with flood-prone citizens to learn if and how they would like to be protected. We found water departments find it very hard to consult rather than sell. Citizens are now included in some operational security activities, such as neighbourhood or dike watch, but are largely absent from hazard management arrangements, which at best remain at the inter-institutional, corporatist level.

States, but also NGOs have a tendency to present groups as vulnerable without consulting them on this (Allan, 2002). Bangladeshi NGOs have patron-client relations with the local poor, and in turn enjoy patronage from international donors. This makes it hard to assess the spontaneity of protests against projects. In Europe initiators and NGOs defended environmental values that were not uniformly shared by local citizens, so that their 'green' moves were not felicitous with the local audience. There may be a very real cry for help (real demand for security), a voluntary offer to be another actor's protégé, but if this is assumed rather than expressed, there is the question of instrumentalisation ('hijacking') of intended beneficiaries. Like fairytales, we thus find neither the security nor the counter-security coalitions are necessarily *democratic*. Positioning oneself as protector attributes agency to the (originator of the) threat, and passivity to the at-risk protégé, even if this passivity is not necessarily warranted.

Invoking History and the Politics of Unease

A positioning approach allows us to account for *change*. Due to interaction and learning, the former antagonists locked in defence dilemmas are now cooperating in consultative bodies, so that the neglected 'princess' now has a voice. Yet, other cases show that learning can also mean learning to reproduce, intensify and develop variations of essentially the same conflict story – with the flood or flood plans as recurring threats. This points us to the importance of a time element.

Buzan et al. (1998: 29) expected *environmental* security speech to be mostly non-felicitous – at most, it results in politicisation. The authors however concede that resonance with historic threats can make all the difference. In the Netherlands, the securitisation of a high-water event that many do not consider a crisis proper triggered crisis legislation if the threat resonates with earlier traumatic events ('saying dikes'), while in Britain, which does not have this historic resonance, floods that killed five residents in Middle England in 1998 did not.

Now that the Dutch are contemplating a risk (adaptivity) rather than a hazard (dikes) approach, proponents of 'dikes' frequently invoke a new threat: climate change. After Bigo (1998) this can be seen as essentially the same narrative. Rather than concentrating on unique (repeated) speech events, Bigo argues we should look for connections that weave them into a more coherent security narrative. He notices a 'politics of unease', in which all manner of threat (e.g. migration and terrorism) are collated to 'sell' technologies of surveillance and identification as the remedy (governmentality). The 'politics of unease' thus legitimises all kinds of security measures that control individual behaviour.

Conceivably, though to my knowledge not contemplated by Bigo, counter-securitising coalitions may well be doing the same thing in their counter-hegemonic strategy. Action-oriented NGOs find (or declare) 'crises' to operate their social or environmental advocacy role. NGOs have broader agendas for social change or environmental conservation, and are constantly on the lookout for any 'mistakes' that create opportunities to delegitimise an adversary and make donors feel uneasy. This, it appears, is easy to do: mega-projects rarely are totally successful and often display glaring weak spots – environmental costs, resettlement, financial irregularities – which would easily be forgiven immediately after an actual crisis context, but not when that context is lacking. Successful protest against large infrastructural water projects in 1990 made international donors nervous – they could not afford to make mistakes.

Incidental conflicts over dikes and zones resonate with other conflict legacies – historic (often centre vs. periphery) grievances and underlying conflicts. Protest against controlled flooding in the Ooij built on earlier mobilisation against dike reinforcement. Limburg protesters were steeped in protest against gravelling. At the international level, protest against FAP-20 and Ilısu resonated earlier successes of locally focussed international INGO protest (e.g. International Rivers Network, and Friends of the Earth) against infrastructural works, such as Narmada, Arun and Pergau. This 'jet stream' may well have provided a window for the counter-securitisation, and hence politicisation, of the flood protection schemes in Bangladesh and Turkey. The careful selection of multiple venues in the political system (forum shopping) enabled the anti-Ilısu and anti-FAP coalitions to find an international hearing for their protests, breaking through the established local 'equilibrium'. Whether within or above the law, they opened the floor to contest the initiator's project frames – as bringing war not peace, destruction not development – which not only delays or halts a project but promotes other agendas.

The strategies used by national NGOs and local platforms in Europe and Asia Tangail and the Ooij polder (lawsuits, dramatic public protests and parliamentary lobbying) were successful in stopping a policy or its follow-up. All projects were seriously compromised or discredited by the opposition. Moreover, as noted, some NGOs and CBOs gained a place at the table in the regime and influenced donor or hegemonic conditionalities imposed on river management schemes. This allowed some actors to have it both ways: to fight the project, but also benefit from it, both in terms of physical protection and of enhanced status resulting from protesting and negotiating enhancements.

Un-securitisation (disarming securitising moves) and desecuritisation (undoing previously successful securitisations) strategies were mounted to take power away from an actor framed as enemy, to delay crucial decisions to prevent action, to take power away from an (institutional) actor, with a view not to getting certain things done. Alternatives were proposed, but none of the options for protection worked out by consultants and retired civil engineers were actually tested and adopted. Calling off the project has not eliminated the risk for the flood-prone regions, and has not introduced an alternative technological frame. Since the flood risk is not 'solved', 'solutions' can be resuscitated. Indeed, the modality for riverine flood management may have become controversial everywhere, all proposed technologies have reappeared in some form. Conflicts, therefore, can be expected to be revived, too.

With some irony, the above argument can be summarised as the ten-step Table 9.1.

9.5 State Overboard?

We have seen that both taming the flood and making peace with the river has easily translated into 'war with stakeholders'. The terms of security provision made sense at the systems level, but rarely at the local level. This invites the question if the systems level, privileged by 'integrated water resource management' is necessarily the appropriate level. A critical perspective questions the state as the key referent of security, arguing the individual or the planet should be privileged. State involvement may reduce but also create and promote risk and vulnerabilities for people and the planet. Throwing the state overboard means relying on social solidarities and/or market forces.

It is legitimate to ask what total non-securitisation of flood risk would mean: a reliance on societal self-help. The effective flood warning and country boat system in Bangladesh shows that emergency can overcome social constraints to include a wide range of actors in flood preparedness and response. The frequent recurrence of floods obviously maintains flood awareness, which is not available in floods that take more than a generation to recur.

The vulnerability school in disaster studies echoes the concern of critical schools in society studies about individual or group security, but distrusts the state or private sector to provide this for different reasons. For both the 'Welsh school' in Aberystwyth (Booth, Wyn Jones, Linklater, etc.) and the 'Paris School'

How to Securitise in Ten Easy Steps	**How to Counter-Securitise in Ten Easy Steps**
1. Select an issue that is sufficiently complex and uncertain	1. Select an issue that is sufficiently complex and uncertain
2. Identify or invent a crisis (injustice) to be overcome	2. Identify or invent a crisis (injustice) to be overcome
3. Present the particular view as the general interest	3. Present the particular view as the general interest
4. Attribute the problem to an 'other'	4. Attribute the problem to an 'other'
5. Present the issue as urgent and solvable	5. Present the issue as urgent and dangerous
6. Present yourself or a favoured actor as the hero of the story	6. Present yourself or a favoured actor as the hero of the story
7. Present yourself or a favoured actor as the victim of the story (e.g. in need of saving)	7. Present yourself or a favoured actor as the victim of the story
8. Mobilise the support of key audiences, including the help of a powerful donor	8. Mobilise the support of key audiences, including the help of a powerful donor
9. Put word into action, if necessary placing yourself above the law	9. Put word into action, if necessary placing yourself above the law
10. If attention flags, bring in a new threat that warrants the same solution	10. If attention flags, bring in a new threat that warrants the same protest

Table 9.1: ***Securitisation and counter-securitisation in ten easy steps***

School	Security is	Referent	Theoretical Background	Regimes Bring
American	Stability of expectations	State	Realism	Stability: strong hegemony
Copenhagen	Peace and cooperation	State/other	Liberal Constructivism with realist roots	Coordination: norms, values and procedures
Welsh/Paris (Critical security studies)	Emancipation	Individual	Radical (Political ecology)	Control mechanisms

Table 9.2: ***Three approaches to security studies***

(Huysmans, Bigo, etc.), governance does not bring the security co-production and alignment envisaged by 'water peace' narrative, but increased control (Table 9.2). Vulnerability analysts, meanwhile, have noted that social resilience to all kinds of hazards is underestimated, and promoted investing in local resilience and preparedness. Disasters are opportunities at the local level too, as they enact social networks and resources (Hilhorst, 2003).

However, we have argued above that resistance to certain projects does not mean local stakeholders do not make use of protection structures and have no demand for protection. Ten thousand Tangaili women protested against FAP-20, but others requested physical protection and those outside the embankments found refuge there in the 1998 flood. The protest against schemes such as Narmada or Maaswerken is not normally oriented against the very idea of development or flood protection, but against its modality and distribution effects.

It is a fine line between control and self-governance: the former can be suffocating, the latter can become synonymous to abandonment, when no one looks out for Others any more in their hour of need. This invites a closer look at the challenge of countering disaster in the 'logic of peace' of networked governance arrangement – one may visualise a 'bazaar' of spontaneously organised social security interaction coexisting with the more customary 'cathedral' of top-down management (Lankford and Hepworth, 2006).

A Case for Conditional Securitisation

In responding to contingencies, perhaps you cannot always privilege 'choice' over 'necessity', 'deliberation' over 'decision'. With our current state of knowledge, an earthquake cannot be deterred. The attraction of disaster securitisation, instead of the politics of neglect, is that it legitimises the human and capital investment in mechanisms to get things done, quick, on a large scale when the 'opponent' does not play by your rules. When a tsunami is coming in your direction, both the certainty and values are clear. With a house on fire, you will be unlikely to deliberate over liability and compensation with your neighbours over collateral damage, but call the fire brigade. The collateral damage to others as a result of dousing the flames can be dealt with later. When someone is an immediate danger to themselves or to others, police and aid workers are allowed to intervene without consultation (outreach).

To avoid being insecure at a crucial time, stakeholders are willing to abandon their sovereignty and delegate their political say to security suppliers. But legitimate intervention need not go completely unchecked. Liberal security analysts, including the Copenhagen School, see the security mode as an undesirable that should at most be transitional. Is it possible to regulate the unregulated period of exception so that rescuers and protectors are accountable for their actions?

The treatment of flood victims, as much as other people temporarily 'placed outside society', requires a discussion on protocols and on rescue ethics – a Geneva Convention for crisis response. In this we can take a cue from Michael Ignatieff (2004), the Canadian social commentator-turned-politician who insists the state of exception is the 'lesser evil' when your adversaries' actions are not as ethical as your own standards, and advocates putting security under democratic control and with a clear time delimitation – thus mixing wartime and peacetime modes of security governance.

In the projects under review, there turned out to be structural links between the securitised and non-securitised 'spheres' that acted as brakes on the suspension of choice and accountability. External actors imposed environmental, financial, socio-economic and political rights and obligations on project initiators – though it merits mentioning that economic conditionalities not only helped but also hurt stakeholder groups. These links however were also levers for donors to pay more attention to local stakeholder interests. It will be argued below that the currently prominent 'integrated security chain' offers opportunities to institutionalise the links between securitised and non-securitised worlds.

Security Chain and Networked Security Governance

This is especially apposite in the context of disaster *preparedness*, where the crisis is not imminent, so that there is time for deliberation as humanitarian crises bring immediate security needs. But water projects are not so much about disaster response as about disaster preparedness. The urgency involved in developing and instating flood protection schemes and policies rarely warrants full securitisation. The research noted that other (social and environmental) agendas were co-opted and adopted in these schemes, and different alternatives possible for which there was no urgent reason to overlook. Flood preparedness provides an opportunity to arrange this institutionally, to guarantee democratic accountability in the aftermath of the next crisis.

An integrated security chain management has the potential of mixing security and non-security modes of risk governance. In the integrated security chain, repression (disaster response) is the fourth phase out of five: *prevention, pro-action, preparation, repression* and *aftercare*.While the initial disaster repression phase is probably best tackled by actors with coercive powers, the other phases are not restricted by urgency. These desecuritised phases widen the range of actors and bring in diversity of likely candidates, whose roles and identities may differ between the stages. Moreover, the stages are likely to overlap and the different links in the chain to be associated with different actors.

A 'water peace' logic fights complexity with complexity but may also suffer from the problems of the water peace logic – a functionalist assumption in the water community that 'good governance' can make actors work well with each other (Friesendorf, 2007).

Currie-Alder (2007) however has warned that participatory resource management can be a foil for resource capture, if it ignores underlying power divergence. In the same vein, Warner, Waalewijn and Hilhorst (2002) qualify their recommendation for a multi-stakeholder approach to disaster preparedness by emphasising the need to understand why such platforms are promoted, and how the interests of less powerful groups are safeguarded. The functional coordination mechanisms in network governance can easily overlook the hegemony element and thus exclude important actor identities, needs and interests.

The research however also found that the vulnerable, whether included or excluded from the regime, do not face a solid 'hegemonic bloc'. One cannot assume the governance system to be consistently cooperative, the epistemic community consensual and the community united. Opposition in one domain can resist the call for consensus co-opting/enrolling dissidents in another domain who can say things that local groups or politicians cannot. Thus we saw *alliances* between community-based platforms and dissenting experts or regional governments.

Such mechanisms however require a level of structural awareness and engagement more likely to be raised in a conflict situation. In 'peacetime', local actors are rarely well-organised and the tendency for all actors not to spend time on the first three phases before the event happens. This privileges the professional state and NGO actors indicated in Table 9.2 – until someone re-securitises the issue.

9.6 Conclusion

Securitisers and counter-securitisers (politicisers) see opportunity in floods and conflicts over flood project to promote certain agendas. They use the same tricks of discursive persuasion and enrolling others for certain goals. Security speech action does not have to be from a position of authority, or even be about speech, but promotes agendas that are otherwise less easily attained. As both initiators and opponents use the language of fear to convince key audiences, flood projects can be expected to lead to securitisation but also counter-securitisation, politicisation and conflict.

Pictured in very broad strokes, securitisers will seek to avoid the political process to get things done and are annoyed when the window of opportunity finally closes, while non- and counter-securitisers will try to avoid securitisers getting certain things done. It is argued that rejecting or relativising security as a construction ignores the express demand for protection in overwhelming disaster events, and politics expresses express concerns about the way this demand is met, so that both modalities should be taken seriously. Both securitisation and counter-securitisation/politicisation are facts of political life and both have their relative merits in relation to different types of policy problems.

While extraordinary powers accruing to state actors can easily have worrying consequences in terms of control and constraints to rights and freedoms, it was proposed not to throw securitisation out with the liberal bathwater. It was noted in the introductory chapter that in a constructivist view, states are not only seen to play power games but also to puzzle (Checkel, 2001). In this puzzling process, not all state actors avoid blame, nor do they always take credit without taking action, and their supply offer appears to be readily met by a demand. A disaster studies approach shows up the pluses of securitisation – swift action, a window for reconstruction breaking through entrenched contexts, but also the minuses.

While the choice between 'going with or without normal political rights' would appear to be easy, both may carry a high price for some actors. Integrated security chain management brings a mix of traditional and non-traditional security actors in the different disaster domains, who will need to find a *modus (co-)operandi* in disaster pro-action, prevention and preparedness.

NOTES

Notes to Chapter 1

1 'Extreme weather brings flood chaos round the world'. *New Scientist*, Environment, 30 July 2007.

2 'Fall in weather deaths dents climate warnings', *The Sunday Times*, December 2, 2007

3 The most severe floods occurred across Northern Ireland, Yorkshire, The Midlands, Gloucestershire, Worcestershire, Oxfordshire and Berkshire.

4 Stephen Davenport, 'Floods around the world', 30 June 2007, MeteoGroup and *New Scientist*. http://www.meteogroup.co.uk/uk/home/weather/weather_news/news_archive/archive/2007/june/ch/0cb69615d9/article/floods_around_the_world.html.

5 Environment Agency, Review of 2007 summer floods, December 2007.

6 U2 and Green Day, The Saints are Coming, pop video, 2006.

7 HKV Lijn in Water and TU Delft (2007), 'Twee jaar na Katrina. De catastrofale overstroming van New Orleans', Delft.

8 Like the Realist conviction that states have always existed, this liberal narrative is not necessarily borne out by history. It appears an instance of another 'invented past'. Western European countries, including Britain have not been top-down but shared power with the middle class and a rich array of local rulers. Trottier (2004) points out that the state in Europe never exercised such a control over resources as it did in 'oriental despotisms'. Water only became a state concern in the nineteenth and twentieth centuries in most European countries (Blokland et al., 1999).

9 Young (1994). As Jägerskog (2003) notes, this is a close cousin to Hajer's (1995) 'emblematic event' raising awareness on social vulnerability.

10 Lees (2001) analyses how calling a 'water crisis' in Israel in the 1990s marginalised farmers and, as a consequence, changed the hydraulic mission.

11 Because a 'securitising move' (a move for closure) and 'a securitisation' are sometimes conflated, I will at times use the stylistic contamination of 'successful securitisation'.

12 The Santiago School, supported by Stafford Beer and others, experimented with a socio-cybernetic system that would communicate feedbacks about people's needs in under Salvador Allende's Chile.

13 A grand narrative or meta-narratives is a narrative about narrative that brings a comprehensive explanation of a historical experience or knowledge. A grand narrative is a 'global and totalising schema which orders and explains knowledge and experiences' (Stephens, 1998).

14 In the tradition of Pierre Bourdieu's [1972] (1977) concepts of 'field' and 'habitus'. Unlike the natural world, human behaviour, is not simply the effect of external forces acting upon it; human beings actively and purposefully act on in response to their environment. The 'security field' to Bigo is a logic integrating heterogeneous practices into a specific concrete manifestation of the rules defining security practices (or 'formation'). Society organises risks by providing an institutional environment, which plays a central role in the production and regulation of particular risks.

Notes to Chapter 2

1 *Al-Ahram Weekly*, 23–29 September 1999, Issue 448.

2 MMWR Weekly, 'International Notes Health Assessment of the Population Affected by Flood Conditions – Khartoum, Sudan', January 06, 1989, 37(51 & 52) 785–788, http://www.cdc.gov/mmwr/preview/mmwrhtml/00001323.htm (last accessed 22 May 2010).

3 International Federation of Red Cross and Red Crescent Societies, www.ifrc.org/docs/appeals/rpts05/SD050810.pdf (last accessed on 22 May 2010).

4 Nevine el-Aref (2007), 'Sending out an SOS', *Al-Ahram Weekly* no. 860, 30 August to 5 September 2007.

5 According to Egyptian hydrologist Sultan, the 'new' lakes in fact took 40 years to form; 'UB Geologist Studies How to Manage Precious Water Amid Volatile Middle-East Politics', Buffalo University news release, 2 April 2003.

6 http://www.eiu.edu/univpub/previous/12/page.html (last accessed on 22 May 2010).

7 Then Prime Minister Kamal el-Ghamzouri, cited in El-Ghamwary and Quinn, 1999.

8 Stages two and three require more pumping stations and irrigation canals to channel to cultivate additional lands west of Lake Nasser, at an additional cost of $6 billion. This latter project apparently involves cooperation with Libya, and 1 million acres would be reclaimed and the desert urbanised. Susan Quinn, 'Egypt's Toshka Project presented to US', *US Arab Tradeline*, 2 October 1998.

9 http://na.unep.net/AfricaLakes/AtlasDownload/Toshka_Project.pdf 2005, which gives a nice pictorial overview.

10 Miral Fahmy, 'Farming Toshka is no pipe dream for Saudi prince', *Middle East Times*, 5 December 1997. p. 35.

11 Quoted in Aaron Gladman (1997), 'Massive Nile River Diversions Planned', *World Rivers Review*, 12 (3).

12 http://www.islamonline.net/English/News/2002-06/04/article83.shtml (last accessed on 22 May 2010).

13 Pratt (2001) notices NGOs now escape control by registering as companies.

14 http://www.hrdc.net/sahrdc/hrfeatures/HRF61.htm. The interpretation of the 'political' is interesting here. When a Member of Parliament asked whether raising funds for Palestine is a political activity, the government answered that as the whole Egyptian population is behind Palestine, it is not a political activity.

15 'No retreat, Toshka Project considered thoroughly, hi-tech implementation'. *Arabic news.com*, 20 December 1999, Mubarak: Toshka project among national priorities', *Arabic News*, Politics, 21 December 1999; ikhwanweb.info; in *al-Jumhurria* of 11 January 1999, quoted in Steve Negy, 'The Toshka Project', *Middle East International*, 12 February 1999; *Al-Alam al-Youm*, A study about Toshka conducted by the Association for Economic Information, "Europe-Egypt", Fribourg/Switzerland, 6 February 2003.

16 Fatemah Farag (2003), 'Green desert – at what cost?', *Al-Ahram Weekly*, 23–29 January, Issue 622.

17 Gamal Essam El-Din (2006), 'Parliament to Scrutinize Tushka Project', *Al-Ahram Weekly*, 8 April 2006.

18 http://www.constructmyfuture.com/hall-aswan.html

19 Fatemah Farag (2000), 'More precious than petrol', *Al-Ahram Weekly*, 17–23 February 2000.

20 Quoted in 'Le second Nile', *Jeune Afrique*, 27 July to 2 August 1999, pp. 56–59.

21 *Al-Ahram Weekly*, 23–29 September 1999.

22 Ahmed El-Ghamrawy and Susan Quinn, 'Egypt's Development Projects Spur Growth', US-Arab Tradeline, 9 July 1999 *Arab World Online*, www.awo.net/newspub/pubs/tradelin/990709a.asp.

23 'Egypt's Toshka Makes Desert Bloom, But for Whom?', *Epoch times*, 20–26 February 2006, p. 3.

24 http://www.sis.gov.eg/En/Publications/343/344/366/369.htm.

25 In Egypt 'irrigation' tends to include both farming and urban water supply (Hvidt 1995, n7).

26 Boutros Boutros-Ghali: UN Secretary General; Ismail Serageldin: World Bank vice-chairman; Mohammed Abu-Zeyd: president, World Water Council.

27 Quoted in Abay Tadala, 'Abay (Nile) in the news', *The Monitor*, 30 September 1999.

28 See for this episode e.g.: R. Louis and R. Owen (1989), *Suez 1956: The Crisis and Its Consequences* (Oxford: Clarendon).

29 'Abu Zeid: African water resources not properly utilized', *Arabic News*, 19 June 1999.

30 Ethiopia is not just home to the headwaters of the Blue Nile, which contributed some 60 per cent to the sum total, but also the Atbara and Sobat (both joining the White Nile in Sudan) – in sum, that's 86 per cent of the Nile flow.

31 http://www.ethiopians.com/abay/nilepolitics.html

32 'As thick as blood', *The Economist*, 23 December 1995.

33 Not all those dams are built on Nile tributaries. Ethiopia also has a number of smaller rivers it can exploit.

34 http://american.edu/ted/ice/bluenile.htm based on Swain (last accessed on May 2010).

35 'East Africans consider pulling out of Nile water treaty', *Sudan Tribune*, 16 January 2004, 'Lake Victoria treaty flawed, says State', *Daily Nation*, 11 December 2003, Cam McGrath and Sonny Inbaraj, 'Water wars loom along the Nile', *News 24*, 16 January 2004.

36 'Nile: Kahama Project "Won't Affect Victoria"', *The East African*, 16 February 2004; Tanzania's Minister of Water Resources Edward Lowasa speaking to *Al-Ahram Weekly*, 10–16 June 2004, Issue No. 694.

37 Amy Dockser Marcus and Marcus Brauchli, 'Greenpolitik: Threats to Environment Provoke a New Security Agenda', *The Wall Street Journal*, 20 November 1997.

38 Hydromet (Hydrometeorological Survey of the Catchments of Lakes Victoria, Kyoga, and Mobutu Sese Seku), an initiative of the East African states, supported by UNDP and the World Metereological Office that took off in 1967. At the sixty-seventh meeting of Undugu in Kampala in December 1992, the Egyptians convinced the other Undugu participants to structure it into a more scientific organisation, the Technical Cooperation Committee for the Promotion of the Development and Environmental Protection of the Nile (Tecconile). Burundi, Eritrea, and Kenya and Ethiopia opted for observer status.

39 *Al-Ahram Weekly*, 26 April to 2 May 2001, Issue No. 531. http://weekly.ahram.org.eg/2001/531/special.htm.

40 'Egypt and the Horn of Africa', *Addis Tribune*, June 26 1998.

41 'Egyptian-Sudanese-Ethiopia project for joint use of Nile water', *ArabicNews*, 17 September 1999.

Notes to Chapter 3

1 Before the Keban dam was built at the confluence of Firat (upper Euphrates) and Murat, the lowest Euphrates flow of 136 m^3/s had been recorded in September 1961, while May 1944 had seen a maximum flood of 6,600 m^3/s.

2 Middle East Watch, 'Genocide in Iraq, the Anfal Campaign against the Kurds' (New York, July 1993), quoted in Jongerden (1994).

3 Zùrcher does not rule out renewed claims on Mosul. Turkish incursions in North Iraq have continued and ambiguous statements on Mosul were made at the time of the 2003 war on Iraq and again in 2007. One version has it that should Iraq be divided, Turkey may stake its claim to the oil rather than the cities ('Former NSC head: If Iraq falls apart, Turkey has rights in Kirkuk, Mosul', *New Anatolian*, March 2007).

4 Arslan, Esan (2005), 'New alternative: Pax Turkistana after pax Turcica', *Turkish Weekly*, 30 June.

5 Not all of these dams are in fact on the Euphrates or Tigris themselves – eight dams are planned under GAP in the valley of the River Munzur in Tunceli and three more on the Greater Zap in Hakkari province (Ronayne, 2005).

6 Israeli maverick Boaz Wachtel also proposed a Peace Channel in the heady days of the Oslo Accords. Turkey has also offered to carry water to Israel through pipelines under the sea.

7 E.g. www.turkishpress.com/turkishpress/news.asp?ID=17281) and www.fas.usda.gov/pecad2/highlights/2001/08/turkey_gap/pictures/turkey_gap.htm.

8 The government only recognises three minorities with a right to practice their customs: Jewish, Greek Orthodox, and Armenian Orthodox communities. The Kurds, an ethnically distinct Sunni Muslim group, are excluded from this protection (Reyes Gaskin, 2005).

9 'Atatürk has a stored capacity of 48.7 km^3, or over *three* years flow of the Euphrates below Atatürk Dam based on the Turkish–Syrian 1987 agreement (an average 500 m^3/s = 15.8 bcm/yr).' (MacQuarrie, 2004).

10 However, the Euphrates is not only charged by Turkish flows. 'The main difference between the Euphrates and Tigris in terms of how their discharge is generated is that the Tigris receives water from a series of major tributaries in the mid-portion of its course. In contrast, on the Euphrates, all of the major tributaries are in the extreme upper part of the basin' (Beaumont, 1999).

11 While Turkey views the Euphrates-Tigris basin as all-Turkish, the state takes the reverse position vis-à-vis the Orontes (or Asi) on which it is downstream (Shapland, 1997). The Orontes rises in Lebanon, then flows through Syria where its flow is heavily regulated. Here, there is a strong material linkage to the continuing Syrian claim to Hatay (province of Alexandretta), which was given to Turkey while still under colonial rule. Syrians have never accepted this decision, and continue to see the province as theirs.

12 The 'one river' concept is undermined by its refusal to accept Syria's claim on the Orontes (Asi), which (now) originates in Syria.

13 The Treaty of Friendship and Good Neighbourliness signed in 1946 by Iraq and Turkey was the first real legal instrument for cooperation. It included a Protocol for the Control of the Waters of the Tigris and Euphrates, and their tributaries. They agreed that flood control structures and storage services should be built upstream on Turkish territory, which was the most effective location. The Turks promised to provide daily hydrological and meteorological data concerning floods (Gruen, 2000).

14 Darwish, Adel, 'Water is behind Turkey-Syria border tension', *Middle East News*, 6 October 1998. Darwish's alarmist journalistic book with John Bullock, *Water Wars* (Bullock and Darwish 1993) fuelled the environmental wars furore in the 1990s, especially in the USA.

15 Moreover, the Bank needs to keep some customers, such as Egypt on board in order to keep moving money; its clout is, to a great degree, a function of its huge budget.

16 Cited in Metin Munir (2004), Turkey: Corruption http://www.globalintegrity.org/reports/2004/2004/country8683.html?cc=tr&act=notebook) (last accessed 22 May 2010).

17 According to the 2005 Update of the Environmental Impact Analysis Report, ten alternatives were considered in 1971, nine of which were in a narrow valley section, one in a wider space. All were tested for watertightness in a limestone area, which made areas rich in karst, gypsum and anhydrite areas unsuitable. The conditions for Ilisu were deemed best in spite of the need for large embankments. To prevent leakage a reduction in dam height by 55 m (from the present 135) would save Hasankeyf but halve the energy capacity. A series of small dams would not reduce costs and reduce effectiveness of flood peak regulation. One or more smaller reservoirs upstream of Hasankeyf combined with a lower dam could channel water into a second basin near Ilisu to feed to turbines, an option that has the Prime Minister's ear. After 2001, an alternative (controversial) rescue plan for Hasankeyf's cultural heritage was developed.

18 On the way to the splendid Anatolia Museum in Ankara you can see a lot of unprotected historic sites on the hill, giving the visitor the impression that there is just too much to properly protect – an embarrassment of riches is certainly in evidence.

19 Efes, near Izmir on the Turkish west coast, is a well-known and well preserved historic site.

20 The biggest problems would be posed by the foundation of 'Little Palace' and the collapse of some of the roofs of the adjacent man-made cave dwellings carved in rock because there is not enough physical support (Akgün, 2005). On 8 July 2005 out of three alternatives for rebuilding the affected parts of Hasankeyf, the alternative was picked that would prove the biggest touristic potential: a museum and an archaeological park will emerge in the upper city.

21 E.g. 'The Ilisu Dam – a human rights disaster in the making', www.thecornerhouse .org.uk/item.shtml?x=52191 (last accessed 20 May 2010).

22 Kristine Drew (2002), 'Recommendations to the U.K. Export Credit Agency, Public Services International Research Unit (PSIRU), University of Greenwich, and UNICORN.'

23 According to its opponents, the reservoir will bring waterborne diseases like malaria to the region, groundwater level will fall and the riverbed will erode in the downstream area. Ecologists also worry that the dam will threaten several bird species (Bosshard, 1999).

24 The Malaysian Pergau dam project, involving ABB and British company Biwater, turned into a scandal when technical development aid turned out to be tied in with British arms deliveries (the Malaysian government did not have to do much more than retract its Buy British Last-policy) and that Biwater had donated great sums to the then Conservative government.

25 www.parliament.the-stationery-office.co.uk/pa/cm199900/cmhansrd/vo000215/halltext/00215h01.htm (last accessed 22 May 2010).

26 A passive revolution is a radical change on the mode of rule with a view to reproducing primacy.

27 Reported in, e.g. Donald Smith (2000), Protests grow over plan for more Turkish Dams', *National Geographic* News, http://news.nationalgeographic .com/news/2000/12/1201_turkey.html (last accessed 22 May, 2010).

28 Laura Smith-Spark, Turkey dam project back to haunt Kurds, 5 August 2006, BBC News; Emíne Kart/Fulya Özerkan, Ilisu Dam: A gold necklace for Tigris or a rope around Hasankeyf's neck, *Turkish Daily News*, 13 August 2006.

29 The press reports professional criticism of a 'mechanical way of dealing with history', Ethem Torunoğlu, the head of an honorary board of the Turkish Union of Engineers and Architects Chambers (TMMOB) Chamber of Environmental Engineers.

30 'Turkije leent miljard voor bouw omstreden dam', *Engineering* 360°, 15 August 2007.

31 Turkey: Final warning for Ilısu Dam from European governments, *Turkish Daily*, 28 October 2008, http://www.turkishdailynews.com.tr/article.php?enewsid=117063.

32 More Speed, Less Haste Results In Turkish Nuclear Tender Fiasco *Eurasia Daily Monitor* 5: 184, 25 Septtember 2008.

33 http://www.livius.org/men-mh/mesopotamia/tigris.html (last accessed 22 May 2010)

34 The below bizarre (and not very factual) 2003 quote from CIA's Stephen Pelletier in the *New York Times* (quoted in Selby, 2005) seems to give an indication of how at least some overheated Americans in high places think:

> We are constantly reminded that Iraq has perhaps the world's largest reserves of oil. But in a regional and perhaps even geopolitical sense, it may be more important that Iraq has the most extensive river system in the Middle East. In the 1990s there was much discussion over the construction of a so-called Peace Pipeline that would bring the waters of the Tigris and Euphrates south to the parched Gulf States and, by extension, Israel. No progress has been made on this, largely because of Iraqi intransigence. With Iraq in American hands, of course, all that could change. Thus America could alter the destiny of the Middle East in a way that probably could not be changed for decades – not solely by controlling Iraq's oil, but by controlling its water.

Notes to Chapter 4

1 In 1995, FAP-20 was rechristened the Compartmentalisation Pilot Project, which confusingly shares its acronym (CPP) with a subsequent Bangladeshi scheme, the Coastal Protection Project. For that reason, the present document will generally refer to FAP-20 despite the name change.

2 Sharmeen Murshid, 'Water Discourse. Where Have All the Women Gone?'; *The Daily Star*; no. 322, 15 July 1998 and 17 November 1999.

3 NGOs cannot escape the spiral of corruption. The NGO desk is under the Prime Minister's Office, which reportedly demands bribes for its services. The desk can decide whether an NGO is eligible for an internationally funded project. Due to the politicisation of aid policy, the desk may be tempted to give the go-ahead to projects that may be harmful to government policies (interviews, BNGO). The national security argument can be exercised, Ahmed (1999) quotes from a 1988 circular: 'The participation of NGOs in development will be encouraged if otherwise not found detrimental to government policy or national security'.

4 'Hague wants to place FAP before JS', *Daily Star*, 4 June 1994.

5 ICCO (The Interchurch Cooperation Organisation) and NOVIB (now Oxfam-Novib) are Dutch development organisations which receive part of their funding from public (government) sources.

6 A good example are the Association of Engineers of Bangladesh Water Development Board's 'Comments on draft Bangladesh Water and Flood Management Strategy proposal by FPCO in March', 1995.

7 Apart from the issue whether they are equipped for this, it is the fundamental prerogative of the executive to set conditions and evaluation standards.

8 Japan is currently the biggest bilateral aid donor followed by the USA (Kronstadt, 2003).

9 http://siteresources.worldbank.org/EXTWSS/Resources/337301-1147283795581/FloodStrategyatWorldBank.pdf (last accessed 22 May 2010).

10 FAO, The State of Food and Agriculture (SOFA) 1997.

11 The resentment and frustration over this Indian move is echoed in the comments by the Bangladesh Association of Water and Power Engineers. A paragraph in

the 1995 National Water Strategy (FPCO) predicting the drying up of the Ganges below Farakka was slammed by the Association as 'suicidal' rather than a realistic resignation to regional geopolitical realities.

12 Troubled by the Farakka dam, Bangladesh raised the Ganges issue with the UN General Assembly in 1976, leading to an agreement in 1977. In 1996 India and Bangladesh signed a water-sharing treaty. India was however slow to renew the agreement. Bangladaesh mooted its own Ganges barrage in the 1970s, but has not yet built it. In 1996 a India and Bangladesh signed a water-shaving treaty India's river linking plan however would transfer water out of the Brahmaputra into the Ganges. Reservoirs have been built in India on the southern Ganga branches (Harun ur-rashid), but not yet on the northern ones that affect Bangladesh.

13 'The arrogance! What he says is right and he won't listen to anyone else [...] He is a liar.' (pers. comm.)

14 The Surface Water Modelling Centre, Dhaka, has continued to model a sequence of compartments along the Jamuna, despite the abandonment of compartmentalisation.

15 FAP Monitor 4, 2(1), RAS (Research and Advisory Services), July 1996.

16 Outraged, Van der Laan protested, but on his return, it was too late to stop it. Anyway, 'The Hague was okay with anything' (interview, Dutch consultant). Euroconsult was unhappy too, and decided to build the sluices without the gates – these would have to await the participatory process (Jansen quoted in Smit, 1993). Piet Wit, who participated in the Dutch ministerial mission, is quoted (in Smit, 1993) as hinting that this stance may well be about the rich pickings to be had from construction. Whichever the case may be, Dirk Frans, the sociologist who devised the alternatives, left the project in a huff over this, but came back several times to help out and is now again involved in the Asian Development Bank's Southwest Area IWRM project.

17 There is of course a predictable overlap in stakeholder identities – boatmen may double as farmers or fishermen, who in turn may be women. Also landowners tend to diversify between plots at different altitudes and had plots inside and outside the project area.

18 To be fair on the French, FAP projects that were eventually adopted by the Franch did include experiments with participation.

19 For example, the Dutch Inspectorate's report on FAP-20 (IOV, 1993) loosely mentions security without explaining it, while the UNDP (Faaland et al., 1995) speaks of 'security, productivity and other development objectives' which places security square in the middle of a modernisation drive. The fifth of the Eleven Guiding Principles requires the 'safe conveyance of the large-scale cross-border flows to the Bay of Bengal' without explaining how safe and for whom it should be safe.

20 While the World Bank put the death toll in those two years at more than 3,000, and the official number was put at 2,379, Saleemul Huq (BCAS) claimed that '(t)he floods claimed only few victims, about 2000' (Salm, 1995), Wood (1999) puts the figure at 1,800 while Proshika puts the number at 'only 1500 – a lot fewer than are killed in traffic each year' (Salm, 1994). FPCO's Kamal Siddiqi quotes the same number. According to Pieter Smit, a critical Dutch political scientist, even that number is strongly exaggerated (Smit, 1993).

21 'Govt urged to suspend FAP activities', *Daily Star*, 26 November 1995.

22 We should not be too idealistic about the *beel* as a 'common pool resource', though. While open access de jure, there are unofficial *de facto* (nested) property rights. These informal rights may take precedence over formal rights.

23 The implication of controlled flooding is to sacrifice less valuable land for the benefit of more valuable land. Parker (1992) for example predicted that the embanking programme would increase the number of homeless as their land would be acquired to accommodate embankments and for sources of earth. This was not communicated.

24 However, conflicts are not always so clear-cut, as people who own land on one side of the embankment may live on the other side.

25 While the FAP case was not selected for the main event, its case generated considerable publicity when it was brought forward at the Second International Water Tribunal in Amsterdam in 1992.

26 It may be countered that NGOs had aligned themselves quite early on in two umbrella organisations, ADAB and CEN, and that they were very well informed 'through the grapevine' about each other's work.

27 Which, for the poor, is almost synonymous to saving lives.

28 To be eligible for services, some interviewees argue, the poor need to sign up to NGO membership, which lands them into a patron–client relationship with the NGO, which as a quid pro quo may require their loyal participation in protest activity.

29 Tangail, however, is a rather different setting. Dakatia is a tidal, undiked area, but Tangail was part-embanked and has no influence from tidal motion.

30 FAP-3.1 (Jamalpur), built on a compartmentalisation concept similar to FAP-20, became controversial as the 1.5 million *char* dwellers living in and in the stretch of the Jamuna immediately adjacent to the project area demanded protection and other protests over impeded fish migration and compensation. It was claimed that in total, FAP-3.1 would displace 6 million people. The original terms were radically revised to provide for flood-proofing (Faaland et al., 1995). When first the European Parliament called for a moratorium on construction (*Bangladesh Environmental Newsletter* 6(2), April–June 1995), and later on the Dutch and German donor balked, pushed by persistent NGO protest, the participation aspect was eventually significantly upgraded.

31 When there is resistance to a project, the Asian Development Bank, the World Bank's regional sister, 'gets the highest managers in and forms a very heavy evaluatory commission. NGOs play on that, it's an instrument of political power.' (interview, Dutch consultant)

32 In the 1994 BELA case, FAP-20 was also claimed to endanger two archaeological sites listed under the Antiquities Act, 1968: the Attia Mosque and the Kadim Mamdani Mosque. Mohiuddin Farooque and Sekandar Ali Mondol vs. Bangladesh (Writ Petition No. 998 of 1994), in UNEP Partnership for the Development of Environmental Law and Institutions in Africa (PADELIA) (2001), Compendium of Judicial Decisions on Matters Related to Environment, Vol. II National issues pp. 112–28.

33 *Bangladesh Observer*, 6 September 1996.

34 The Court however ruled in 1997 that the Minister should draft new bye-laws to regulate compensation.

35 This 50–50 partition is for the dry season (March–June). In case the flow below Farakka is 70,000 cubic feet per second (cusecs) or less – if the amount is between

70,000 and 75,000, Bangladesh receives 35,000 and India the balance; if over 80,000 cusecs Bangladesh gets 40,000 and India again gets the balance (Sands, 1997).

36 Natural causes were claimed by officials. Alternative stories quickly emerged: some Bangladeshi interviewees claim to have heard explosions, reinforcing a local feeling their area was the site of a real-life experiment. Others (mainly Dutch) say one bank may have been strategically eroded so that it would collapse at the next major wave action in due course, while the then Team Leader claims it was unclogged by hand paid for by the World Food Programme.

37 Bangladesh Ministry of Water Resources, 'Report on the Flood Action Plan', 1994.

38 The Indian Farakka Dam was built on the Ganges without prior consultation with Bangladesh in 1975, to conserve water from the river Hooghly for the winter season. Even bigger projects to solve Bangladesh's flood problems include international schemes, notably upstream dams in Nepal and Assam. A problem however is that these will have a marginal effect on the water level (Berne University, 1995).

39 This aspect was indeed firm in the minds of the local population: the FAP-20 recipients identified 'flood control' as the project's number one objective, rather than 'water management' (Shamunnay, 1996).

40 Mirza Shakil, 'Encroachers turn Louhajang river into a narrow stream', *Daily Star*, 10 July 2006; 'No step yet to free Louhajang, Bairan rivers from grabbers. Tangail AC says list of encroachers being prepared', *Daily Star*, 23 April 2007.

41 The 'epistemic community' approach to regimes developed by P. Haas (1992) sees regimes as a way of reducing 'noise' in providing a clearing house for information, enabling the participating actors to learn. New functional knowledge may lead to evolutionary change, changing rules and procedures as the regime 'learns', or revolutionary change, generating new principles and norms. 'Epistemic communities' converge on a body of accepted scientific procedure and evidence.

42 This fulfilled the catastrophic potential of rivers predicted by the Bengali professor Mahalanobis in 1927 and later in 1964, by the Dutch Professor Thijsse. This cast new doubt on the control paradigm that was already sown when the Mississippi flood showed the impossibility of taming some floods – a message that was carried over into the Hughes report on Bangladesh, on which Shapan Adnan co-authored (Hughes et al., 1994).

43 For powerful pumps to support the drainage of polders – in this respect the experiences are not very different from the mixed results of poldering in Bangladesh.

44 www.emergency-management.net/flood.htm (last accessed 22 May 2010).

45 Water security is now defined to mean that all people, including the world's poor,

- have access to water services to meet their basic needs;
- are able to take advantage of the opportunities that water resources provide;
- are protected from water-related hazards; and
- have recourse where conflicts over water arise.

Notes to Chapter 5

1 Still, one interviewee was disappointed that Van der Ven's challenges did not generate a more lively exchange of views. 'It is telling how his criticism was not picked up in the press and the debate died down. In a way that is unfortunate'.

2 'Irritatie, ergernis en zorg over te lage Maasdijken', *De Gelderlander*, 15 June 1999.

3 'Van Voorst tot Voorst: Maas had hoger gemogen', *De Limburger*, ed. Zuid, 21 January 2000; 'Geen magere alternatieven voor de Maas', *De Gelderlander*, 10 June 1999.
4 On KNAG Discussieforum, response to article by G.P. van der Ven.
5 Cllr Math Vestjens was one of the most fervent defenders against deprioritisation of the project ever since taking office in the Provincial Council in 1995 and the Provincial authority in 1998.
6 Peet Adams, 'Lobby-offensief voor Grensmaas', *De Limburger*, 3 July 2003.
7 Equivalent to the Department of Trade and Industry in the UK.
8 Despite the policy guideline, RWS was negotiating with municipalities to allow only very limited construction in the flood plain, the Minister for Transport granted Oolder Veste, a new residential area, 'pipeline status' which means dispensation from the moratorium on building in the flood plain (Wolsink 2006). T de Haan, then Chief Inspector for Limburg, is unhappy about it from a river management perspective. 'But once the Minister has decided, this is a "hard fact" for us we cannot contravene' ('"Slaapverwekkend of rond-Hollands" betogen over Oolder Veste', *De Limburger*, 23 December 1999.
9 http://www.rijkswaterstaat.nl/wateroverzicht/maaswerken/, accessed March 2006.
10 *Nieuwsnet Limburg*, 27 May 1999.
11 'Maaswerken van start. ik durf nu hier te blijven', *De Limburger*, 18 June 2005. The municipality of Haelen contracted of its own accord Kupers, a private company, to provide big inflatable bags, which can be in place within 36 hours in case of emergency (*De Limburger*, 1 February 2002). Meanwhile, Roermond now has a mobile water dam, shaped like an 'inflatable sausage' (*De Limburger*, 25 October 2001).
12 'Arcen en Velden voert overleg over strategie Zandmaas', *De Limburger*, 28 November 1998.
13 *De Gelderlander*, 13 August 1999.
14 Geo-Control B.V., Exploitatiemaatschappij L'Ortye Stein B.V., Vereniging tot behoud van Natuurmonumenten in Nederland, Boskalis B.V., HAM-Van Oord-Werkendam B.V., Ballast Nedam Baggeren B.V. en Van den Biggelaar Aannemingsbedrijf B.V.
15 Arthur Sassen, 'Geulle zegt 'NEE' tegen ontgrinding', http://www.geulle.com/geulle/nieuws/250401nieuws.html (last accessed 11 July 2010).
16 http://home.hetnet.nl/~milieustichting/achttien.htm *Limburger* 10-7-2002. (last accessed 23 May 2010).
17 Peet Adams, 'Een brave straatvechter', *De Limburger*, 5 June 2002.
18 Bosscherveld – Geulle aan de Maas – Meers – Maasband – Urmond; – Nattenhoven – Roosteren
19 'CDA wil natuur schrappen in Zandmaas', *De Limburger*, 18 January 2003.
20 'Provincie wil Grensmaas niet openbaar', *De Limburger*, 15 November 2001.
21 'Under Dutch law, expropriation is not an option if the landowner is able to carry out the desired work, and gravel extraction companies can arguably carry out river widening measures'.
22 The so-called *Pikmeerarrest* established public servants and agencies cannot be prosecuted for carrying out legally prescribed administrative tasks. When the ruling was

reviewed in 1998, the Supreme Court decided only national authorities enjoyed this immunity.

23 Peet Adams and Bjorn Oostra, 'Topberaad over stort Maaswerken', *De Limburger,* 2 Febuary 2002. Also see Van der Meulen et al. (2006: 166).

24 Peet Adams, 'Volledige top van De Maaswerken weg', *De Limburger*, 25 January 2002.

25 'Rijk dreigt Grensmaas af te blazen', *Bodemnieuws Nieuwsbrief*, March 2005.

26 Peet Adams, 'Akkoord beveiliging Maas in M-Limburg'; *De Limburger* 2 July 2004.

27 *De Water*, No. 108, July 2005.

28 Sometimes conflated: Landscape is 'securitised' by one stakeholder as part of the cultural heritage.

29 Paul Bots, 'Gaten in kaden dichten gaat niet zomaar', *De Limburger/Limburgs Dagblad*, 6 November 2007.

Notes to Chapter 6

1 E.g. '. . . participatory approaches generating consensus and enthusiasm within the community for adoption of IFM; autonomous management; and mechanisms for equitable distribution of benefits.' (www.nisp.org).

2 It is acknowledged with thanks that the study was sponsored by Wageningen University's Boundaries of Space programme, and carried out together with Dik Roth and Madelinde Winnubst. A slightly shorter version of the present chapter appears in the *International Journal of Water Resources Development* in March 2008.

3 When a concerned Prince William Alexander inquired what the flood had been like, people responded; 'what flood?' (http://www.wrlent.nl/downloads/achtergrond 26april.pdf). The Prince also appeared to believe that controlled flood storage would save Rotterdam, but this does not make much hydrological sense (interviews).

4 Note that the respondent does not talk about conferring with stakeholders.

5 It was a variety of the legal concept of a 'calamitous polder', a polder that so often has to cope with flooding that polder inhabitants cannot raise the cost of damage and recovery themselves (Klijn and van der Most 2001: 2–6).

6 Experts like Wim Silva (RIZA), and Matthijs Kok (HKV Lijn in Water, formerly WL | Delft) and Richard Jorissen (DWW) were among the key people involved in this.

7 Presentation at 'Ruimtelijke bijdrage aan gevolgenbeperking', an expert meeting on flood impact mitigation, NIROV/Spatial Planning Department, The Hague, 10 October 2007.

8 Technische Adviescommissie Waterkeringen, draft advice to the Luteijn Commission, 13 September 2002 and eventual advice, 8 October 2002.

9 In November 2007 a study by Aachen University was announced on how to handle a dike break at Erlecom (Figure 6.2). Such a calamity would flood both the Dutch and German sides of the Ooij and Duffelt polder. The study involved the reinstatement of the compartmentalisation of the polder, abandoned in the 1920s. The Ooij platform responded saying it would not protest the study, as compartmentalisation is about reducing impact rather than cutting dikes to save others. Geert Willems, 'Querdamm en Kapitteldijk hoger', *De Gelderlander*, 15 November 2007.

Notes to Chapter 7

1 RPS Landscape Management and Planning Consultants, Clouston, Didcot.

2 Appalling pollution in the Thames gave rise to the first European water policy (Newson) culminating in the 1951 Report of the Peppard Committee to improve water quality sufficiently for the salmon to return.

3 http://www7.caret.cam.ac.uk/windsor_maid_intro.htm (last accessed 25 May 2010).

4 The pattern of main or non-main rivers follows no set rule. 'Enmaining' (legally reclassifying 'critical ordinary watercourses' as 'main river') must be accepted by the Regional Flood Defence Committee, and 'committees have sometimes refused applications for rivers whose flood defences are in poor condition or absent' (Oxera/MAFF, 2001: 14). The upshot is that the (minor) Clapper Stream, another source of occasional local flooding in the project area, cannot be handled by the Environment Agency, since the institution has no authority over it, it being non-main water (Venables, 2000).

5 'The local authority appointees who sit on the RFDCs are bound to act as members of an EA committee, not as representatives of local authorities, although it is not clear that this distinction is always made in practice, and if it were, an element of local accountability that appears to exist *de facto* from current practice might be lost'. [2nd interim report 2001] The Drainage Boards, established in 1930 have permissive powers to 'enter land' and carry out works on non-main channels (Scrase and Sheate, 2005). While flood-defence work on non-main rivers outside the areas covered by Internal Drainage Districts are the realm of Local Authority. National grant-aid supplemented the levies raised by catchment organisations, IDBs and local authorities until 2003. The committees are formally part of the EA but have a larger mandate beyond that of either of its constituents.

6 The Land Drainage Act of 1991 lays down the IDB's drainage mandate, while the Water Resources Act 1991 relates to the functions and powers of the EA and the flood-defence committees.

7 Interviewees noted that the same held true for Railtrack, with whom the EA worked together to enable the jacking of an underpass under the railway embankment.

8 Memorandum submitted by The Environment Agency (F21) to Select Agricultural Committee, House of Commons, Minutes of Evidence, 1998.

9 '. . . as rivers keep on rising', *The Independent*, 9 February 1990.

10 Cost estimates rose from £51 million (NRA 1989) and £83.5 million or £14,000 per protected house including to £43.75 million for implementation and O&M for 65 years (EA, 1998), to £110 million. This was largely covered by an increase in the council tax (community charge) levy by 6.3 per cent for the fiscal year 1999–2000, which brings in £62.5 million. 'Danger alert along river as levels rise' (*Maidenhead Advertiser*, 22 January 1999).

11 Middlesex University's submission to the 1998 Agricultural Select Committee notes that MAFF's scoring system had become even harder for new projects than the existing Project Appraisal Guidance Note (PAGN, 1995), requiring a cost-benefit ratio of 4 to 1 – to achieve a high priority in funding (Memorandum 22, Agricultural Select Committee, 1998), or as Crichton (2005) has it: 'Benefits have to exceed costs by at least a factor of three, with a national target of a factor of five'.

12 Maidenhead, Windsor and Eton Flood Alleviation Scheme – Environmental Statement Part I. National Rivers Authority, Thames Region.
13 http://www.spelthorne.gov.uk/contrast/pdf_floodreportjan2003.pdf. (last accessed 25 May 2010).
14 The CBA yields a *ratio*, rather than a difference, so it can make a difference whether an item appears as a negative cost or a positive benefit in the equation, even though the value is the same (Cited Green, pers. comm., 2001).
15 Though still 'relatively slow' compared to some upland rivers (Johnson, 2005).
16 'With the high ground of Windsor Castle on one side and the M4 Motorway on the other it is difficult to see any other realistic alternative solutions.' (RPS, 1993).
17 'While risk reduction is central to the DEFRA/NAW policy and implicit in current decision-making practice, explicit assessment of risks has in the past tended to be limited to the appraisal of major decisions to invest in flood defense infrastructure [. . .] The contribution that a wide range of interventions, including land-use planning, control of runoff, flood storage, flood warning, insurance, improving flood resistance of property, and operation and maintenance of flood defenses, makes to flood risk management has only recently begun to be analysed in a systematic way' (Hall et al., 2003: 226).
18 The Datchet, Wraysbury, Staines and Chertsey Floodplain Plan Study.
19 Matthew Gorman, 'EA admits at-risk flood areas need more protection', *Windsor Reporter*, 21 April 2005.
20 'Problems' S. 13, Memorandum 22 (F34), Select Agricultural Committee, 1998.
21 Note of Conference with Counsel, 19 September 1988.
22 Another formal objector to a Compulsory Planning Order was the *Department of Transport*. The MWEFAS needed a diversion on the M4 motorway, which got in the way of its Transport Ministry's own M4 motorway widening project. This and other complaints from landowners and agencies led to intense consultations between the DETR, Berkshire and Buckinghamshire.
23 Dorney Lake was the site for the BearingPoint Rowing World Cup 2005, the World Rowing Championships 2006 and has been selected for rowing and sprint canoeing in the Olympic Games 2012.
24 'Flooded with relief', *Quarrying Today*, Spring 2004, Issue 13. pp. 8–9. http://www.mineralproducts.org/documents/qtoday13.pdf (last accessed 25 May 2010).
25 Quoted in 'Trench threat to common ends', *Windsor, Slough and Eton Express* (WSEE), 31 March 1989.
26 'Villagers are told: Keep up the fight', *Maidenhead Advertiser*, 5 May 1995.
27 'Gravel pipeline backed', *Maidenhead Advertiser*, 9 June 1995.
28 'Flood channel will still go with the flow', *Maidenhead Advertiser*, 12 February 1999.
29 House of Commons, Select Committee on Agriculture, Sixth Report.
30 British policy discourse makes an interesting distinction between *statutory* rules, institutionalising protection from threats and *permissive*, discretionary measures. While spending on flood protection is *permissive*, Local Authorities and the Environment Agency *may* choose to do it – protecting the birds is *statutory* (Venables, 2000). The upshot is a lack of EA mandate for flood protection works.
31 It was officially opened by HRH Prince Andrew in July 2002, in honour of Queen Elizabeth's golden Jubilee. Among others, the project protects her Windsor castle and deer parks.

32 'Merit award swells Jubilee River trophies', *New Civil Engineer,* 19 September 2002: 39.

33 'Groups in flood role', *River views*, Environment Agency newsletter, September/October 2003. Huxley to Wraybsury, Wraysbury to Teddington and one dealing with Chertsey Bourne, which meets the Thames in the MWEFAS project area.

34 'Mechanisms of Flooding', Flood Risk Action Groups, Volume 1, 11.3.25, http://www.frags.org.uk/mech_vol1.htm (last accessed 25 May 2010). Subcontractor Arup also took flak for changing specifications of their role in the project in its work for MWEFAS in 1997–98. 'Channel Closure stokes Jubilee River row', *New Civil Engineer*, 6 May 2004, p. 12.

35 The borough comprises Ashford, Charlton, Halliford, Laleham, Littleton, Shepperton, Staines, Stanwell, Stanwell Moor and Sunbury.

36 *The Times,* 30 August 2004.

37 Francis Batt, 'Fears over flood showdown', icBerkshire, 3 June 2004; Francis Batt, 'Flood, sweat and jeers', 13 August 2004, icBerkshire; Mark Hansford, 'Arup denies downplaying its role on Jubilee river', *New Civil Engineer International*, 30 September 2004.

38 'Two-year-old flood relief channel already needs major repairs', *Ground Engineering*, 1 August 2004.

39 'Soft engineering comes up short', *New Civil Engineer International*, 1 October 2004.

40 'Repaired Jubilee river flood defence still 10 per cent under capacity', *New Civil Engineer* +, 21 September 2006.

41 *Windsor, Ascot and Maidenhead Observer*, 22 April 2005.

42 This progressive insight is reflected in the rather different answers to questions in the Commons asked in 2003 and 2006. When Parliamentary questions were posed by various regional Members on 15 January 2003 and 4 February 2003, Mr Morley (Minister of State for Climate Change and Environment) stated there was 'no effect on Medmenham and Marlow' and that a rerun of an updated hydrological model had been done which showed no significant effect. When on 6 June 2006, Adam Afriyie, MP for Windsor, asked again about Jubilee River and MWEFAS as a whole, Ian Pearson admitted the channel was functioning below standard. (http://www.publications.parliament.uk/pa/cm200506/cmhansrd/cm060626/text/60626w1189.htm) (last accessed 25 May 2010).

43 'EA sues designers of failed Jubilee River flood defence', *New Civil Engineer*+, 15 June 2006.

44 Michael Horsnell, 'Anger swells over claims that flood relief river shifts damage', *The Times*, 30 August 2004.

45 http://www.environment-agency.gov.uk/commondata/acrobat/lowerthames_strategy_948936.pdf (last accessed 25 May 2010).

46 'Repaired Jubilee river flood defence still 10 per cent under capacity', *New Civil Engineer* +, 21 September 2006.

47 'Locals may pay £200 flood scheme', BBC News, 7 December 2006.

48 www.publications.parliament.uk/pa/cm200607/cmhansrd/cm070724/debtext/70724–0008.htm (last accessed 11 July 2010).

49 www.jubileeriver.co.uk, www.environment-agency.gov.uk/news/113706.aspx. (both accessed 25 December 2009).

50 *Maidenhead Advertiser*, 5 May 1995.

51 'Downstream Flooding – Residents remain angry', thamesweb, 16 January 2004. Parliamentary questions on 4 February 2003 also give examples of constituency correspondents frequently mentioning the word 'sacrifice'.

52 This can be seen as a new step in a more inclusive trajectory. After the 2000 floods, the 'Flooding. You can't prevent it. You can prepare for it' campaign was launched. The year 2001 saw the publication of the civil engineering report, 'Learning to Live With Rivers', and in 2004 DEFRA issued a consultation document, 'Making Space for Rivers' which explicitly advocates stakeholder involvement, where 'stakeholder' is defined as 'all those individuals and groups affected by flood and coastal erosion risks and/or able to influence the development of approaches to flood or coastal erosion risk management decision making' (Defra, 2004b: 2). It claims 'members of the community should have input both of their knowledge of the local characteristics of flooding and the community in terms of their preferences and priorities for flood' (Speller, 2005).

53 'The town at greatest risk of flooding', *The Times*, 3 December 2007.

Notes to Chapter 8

1 This is not a necessary course of action. The US Corps of Engineers made a public apology for the New Orleans flood and admitted error of judgment and construction faults.

2 Also, the campaign to save the wild hamster (*creticus creticus, korenwolf*) for the Netherlands came at a time neighbouring Germany experienced a wild hamster plague.

3 But revealing this appears to have been a public taboo. The project Security Map for the Netherlands (VKN) would mercilessly reveal differences in protection. Only after a government-commissioned report (Bannink et al., 2004) in 2004 decried the lack of knowledge and poor state of many dikes, the Vice-Minister allowed the publication (declassification) of the Security map.

4 Graeme Wearden (2007), 'Insurers say authorities partly to blame for flood damage', *Guardian,* 20 August.

BIBLIOGRAPHY

Abdelazim, Saleh S. (2002). *Structural Adjustment and the Dismantling of Egypt's Etatist System*, PhD Dissertation, Blacksburg, Va.: Virginia Polytechnic.

Adnan, S., Ghani, M., Uddin, S., Khandaker, S., Dewan, A., Zaker, S., Suflyan, A., Manic, S., Hossain, A. and Akhter, S. (1991). *Floods, People and the Environment: Institutional Aspects of Flood Protection Programmes in Bangladesh*, 1990. Dhaka: Research and Advisory Services, Dhaka.

Adnan, Shapan. (1992). *People's participation, NGOs, and the Flood Action Plan. An independent review*. Dhaka: Research & Advisory Services/Oxfam.

Aerts, J. (2006). 'Bewoner van riviergebied extra belasten'. *De Gelderlander*, 22 December.

Agamben, Giorgio (1998). *Homo Sacer*, Stanford, Ca.: Stanford University Press.

Ahmad, Q. K., Chowdhury, A. K. A., Imam S. H. and Sarker, M. (ed.), *The Perspectives on Flood 1998*, Dhaka: University Press.

Ahmed, M. (1999). *Bottom Up. The NGO Sector in Bangladesh*. Dhaka: Community Development Library.

Ahmed, Raqub. (1998). 'Land, soil and landscape' in Gain, Philip (ed.), *Bangladesh: Facing the 21st Century*, Dhaka: Society for Environment and Human Development.

Akgün, H. (2003). 'Remediation of the geotechnical problems of the Hasankeyf historical area, Southeastern Turkey', *Environmental Geology* 44 (5): 522–9.

Alam, Khorshed. 'An experience of FAP-20 pilot project', presented at the Conference on Food Security, FAP and Bangladesh, 5–6 December 1996, Brussels: European Parliament.

Alam, S., Chadwick, M. and Soussan, J. (1998). 'Understanding Water Resources: Resource Characteristics and Water Sector Planning in Bangladesh', National Resources Systems Programme, Report No. 577, Leeds: University of Leeds.

Ali, M., Hoque, M. M., Rahman, R. and Rashid, S. (eds.) (1998). *Bangladesh Floods – View from Home and Abroad*, Dhaka: University Press.

Ali, Tariq and Hossain, Naomi. (2006). 'Popular Expectations of Government: Findings from Three Areas', Dhaka: Bangladesh Rural Advancement Committee/Bangladesh Institute for Development Studies.

Alim, Md Abdul. (2004). '*Shalish* and the Role of BRAC's Federation: Improving the Poor's Access to Justice', Institute of Social Studies research paper, SSRN series. The Hague: Institute of Social Studies.

Allan, J. Anthony. (1990). 'The Nile basin: Evolving Approaches To Nile Waters Management', SOAS, University of London, Occasional Paper 20, SOAS Water Issues Group, June 1990, http://www.soas.ac.uk/waterissues/occasionalpapers/OCC20.PDF

Allan, J. Anthony. (1997). '"Virtual Water": A Long Term Solution for Water Short Middle Eastern Economies?' Occasional Paper 3, SOAS Water Issues Group, September.

Allan, J. Anthony. (2001). *The Middle East Water Question: Hydro-Politics and the Global Economy*, London: I.B.Tauris.

Allen, Katrina. (2002). Meanings and Constraints: Processes Shaping Vulnerability Reduction in Philippine National Red Cross, PhD Dissertation, Flood Hazard Research Centre, Middlesex University.

Allen, Katrina. (2003). 'Vulnerability reduction and the community-based approach: a Philippines study'. In: Mark Pelling (ed.), *Natural Disasters and Development in a Globalizing World*, London: Routledge, 170–85.

Allouche, Jeremy. (2003). Water Nationalism. An explanation of the past and present conflicts in Central Asia, the Middle East and the Indian subcontinent, Thesis No 605, Geneva: Institut Universitaire des Hautes Études Internationales, University of Geneva.

Alterman, Jon B. (1998). 'Sudan may emerge as irritant to US', *Policywatch*, No 311.

Amare, Girma (2000). 'Nile Waters Hydrological Co-operation Vs. Hydropolitics': Proceedings of the eighth Nile 2002 Conference (June 26–29) Addis Ababa.

Aradau, C. (2001). 'Beyond Good and Evil: Ethics and Securitization/Desecuritization Techniques', *Rubikon*, December.

Arendt, H. (1985). 'Decline of the nation-sate: End of the rights of man', in Arendt, *The Origins of Totalitarianism*, New York/Orlando, FL: Harcourt, pp. 267–302.

Arts, Bas, and Tatenhove, Jan van. (2000). 'Environmental policy arrangements: A new concept', in H. Goverde (ed.) *Global and European Polity? Organizations, Policies, Contexts*, Aldershot: Ashgate.

Associated Programme on Flood Management. (2006). 'Integrated Flood Management'. Concept paper, World Meteorological Organisation/Global Water Partnership.

Austin, J. L. (1962). *How To Do Things with Words: The William James Lectures Delivered at Harvard University in 1955*, Oxford: Clarendon.

Aydin, Mustafa. (2003). 'Securitization of history and geography: Understanding of security in Turkey', *Journal of Southeast European and Black Sea Studies* 3 (2): 163-84.

Bachrach, Peter and Baratz, Morton S. (1970), *Power and Poverty, Theory and Practice*. London, New York: Open University Press.

Bak, Per. (1996). *How Nature Works*. New York: Springer-Verlag.

Baker, Marcia Merry. (1997). 'Mubarak: Tushka Project opens way towards new civilization in Egypt', *The Executive Intelligence Review*, December.

Bakker, Karen. (1999). 'The politics of hydropower: Developing the Mekong, *Political Geography* 18: 209–232.

Bakker, Karen, Babiano, Luis and Giansante, Consuelo. (2006). 'La Mercantiliación del Agua.' In Carlos Crespo & Susan Spronk, *Despùes de las guerras del agua*, Cochabamba/La Paz: Universidad M. de San Simón (CESU)/Plural, 25–70.

Bakker, K., Downing, T., Garrido, A., Giansante, C., Iglesias, E., Moral, L. del, Pedregal, B., Riesco, P. and the SIRCH Team (eds.). (1999). 'Societal and Institutional Responses to Climate Change and Climatic Hazards: Managing Changing Flood and Drought Risk', SIRCH Working Paper #3: A Framework for Institutional Analysis., Oxford: Oxford University.

Bakker, K., Downing, T., Handmer, J., Crook E. and Penning-Rowsell, E. (n.d), 'Hydrological risk in the Thames Valley', Background Monograph for the SIRCH project.

Balat, M. (2003). 'Southeastern Anatolia Project (GAP) of Turkey and Regional Development Applications'. *Energy Exploration & Exploitation* 21 (5–6): 391–404(14).

Balzacq, Thierry. (2005). 'The three faces of securitization'. *European Journal of International Relations* 111 (2): 171–201.

Bannink, Bert A. and ten Brinke, Wilfried B. M. (2004). *Risico's in bedijkte termen, een thematische evaluatie van het Nederlandse veiligheidsbeleid tegen overstromen*, De Bilt:

Rijksinstiutuut voor Volksgezondheid en Milieuhygiëne, http://www.rivm.nl/bibliotheek/rapporten/500799002.html (last accessed 10 July 2010).

BARC. (1989). *A Policy Brief on "Floodplain Agriculture."* Dhaka: Bangladesh Agricultural Research Council.

Barkey, H. J. and Fuller, G. E. (1998). Turkey's Kurdish Questions, New York: Rowman & Littlefield.

Bari, Z. (1977), 'Syrian-Iraqi disputes over the river Euphrates', *International Studies* 16 (2): 227–244.

Barnett, Michael N. (1999). 'Culture, strategy and foreign policy change: Israel's road to Oslo'. *European Journal of International Relations* 5: 5–36.

Bate, Roger. (2001). 'The environment: Bangladesh: basket-case of choice for green alarmists', *Economic Affairs* 21 (2): 56.

Bauman, Zygmunt. (1999). *In Search of Politics*, London: Polity Press.

Baumgartner, Frank R. and Jones Bryan D. (1991). 'Agenda dynamics and policy subsystems'. *Journal of Politics* 53 (4): 1044–74.

Beaumont, Peter (1998). 'Restructuring of water usage in the Tigris-Euphrates basin: The impact of modern water management policies', Conference: Middle Eastern Natural Environments. *Yale University School of Forestry and Environmental Studies Bulletin* 103: 168–86 http://environment.research.yale.edu/documents/downloads/0-9/103beaumont.pdf (last accessed 10 July 2010).

Beaumont, Peter. (1991). 'Transboundary Water Disputes in the Middle East', International Conference on Transboundary Waters in the Middle East: Prospects for Regional Co-operation, Sept. 2-3, Ankara: Bilkent University.

Beblawi, Hazem and Luciani, Giacomo. (eds.). (1987). *The Rentier State*, London: Croom Helm.

Beck, U. G. and Lash, S. (1994). *Reflexive Modernisation*, Cambridge, Polity Press.

Beetham, David. (1991). *The Legitimation of Power*, Basingstoke: Macmillan.

Behnke, Andreas. (2007). 'Presence and creation: A few (meta-)critical comments on the c.a.s.e. manifesto', *Security Dialogue* 38 (1): 105–111.

BELA (Bangladesh Environmental Lawyers Association), 'FLOOD and FAP. The transnational twins', *BELA Bulletin. A quarterly bulletin on people & the FAP-20*, 1(3), March–May 1999.

Béland, Daniel. (2005). Insecurity, citizenship, and globalization: The multiple faces of state protection, *Sociological Theory*, 23 (1): 25: 41, http://www.danielbeland.org/pubs/Beland2005(SociologicalTheory).pdf (last accessed 10 July 2010).

Belshaw, Deryke and Belshaw, Roger. (1999). 'Rising Natural Resource Scarcity and Geopolitical Tension in the Nile basin: Poverty Reduction and Conflict Prevention through Multi-national Water Agreements', paper for the Spring Seminar, Conflict and Security Group, Development Studies Association, London, March 1999.

Berger, Peter L. and Luckmann, Thomas. (1966 [1991]). *The Social Construction of Reality: A Treatise in the Sociology of Knowledge*, Garden City, New York: Anchor Books.

Berman, Ilan and Wihbey, Paul Michael. (1999). 'The new water politics of the Middle East', *JINSA Online*, August 26 / *Strategic Review* 27: 45–52.

Beyene, Zewdineh and Wadley, Ian L. (2004). *Common Goods and the Common Good: Transboundary Natural Resources, Principled Co-operation, and the Nile basin Initiative*, Center for African Studies, Breslauer Symposium on Natural Resource Issues in Africa, Berkeley: University of California.

Bially Mattern, Janice. (2005). Why 'Soft Power' isn't so soft. Representational force and the sociolinguistic construction of attraction in World Politics, *Millennium: Journal of International Studies* 33 (3): 583–612.

Biçak, Hasan Ali and Jenkins, Glenn. (2000). 'Transporting water by tanker from Turkey to North Cyprus: Costs and pricing policies', in: David Brooks and Ozay Mehmet, *Water Balances in the Eastern Mediterranean, Ottawa*, Ontario: International Development Research Centre. (IDRC), Chapter 7, http://www.idrc.ca/en/ev-33232-201-1-DO_TOPIC.html (last accessed 10 July 2010).

Bidaseca, Karina. (2004). 'La lucha por no silenciar el río y por recuperar el control del agua. Resistencias locales y globales en Narmada y Cochabamba', in Jeroen Warner and Alejandra Moreyra (eds.), *Conflictos y Participacion. Uso Multiple del Agua*, Montevideo: Nordan, pp. 65–78.

Bierschenk, Thomas. (1988). 'Development projects as arenas of negotiation for strategic groups', *Sociologia Ruralis*, Vol, XXVIII-2/3, p. 146ff.

Bigo, Didier. (2002). 'Security and immigration: Toward a critique of the governmentality of unease', *Alternatives* 27: 63–92.

Bijker, Wiebe E. (1995). *Of Bicycles, Bakelites, and Bulbs: Toward a Theory of Sociotechnical Change*, Cambridge, Mass.: MIT Press.

Bijker, Wiebe E. (2007). 'Dikes and dams, thick with politics', *Isis*, University of Chicago, (98) 1: 109–123.

Birkland, Thomas A. (2006). *Lessons of Disaster: Policy Change after Catastrophic Events*, Georgetown University Press.

Blaikie, Piers, Cannon, Terry, Davis, Ian and Wisner, Ben. (1994). *At Risk: Natural Hazards, People's Vulnerability and Disasters*, London: Routledge.

Blokland, M., Braadbaart, O. and Schwartz, K. (eds.). (1999). *Private Business, Public Owners: Government Shareholdings in Water Companies*, Delft: Institute for Infrastructural, Hydraulic and Environmental Engineering (IHE).

Boer, E. De. (2003). *Het noodoverloopgebied: airbag of luchtzak? Een kritiek op het rapport van de Commissie Luteijn*, Delft: Technische Universiteit Delft, Faculteit Civiele Techniek en Technische Geowetenschappen.

Booher, Judith E. and Innes, David E. (2002), 'Network power in collaborative *planning', Journal of Planning Education and Research* 21 (3): 221–36.

Boorsma, K. (1999). 'Sluit de Waddenzee af. Terugkeer naar veerkrachtstrategie onzinnig', *De Ingenieur* 111 (12), pp. 14–15.

Bosshard, Peter. (1999). 'The Ilısu Hydroelectric Project (Turkey): A test case of international policy coherence', Berne Declaration, November 1998.

Bourdieu, Pierre. [1972] (1977). *Outline of a Theory of Practice*, Cambridge: Cambridge University.

Boyce, James. K. (1990). 'Birth of a mega-project. Political economy of flood control in Bangladesh, *Environment Management* 14 (4): 419–28.

Bradnock, R. W. and Saunders, P. L. (2000). 'Sea-level rise, subsidence and submergence: The political ecology of environmental change in the Bengal delta' In: Stott, P. and Sullivan S. (eds). *Political Ecology: Science, Myth and Power.* London: Arnold, 66–90.

Brammer, Hugh. (1990). 'Floods in Bangladesh: II. Flood mitigation and environmental aspects', *Geographical Journal* 156 (2): 158–65.

Brennsell, Ariane. (2005). 'Ilısu Staudamm zu verkaufen', *Tageszeitung taz*, 24 September.

Briscoe, John. (1997). 'Managing Water as an Economic Good: Rules for Reformers', keynote paper to: The International Committee on Irrigation and Drainage Conference on Water as an Economic Good', http://cdi.mecon.gov.ar/biblio/docelec/MU1401.pdf (last accessed 10 July 2010).

Brismar, Anna. (2002). 'The Atatürk Dam Project in South-East Turkey: Changes in objectives and planning over time'. *Natural Resources Forum* 26: 100–112.

Brouma, Anthi Dionissia (2003a), Water and Security in International Relations: A Non-Conflictual Discourse. In: Saskia Kastelein (ed.): Proceedings, International Conference '*From Conflict to Co-operation in International Water Resources Management: Challenges and Opportunities*', 20–22 November 2002, Delft: UNESCO-IHE Institute for Water Education, 228–240. http://webworld.unesco.org/water/wwap/pccp/cd/pdf/conference_proceedings/conf_proceedings.pdf (last accessed 10 July 2010).

Brouma, Anthi Dionissia. (2003b). *Bridging the GAP: Modernity versus Post-Modernity*, Kokkalis Program Workshop, Harvard, 7 February.

Brown, Thomas Ford. (1997). 'Ideological hegemony and global governance'. *Journal of World-Systems Research*, 3: 250–8.

de Bruin, D., Hamhuis, D., van Nieuwenhuijze, L., Overmars, W., Sijmons, D., and Vera, F. (1987). *Plan Ooievaar. De toekomst van het rivierengebied*, Arnhem: Stichting Gelderse Milieufederatie.

Brunnée, Jutta and Toope, Stephen J. (2002). 'The changing Nile basin regime: Does law matter?' *Harvard International Law Journal* 43 (1): 105–59.

Bryant, Raymond L. and Bailey, Sinéad. (1997). *Third World Political Ecology*, London: Routledge.

Bulloch, John and Darwish, Adel. (1993). *Water Wars: Coming Conflicts in the Middle East*, London. Gollancz.

Burke, Anthony. (2007). 'What security makes possible. Some thoughts on critical security studies', working paper, Canberra: Australian National University, Department of International Relations.

Burton, Frank and Carlen, Pat. (1979). *Official Discourse: On Discourse Analysis, Government Publications, Ideology and the State*, London: Routledge & Kegan Paul.

Burton I., Kates, R. W and White, G. F. (1978). *The Environment as Hazard*, New York: Oxford University Press (reissued with new introduction, Guilford Press, 1993).

Bush, R. C. (1999). *Economic Crisis and the Politics of Reform in Egypt*. Boulder, CO: Westview Press.

Bush, R. C. (2007). 'Politics, power and poverty: Twenty years of agricultural reform and market liberalisation in Egypt'. *Third World Quarterly* 28 (8): 1599–1615.

Bush, Ray. (2004). 'Civil Society and the Un-Civil Politics of the Egyptian State, Land Tenure Reform and the Crisis of Rural Livelihoods', Civil Society and the Social Movement Paper No. 9, UNRISD (United Nations Research Institute for Social Development).

Bush, Ray. (2005). *Mubarak's Legacy for the Poor: Returning Land to Landlords*, The Hague: Institute for Social Studies.

Bustamante, Rocio and Palacios, Paulina. (2005). 'Gobernanza, Gobernabilidad y Agua en Los Andes, Un análisis conceptual y contextual', Linea Tematica 2, Proyecto '*Construyendo la Visión social del agua desde los Andes*', position paper, September 2005; http://www.negowat.org/curso/Modulo%20II/Documentos/Visiones%20Gobernanza.pdf (last accessed 10 July 2010).

Buzan, Barry. (1991). *People, States and Fear, an Agenda for International Security studies in the Post-Cold War Era*, Hemel Hampstead: Harvester Wheatsheaf, 2nd ed.

Buzan, Barry, Wæver, Ole, and de Wilde, Jaap. (1998). *Security. A New Framework for Analysis*, Hemel Hampstead: Harvester Wheatsheaf.

Caldwell, John C., Barkat-e-Khuda, Caldwell Bruce, Pieris Indrani, Caldwell Pat. (1999). 'The Bangladesh fertility decline: An interpretation'. *Population and Development Review*, 25 (1): 67–84.

Callon, Michel. (1986). 'Some elements of a sociology of translation: Domestication of the scallops and the fishermen of St Brieuc Bay'. In J. Law (ed.), *Power, Action and Belief: A New Sociology of Knowledge?* London: Routledge, pp. 196–223.

Cannon, Terry, Twigg, John and Rowell, Jennifer. (n.d.). Social Vulnerability, Sustainable Livelihoods and Disasters. A Report to DFID. Conflict and Humanitarian Assistance Department (CHAD) and Sustainable Livelihoods Support Office. http://www.proventionconsortium.org/themes/default/pdfs/CRA/DFIDSocialvulnerability.pdf (last accessed 10 July 2010).

Cerem, Cem. (2006). 'DSI pushes Treasury on Ilısu project', *The New Anatolian*, 16 April 2006.

Cernea, Michael. (2006). 'Comments on the Resettlement Action Plan and HEPP Project', Prepared for the Berne Declaration and the Ilısu Campaign Europe. February 2006.

Chadwick, Matthew and Datta, Anjan. (n.d.), 'Water Resources Management in Bangladesh. Improving Policy – Livelihood Relationships in South Asia'. Policy Review Paper 1. DFID.

Chadwick, Matthew, Soussan, J., Mallick, D. and Alam, S. (1998). *Understanding Indigenous Knowledge: Its Role and Potential in Water Resource Management in Bangladesh*. Leeds: University of Leeds.

Chadwick, M. T., Soussan, J. G., Martin, T. C., Mallick, D. and Alam, S. S. (2001). 'Bank robbery: The real losers in the 1998 Bangladesh flood'. *Land Degradation & Development* 12: 251–60.

Chandler, Daniel. (2007). *The Basics of Semiotics*, London & New York: Routledge.

Chatterjee, Bipul, Davis, Junior R., Eusuf, M. Abu, Harriss, John and Purohit, Purnima. (2006). 'Institutions and Pro-Poor Growth in Bangladesh'. IPPG (Institute for Pro-poor Growth), Inception Phase Study 2006, working paper Series No. 2.

Checkel, Jeffrey T. (1999). 'International Institutions and Socialization', Arena working paper WP 99/5. University of Oslo: ARENA.

Checkel, Jeffrey T. (2001). 'Why comply? Social learning and European identity change'. *International Organization* 55 (3): 553–588.

Chowdhurry, Jahir Uddin. (1992). 'Six comments on the Bangladesh Flood Action Plan', *Natural Hazards* 6 (3): 287–98.

Christie, Frances and Hanlon, Joseph. (2001). *Mozambique and the Great Flood of 2000*. Oxford: James Currey Ltd.

Cizre, U. (2000). 'Politics and Military in Turkey into the Twenty-first Century', Working Paper, No. 2000/24, Florence: Robert Schuman Centre, European University Italy (EUI).

CNN. (2003). Pentagon: Iraq could flood Tigris for defense. Tactic was used to slow Iranian forces during Iran-Iraq War, 21 March 2003.

Cohen, M. D., March, J. G., and Olsen, J. (1972). A garbage can theory of organizational choice. *Administrative Science Quarterly* 17: 1–25.

Collingwood Environmental Planning. (1999). 'Datchet, Wraysbury, Staines and Chertsey Flood Alleviation Scheme – Options appraisal (for the Environment Agency).

Collins, K. and Ison, R. (2006). Dare we jump off Arnstein's ladder? Participation and social learning as a new policy paradigm. PATH conference, Edinburgh, 4–7 June. http://oro.open.ac.uk/8589/1/Path_paper_Collins_Ison.pdf or http://www.macaulay.ac.uk/PATHconference/outputs/PATH_abstract_3.1.2.pdf (last accessed 10 July 2010).

Collins, Robert O. (2003). 'The Inscrutable Nile at the Beginning of a New Millennium', unpublished paper, University of California Santa Barbara, http://www.history.ucsb.edu/faculty/Inscrutable%20Nile1.pdf (last accessed 10 July 2010).

Comfort, L., Wisner, B., Cutter, S., Pulwarty, R., Hewitt, K., Oliver-Smith, A., Weiner, J., Fordham, M., Peacock, W. and Krimgold, F. 1999. 'Reframing disaster policy: The global evolution of vulnerable communities'. *Environmental Hazards* 1 (1): 39–44.

Commissie Noodoverloopgebieden. (2002). *Gecontroleerd Overstromen*, Den Haag.

Cook, Steven A. (2007). *Military ruling but not governing*, Council on Foreign Relations. http://www.cfr.org/publication/13003/ruling_but_not_governing.html (last accessed 10 July 2010).

Cooperman, Alan. (1997). *Making the Desert Bloom – or Making Wells go Dry*, US News and World Report, 22 (19): 33, 19 May.

Coskun, Bezen B. (2005). 'Power structures in water regime formation: Jordan and Euphrates-Tigris River Basins'. *The Interdisciplinary Journal of International Studies* 3 (1): 1–21.

Cowper, Richard. (2000). *Egypt Survey. MEGA-PROJECTS: Draining away resources*, *Financial Times* Country Survey.

Cox, Robert W. (1981). 'Social forces, states and world orders', *Millennium: Journal of International Studies*, 10 (2): 126–155.

CPP (Compartmentalisation Pilot Project). (2000). Final Report, 5 Volumes, Dhaka.

Crichton, D. (2002). 'The flood tax – is the government out of it depth?', *Town and Country Planning*, 72: 66–68.

Crichton, D. (2005). 'Flood Risk and Insurance in England and Wales: Are There Lessons To Be Learnt from Scotland?', Technical Paper Number 1, London: University College London, Benfield Greig Hazard Research Centre, Department of Earth Sciences.

Crow, Ben. (1995). *Sharing the Ganges: The Politics and Technology of River Development*, London: Sage.

Crozier, Michel. (1964). *The Bureaucratic Phenomenon*, Chicago: University of Chicago Press.

Cullather, Nick. (2002). 'From New Deal to New Frontier in Afghanistan', Working Paper, No. 6, New York: New York University, International Center for Advanced Studies.

Cullingworth, John B. and Nadin, Vincent. (1997). *Town and Country Planning in the UK*, London: Routledge.

Currie-Alder, Bruce. (2007). 'Unpacking participatory NRM: Distinguishing resource capture from democratic governance', in J. Warner (ed.), *Multi-Stakeholder Platforms for Integrated Water Management*, Aldershot: Ashgate, pp. 245–59.

Czarniawska-Joerges, Barbara and Joerges, Bernard. 'How to control things with words: Organizational talk and control. *Management Communication Quarterly*, 1988; 2: 170–93.

Czarniawska, Barbara. (2001). Metaphors and the Cultural Context of Organizing, GRI-report 2001:3, Gothenburg: Gothenburg Research Institute, http://gupea.ub.gu.se/bitstream/2077/2968/1/2001_3_Metaphors_BC.pdf (last accessed 10 July 2010).

Daily Star. (1995). 'Villagers protest FAO-20 in Tangail', 26 November 1995.

Dalby, Simon. (2000). 'Geopolitical Change and Contemporary Security Studies: Contextualizing the Human Security Agenda', Institute of International Relations,

University of British Columbia, Working Paper No. 30, April 2000, http://www.iir.ubc.ca/site_template/workingpapers/webwp30.pdf

Daoudy, Marwa. (2005). 'Turkey and the Region: Testing the Links Between Power Asymmetry and Hydro-Hegemony'. Presentation given at First Workshop on Hydro-Hegemony, 21/22 May 2005, King's College London, London, UK.

Dasgupta, Tapati and Chattopadhyay, R. N. (2004). 'Ecological contradictions through ages: Growth and decay of the Indus and Nile Valley Civilizations, *Journal of Human Ecology*, 16 (3): 197–201.

Day, Richard J. F. (2006). *Gramsci is Dead, Anarchist Currents in the Newest Social Movements.* Pluto Press, London, UK.

DEFRA (2002), 'Flood and coastal defence funding review. Report on the outcome of consultation London. Department for Environment, Food and Rural Affairs.

DEFRA. (2005). Making space for water. Taking forward a new Government strategy for flood and coastal erosion risk management in England First Government response to the Autumn 2004 *Making space for water* consultation exercise, March 2005. London: Department for Environment, Food and Rural Affairs, http://library.coastweb.info/269/1/1stres.pdf (last accessed 10 July 2010).

DFID. (1999). Livelihood Connect, Sustainable Livelihoods Guidance Sheets, IDS Discussion Paper 196, Institute for Development Studies, Sussex, UK Department for International Development http://www.nssd.net/references/SustLiveli/DFIDapproach.htm#Guidance (last accessed 10 July 2010).

Dicke, Willemijn. (2001). *Bridges and Watersheds. A Narrative Analysis of Water Management in England, Wales and the Netherlands*, Amsterdam: Aksant.

Diez, Thomas. (2000). The Imposition of governance. 'Transforming Turkish Foreign Policy through EU Enlargement', CIAO (Columbia International Affairs Online) Working paper 11/00, August 2000.

Dijkman, T., *et al.* (1998). De Rijn op Termijn, WL Delft, rijnoptermijn.wldelft.nl

Dinar, S. (2009). Power Asymmetry and Negotiations in International River Basins. *International Negotiation* 14 (2): 329–60.

Disco, Cornelis. (2002). 'Remaking "Nature" the ecological turn in Dutch water management', *Science, Technology & Human Values* 27 (2): 206–35.

Dockser Marcus, Amy and Brauchli, Marcus. (1997). 'Greenpolitik: Threats to environment provoke a new security agenda', *The Wall Street Journal*, 20 November 1997.

Dodds, Richard and Venables, Roger. (eds.). (2005). *Engineering for Sustainable Development: Guiding Principles*, London: The Royal Academy of Engineering.

Dohmen, J. (1996). De vriendenrepubliek. Nijmegen: SUN.

Dolfing, B. (1996a, b). 'Waterkering en planologie: (g)een maatregel teveel', *Het Waterschap*, 1996 (2) and (3), pp. 82–9.

Donahue, John M. and Johnston, Barbara Rose. (eds.). (1998). *Water, Culture, & Power, Local Struggles in a Global Context*, Washington: Island Press.

Dore, John. (2007). 'Mekong Region water-related MSPs – unfulfilled potential', in Jeroen Warner (ed.), *Multi-Stakeholder Platforms for Integrated Water Management*, Aldershot: Ashgate, 205–235.

Dorman, W. Judson. (2007). *The Politics of Neglect. Cairo 1952–1998.* PhD dissertation, London: School of Oriental and Asian Studies, University College London.

Dosi, G. (1982). 'Technological paradigms and technological trajectories: A suggested interpretation of the determinants and directions of technical change', *Research Policy* 11: 147–62.

Douglas, Mary. (1994). *Risk and Blame: Essays in Cultural Theory*, London: Routledge

Douglas, Mary and Wildavsky, Aaron. (1983). *Risk and Culture: An Essay on the Selection of Technological and Environmental Dangers*, Berkeley: University of California Press.

Dove, Michael R. (1998). 'Local dimensions of "global" environmental disasters', in: Anne Kalland & Gerald Persoon (eds.), *Environmental Movements in Asia*, Richmond, Surrey: Curzon, pp. 44–65.

Driessen. P. P. J. and de Gier, A. A. J. (1997a). 'Deltawet Grote Rivieren. Een evaluatie van een bijzondere wet na de wateroverlast van 1995', *Bestuurskunde* 7 (2), pp. 44–86.

Driessen, P. P. J. and de Gier A. A. J. (1997b). *Uit nood geboren; een bestuurlijk-juridische evaluatie van de dijkversterkingen en kadenaanleg onder de Deltawet grote rivieren*, Den Haag: VUGA, pp. 15–27.

Drorian, Sevgi. (2005). 'Turkey, security, state and society in troubled times', *European Security*, 14(2), pp. 255–75.

Dryzek, J. S. (2002). *Deliberative Democracy and Beyond. Liberals, Critics, Contestations*, New York: Oxford University Press.

Dubbeldam, H. (1999). *Maatschappelijke golven in de waterbouwkunde*, PhD thesis, Delft: Delft University Press.

Duivenvoorden, A. (1997). *In de Maas verdiept, een regionaal geografische verkenning van bron tot monding*. Amsterdam ± NIVON.

Du Plessis, Anton. (2000). 'Charting the course of the water discourse through the fog of international relations theory'. In: H. Solomon and A. Turton (eds.), *Water Wars: Enduring Myth or Impending Reality. Africa Dialogue Series.* Vol 2, Durham-Pretoria: ACCORD, Green Cross International and the African Water Issues Research Unit, Pretoria, 9–34.

Duyne, Jennifer. (1998). 'Local initiatives: People's water management practices in rural Bangladesh', *Development Policy Review*, 16 (3): 265–80.

Dye, Thomas, Zeigler, Harmon and Lichter, Robert. (1992). American Politics in the Media Age, 4th Edition. Pacific Grove, CA: Brooks Cole.

Easton, David. (1965). *A Framework for Political Analysis*, Englewood Cliffs: Prentice Hall.

Eeten, M. J. G. van. (1997). 'Sprookjes in Rivierenland: Beleidsverhalen over wateroverlast en dijkversterking (Tales from Riverland: Policy narratives about flooding and dike improvement)'. *Beleid en Maatschappij*, 14 (1): 32–43.

Egyptian State Information System. (2007). *Ministry of Agriculture: Tushka Project Best Model of Agricultural Investment*, 2 April 2007.

Ekengren, Magnus. (2004). 'From a European Security Community to a Secure European Community. Analysing EU "Functional" Security – The Case of EU Civil Protection', SGIR Conference, Fifth Pan-European Conference, The Hague, Netherlands, 9–11 September 2004.

El-Aref, Nevine. (2007). 'Sending out an SOS', *Al-Ahram Weekly*, Issue 860.

El-Din, Gamal Essam. (1999). 'Mega-projects under scrutiny', *Al-Ahram Weekly*, No. 459, 9–15 December.

El-Fadel, M., El Sayegh, Y., Abou Ibrahim, A., Jamali, D. and El-Fadl, K. K. (2002). 'The Euphrates-Tigris Basin: A case study in surface water conflict resolution', *J. Nat. Res. Life Sci. Educ.*, vol 31, pp. 99–110.

El-Ghamrawy, Ahmed and Quinn, Susan. (1999). *Egypt's Development Projects Spur Growth*, US-Arab Tradeline, 9 July 1999.

El-Khodari, Nabil M. (2003a). 'Agricultural projects and the Egyptian Bedouin', *Water Nepal*, 10 (1): 409–19.

El-Khodari, Nabil (2003b). 'Diverse interests in the Nile basin Initiative', in Jannik Boesen and Helle Munk Ravnborg (eds.), From water 'wars' to water 'riots'? Lessons from transboundary water management proceedings of the international conference, December 2003, Copenhagen: Dansk Institut fòr Internationale Studier, pp. 140–54.

Elsenhans, Hartmut. (1983). 'Rising mass incomes as a condition of capitalist growth; implications for the world economy', *International Organization* 537 (1): 1–37.

Erhan, Selahattin. (1997). 'The social structure in the GAP region and its evolution', *International Journal of Water Resources Development* 13 (4): 505–22.

Ericksen, N. J., Ahmad, Q. K. and Chowdhury, A. R. (n.d.). 'Socio-Economic Implications of Climate Change for Bangladesh. Dhaka: BUP (Bangladesh Unnayan Parishad), Briefing Document No. 4.

Euroconsult, Lahmeyer International, Bangladesh Engineering and Technological Services, House of Consultants. (1995). *Compartmentalization Pilot project: Water Management. Workshop, Experience of the 1995 Monsoon*, Technical Note 95/07 (December 1995).

European Parliament and Council. (2007). Directive 2007/60/EC of the European Parliament and of the Council of 23 October 2007 on the assessment and management of flood risks. Published in the Official Journal on 6 November 2007, p. 27.

Faaland, J. and Geoff Wood (1995). *Flood and Water management. Towards a Public Debate, Report by the Independent FAP Review Mission*, United Nations Development Programme.

Fahmy, Miral. (1997). 'Farming Toshka is no pipe dream for Saudi prince', *Middle East Times*, 5 December.

Faisal, Islam M. and Parveen, Saila. (2004). 'Food security in the face of climate change, population growth, and resource constraints: Implications for Bangladesh', *Environment Management*, 34 (4): 489–98.

FAO. (1997). *Irrigation potential in Africa, a basin approach*, FAO Land and Water bulletin 4, Rome.

Farooque, Mohiuddin and Sekandar Ali Mondol vs. Bangladesh (2001), Writ Petition No. 998 of 1994, in UNEP Partnership for the Development of Environmental Law and Institutions in Africa (PADELIA) (2001), Compendium of Judicial Decisions on Matters Related to Environment, Vol. II: National issues, pp. 112–28, http://www.unep.org/dec/PDF/UNEPCompendiumSummariesJudgements Environment-relatedCases.pdf (last accessed 10 July 2010).

Feitelson, Eran. (1999). 'Social norms, rationales and policies: Reframing farmland protection in Israel', *Journal of Rural Studies*, 15, 431–46.

Ferguson, James. (1994). *The Anti-Politics Machine: "Development", Depoliticization, and Bureaucratic Power in Lesotho*. Minneapolis, MN.: University Of Minnesota Press.

Floyd, Rita. (2007). Towards a consequentialist evaluation of security: Bringing together the Copenhagen and Welsh schools of security studies, *Review of International Studies* 33: 327–50.

Flyvbjerg, Bent. (1998). *Rationality and Power: Democracy in Practice*, Chicago and London: The University of Chicago Press.

Ford Brown, Thomas. (1997). 'Ideological hegemony and global governance', *Journal of World Systems Research*, 3 (2): 250–8.

Fordham, Maureen. (1998/99). 'Participatory planning for flood mitigation: Models and approaches', *Australian Journal of Emergency Management*. Summer 1998/99; 13 (4): 27–35.

Forsyth, Tim. (2003). *Critical Political Ecology. The Politics of Environmental Science*, London: Routledge.

Fox, Nick J. (1999). 'Postmodern reflections on "risk", "hazards", and "life choices"'. In Lupton, D. (ed.), *Risk and Sociocultural Theory: New Directions and Perspectives.* Cambridge: Cambridge University Press, Ch.1.

Frey, F. (1993). 'The political context of conflict and cooperation over international river basins'. *Water International* 18: 54–68.

Friedman, Thomas L. (2005). *The World is Flat. A Brief History of the 21st Century*, London: Penguin Books.

Friesendorf, Cornelius. (2007). 'Pathologies of security governance: Efforts against human trafficking', *Security Dialogue* 38 (3): 379ff.

Friis, Karsten. (2000). 'From liminars to others: Securitization through myths'. *Peace and Conflict Studies*, 7 (2): 1–17.

Frijters, I. D. and Leentvaar, J. (2001). 'Participatory planning for flood management in the Netherlands', http://www.unescap.org/esd/water/disaster/2001/netherlands.doc (last accessed 10 July 2010).

Frisch, Hillel. (2001). 'Guns and butter in the Egyptian army', *MERIA Journal* 5 (2), http://meria.idc.ac.il/journal/2001/issue2/jv5n2a1.html (last accessed 10 July 2010).

Fryer, G. A. (1999). 'Maidenhead, Windsor and Eton Flood Alleviation Scheme: Engineering Design' Paper presented to the CIWEM Rivers and Coastal Group, London, September 1999.

Furlong, Kathryn. (2006). 'Hidden theories, troubled waters: International relations, the "territorial trap", and the Southern African Development Community's transboundary waters'. *Political Geography* 25 (4): 438–58.

Galetti, Mirella. (1999). 'The Kurdish issue in Turkey', *International Spectator*, 34 (1), Jan-Feb 1999.

GAP-RDA (Greater Anatolia Project, Regional Development Administration). (2002). *Master Plan.* Background of the Southeast Anatolia Project.

Gardiner, J. L. (1988). River Thames Flood Defence, a Strategic Initiative, paper, Institution of Water and Environmental Management, Central Southern Branch Meeting 29 June 1988.

Gardiner, J. L. (1992). 'The River Thames Strategic Flood Defence Initiative. A New Approach to Flood Control Measures'. Paper presented at NATO scientific conference 'Defence from Floods and Floodplain Management, September 1992.

Gardiner, J. L. Strarosolszky, O. and Yevjevich, V. (eds.). (1995). *Defence from Floods and Floodplain Management*, NATO ASI Series, 299, Dordrecht: Kluwer.

Geels, Frank W. (2004). 'From sectoral systems of innovation to socio-technical systems. Insights about dynamics and change from sociology and institutional theory', *Research Policy*, 33 (6–7): 897–920.

Geldof, Govert D. (1994). *Adaptief waterbeheer; artikelen uit het blad Het Waterschap september 1993 t/m juli 1994*, Deventer: Tauw Civiel en Bouw.

George, Alan. (1998). 'Friction flows over Nile waters', *The Middle East*, May 1998, No. 278: 15.

Giddens, Anthony. (1999a). 'Risk and responsibility', *Modern Law Review*, 62 (1): 1–10.

Giddens, Anthony. (1999b). 'Risk', Reith lectures 1999, BBC Radio 4, Lecture 2.

Gigch, van, John P. (1987). *Decision making about decision making. Metamodels and metasystems*; with a foreword (Metacomment) by Stafford Beer. Cambridge, MA: Abacus Press.

Girma, Amare. (2000). *Nile Waters – Hydrological Co-operation vs. Hydropolitics*, Proceedings of the eighth Nile Conference, 26–29 June Addis Ababa.

Giroux, Henry A. (2005). 'Stormy Weather: Katrina and the Politics of Disposability', http://www.henryagiroux.com/online_articles/Pol_Disposibility.htm (last accessed 10 July 2010).

Gleick, H. P. (ed.). (1993). *Water in Crisis*, Pacific Institute for Studies in Development, Environment & Security, Stockholm Env. Institute, New York: Oxford University Press.

Gleick, H. P. (2002). *The World's Water: The Biennial Report on Freshwater Resources*, Washington D.C.: Island Press.

Gould, Stephen Jay and Eldredge, Niles. (1977). 'Punctuated equilibria: The tempo and mode of evolution reconsidered'. *Paleobiology* 3: 115–151.

Graeff, de, J. (n.d.). *Water boards in the Netherlands*, http://content.alterra.wur.nl/Internet/webdocs/ilri-publicaties/special_reports/Srep3/Srep3-h9.pdf (last accessed 10 July 2010).

Gramsci, Antonio. (1971) [1922]. *Selections from the Prison Notebooks*. Edited and translated by Q. Hoare and G. N. Smith, London: Lawrence and Wishart.

Green, C. and Warner, J. (1999). 'Flood Management: Towards a New Paradigm'. Conference paper presented at the Stockholm Water Symposium, 9–12 August 1999.

Gromes, Thorsten and Bonacker, Thorsten. (2007). 'The Concept of Securitization as a Tool for Analysing the Role of Human-Rights-Related Civil Society in Ethno-Political Conflicts', SHUR: Human Rights in Conflict: The Role of Civil Society. Working paper 05/07, March 2007.

Gruen, George E. (2000). *Turkish waters: Source of regional conflict or catalyst for peace? Water, Air and Soil Pollution*, 123 (1–4): 565–79.

Gruen, George E. (2004). 'Turkish Water Exports: A Model For Regional Co-operation in the Development Of Water Resources'; 2nd Israeli-Palestinian International Conference, 10–14 October 2004, http://www.ipcri.org/watconf/papers/george.pdf

Guner, Serdar. (1997). 'The Turkish-Syrian War of Attrition: The Water Dispute'. *Studies in Conflict & Terrorism*, 20 (1): 105.

Guzzini, Stefano. (2005). The concept of power: A constructivist analysis. *Millennium* 33 (3): 495–522.

Haas, Peter M. (1992). 'Introduction: Epistemic communities and international policy co-ordination', *International Organisation*, 46 (1): 1–35.

Hagens, Janneke E. (2007). 'Principles of Spatial Conceptualisation – Examples From Ijmeer: A Dutch Regional Planning Case', International Conference 'New concepts and approaches for Urban and Regional Policy and Planning?' ESDP & SP2SP, 2 April, Leuven, Belgium.

Haggart, K. (ed.). (1994). *Rivers of Life*. Dhaka: Bangladesh Center for Advanced Studies (BCAS).

Hajer, Maarten A. (1995). *The Politics of Environmental Discourse*, Oxford: Oxford University.

Hajer, Maarten A. (2005). 'Setting the stage. A dramaturgy of policy deliberation'. *Administration & Society* 36 (6), 624–47.

Hall, Jim W., Evans, Edward P., Penning-Rowsell, Edmund C., Sayers, Paul B., Thorne, Colin R. and Saul, Adrian J. (2003). 'Integrated flood management in England and Wales', *Natural Hazard Research*, 4 (33): 126–35.

Hamilton, Ashley. (2003). 'Resource Wars and the politics of abundance and scarcioty', *Dialogue*, 1 (3): 27–38.

Hanchett, Suzanne. (1997). 'Participation and policy development. The case of the Bangladesh Flood Action Plan'. *Development Policy Review* 15: 277–95.

Hanchett, Suzanne and Nasreen, Mahbuba. (1992). 'Gender Issues in the Flood Action Plan'. A paper presented at the workshop of *Flood Response Study* (*FAP 14*) organised by Bangladesh Flood Action Plan, Dhaka, 9 November 1992.

Hansen, Thomas Blom and Stepputat, Finn. (2001). *States of Imagination: Ethnographic Explorations of the Postcolonial State*, Durham, NC: Duke University.

Hardt, Michael and Negri, Antonio. (2000). *Empire*. Cambridge, MA: Harvard University Press.

Harries, Tim and Borrows, Peter. (n.d.). 'Can people learn to live with flood risk?' Floodscape (EDRF Interreg IIIb project) 01-3, Flood Hazard Research Centre, Enfield/Environment Agency.

Harris, Leila M. (2002). Water and conflict geographies of Southeastern Anatolia Project, *Society and Natural Resources*, 15, pp. 743–59.

Hasenclever, Andreas, Mayer, Peter and Rittberger, Volker. (1997). *Theories of International Regimes*, New York: Cambridge University Press.

Haufler, Virginia. (1993). 'Crossing the boundary between public and private: international regimes and non-state actors'. In Volker Rittberger (ed.) *Regime Theory and International Relations*, Oxford: Clarendon Press/Oxford University Press.

Havekes, H., Koemans, F., Lazaroms, R., Poos, D., and Uijterlinde, R. (2005). *Water governance: the Dutch water board model.* Dutch Association of Water Boards., The Netherlands www.uvw.nl/content/TRIBAL_tsShop/files/123_watergovernance.pdf

Haynes, Kingsley E. and Whittington, Dale. (1981). 'International management of the Nile-Stage Three?' *The Geographical Review* 71 (1): 17–32.

Healey, Patsy. (1997). *Collaborative Planning. Shaping Places in Fragmented Societies*, 2nd Edition, Basingshoke, Hants: Palgrave Macmillan.

Held, David. (1984). 'Power and legitimacy in contemporary Britain', in G. McLennan, D. Held and S. Hall (eds.), *State and Society in Contemporary Britain: a Critical Introduction*, London: Polity Press.

Helleman, Luuk. (2005). *Interactieve beleidsvorming in integraal perspectief*, MSc thesis, Public Administration, Erasmus University.

Helmer, W., Klink, A., Overmars, W. and Litjens G. (1992). *Levende Rivieren.* Zeist: Wereld Natuur Fonds.

Hemert, Mieke van. (1999). 'Ruimte voor de ingenieur. Rivierbeheer in Nederland eind jaren negentig', *K&M, Tijdschrift voor empirische filosofie*, 23 (4): 361–87.

Hemmati, M. (2002). *Multi-Stakeholder Processes for Governance and Accountability*, London: Earthscan

Hermans, Leon. (2005). *Actor analysis for water resources management. Putting the promise into practice.* PhD Dissertation, Delft University. Chapter 8: Implementation of the EU Water Framework Directive in Turkey, pp. 121–39.

Herz, John. (1951). *Political Realism and Political Idealism*, Chicago, IL: Chicago University Press)

Hewitt, Kenneth. ([1983] 1997). *Regions of Risk: A Geographical Introduction to Disasters*, Essex, England: Addison Wesley Longman.

Hilhorst, D. (2003). Responding to disasters: Diversity of bureaucrats, technocrats and local people, *Journal of Mass Emergencies and Disasters*, 21 (3), pp. 37–55.

Hill, Enid. (2000). *Discourses in Contemporary Egypt. Politics and and Social Issues*, Cairo: American University in Cairo Press.

Hillel, Daniel. (1994). *Rivers of Eden. The Struggle for Water and the Quest for Peace in the Middle East.* New York: Oxford University Press.

Hisschemöller, M. and Hoppe, R. (1998). 'Weerbarstige beleidscontroverses: een pleidooi voor probleemstructurering in beleidsontwerp en –analyse'. In: R. Hoppe and A. Pieterse (Ed.) *Bouwstenen voor een argumentatieve beleidsanalyse.* Den Haag: Elsevier.

Homer-Dixon, Thomas F. (1994). 'Environmental scarcities and violent conflict: Evidence from cases', *International Security* 19 (1): 5–40.

Homer-Dixon, Thomas F. (1995). 'The ingenuity gap: Can poor countries adapt to resource scarcity?', *Population and Development Review* 21 (3): 587–612.

Homer-Dixon, Thomas F. (1999). 'The myth of global water wars', in S. Fleming (ed.), *War and Water.* Geneva: ICRC Publication Division.

Hood, Christopher, Rothstein, Henry and Baldwin, Robert. (2001). *Government of Risk*, Oxford: Oxford University Press.

Hornstein, Donald T. (1999). *Environmental Sustainability and Environmental Justice at the International Level: Traces Of Tension And Traces Of Synergy*, Duke Envtironmental Law & Policy Forum, p. 291ff.

Hough, Peter. (2004). *Understanding Global Security*, London: Routledge.

Houscht, Martin Peter. (n.d.). Der Flutaktionsplan in Bangladesh, Genese, Entwicklung und Perspektiven einer umstrittenen Entwicklungsvorhabens, In: Thomas Hoffmann (ed.) *Elementare Konflikte Wasser in Asien.* Essen: Asienhaus. pp 410–419. www.gbv.de/dms/spk/sbb/recht/toc/280104715.pdf (last accessed 10 July 2010).

House of Commons. (1998). Select Committee on Agriculture, Sixth Report.

Howell, P. P. and Allan, J. A. (1994). *The Nile, Sharing a Scarce Resource: A historical and Technical Review of Water Management and of Economical and Legal Issues*, Cambridge; New York: Cambridge University Press.

Huber, Michael. (2005). 'Reforming the UK Flood Insurance Regime. The Breakdown of A Gentleman's Agreement', ESRC/LSE, Discussion paper no. 18, www.lse.ac.uk/collections/CARR/pdf/Disspaper18.pdf (last accessed 10 July 2010).

Hughes, R., Adnan, S. and Dalal-Clayton, B. (1994). *Floodplains or Flood Plans? A Review of Approaches to Water Management in Bangladesh*, London: IIED and RAS.

Huq, Saleemul. (1994). 'FAP: From Debate to Dialogue, *Daily Star*, 19 November.

Huq, Saleemul. (n.d.). 'Environmental Shocks as Policy Drivers: A Case Study of Floods and Coastal Cyclones in Bangladesh. Improving Policy-Livelihood Relationships in South Asia', Issue Paper 5. London: DFID.

Huq, Saleemul and Reid, Hannah. (2004). 'Climate Change and Development Consultation On Key Researchable Issues Section 4.1, South Asian Regional Scoping Study', Project Report No. 2004GW35, London: Teri/DFID; www.iied.org/pubs/pdfs/14516IIED.pdf (last accessed 10 July 2010).

Huysmans, Jef. (1998a). 'Security! What do you mean? From concept to thick signifier', *European Journal of International Relations* 4 (2): 229–58.

Huysmans, Jef. (1998b). 'Revisiting Copenhagen, or, On the Creative Development of a Security Studies Agenda , *European Journal of International Relations.* 4: 479–505.

Hvidt, Martin. (1995). 'Water resource planning in Egypt', in Eric Watkins (ed.), *The Middle East Environment*, Cambridge: St Malo Press, pp. 90–100.

Ignatieff, M. (1993). *Blood and Belonging*, London: Chatto & Windus.

Ignatieff, Michael. (2004). *The Lesser Evil: Political Ethics in an Age of Terror*, Princeton, N.J.: Princeton University Press.

Ilısu Engineering Group. (2001). *Ilısu Dam and HEPP – Environmental Impact Assessment Report, 2001.*

Immink, Irene. (2007). 'Established and recent policy arrangements for river management in The Netherlands: An analysis of discourses', PhD Dissertation, Wageningen University http://library.wur.nl/ojs/index.php/frontis/article/viewFile/1134/705 (last accessed 10 July 2010).

Independent. (1995). 'FAP-20 and Jamuna Bridge', 15 September 1995.

Ingen-housz, Famke. (2007). *Een kanteling in het denken over overstromingsbeheer in Engeland.* Een *studie naar de recente veranderingen in het Engelse overstromingsbeheer.* Wageningen University, MSc thesis.

IOV (Inspectie Ontwikkelingssamenwerking te Velde). (1993). *The Flood Action Plan.* The Hague: Dutch Ministry of Foreign Affairs.

Islam, S. Aminul. (2004). 'Overcoming poverty in Bangladesh: Search for a new paradigm', *Bangladesh e-Journal of Sociology* 1 (2), July, 2004.

Islam, S. Aminul. (2006). 'The predicament of democratic consolidation in Bangladesh', *Bangladesh e-Journal of Sociology* 3 (2), July 2006.

ISPAN. (1992). Environmental Impact Assessment, (Case Study), Compartmentalisation Pilot Project. FAP 16 Report prepared for USAID and Ministry of Irrigation, Water Development and Flood Control, Government of Bangladesh, Dhaka.

Jacoby, Tim. (2005). 'Semi-authoritarian incorporation and autocratic militarism in Turkey', *Development and Change*, Vol. 36 (4): 641–65.

Jägerskog, Anders. (2003). *Why states co-operate over shared water. The water negotiations in the Jordan River Basin*, PhD Dissertation, Studies in Arts and Science, No. 281, Linköping: Linköping University, Department of Water and Environmental Studies.

James, L. D. and Pitman, K. (1992). 'Six comments on the Bangladesh Flood Action Plan', *Natural Hazards* 6 (3) 287–98.

Jasanoff, Sheila. (1999). 'The songlines of risk.' *Environmental Values* 8 (2): 135–52.

JMP Consultants Ltd. (2003). Flood Analysis Report, Final 10-5032-B, 10-5042-A, 10-5047-A R.001 V3, Flood Analysis Report.

Johnson, Clare, Tunstall, Sylvia and Penning-Rowsell, Edmund. (n.d.). Crises as Catalysts for Adaptation: Human Response to Major Floods. Research Report. ESRC Environment and Human Behaviour New Opportunities Programme, Flood Hazard Research Centre, Publication No. 511, http://www.safecoast.nl/editor/databank/File/crisis%20as%20catalysts%20for%20adaptation%20-%20human%20respons%20to%20major%20floods.pdf (last accessed 10 July 2010).

Jongerden, Joost. (2006). 'From Productive Power to Blunt Control: Theses on the Technology of (Re)settlement in Turkey and the Kurds', paper presented at the Kurdish Studies Conference, the Kurdish Institute of Paris and Salahaddin University, Arbil, Iraqi Kurdistan, 6–9 September 2006, http://www.internal-displacement.org/8025708F004CE90B/(httpDocuments)/580FAD726479B303C125725D005C1B45/$file/Paper_Resettlement_Jongerden.pdf

Jongerden, Joost, m.m.v. Guido van Leemput. (1994). *Het recht op dromen. Ontwikkelingen naar een zelfstandig Koerdistan*, Breda: De Papieren Tijger.

Jongerden, Joost, Oudshoorn, René and Laloli, Henk. (1997). *Het verwoeste land, Berichten van de oorlog in Turks Koerdistan*, Breda: De Papieren Tijger.

Jouvé, Bernard. (2005). 'From government to urban governance in Western Europe: A critical analysis', *Public Administration and Development* 25 (4): 285–94.

Kalimullah, Nazmul Ahsan, Alam, Khorshed and Parvez, Altaf. (1995). 'Report on the Quality of People's Participation in Tangail FAP 20', Dhaka: UST (Unnayan Shahyogi Team).

Kalin, Michael. (2006). *Pharaohs: Egypt, Engineers and the Modern Hydraulic*, Mphil thesis, Dublin: Trinity College.

Kagwanja, P. (2007). 'Calming the waters. The East African community and conflict over the Nile resources'. *Journal of Eastern African Studies* 1 (3), 321–37.

Kalpakian, Jack. (2004). *Identity Conflict and Co-operation in International River Systems*, Aldershot: Ashgate.

Kamrava, Mehran. (1993). *Politics and Society in the Third World*, London: Routledge.

Kaplan, Robert. (1994). 'The coming anarchy', *The Atlantic Monthly*; February 1994; 273 (2): 44–76. http://www.theatlantic.com/magazine/archive/1994/02/the-coming-anarchy/4670/2/ (last accessed 10 July 2010).

Kazan, Işil. (2005). 'Turkey, where geopolitics still matters', *Contemporary Security Policy*, 26 (3), pp. 588–604.

Keeley, James F. (1990). 'Toward a Foucauldian analysis of international regimes', *International Organization* 44 (1): 83–105.

Kemp, J. W. J. (2004). *Bangladesh in the 1990s: Make or Break*. Edinburgh: Lame Duck Press.

Kendie, Daniel. (1999). 'Egypt and the hydro-politics of the Blue Nile River', *Northeast African Studies* 6 (1): 141–69.

Kenon, Herb. (2003). 'Deal to buy water from Turkey finalized', *Jerusalem Post*, 23 July 2003.

Kerr, Pauline. (2003). 'The Evolving Dialectic between State-Centric and Human-Centric Security', working paper 2003/2, Department of International Relations, RSPAS, Melbourne, Canberra: Australian National University/Sydney.

Keynes, J. M. (1936). *The General Theory of Employment, Interest and Prices*, London: Macmillan. http://cepa.newschool.edu/het/essays/keynes/general.htm (last accessed 10 July 2010).

KfW (Kreditanstalt für Wiederaufbau). (2004). Evaluation, http://www.kfw-entwicklungsbank.de/EN_Home/Ex-post_Evaluation_at_KfW/Ex-post_evaluation_reports/PDF-Dokumente_A-D/bangladesh_com.pdf (last accessed 10 July 2010).

Khalequzzaman, Md. (1994). 'Recent floods in Bangladesh: Possible causes and solutions', *Natural Hazards*, 9 (65–80).

Khayyam, Omar. (n.d.). *Rubaiyat*, Translated by Edward FitzGerald, 5th edition. http://www.iranonline.com/literature/index-khayyam.html (last accessed 10 July 2010).

KHRP (Kurdish Human Rights Project), Corner House, Ilısu Dam Campaign. (2002). *Downstream Impacts of Turkish Dam Construction on Syria and Iraq*, London.

Kibaroğlu, Ayşegül. (1996). 'Prospects for co-operation in the Euphrates-Tigris Basin', in Peter Howsam and Richard Carter (eds.), *Water Policy: Allocation and Management in Practice*, London: E & FN Spon, September 1996, 31–9.

Kibaroğlu, Ayşegül. (2002). 'Building bridges between key stakeholders in the irrigation sector: GAP-RDA's Management Operation and Maintenance Model', in Olcay Ünver and Rajiv K. Gupta (eds.), *Water Resources Management: Crosscutting Issues*, Ankara: METU Press.

Kibaroğlu, Ayşegül. (2003). Settling the Dispute Over The Water Resources in the Euphrates-Tigris River Basin, *Stradigma, Middle East -Journal Of Strategy and Analysis*, No: 6, http://www.stradigma.com/english/july2003/articles_01.html (last accessed 10 July 2010).

Kingdon, J. W. (1984). *Agendas, Alternatives, and Public Policies*, New York: Harper Collins Publishers.

Kirschenbaum, A. (2004). *Chaos Organization and Disaster Management*, New York: Marcel Dekker.

Klein, Naomi. (2007). *De shockdoctrine. De opkomst van rampenkapitalisme*, 2007, Breda: De Geus.

Klijn, F. and van der Most, H. (2001). 'Calamiteitenpolders een ruimteclaim in het rivierengebied?; report, Delft: WL Delft Hydraulics.

Klink, A. G. (1985). *De hydrobiologie van de Grensmaas; huidig functioneren, potenties en bedreigingen*, Rapporten en mededelingen, 39, Wageningen: hydrobiologisch adviesbureau Klink.

Klink, A. G. (1986). *Literatuuronderzoek naar enige factoren die invloed hebben op het biologisch herstel van de Grensmaas*, Rapporten en mededelingen, 24, Wageningen: hydrobiologisch adviesbureau Klink.

Knaub, Horand. (1996). 'Bonn says good-bye to development aid which is not acceptable', *Badische Zeitung*, 20 March 1996, trans. in *FAP Monitor* 5 (2), September 1996.

Knight, Frank H. (1921). *Risk, Uncertainty, and Profit*, Ph.D. First edition. Hart, Schaffner & Marx; Boston: Houghton Mifflin Company, The Riverside Press.

Kochanek, Stanley. (1993). *Patron-Client Politics and Business in Bangladesh*, New Delhi: Sage.

Kochanek, Stanley. (2000). 'The growing commercialisation of power', in Jahan, Rounaq (ed.). *Bangladesh: Promises and Performances*. Dhaka: University Press Limited, pp. 149–79.

Kolars, John F. and Mitchell, William A. (1991). *The Euphrates River and the Southeast Anatolia Development Project*, Carbondale, IL: Southern Illinois University Press.

Kooiman, J., Martijn van Vliet L. and Jentoft, Svein. (eds.). (2000). *Creative Governance Opportunities for Fisheries in Europe*, Aldershot: Ashgate.

Koppen, B. van. (1998). 'Water rights, gender and poverty alleviation: Inclusion and exclusion of women and men smallholders in public irrigation infrastructure development', *Agriculture and Human Values* 15 (4): 361–74.

Krahmann, E. (2003). 'Conceptualizing security governance', *Co-operation and Conflict*, 38 (1): 5–26.

Krasner, Stephen D. (ed.). (1983). *International Regimes*, Cambridge, MA: Cornell University Press.

Krause, Keith and Williams, Michael. (1997). *Critical Security Studies: Concepts and Cases*, London and New York: Taylor and Francis.

Kronstadt, K. Alan. (2003). 'CRS Report for Congress', Order Code RS20489. Updated 30 January 2003 http://fpc.state.gov/documents/organization/19701.pdf (last accessed 10 July 2010).

Kvaloy, F. (1994). NGO's and People's Participation in Relation to the Bangladesh Flood Action Plan, Oslo. Mankodi.

Kwadijk, J., van der Poel, Lenie. (2005). *Technical Assistance Services Nasser Flood and Drought Control/Integration of Climate Change Uncertainty and Flooding Risk*, Project Description, Delft: WL Delft Hydraulics.

Lankford, B. A., Hepworth, N. (2006). 'The Cathedral and the Bazaar: Centralised versus Decentralised River Basin Management'. Workshop 4: 'Benefits and Responsibilities of Decentralised and Centralised Approaches for Management of Water and Wastewater', World Water Week 2006. Stockholm International Water Institute.

Larcombe, Ewan. (2005). 'The Rise and Fall of the Jubilee River', www.jubileeriver.co.uk/papers.html (last accessed 10 July 2010).

Lasswell, H. D. and Kaplan, A. (1950). *Power and Society: A Framework for Critical Inquiry*, New Haven: Yale University Press.

Latour, Bruno. (1987). *Science In Action: How to Follow Scientists and Engineers Through Society*, Cambridge, MA: Harvard University Press.

Leenders, Michael. (2004). *De kennismakelaar. Matching van vraag en aanbod van expert kennis, ervaringen uit de praktijk*, Proceedings, conference Lof der Verwarring, Rotterdam: Erasmus Universiteit, pp. 151–6.

Leeuwen, Eveline van, Dalhuisen, Jasper, Vreeker, Ron and Nijkamp, Peter. (2002). The Grensmaas Project, Integrated Evaluation for Sustainable River Basin Governance, 'Advisor', Energy, Environment and Sustainable Development Programme. Work Package 1 – Case Studies Reviews, Report. April 2002.

Leeuwis, Cees. (2004). *Communication for Rural Innovation: Rethinking Agricultural Extension*, Oxford: Blackwell Science.

Leiss, William and Chociolko, Christina. (1995). *Risk and Responsibility*, Montreal: McGill-Queen's University Press.

Léonard, Sarah. (2004). 'The "Securitization" of Asylum and Migration in the European Union: Beyond the Copenhagen School's Framework'. The Transformation of Internal Security in Europe, paper, SGIR Fifth Pan-European International Relations Conference, the Hague, 9–11 September 2004.

Lewins, Roger with Sarah Robens. (2004). 'Participation in Integrated Floodplain Management in Bangladesh, R8195: FTR – Annex B-vii: Integrated floodplain management – Institutional environments and participatory methods.

Lewis, C.S. (1947). *The Abolition of Man*, New York: Macmillan.

Lindahl, Anna and Sundset, Vivian. (2003). 'The Grammar of Threat and Security in HIV/AIDS: An Analysis of the South African Government's Discourse on HIV and AIDS Between 1998 and 2002'.

MFS report no. 72, Linkòping: Department of Management and Economics, Linköping University.

Lindemann, Stefan. (2005). 'Water Regime Formation in Europe: A Research Framework with Lessons from the Rhine and Elbe River Basins, paper presented for the German-Israeli-Palestinian project 'From conflict to collective action: Institutional change and management options to govern transboundary watercourses', Berlin: Forschungsstelle für Umweltpolitik (ffu).

Lindholm, Helena. (1995). 'Water and the Arab-Israeli conflict', in Leif Ohlsson (ed.), *Hydropolitics: Conflicts over Water as a Development Constraint*, London: Zed Books), pp. 55–90.

Lipschutz, Ronnie. (1995). *On Security*, New York: Columbia University Press.

Litfin, Karen. (1999). 'Constructing environmental security and ecological interdependence', *Global Governance* 5: 359–77.

Lonergan, S. and Wolf, A. (2001). 'Moving water to move people: The Toshka project in Egypt,' *Water International*, 26 (4): 589–96.

Long, Norman. (2001). *Development Sociology. Actor Perspectives*, New York: Routledge.

Loucks, Daniel P. (2006). 'Why People Gamble with Natural Hazards', *Geophysical Research Abstracts*, Vol. 8, 01071.

Louis, R. and Owen, R. (1989). *Suez 1956: the Crisis and Its Consequences*, Oxford: Clarendon.

Lowi, Miriam R. (1993). *Water and Power. The Politics of a Scarce Resource in the River Jordan Basin*, New York: Cambridge University Press.

Lowry, William. (2006). 'Potential focusing projects and policy change', *Policy Studies Journal* 34 (3): 313–35.

Lukes, Steven. (1974). *Power: A Radical View*, London: Macmillan.

Lukes, Steven. (2005). 'Questions About Power: Lessons from the Louisiana Hurricane'. Understanding Katrina. Perspectives from the Social Sciences. presented as the Vilhelm Aubert Memorial Lecture at the Institutt for Samfunnsforskning in Oslo, Norway, 22 September 2005. http://understandingkatrina.ssrc.org/Lukes/ (last accessed 10 July 2010).

Lünnemann, Katinka. (2003). 'Schaarste en veiligheid: het onverzadigbare verlangen naar veiligheid', essay prepared for RMO for policy advice to the Dutch Administration, Den Haag, 14 February 2003.

Lupton, Deborah. (1999). *Risk*. New York: Routledge.

Lustick, Ian. (1997). 'Lijphart, Lakatos, and consociationalism'. *World Politics* 50 (1): 88–117.

Maaswerken, De. (2003). Milieu-effect rapport Grensmaas, Hoofdrapport, Maastricht.

MacDonald, Matthew. (2000). 'The Environment and Security: The Euphrates River', APSA Conference 2000, http://apsa2000.anu.edu.au/confpapers/macdonald.doc (last accessed 10 July 2010).

MacNeill, Jim, Yakushiji, Taizo and Winsemius, Pieter. (1991). *Beyond Interdependence: The Meshing of the World's Economy and the Earth's Ecology*. Oxford: Oxford University Press.

MacQuarrie, Patrick. (2004). 'Water Security in the Middle East. Growing Conflict Over Development in the Euphrates-Tigris Basin', MSc thesis, Peace Studies, Dublin: Trinity College, http://waterwiki.net/images/1/1e/MacQuarrie2004.pdf (last accessed 10 July 2010).

Manuta, J., Khrutmuang, S., Huaisai, D. and Lebel, L. (2006). Institutionalized incapacities and practice in flood disaster management in Thailand. *Science and Culture* 72 (1-2): 10–22.

Martin, Colin. (2005). 'The Maidenhead, Windsor and Eton Flood Alleviation Scheme – the background to the scheme, in Ewan Larcombe, *The Rise and Fall of the Jubilee River* http://www.jubileeriver.co.uk/riseandfall/TRAFOTJR050916.doc (last accessed 10 July 2010).

Marullo, Sam, Pagnuccos, Ron and Smith, Jackie. (1996). 'Frame changes and social movement contraction: US peace movement framing after the Cold War', *Sociological Inquiry* 66: 1–28.

Mason, Simon A. (2004). 'From Conflict to Co-operation in the Nile basin, Interaction Between Water Availability, Water Management in Egypt and Sudan, and International Relations in the Eastern Nile basin'. Conflict Sensitive Interviewing and Dialogue Workshop Methodology, Zurich Center for Security Studies (CSS), ETH Zurich Swiss Federal Institute for Environmental Science and Technology (EAWAG).

McDowall, David. (1996). *A Modern History of Kurdistan*, New York: I.B.Tauris.

Mearsheimer, John. (2001). *The Tragedy of Great Power Politics*, New York: WW Norton.

Meijerink, Sander. (2005). 'Understanding policy stability and change. The interplay of advocacy coalitions and epistemic communities, windows of opportunity, and Dutch coastal flooding policy 1945–2003'. *European Public Policy* 12 (6): 1060–77.

Meinecke, Michael. (1996). 'Hasankeyf/Hisn Kaifā on the Tigris. A Regional Centre on the Crossroad of Foreign Influences', in Meinecke, *Patterns of Stylistic Changes in Islamic Architecture: Local Traditions Versus Migrating Artists*, New York University Press, pp. 55–89.

Meissner, Richard, and Turton, Anthony R. (2003). 'The hydrosocial contract theory and the Lesotho Highlands Water Project', *Water Policy* 5 (2): 115–26.

Meulen, Michiel J. van der, Rijnveld, Marc, Gerrits, Lasse M., Joziasse, Jan, Heijst, Max W. I. M. van and Gruijters, Stephan H. L. L. (2006). 'Handling sediments in Dutch river management: The planning stage of the Maaswerken River Widening Project', *Journal of Soils and Sedimentology* 2006 (3): 163–72.

Middle East Times. (2006). Turkey, Israel scrap water project, 7 April 2006.

Migdal, Joel S. (1988). *Strong Societies and Weak States: State-Society Relations and State Capabilities in the Third World*, Princeton, NJ: Princeton University Press.

Miller, Donald L. (1986). *The Lewis Mumford Reader*, New York: Pantheon Books.

Miniotaite, Grazina. (2000). 'The Security Policy of Lithuania and the "Integration Dilemma"', CIAO Working Paper 6/2000, Copenhagen.

Ministerie van Binnenlandse Zaken. (1993). *Integrale veiligheidsrapportage*, Den Haag: Directoraat-Generaal Openbare Orde en Veiligheid.

Ministerie van Verkeer en Waterstaat. (2000). *Anders omgaan met water. Waterbeleid in de 21ᵉ eeuw*, Den Haag: Ministerie van Verkeer en Waterstaat, Directoraat-Generaal Rijkswaterstaat.

Ministerium für Umwelt und Naturschütz, Landwirtschaft und Verbraucherschütz des Landes Nordrhein-Westphalia, the province of Gelderland, Public Works Department (eds.) (2002), *Grensoverschrijdende effectmn van extreem hoogwater op de Niederrhein*, Düsseldorf, Arnhem.

Mirkasymov, Bakhtiyar. (2006). 'Water resources in the Middle East Conflict', *Journal of Middle Eastern Geopolitics*, 2 (3): 51–63.

Mitchell, Bruce. (ed.). (1990). *Integrated Water Management: International Experiences and Perspectives*; London: Belhaven Press.

Mitchell, Gordon R. (1998). 'Pedagogical possibilities for argumentative agency in academic debate', *Argumentation and Advocacy* 35: 41–60.

Mitchell, Timothy. (1995). 'The Object of Development. America's Egypt'. Discourse of the Development Industry, in Jonathan Crush (ed.), *Power of Development*, London: Routledge, pp. 129–58.

Mitchell, Timothy. (2002). *Rule of Experts: Egypt, Techno-Politics, Modernity*, Berkeley, CA: University of California Press.

Mitzen, Jennifer. (2005). 'Ontological security in world politics: State identity and the security dilemma', *European Journal of International Relations*, 12 (3): 341–70 http://psweb.sbs.ohio-state.edu/faculty/jmitzen/selected/mitzen_ontological.pdf (last accessed 10 July 2010).

Moll, Yasmin. (2004). 'Paradise lost', *Egypt Today*, May.

Morvaridi, Behrooz. (1999). 'Social Review of the Ilısu Dam Resettlement Action Plan', BCID Research Paper No.16, Bradford: University of Bradford.

Mouffe, C. (2000). 'Deliberative democracy or agonistic pluralism?', Reihe Politikwissenschaft, 72, Wien: Institut für Höhere Studien (IHS) www.ihs.ac.at/publications/pol/pw_72.pdf (last accessed 10 July 2010).

Mouffe, C. (2005). *On the Political*, London: Routledge

Mourits, K., and Potten, M. (1998). *Maatschappelijke Kosten en Baten van de Maaswerken. Een Verkenning.* Reeks Achtergrondstudies Interfacultair Onderzoeksproject Grensmaas, Maastricht Wetenschapswinkel, Universiteit Maastricht, Part 8.

Muller, B., (2004). '(Dis)qualified bodies: Securitization, citizenship and "identity management"', *Citizenship Studies*, 8 (3): 279–94.

Mumford, Lewis. (1963). *Technics and Civilisation*, New York: Harcourt Brace & Co.

Murakami, Masahiro. (1999). *Managing Water for Peace in the Middle East: Alternative Strategies*, United Nations University, UNU Press.

Mutlu, Servet. (1996). 'The Southeastern Anatolia Project (GAP) of Turkey: Its context, objectives, and prospects'. *Orient* 37 (1): 59–86.

Myers, Norman. (1995). *Ultimate Security*, New York: W.W. Norton.

Nadelmann, Ethan A. (1990). 'Global prohibition regimes: The evolution of norms in international society', *International Organization* 44: 479–526.

Napoli, James and Amin, Hussein. (1997). 'Press freedom in Egypt', in William Jong-Ebot and Festus Eribo (Eds.), *Communication and Press Freedom in Africa*, Trenton, NJ: Africa World Press, Inc.

Nasreen, Mahbuba. (2004). Disaster research: Exploring the sociological approach to disaster in Bangladesh, *Bangladesh e-Journal of Sociology*. Vol. 1. No. 2. July.

Neumann, Iver B. (1999). 'Identity and the outbreak of war: Or why the Copenhagen School of Security Studies should include the idea of "Violisation" in its framework of analysis', *International Journal of Peace Studies*, 3 (1), http://www.gmu.edu/programs/icar/ijps/vol3_1/Neuman.htm (last accessed 10 July 2010).

Nicolassen, Lidy. (1993). 'Inpoldering Bengaalse delta wekt veel verzet', *Volkskrant*, 28 May 1993.

Noeman, Rachel. (2000). 'Egypt pours money into desert reclamation', Reuters, Planet-Ark, 17 December 2000.

NRC Handelsblad. (2002). 'Commissie kiest drie "calamiteitenpolders"', 29 May.

ODA (Overseas Development Assistance), 'Fisheries and the Flood Action Plan: Report and Recommendations of the ODA Project Identification Mission to Bangladesh' (2 vols.), May 1990.

OECD. (2004/2005). *African Economic Outlook 2004/2005*, Egypt.

Oğuzlu, T. (2007). 'Soft power in Turkish foreign policy', *Australian Journal of International Affairs* 61 (1): 81–97.

Ohana, Uzzi. (2007). 'The Securitization of Others: Fear, Terror, Identity', paper prepared for the 6th Pan-European Conference On International Relations: Making Sense Of A Pluralist World 12–15 September 2007, University Of Turin, Italy, www.Sgir.Org/Archive/Turin/Uploads/Ohana-Sgir%20conference%202007.pdf

Ohlsson, Leif. (1998). 'Water and Social Resource Scarcity'. An issue paper commissioned by the FAO, Rome: AGLW.

Ohlsson, Leif and Turton, Anthony R. (1999). 'The Turning of a Screw'. Paper presented in the Plenary Session of the 9th Stockholm Water Symposium 'Urban Stability through Integrated Water-Related Management', hosted on 9–12 August by the Stockholm Water Institute (SIWI) in Stockholm, Sweden. http://www.soas.ac.uk/waterissues/papers/file38362.pdf (last accessed 10 July 2010).

Okidi, C. (1994). *History of the Nile and Lake Victoria Basins through Treaties*, Cambridge: Cambridge University Press.

OMCT (World Organisation against Torture). (2006). 'Agrarian Policy, Human Rights and Violence in Egypt. Information and Recommendations for the European Union, in the Context of the Association Agreement between the European Union and Egypt', http://www.omct.org/pdf/omct/2006/report/Egypt_Farmers_OMCT_Paper_for_EU_final.pdf (last accessed 10 July 2010).

Outshoorn, Eric. (2006). 'De Tigris zal Hasankeyf verzwelgen', *De Volkskrant*, 20 November 2006.

Overseas Development Institute, Arcadis, Euroconsult. (2001). 'Transboundary Water Management as an International Public Good', prepared for the Ministry for Foreign

Affairs, Sweden, http://www.odi.org.uk/resources/download/2972.pdf (last accessed 10 July 2010).

OXERA/Ministry of Agricultural, Fisheries and Food. (2001). *Flood and Coastal Defence Funding Review, Second Interim Report* (unpublished), Oxford, 24 April.

Özok-Gündoğan, Nilay. (2005). '"Social Development" as a governmental strategy in the Southeastern Anatolia Project', *New Perspectives on Turkey*, 32, Spring 2005, pp. 93–111.

Paltemaaĝü, Lauri and Vuori, Jahu. (2006). 'How cheap is identity talk? – A framework of identity frames and security discourse for the analysis of repression and legitimization of social movements in Mainland China', *Issues & Studies*s, 42 (3) (September 2006): 47–86. http://iir.nccu.edu.tw/attachments/journal/add/4/42-3-047-86.pdf (last accessed 10 July 2010).

Pamukcu, Konuralp. (2003). 'Water trade between Israel and Turkey: A start in the Middle East? *Middle East Policy* 10 (4): 87–99.

Parker, Dennis J. (1992). 'Six comments on the Bangladesh Flood Action Plan', *Natural Hazards*, 6 (3): 287–98.

Parker, Dennis J. (ed.). (2000). *Floods*, London: Routledge.

Pearce, Laurie. (2003). Disaster Management and Community Planning, and Public Participation: How to Achieve Sustainable Hazard Mitigation, *Natural Hazards*, 28 (3): 211–28.

Pelletiere, Stephen C. (2003). 'A war crime or an act of war?', *New York Times*, 31 January.

Pelling, Mark. (ed.). (2003). *Natural Disasters and Development in a Globalizing World*, London: Routledge.

Pelling, Mark and Dill, Kathleen. (2006). '"Natural" Disasters as Catalysts of Political Action', Chatham House ISP/NSC (New Security Challenges) Briefing paper, 06/01, February.

Penning-Rowsell, Edmund C., Winchester, Peter and Bosman-Aggrey, Peter. (1987). *Flood at Maidenhead, England. An evaluation of three levels of non-structural protection*, Middlesex Polytechnic, Enfield.

Penning-Rowsell, E. C., Parker, D. J. and Harding, D. M., (1986). *Floods and Drainage. British Polices for Hazard Reduction, Agricultural Improvement and Wetland Conservation*, London: Routledge.

Perrow, Charles. (2007). *The Next Catastrophe. Reducing Our Vulnerabilities to Natural, Industrial, and Terrorist Disasters*, Princeton, NJ: Princeton University Press.

Petrella, Riccardo. (1998). Le Manifeste de l Eau. Pour un Contrat Mondial, Namur: Labor.

Phillips, David, Daoudy, Marwa, Öjendal, Joakim, Turton, Anthony and McCaffrey, Stephen. (2006). *Trans-Boundary Water Co-operation as a Tool for Conflict Prevention and for Broader Benefit-sharing*, Stockholm: Ministry of Foreign Affairs, Sweden; http://www.bvcooperacion.pe/biblioteca/bitstream/123456789/5964/1/BVCI0005744.pdf (last accessed 10 July 2010).

Pia, Emily and Diez, Thomas. (2007). 'Conflict and Human Rights – a Conceptual Paper'. SHUR paper 1/07, European project 'Human Rights in Conflicts. The Role of Civil Society (SHUR)', Italy, http://www.luiss.it/shur/wp-content/uploads/2008/10/shurwp01-07.pdf (last accessed 10 July 2010).

Pinch, Trevor J. and Bijker, Wiebe E. (1984). 'The social construction of facts and artefacts: Or how the sociology of science and the sociology of technology might benefit each other', *Social Studies of Science* 14: 399–441.

Pitman, Keith. (1994). 'Improving Technical Rigor Through Participation'. *The Participation Forum*, USAID, No. 6, July 21; www.info.usaid.gov/about/patt_devel/docs/

prtform6.htm, accessed 30 November 1999. Now only on http://pdf.dec.org/pdf_docs/pnacb006.pdf

Pols, Bram. (1994). '"Duurzaam Boeren" in Bangladesh geeft betere oogst', *NRC* 16 March 1994.

Pols, Leo, Kronberger, Pia, Pieterse, Nico and Tennekes, Joost. (2007). *Overstromingsrisico als Ruimtelijke Opgave*, Den Haag: Ruimtelijk Planbureau.

Pratt, Nicola. (2001). *Globalization and the Post-Colonial State: Human Rights, NGO's and the Prospects for Democratic Governance in Egypt*, PhD Thesis, Birmingham: University of Birmingham.

Proost, Jet and Leeuwis, Cees. (2007). 'Learning alliances between power and impotence: Underpinnings and pitfalls from innovation and social learning theory', in Stef Smits, Moriarty, Patrick and Sijbesma, Christine (eds), *Learning Alliances. Scaling up Innovation in Water, Sanitation and Hygiene*, Delft: IRC, 19–37.

Puchala, Donald J. and Hopkins, Raymond F. (1983). 'International regimes: Lessons from inductive analysis'. *International Organization* 36: 427–69.

Quinn, Susan. (1998). *Egypt's Toshka project presented to US, Arab World Online*, 2 October 1998, www.awo.net/newspub/pubs/tradelin/981002b.asp

Rahman, Atiq (n.d.). *Civil society and sustainable development: Perspectives on participation in the Asia and Pacific Region, Approaches to Sustainability, Capacity 21 Resource Library*, New York: United Nations Development Programme, pp. 7-18. http://stone.undp.org/maindiv/bdp/dl/documents/cap21libdoc166en.pdf (last accessed 10 July 2010).

Ramadan, Rania. (n.d.). *Water Poverty in Egypt: Using Geographic Information Systems in Tracking the Relation between Water Poverty and Development Indices*, Cairo: IRD (Institut de Recherche pour le Développement)/Sakia, http://balwois.mpl.ird.fr/balwois/administration/full_paper/ffp-490.pdf

Rangpur Dinajpur Rural Service (RDRS), Flood Action Plan (GAP) RDRS Position Paper, July 1995.

Rasid, Harun. (1993). 'Preventing flooding or regulating flood levels? Case studies on perception of flood alleviation in Bangladesh', *Natural Hazards*, 8 (1): 39–57.

Reisner, Mark. (1993). *Cadillac Desert: The American West and its Disappearing Water*. Revised edition. New York: Penguin.

Reyes-Gaskin, Roberto. (2005). 'Distorted Governmentality: 'The embedded biopolitics of dam resettlement', *Journal of Politics & Society*, essay 3, Colombia University, 16 (3): 69–87. http://www.helvidius.org/files/2005/2005_Reyes-Gaskin.pdf (last accessed 10 July 2010).

Richards, Alan and Waterbury, John. (1990). *A Political Economy of the Middle East*, Boulder, CO: Westview Press.

Roberts, John, and Fagernäs, Sonja. (2004). 'Why is Bangladesh Outperforming Kenya? A Comparative Study of Growth and Its Causes since the 1960s', Economic and Statistics Analysis Unit (ESAU) Working Paper 5, London: Overseas Development Institute.

Roe, Paul. (2004). 'Securitization and minority rights: Conditions of desecuritization'. *Security Dialogue* 35 (3): 279–94.

Rogers, P., Lydon, P. and Seckler, D. (1989). *Eastern Waters Study: Strategies to Manage Flood and Drought in the Ganges-Brahmaputra Basin*, Prepared for the Office of Technical Resources, Agriculture and Rural Development Division, US Agency for International Development, Washington, DC, April.

Röling, N. and Woodhill, J. (2001). 'From Paradigms To Practice: Foundations, Principles and Elements for Dialogue on Water, Food and Environment'. Background

Document for National and Basin Dialogue Design Workshop, Bonn, December 2001, Secretariat for Global Dialogue on Water, Food and Environment.

Rolloos, Hans. (1995). 'Nieuwe dijken moeten overstromingen beheersbaar maken', *Internationale Samenwerking*, 2–3 June.

Ronayne, Maggie. (2005). The Cultural and Environmental Impact of Large Dams in Southeast Turkey: Fact-Finding Mission Report, Fact-finding Mission Report, National University of Ireland/Kurdish Human Rights Project, www.khrp.org

Rosenau, James N. (1997). *Along the Domestic-Foreign Frontier. Exploring Governance in a Turbulent World*, Cambridge: Cambridge University Press.

Rosenthal, Uri and 't Hart, Paul. (1998). *Flood Response and Crisis Management in Western Europe. A Comparative Analysis*, New York/Heidelberg: Springer.

Roth, Dik, Warner, Jeroen, and Winnubst, Madelinde. (2006). 'Een noodverband tegen hoogwater. Waterkennis, beleid en politiek rond noodoverloopgebieden', Boundaries of Space Series, Wageningen: Wageningen University.

Rubin, Barry. (1998). 'The geopolitics of Middle East conflict and crisis', *MERIA Journal* (3) http://meria.idc.ac.il/journal/1998/issue3/jv2n3a7.html (last accessed 10 July 2010).

Rubin, Corey. (2004). *Fear. The History of a Political Idea*, New York: Oxford University Press.

SAARC. (1992). 'Meeting the Challenge': Kathmandu: Independent South Asian Commission on Poverty Alleviation.

Salm, Harriët (1994), 'Ruzie over plan tot redding van verstopte rivierdelta', *Trouw*, 18 July 1994.

Salm, Harriët. (1995). 'Mega-project met hoge dijken in Bangladesh gedoemd te mislukken,' *Trouw*, 13 May.

Sands, Philippe. (1997). Bangladesh-India Treaty on sharing of the Ganges waters at Farakka. Introductory Note, I.L.M. 519.

Schiffler, Manuel. (1997). Konflikte um den Nil oder Konflikte am Nil?, in Jörg Barandat (red.), *Wasser – Konfrontation oder Kooperation. Ökologische Aspekte der Sicherheit am Beispiel eines weltweit begehrten Rohstoffs*, Baden-Baden: Nomos, pp. 137–50.

Schleifer, Abdallah and Bursch, Barbi. (2005). 'Before the flood', *Al-Ahram Weekly*, 10–16 February, Issue No. 729.

Schmitt, Carl. (1922). *Politische Theologie. Vier Kapitel zur Lehre von der Souveränität*. Berlin: Duncker & Humblot.

Schmuck, Hanna. (2000). '"An Act of Allah": Religious explanations for floods in Bangladesh as survival strategy'. *International Journal of Mass Emergencies and Disasters* March 2 W, 18 (1): 85–95.

Schön, D.A. and Rein, M. (1994). *Frame Reflection. Towards the Resolution of Intractable Policy Controversies*, New York: Basic Books.

Schultz van Haegen, M. (2003). Cleveringa Lezing (Public lecture by Vice Minister for Water Management), 27 November, http://www.verkeerenwaterstaat.nl/actueel/toespraken/toespraakarchief

Schulz, Michael. (1995).'Turkey, Syria and Iraq: A hydropolitical security complex', in Ohlsson, L (ed.), *Hydropolitics: Conflicts over Water as a Development Constraint*, London: Zed Books pp. 107–13 .

Scott, James. (1998). *Seeing Like a State: How Certain Schemes to Improve the Human Condition Have Failed*, New Haven: Yale University Press.

Scrase, J. Ivan and Sheate, William R. (2005). 'Re-framing flood control in England and Wales'. *Environmental Values* 14 (1): 113–37.

Selby, Jan. (2003). 'Dressing up domination as "Co-operation": The case of Israeli-Palestinian water relations', *Review of International Studies* 29 (1): 121–38.

Selby, Jan. (2005). 'The geopolitics of water in the Middle East: Fantasies and realities', *Third World Quarterly* 26 (2): 329–49.

Sen, Amartya. (1980). 'Famines'. *World Development* 8 (9): 613–21.

Sen, Amartya. (1981). 'Ingredients of famine analysis: Availability and entitlements, *Quarterly Journal of Economics*: 433–64.

Sener, Ipek Nese. (2004). *An Innovative Method for Relocation of Historical Masonry Monuments: A Case Study in Hasankeyf*, Thesis submitted to the Graduate School of Natural and Applied Science, Middle East Technical University.

Shalin, Monte. (1992). 'Paradigm Shift', National Voluntary Organisations Active in Disaster, http://www.nvoad.org/articles/paradigm.php 14 September

Shapland, Greg. (1995). 'Policy options for downstream states in the Middle East', in Tony Allan and Chibli Mallat (eds.), *Water in the Middle East. Legal, Political and Commercial Implications*, London: I.B.Tauris, 301–23.

Shapland, Greg. (1997). *Rivers of Discord: International Water Disputes in the Middle East*, New York, St. Martin's Press.

Shiva, Vandana. (2002). *Water Wars. Privatization Pollution and Profit*, Boston: South end Press.

Shoup, Daniel. (2006). 'Can archeology build a dam? Sites and politics in Turkey's Southeast Anatolia Project'. *Journal of Mediterranean Archeology*, 19(2): 231–58.

Silva, W. (2001). 'Hoogwaterbescherming langs de Rijntakken. Onzekerheden en omgaan met onzekerheden', RWS/RIZA Werkdocument nr. 2000.179X.

Sjöberg, Lennart, Moen, Bjørg-Elin and Rundmo, Torbjørn. (2004). 'Explaining risk perception. An evaluation of the psychometric paradigm in risk perception research', *Rotunde* 84, Trondheim.

Sjursen, H. (2004). 'Changes to European security in a communicative perspective', *Co-operation and Conflict* 39: 107–28

Slocum, Nikki and Langenhove, Luk van. (2003). 'The Meaning of Regional Integration: Introducing Positioning Theory in Regional Integration Studies', United Nations University, Comparative Regional Integration Studies (UNU-CRIS) Working paper 2003–5.

Smircich, Linda, and Morgan, Gareth. (1982). 'Leadership: The management of meaning', *Journal of Applied Behavioral Science*; 18 (3): 257–73.

Smit, Pieter. (1993). 'Het gevecht rond een masterplan', *onze Wereld*, June.

Smith, Steve and Hollis, Martin. (1990). *Explaining and Understanding International Relations*, Oxford: Clarendon Press.

Snow, David A., Rochford, E. Burke, Jr., Worden, Steven K. and Benford, Robert D. (1986). 'Frame alignment processes, Micromobilization, and movement participation'. *American Sociological Review*, 51: 464–81.

Soek-Fang Sim (2004). 'Dewesternising Theories of Authoritarianism: Economics, Ideology and the Asian Economic Crisis in Singapore', Working Paper No. 103, St Paul, Minn.: Macalester College, June.

Sommen J. J and MER-Coördinatieteam (1999). *Werken aan de Maas van morgen*, Milieu Effect Rapportage Grensmaas, Maastricht: IWACO/CSO/WL.

Soussan, J. G. *et al.* (1999). *Integrated Coastal Zone Management in Bangladesh – A Concept Note and Development Process*, Dhaka: World Bank/NEDA/WP.

Speller, G. M. and Twigger-Ross, C. L. (2005). *Improving community and citizen engagement in flood risk management decision making, delivery and flood response.* R&D Technical Report

SC040033/SR4. Bristol: Environment Agency http://publications.environment-agency.gov.uk/pdf/SCHO1005BJTC-e-e.pdf

Staatsbosbeheer. (2003). *Lonkend Rivierenland. Visie van Staatsbosbeheer op de Rivieren.*

Stahl, Bernhard. (2007). 'Who Securitized What, When, and How? A Comparative Analysis of Eight EU Member States in the Iraq Crisis', paper prepared for presentation at the ECPR conference in Turin, 12–15 September 2007 archive.sgir.eu/uploads/Stahl-iraq_securitization.pdf (last accessed 10 July 2010).

Starr, Joyce. (1991). 'Water wars', *Foreign Policy* 82 (Spring): 17–36.

Starr, Joyce and Stoll, Daniel. (1988). *The Politics of Scarcity. Water in the Middle East,* Boulder: Westview Press.

Stassen, Peter. (2005). 'Natte archeologie in de Maaswerken', in Henk Stoepker (ed.), 'Synthese en evaluatie van het inventariserend archeologisch onderzoek in de Maaswerken 1998–2005 Lezingen gehouden op het Maaswerken-archeologie symposium te Maastricht op 14 oktober 2005', e-depot.

Stephens, John and McCallum, Robyn. (1998). *Retelling Stories, Framing Culture: Traditional Story and Metanarratives in Children's Literature*, New York: Garland.

Stiles, Kendall W. (2002). *Civil Society by Design: Donors, NGOs, and the Intermestic Development Circle in Bangladesh*, Westport, CT: Praeger.

Stoker, Gerry. (1998). 'Governance as theory: Five propositions', *International Social Science Journal*, 50 (1): 17–28.

Strange, Susan. (1987). 'The persistent myth of lost hegemony', in Tooze, Roger and Chris May (eds.) *Authority and Markets – Susan Strange's Writings on International Political Economy*, Hampshire: Palgrave Macmillan.

Stroh, Kassian. (2003). 'Konflikt und Kooperation um Wasser, Eine Fallstudie über den Nil', Arbeitspapiere zu Problemen der Internationalen Politik und der Entwicklungsländerforschung, Forschungsstelle Dritte Welt am Geschwister-Scholl-Institut für Politische Wissenschaft der Lud-wig-Maximilians-Universität München.

Stroming. (1990). *Toekomst voor een grindrivier*, Hoog-Keppel: Stroming.

Stucki, Philippe. (2005). 'Water Wars or Water Peace?' PSIS Occasional Paper No. 3/2005, Programme for Strategic and International Security Studies. Geneva, Switzerland.

Swain, Ashok. (Winter 1998). 'A new challenge: Water scarcity in the Arab world', *Arab Studies Quarterly* (ASQ).

Swyngedouw, Erik. (1999). 'Modernity and hibridity: Nature, *Regeneracionismo*, and the production of the Spanish waterscape, 1890–1930'. *Annals of the Association of American Geographers*, 89 (3): 443–65.

Swyngedouw, Erik. (2007). 'TechnoNatural revolutions – the scalar politics of Franco's hydro-social dream for Spain, 1939–1975', *Transactions, Institute of British Geographers* 32: 9–28.

Szerszynski, Bronislaw. (2002). 'Ecological rites. Ritual events in ecological protest events', *Culture, Theory and Society* 19 (3): 51–69.

Tamir, Moustafa. (2003). 'Law versus the State: The judicialization of politics in Egypt', *Law and Social Inquiry*, 28: 883–930.

Tansey, J and O'Riordan, T. (1999). 'Cultural theory and risk: A review', *Health, Risk and Society*, 1, 71–90.

Tarrow, S. (1994). *Power as Movement. Social Movements and Contentious Politics*, Cambridge: Cambrige University Press.

Task Force. (1991). *Report on Bangladesh Development Strategies for the 1990's*, Dhaka: University Press.

TAW. (1995). *Druk op de dijken 1995, De toestand van de rivierdijken tijdens het hoogwater van januari/februari 1995*, Delft: Technische Adviescommissie Waterkeringen.

Teisman, Geert R. (1995). 'Het project Grensmaas', *Bestuurskunde*, 4 (8): 370–80.

Tennekes, Joost. (2005). *Wat donoren zien in Good Governance. Discoursanalyse van het ontwikkelingsbeleid van Nederland en Duitsland.* PhD thesis, TU Twente.

Thompson, Michael and Warburton, Michael. (1985). 'Decision making under contradictory certainties: How to save the Himalayas when you can't find out what's wrong with them', *Journal of Applied Systems Analysis*, 12, 3–34.

Thompson, Paul M. and Sultana, Parvin. (1996). 'Distributional and social impacts of flood control in Bangladesh', *The Geographical Journal*, 162: 1–13.

Tilly, Charles. (1985). 'War making and state making as organized crime', in P. B. Evans, D. Rueschmeyer, and T. Skocpol (eds.). *In Bringing the State Back In*, Cambridge: Cambridge University Press, pp. 169–91.

Trottier, Julie. (1999). *Hydropolitics in the West Bank and Gaza Strip*, Jerusalem: PASSIA.

Trottier, Julie. (2003). 'Exploring the making of the water war and water peace belief within the Israeli–Palestinian conflict', UNESCO/Green Cross PC-CP series http://webworld.unesco.org/water/wwap/pccp/cd/pdf/history_future_shared_water_resources/water_wars_hegemonic_concept.pdf (last accessed 10 July 2010).

Tunstall, S., Tapsell, S. and Fernandez-Bilbao, A. (2005). 'Objective 13: the damage-reducing effects of flood warnings: Results from new data collection, London: Defra/EA.

Tunstall, Sylvia, Johnston, Clare and Penning-Rowsell, Edmund. (2004). 'Flood Hazard Management in England and Wales: From Land Drainage to Flood Risk Management'. Paper presented to the World Congress on Natural Disaster Mitigation, 19–21 February 2004.

Tunstall, Sylvia and Green, Colin (2003). *From listener to talker. The changing role of the citizen in England and Wales.* Report prepared for the 4th work package of HarmoniCOP, December 2003. http://www.harmonicop.uni-osnabrueck.de/_files/_down/UK.pdf (last accessed 10 July 2010).

Turner, B. (1976). 'The organizational and interorganizational development of disasters', *Administrative Science Quarterly*, 21: 378-397.

Turnhout, Esther and Leroy, Pieter. (2004). 'Participeren in onzekerheid. Literatuuronderzoek naar het inzetten van participatie in wetenschappelijke beleidsadvisering', RIVM Rapport 550002008/2004.

Turton, A. (2001). 'Towards Hydrosolidarity: Moving From Resource Capture to Cooperation and Alliances', *Keynote Address SIWI Seminar*, 18 August 2001.

Turton, Anthony R. (2003). 'The Political Aspects of Institutional Development in the Water Sector. South Africa and its International River Basins. Submitted in partial fulfilment of the requirements for the degree of Doctor Philosophiae (International Politics), Faculty of Humanities, University of Pretoria, 31–74, http://upetd.up.ac.za/thesis/available/etd-06042004-110828/unrestricted/02chapter2.pdf (last accessed 10 July 2010).

Turton, Anthony R. (n.d.). 'Transboundary River Basins: Proposed Principles and Discussion Papers', http://www.dams.org/docs/kbase/contrib/ins224.pdf (last accessed 10 July 2010).

Turton, Anthony R., Schreiner, Barbara and Leestemaker, Joanne. (2001). 'Feminization as a critical component of the changing hydrosocial contract', *Water Science & Technology*, 43 (4): 155–63.

UNDP (United Nations Development Programme). (1989). Bangladesh Flood Policy Study. Final Report, Dhaka: Ministry of Irrigation, Water Development and Flood Control.

UNDP. (1994). *Human Development Report*, New York: Oxford University Press.

UNDP. (2005). *Human Development Report*, New York origin-hdr.undp.org (last accessed 10 July 2010).

UNESCO. (2001). Taming the Nile's serpents, *Unesco Courier*, 10 http://www.geckosadventures.com/middle-east-north-africa/egypt (last accessed 10 July 2010).

ur-Rashid, Harun. (2005). 'How can Bangladesh respond to Indian river-linking proposal?', *Daily Star*, Dhaka, 5 January 2005.

Vance Haynes, C. (1980). 'Geochronology of Wadi Tushka: Lost tributary of the Nile', *Science*, 210 (4465): 68–71.

Van Dijk, Han and Bruijn, Mirjam de. (1995). *Arid Ways. Cultural Understandings of Insecurity Among the Fulbe People, Central Mali*, Dissertation (CERES series), Wageningen Landbouw Hogeschool, Wageningen.

Ven, G. van der and van Dooren N. (1998). *De Nieuwe Rivieren, Dijkversterking als ontwerpopgave*, Rotterdam: NAI.

Venables, Roger. (2005). 'Civil engineering – Jubilee River', in Richard Dodds & Roger Venables (eds.), *Engineering for Sustainable Development: Guiding Principles*, London: The Royal Academy of Engineering.

Vidal, John. (2004). 'Israeli "water for arms" deal with Turkey', *The Guardian*, 6 January.

Villiers, de Marq. (1999). *Water Wars. Is the World's Water Running Out?* London: Weidenfeld and Nicolson.

Viotti, Paul and Kauppi, Mark. (1999). *International Relations Theory*, 3rd Edition, Boston: Allyn and Bacon.

Volkskrant, 'Laat de polder niet verzuipen', Science section, 27 December 2003.

VROM-raad. (2007). *De hype voorbij. Klimaatverandering als structureel ruimtelijk vraagstuk*, Advies 060.

Vultee, Fred. (2007). *Securitization as a theory of media effects. The contest over the framing of political violence.* DPhil Dissertation, University of Missouri-Columbia.

Wæver, Ole. (1995). 'Securitization and desecuritization', in Ronnie D. Lipschutz (ed.) *On Security*, 46–86

Wahby, Wafeek S. (2004). 'Technologies applied in the Toshka project of Egypt', *Journal of Technology Studies* 30 (1): 86–91.

Walford, D. (1998). 'The M4 flood relief scheme', *Concrete*, 32 (10): 38–9.

Wallensteen, Peter. (2002). *Understanding Conflict Resolution. War, Peace and the Global System*, London: Sage.

Ward, Colin. (1997). *Reflected in Water. A Crisis of Social Responsibility*, London: Cassell, p. 113.

Warner, J., Waalewijn, P. and Hilhorst, D. (2002). 'Public Participation for Disaster-Prone Watersheds, Time for Multi-Stakeholder Platforms? Water and Climate Dialogue Thematic Paper. *Disaster Sites*, No. 6, Wageningen, Wageningen University.

Warner, Jeroen. (1992). 'The Politics of Diversion - Bridging troubled water in the Middle East'. Master's Thesis submitted to the Department of International Relations, University of Amsterdam.

Warner, Jeroen (1999), 'Schaken om dammen. Turkije als waterhegemoon', *Transaktie.* 28 (4): 510–525.

Warner, Jeroen. (2000a). 'Global environmental security', in Ph. Stott & S. Sullivan (eds.), *Political Ecology*, London: Edward Arnold, 2000, Ch. 11.

Warner, Jeroen. (2000b). 'Integrated Management Requires an Integrated Society. Towards a New Hydrosocial Contract for the 21st Century', AWIRU Occasional Paper, http://www.awiru.co.za/OccasionalP.asp (last accessed 10 July 2010).

Warner, Jeroen. (2004a). 'Plugging the GAP. Working with Buzan, The Ilısu Dam as a Security Issue', SOAS Occasional Paper No. 67, School of Oriental and Asian Studies, University College London.

Warner, Jeroen. (2004b). 'Water, Wine, Vinegar, Blood: On Politics, Participation, Violence and Conflict over the Hydrosocial Contract', paper presented at the World Water Council conference on 'Water and Politics' in Marseilles, 26–27 February 2004. http://www.worldwatercouncil.org/fileadmin/wwc/Library/Publications_and_reports/Proceedings_Water_Politics/proceedings_waterpol_full_document.pdf (last accessed 10 July 2004).

Warner, Jeroen. (2006a). 'Multi-stakeholder platforms for integrated catchment management – more sustainable participation?', *International Journal of Water Resources Development* 22 (1), pp. 15–35.

Warner, Jeroen. (2006b). 'Risk, representation and legitimacy of flood management schemes in Bangladesh. The case of FAP-20', *Journal of Health, Social and Environmental Issues* 7 (1): 31–47.

Warner, J. F., and Simpungwe, E. (2003). 'Stakeholder Participation in South Africa: Power to the People?' Paper presented 2nd International Symposium on Integrated Water Resources Management (IWRM): Towards Sustainable Water Utilization in the 21st Century', ICWRS/IAHS, Stellenbosch, Western Cape, South Africa, 22–24 January 2003.

Warner, Jeroen, Meijerink, Sander and Needham, Barrie. (2007). 'Sturen in de Ruimte. Een evaluatie van beleidsinstrumenten ter beperking van gevolgen bij overstromingen'. Report commissioned by the Netherlands Public Works Department. Nijmegen: Centre for Water and Society, Radboud University.

Waterbury, John. (1979). *Hydropolitics of the Nile Valley*, Syracuse, NY: Syracuse Press.

Waterbury, John. (1993). *Exposed to Innumerable Delusions: Public Enterprise and State Power in Egypt, India, Mexico and Turkey*, Cambridge: Cambridge University Press.

Waterbury, John. (1997). 'Between unilateralism and comprehensive accords: Modest steps toward co-operation in international river basins', *International Journal of Water Resources Development* 13 (3): 279–89.

Waterbury, John. (2002). *Nile basin: National Determinants of Collective Action*, New Haven: Yale University Press.

Waterbury, John, and Whittington, Dale. (1998). 'Playing chicken on the Nile? The implications of micro-dam development in the Ethiopian highlands and Egypt's New Valley Project', *Natural Resources Forum*, 22 (3): 155–64.

Weber, Max. (1947). *The Theory of Social and Economic Organisations*, New York: The Free Press (trans. A.M. Henderson & T. Parsons).

Weinbaum, M. G. (1982). *Food Development and Politics in the Middle East*, Boulder, CO: Westview.

Wendt, Alexander. (1999). *Social Theory of International Politics*, Cambridge: Cambridge University Press.

Werner, Louis and Bubriski, Kevin. (2007). 'Seas beneath the Sand', *Aramcoworld*, 58 (1), January/February 2007, http://www.saudiaramcoworld.com/issue/200701/seas.beneath.the.sands.htm (last accessed 10 July 2010).

Werritty, Alan. (2006). Sustainable flood management: Oxymoron or new paradigm?, *Area* 38.(1), 16–23, http://www.rgs.org/NR/rdonlyres/015A865F-69D0-410E-80CF-994FFAE539DD/0/SustainablefloodmanagementArea.pdf (last accessed 10 July 2010).

Wesselink, Anna J. (2007). *Integraal Waterbeheer: de verweving van expertise en belangen*. PhD thesis, Enschede: Twente University.

Wester, Philippus. (2008). Shedding the Waters. Institutional Change and Water Control in the Lerma-Chapala Basin, Mexico, PhD dissertation, Wageningen: Irrigation and Water Engineering group, Wageningen University.

Wester, Philippus and Bron, Jan. (1998). 'Coping with Water. Water Management in Flood Control and Drainage Systems in Bangladesh', Liquid Gold Paper 4, Wageningen : ILRI. http://www.alterra.wur.nl/NL/publicaties+Alterra/ILRI-publicaties/Downloadable+publications/ (last accessed 10 July 2010).

Wester, Philippus and Warner, Jeroen. (2002). River basin management reconsidered, in A. Turton; R. Henwood (eds.). *Hydro-Politics in the Developing World – A Southern African Perspective.* Pretoria: African Water Issues Research Unit.

Westermann, Olaf. (2003). 'Interstate Collaboration, Local Conflicts and Public Participation in the Nile River Basin' in Jannik Boesen and Helle Munk Ravnborg (eds.) (2003), From water 'wars' to water 'riots'? Lessons from transboundary water management proceedings of the international conference, December 2003, Copenhagen: Dansk Institut for Internationale Studier, pp. 113–140.

Westermann, Olaf. (2004). 'Privatisation of Water and Environmental Conflict – with Case Study of the Cochabamba "Water Riot"', in Helle Munk Ravnborg (ed.), 'Water Conflict: Conflict Prevention and Mitigation in Water Resource Management', DIIS Report 2004 / 2, Copenhagen: Dansk Institut fòr Internationale Studier.

White, Gilbert F. (1974). *Natural Hazards: Local, National, Global*, Oxford University Press.

Wilde, Jaap de, and Wilberg, Håkan. (eds.). (1995). *Organised Anarchy in Europe – the Role of Intergovernmental Organizations*, London: I.B.Tauris.

Wilkinson, Clare. (2007). 'The Copenhagen School on tour in Kyrgyzstan: Is securitization theory useable outside Europe?', *Security Dialogue* 38: 5–23.

Williams, Michael C. (2003). 'Words, images, enemies: Securitization and international politics', *International Studies Quarterly* 47 (4): 511–31.

Williams, Philip B. and Associates Ltd. (2001). *A Review of the Hydrologic and Geomorphic Impacts of the Proposed Ilısu Dam*, Prepared for The Corner House, 31 August 2001, San Francisco.

Williams, Paul. (2001). 'Turkey's H20 diplomacy in the Middle East', *Security Dialogue* 32, 27–40.

Williams, Paul. (2002). 'Nile co-operation through hydro-realpolitik?', *Third World Quarterly* 23 (6), pp. 1189–96, 1 December 2002.

Williams, Paul. (2003a). 'The Security Politics of Enclosing Transboundary River Water Resources', paper presented at the International Conference on Resource Politics and Security in a Global Age, University of Sheffield (UK), 26-28 June 2003.

Williams, Paul. (2003b). 'Global (mis)governance of regional water relations', *International Politics* 40 (1): 149–58.

Winner, Langdon. (1980). 'Do artifacts have politics?', *Daedalus* 109 (1): 121–36.

Wishnick, Elizabeth. (2005). 'The Securitization of Chinese Migration to the Russian Far East', paper presented at the annual meeting of the International Studies Association, Hilton Hawaiian Village, Honolulu, Hawaii.

Wittfogel, K.A. (1957). *Oriental Despotism: A Comparative Study of Total Power*, New Haven, Conn: Yale University Press.
Wolf, Aaron T. (1998). 'Conflict and co-operation along international waterways', *Water Policy* 1: 251–65.
Wolfe, Alan. (1979). *The Rise and Fall of the Soviet Threat*, Domestic Sources of the Cold War Consensus, Washington D.C.: Institute of Policy Studies.
Wolsink M. (2003). 'Reshaping the Dutch planning system: A learning process?', *Environment and Planning A* 35 (4): 705–23.
Wolsink, M. (2006). 'River basin approach and integrated water management: Governance pitfalls for the Dutch Space-Water-Adjustment Management Principle', *Geoforum* 37: 473–87.
Wood, Geoff D. (1994). *Bangladesh: Whose Ideas, Whose Interests?* Dhaka: University Press.
Wood, Geoff D. (1999). 'Contesting water in Bangladesh: Knowledge, rights and governance, *Journal of International Development* 11: 731–54.
World Bank. (1989). 'Bangladesh Action Plan for Flood Control', Dhaka: International Bank for Reconstruction and Development.
Worster, Donald. (1985). *Rivers of Empire. Water, Aridity, and the Growth of the American West*, New York: Oxford University Press.
Young, Emma. (1999). 'Just a mirage?', *New Scientist*, 18 December, p. 19.
Young, Oran R. (1994). *International Governance: Protecting the Environment in a Stateless Society*, Ithaca, NY: Cornell University Press.
Young, Oran R. (1994). 'The politics of international regime formation: Managing natural resources and the environment', in Kratochwil, F. and Mansfield E. (eds.), *International Organization: A Reader*, New York: Harper Collins.
Zawahri, Neda A. (2008), 'Capturing the nature of co-operation, unstable co-operation, and conflict over international rivers: The story of the Indus, Yarmouk, Euphrates, and Tigris rivers', *International Journal of Global Environmental Issues* 8 (3), 286–310.
Zeitoun, Mark and Jeroen Warner. (2006). 'Hydro-hegemony: A framework for analysis of transboundary water conflicts', *Water Policy* 8: 435–60.
Zürcher, Erik (1998) [1993], *Turkey. A Modern History*, London: I.B.Tauris.

INDEX

Note: Page numbers followed by f and t indicate figures and tables respectively